Making Haste Slowly
The Troubled History of Higher Education in Mississippi

Making Haste Slowly

The Troubled History
of Higher Education in Mississippi

David G. Sansing

UNIVERSITY PRESS OF MISSISSIPPI
Jackson and London

Copyright © 1990 by the University Press of Mississippi
All rights reserved
Manufactured in the United States of America

93 92 91 90 4 3 2 1

Publication of this book has been made possible in part by a grant from
University of Mississippi.

Designed by Sally Horne

Library of Congress Cataloging-in-Publication Data

Sansing, David G.
    Making haste slowly : the troubled history of higher education in
Mississippi / David G. Sansing.
        p.   cm.
    Includes bibliographical references and index.
    ISBN 0-87805-458-8 (alk. paper)
        1. Universities and colleges—Mississippi—History.   2. Education,
Higher—Social aspects—Mississippi.   I. Title.
LA313.5.S26   1990
378.762—dc20   90-37004
                                                                    CIP

British Library Cataloguing-in-Publication data available

To
Verner Smith Holmes
who honored his public trust with a faithful fidelity
and to
Emma Bauer Holmes
who made the world a better, sweeter place

Contents

Preface ix

CHAPTER 1   Jefferson College and the Origins
of Higher Education, 1802–1830   3

CHAPTER 2   Old-Time Colleges in Mississippi,
1830–1840   18

CHAPTER 3   Founding the State University, 1840–1865   34

CHAPTER 4   Expansion of Higher Education,
1865–1900   55

CHAPTER 5   A State System of Higher Education,
1900–1928   77

CHAPTER 6   The Bilbo Purge, 1928–1932   91

CHAPTER 7   A Constitutional Board of Trustees,
1932–1944   111

CHAPTER 8   The College Boom, 1944–1954   125

CHAPTER 9   Race, Rights, Riots, Role and Scope,
1954–1962   140

CHAPTER 10   The Meredith Crisis: NEVER   156

CHAPTER 11   The Meredith Crisis: ИƎ∀ƎN   177

CHAPTER 12   In Defense of Yesterday, 1962–1972   196

CHAPTER 13   A System of Universities, 1972–1990   215

Afterword   236

Notes   239

Bibliography   281

Index   297

Preface

Since Bernard Bailyn's admonition of thirty years ago, in which he defined education as the "entire process by which a society transmits itself across the generations" and encouraged American historians to study education "in its elaborate, intricate involvements with the rest of society," there has been a renaissance in the history of education. That renaissance has produced an "imaginative and mature . . . historical scholarship," but unfortunately it has not yet made its way south of the Mason-Dixon line. With the possible exception of studies of education for blacks and a few good institutional histories, southern education remains a neglected field of historical scholarship.[1] It seems to me that if we are to understand the American character and its devotion to republican ideals, in particular the American dream, we must examine the institutions we create to perpetuate those ideals and to keep that dream alive. Moreover, if we are to understand the southern expression of that dream, the "Southern Way of Life," we must look to the southern schoolhouse and determine what is happening there. We may know more about some Civil War skirmishes and the economic consequences of a capricious cotton market than we actually need to know. But southern historians have left the relationship between the schoolhouse and the society that supports it, or does not support it, largely unexplored.

This book, if I may paraphrase Frederick Rudolph, is an attempt to redress the balance, as far as one southern state's experience with higher education is concerned. I have consciously, perhaps unconsciously as well, patterned this book after Rudolph's classic study of the American college and university, though mine may suffer by comparison.[2] And I must acknowledge, as he did, the shortcomings of a study embracing such a long period of time and such a broad range of issues, personalities, and institutions.

There are many topics, such as the role of the federal government in shaping higher education, the rise of athletics and alumni organizations, the expanding role of the community colleges, and the relation-

ship between public institutions and private colleges that are not given
the extended treatment they warrant. But this volume is not intended
as a definitive study. It is meant to serve as an introduction to a range
of topics that invite, or plead, for further research. Socialization as a
function of higher education, the relationship between higher education and modernization, the college as local industry, the separation of
the junior colleges from the senior institutions, the maintenance of a
university for women that is coeducational, the role of black colleges
in the post–civil rights era, and the renewed popular support for liberal education are but a few topics that need to be studied.

The purpose of this book is to help the reader understand where the
state's present system of higher education came from and how it got
here. I have traced the evolution of institutional autonomy, a tradition
that spawned rivalry, competition, duplication, and waste and that frustrated the effort to coordinate the eight universities and the fifteen
public junior colleges into a state system of higher education. I have
written about the racial dimension and the dynamics of class and have
detailed the influence of those forces on the development of higher
education. I have chronicled the incursion of politics into academia and
have documented its consequences. The public colleges were never
cloistered in Mississippi, or anywhere else in America. The "republic
of letters," sovereign and independent, was an ideal to be sought but a
goal never reached.

During the ten years that this study was underway, I became in-
debted to many people. Unfortunately, I can express my appreciation
to only a few of them. Former Chancellor Porter L. Fortune, Jr., first
introduced me to Dr. Verner Smith Holmes and suggested that I chronicle his experiences on the board of trustees of Mississippi state institutions of higher learning, especially during the James Meredith crisis at
Ole Miss. I readily agreed to do so, and from that happy circumstance
a friendship developed with Dr. Holmes and Emma, and Vern, and
with Lisa, Lynn and Jim Covington. It was largely at Holmes's urging
that I broadened my initial endeavor into this present study. I could
not, or would not, have been able to complete this book without his
and Emma's support and encouragement. Dr. Holmes, the only person
in the board's history to serve two full twelve-year terms, was a member of the board of trustees from 1956 to 1980 and was twice elected
president. He is a scion of Old Mississippi. Imbued and buoyed by the

American dream, his forebears emigrated from Ireland, by way of the Old Dominion to the new settlements in Georgia, and thence to the Old Southwest when Mississippi was still a wilderness territory. He is a man of rare and noble character, he represents the best of Mississippi, and his contributions to higher education will be as the rippling effects of a widening circle.

Chancellor Fortune and the University of Mississippi provided financial support during the early stages of the study. George Street and Rufus Jones, director of university relations and director of development at the University of Mississippi, made very significant contributions to the study during its beginning, and Betty Galloway transcribed with diligence and dispatch most of the interviews cited in the latter chapters.

Claude Fike, Henry Simmons, and Terry Latour of the William D. McCain Library, University of Southern Mississippi; the late Jimmy G. Shoalmire, Mitchell Memorial Library, Mississippi State University; Sammy Cranford, curator of the Walter Sillers Papers, Delta State University; Elbert Hilliard and his staff at the Mississippi Department of Archives and History; Dr. Thomas Verich, Naomi Leavell, Mary Crestman, Sharron Sarthou, Scott Barber, and Susan Avery of the Special Collections Division, John Davis Williams Library, University of Mississippi all made my visits to their collections pleasant as well as profitable.

I also wish to thank E. E. Thrash, former executive secretary of the board of trustees of institutions of higher learning, for reading large portions of the manuscript; Willie Morris, the writer-in-residence at the University of Mississippi, who read an early version of the manuscript; Frank Moak, professor of higher education at the University of Mississippi, who has made his own research and understanding of higher education always available to me; my colleagues in the history department, especially Charles Eagles, who pointed me to several useful sources, and Chairman Robert Haws, who read portions of the manuscript; and the departmental secretaries Virginia Williams and Janet Smith for their cheerfulness under stress and for never saying that they could not do something "today." I also want to thank Seetha Srinivasan, editor-in-chief of the University Press of Mississippi, who guided this book through a lengthy process to a happy conclusion and Richard Abel, director of the university press.

To Julius J. Hayden, former president of Mississippi Gulf Coast Community College, and to Lillian Hayden, I owe a great debt, which I gratefully acknowledge but can never fully repay. Among other things, President Hayden gave me my first teaching job. I also wish to express my deep appreciation to Governor Bill Waller and Carroll Waller.

To Nell Thomas, my high school history teacher, I owe the most. She is the single most important influence in my academic career. My loftiest ambition as a teacher is some day to have a student feel toward me as I do toward her.

And to my family, Lib, David and Cindy and Cherish, Beth and Mary Love and John, Jeannie and Perry, who lived with me and this book for a long time, and seemed never to weary of either, I promise not to take this long again.

Making Haste Slowly
The Troubled History of Higher Education in Mississippi

Jefferson College and the Origins of Higher Education, 1802–1830

The cause of education is the cause of our country.
— Jackson *Mississippian*

By the time Mississippi was established as a territory in 1798, higher education in America had already entered its second stage of development. During the colonial period the American college had been a "child of the church" and a "nursery for ministers." Even at the venerable Harvard, according to its 1646 student code, the "main End of [education is] to know God and Jesus Christ which is Eternal life" (John 17:3). A century later President Thomas Clap of Yale reaffirmed the notion that educational institutions were essentially religious in nature and function. "Colleges," he wrote in 1754, "are Societies of Ministers, for training up persons for the work of the Ministry." But the Enlightenment and the American Revolution changed the function of higher education in America. During the ascendancy of democracy and free enterprise, colleges turned from piety to polity and assumed a commitment to the republic as a guiding obligation. To the founders of the new republic "the true use of Education, is to qualify Men for the Employments of Life," to "infuse them with a Public Spirit" and a "Benevolence for Mankind," and "to make them more extensively serviceable to the Commonwealth." Evangelical denominations resisted the transition of the college from "child of the church" to "child of the state," and their clergy sermonized against the secularization of education.[1] But in the end it was the Enlightenment, rather than the Covenant, that shaped the American college.

Preeminent among America's apostles of Enlightenment was Thomas Jefferson, one of the new nation's earliest advocates of public education. In 1776 Jefferson introduced a bill in the Virginia legislature to revoke the private charter of William and Mary College and re-charter the school as a public university to train the sons of Virginia in the art of statecraft. Although that bill was defeated, Jefferson was de-termined to remodel William and Mary. When he later became a mem-ber of its board of visitors, he tried unsuccessfully to restructure its curriculum and replace the chair of divinity with a chair of science.[2] Most of Jefferson's early efforts at collegiate reform were unsuccessful, but the innovative curriculum that he later installed at the University of Virginia became a model for other American colleges and influenced academic discussion in the United States for the next fifty years.

Mr. Jefferson's disciple in the Old Southwest was W. C. C. Clai-borne, the twenty-six-year-old governor of the Mississippi Territory. Like President Jefferson who appointed him governor of the territory in 1801, Claiborne believed that education was a function of the state and that an enlightened citizenry was absolutely essential to the suc-cess of the republic. "The very preservation of Republican Govern-ment in its genuine purity and energy," he wrote, "depends upon a diffusion of knowledge among the body of society."[3] Acting on that belief, Governor Claiborne sent a message to the territorial legislature on May 4, 1802, recommending the establishment of a state-supported "seminary of learning." The legislature responded quickly; nine days after receiving Claiborne's message, it sent the governor a bill estab-lishing Jefferson College. Governor Claiborne signed the bill on May 13, 1802.[4]

Governor Claiborne's recommendation for a state-supported in-stitution made no mention of the need to train ministers or provide moral instruction. Claiborne's conception of man—like that of many other southerners, especially from Mr. Jefferson's Virginia—was more influenced by French liberalism than by New England Puritanism. French liberalism, which rejected the Puritan dogma of human de-pravity, flourished among southerners in the post-Revolutionary pe-riod. More than a few southern men must have given counsel to their sons, in actions if not in words, similar to the advice that Mr. Jefferson gave his nephew in 1787: "Question with boldness even the existence of God, because if there be one, he must more approve of the homage of reason, than that of blindfold fear."[5]

The Almighty might have approved of Mr. Jefferson's advice but the Scottish Presbyterians, whom Jefferson called "the most intolerant of all sects," did not. Furthermore, the general assembly of the Presbyterian church declared in 1811 that education was "the legitimate business of the church, rather than the state." A resurgence of orthodoxy and intolerance swept the Old Southwest in the opening decades of the nineteenth century, and the evangelical denominations used higher education, even at state-supported institutions, as a weapon against rationalism, secularism, and religious liberalism. The shifting emphasis at the University of Georgia is a testament to the success of southern evangelicals. The university was founded in 1785 for the young men of Georgia in order that "they [might] be molded to the love of virtue and good order." Those republican ideals were predicated on the belief that mankind was good and noble and capable of ordering society with just and equitable laws. But later, under its Presbyterian minister-president, Robert H. Finley, the university's primary purpose was "to militate the condition of man and direct his heart to heaven."[6] The tension between church and state over control of the colleges was a central theme in the early history of higher education in Mississippi. It significantly influenced the development of Jefferson College and of the state's other antebellum institutions.

The law establishing Jefferson College placed the institution under the governance of a thirty-four-member, self-perpetuating board of trustees and directed the board to locate the college at a "healthy and central situation." The board was given complete governance over the academic affairs of the college, including admission standards, curriculum, degree requirements, and student examinations. The board of trustees was also empowered to "engage a president and other professors" and to "displace or supersede them at pleasure." Since academic credentials were not standardized in the early nineteenth century, trustees routinely examined prospective faculty members in their subject areas. Board members also questioned applicants about their philosophical beliefs, politics, and religious preferences. But trustees took "effectual care that students of all denominations received fair, just, and impartial treatment during their residence at the college."

Professors, tutors, and students at Jefferson College were exempt from militia duty "except in a general invasion of the territory."[7]

The Jefferson College board of trustees held its first meeting on January 3, 1803. At that meeting the board received citizens' petitions to locate the college in the towns of Washington and Greenville. Mordecai Throckmorton offered the college twenty acres of choice land in Greenville, twenty-eight miles north of Natchez, and other townsmen agreed to contribute varying sums of money. A counter offer came from John and James Foster, Randall Gibson, and other residents of Washington, six miles east of Natchez. The board of trustees appointed David Ker, a former president of the University of North Carolina, chairman of a committee to study the two possible sites.[8]

At the board's next meeting, which was held in Washington on March 14, the site selection committee recommended Greenville. That town's partisans were well represented and, with little difficulty, carried the motion to establish Jefferson College at Greenville. Some trustees who had not attended the meeting, however, accused David Ker of deception, claiming that he had misled them into thinking that a vote on the location of Jefferson College would not be taken at the March meeting. He was also accused of understating the number of acres in the Foster grant at Washington and of "addressing himself to motives of personal interest."[9]

A month later, on April 11, the board of trustees held a stormy session at Greenville. Both factions, those wanting to locate the college at Washington and those who wanted it at Greenville, came to the meeting in full strength. After extended discussions, which served only to intensify the bitterness and push both sides farther apart, it was decided that another committee should be appointed to reconsider the matter of locating the college.[10]

The new site selection committee reported to the board on June 6 that a choice between Washington and Greenville could not be made. It therefore recommended selecting an alternate site at Selserton, approximately halfway between Washington and Greenville. The board deferred voting on the matter until its July meeting. With twenty of the thirty-four board members present at the July session, both sides were again ready for a showdown vote. The six-member site selection committee once more recommended that Jefferson College be located at Selserton.[11] The board rejected the committee's proposal and voted in favor of Washington. Although the records are not clear on the matter, its choice may have been influenced by the additional land and monetary pledges made in behalf of the town of Washington.

An announcement published shortly before the July board meeting that Governor W. C. C. Claiborne had established his official residence in Washington gave the town an additional advantage. The same announcement indicated that the territorial judges and the federal land office would also be located in Washington.[12] Moreover, it was probably known by then that the United States government planned to build Fort Dearborn adjacent to the town. For whatever combination of reasons, the board voted to establish Jefferson College at Washington and asked the legislature to fix the site of the college by statute, which the legislature did on November 11, 1803.

With the site of Mississippi's first public institution of higher learning settled, the board of trustees directed its attention and a considerable amount of effort toward matters of finance. The board faced the bewildering task of establishing a college without funds, because the law establishing Jefferson College had not included an appropriation for either capital construction or operating expenses. Governor Claiborne recommended a special tax on marriage licenses to endow Jefferson College, but the legislature did not pass the tax.[13]

The task of initiating a fund-raising campaign for an institution that had no students, no faculty, and no alumni would have dismayed ordinary men. But those trustees were extraordinary and undaunted, even optimistic. "Indeed," their first public statement read, "when we look forward to the consequence of a successful attempt to raise a respectable school for the education of the youth of this Territory, we trust the enlightened citizens will not be wanting in furnishing the means essentially necessary."[14] But to their great disappointment, private support for Jefferson College was minimal.

Consequently, the board of trustees decided to conduct a $10,000 lottery. Lottery tickets were printed and an extensive sales campaign conducted. But so few tickets were sold that the lottery had to be abandoned in May 1805 and the ticket money refunded. Neither the private contributions nor the lottery produced enough revenue for the college to begin operation. A much more promising source of funds had become available on March 3, 1803, when Congress granted Jefferson College a township of land (about 23,000 acres) in the unsettled area along the lower Tombigbee River in what is now Alabama. Generous as the grant was, Jefferson College did not receive any immediate benefit from it. The township was not surveyed until several years later, and even then so few acres were sold that the proceeds fell far short of what college officials had anticipated.[15]

The 1803 federal land grant also included two town lots located within the corporate limits of Natchez and a thirty-acre plot adjacent to the city. Although these lots appeared to offer more immediate benefits than the township along the Tombigbee, the end results were equally disappointing. On January 28, 1804, Acting Governor Cato West informed the Jefferson College board of trustees that the town lots and the out-lot of thirty acres had been located but that the city of Natchez and Adams County had already constructed public buildings on the lots. The board of trustees demanded that the city of Natchez and Adams County relinquish their claims and vacate the buildings, but both refused to do so. Because Jefferson College did not realize any revenue from these lots, its opening was postponed indefinitely and the board of trustees did not meet from December 21, 1805, to April 28, 1810. During that interim the Reverend James Smylie, a Presbyterian minister, conducted the Washington Academy in a temporary frame structure on the site of Jefferson College.[16]

In 1810 the board of trustees renewed its efforts to open Jefferson College. Although the records are not clear concerning why the effort was made at that time, the appointment of David Holmes as governor of the territory in 1809 was likely a factor in the board's decision. Holmes was a popular governor, and his appointment ended a long period of bitter factionalism in the Mississippi Territory. Under his leadership the board of trustees, "their expectations humbled by the experiences of the past eight years," announced that Jefferson College would open as a sub-collegiate academy on January 1, 1811. With no funds immediately available, the board was able to open the college only by continuing the policy Smylie had initiated of paying faculty and staff members out of the tuition fees collected from the students.[17] That procedure, however tenuous and unpredictable, enabled the board to open Jefferson College at last.

About a year after it opened the college began receiving financial support from the territorial legislature in the form of proceeds from all escheats. During the ten years that the law was in effect, Jefferson College received approximately $6,000.[18] The legal expenses to prosecute the college's claim to the escheats, however, consumed a substantial amount of the monies collected. Because of such limited funding, Jefferson College remained a preparatory academy during its first five years.

In 1816 the legislature made additional financial support available to Jefferson College in the form of a $6,000 loan. The law authorizing the loan required the president of the Jefferson College board of trustees to file an annual report with the legislature giving detailed information about the general and financial condition of the college. The loan enabled the board to open the collegiate department, and in June 1817 the trustees appointed James McAllister president of Jefferson College. According to the board's statement announcing his appointment, McAllister was "advantageously known in the United States for his profound learning."[19]

President McAllister's tenure began under the most favorable circumstances. When Mississippi was admitted to statehood on December 10, 1817, immigration into the lower Tombigbee Valley prompted a swell in land prices. The board of trustees sent an agent to St. Stephens to begin leasing portions of the land grant. The first installment on the new leases netted Jefferson College about $8,000, and future installments were estimated at $25,000. On the basis of that anticipated revenue, the board of trustees secured a bank loan and proceeded to complete several buildings that were in various stages of construction. An air of excitement permeated the campus, enrollment reached a record high of sixty-six in 1818, and college officials were enthusiastic about the school's future.[20] But at the very time when its future seemed so bright, Jefferson College suffered a serious and unexpected setback. During the Panic of 1819 Mississippi's impoverished farmers were unable to pay the installments on their leases. Even though the board of trustees offered an abatement of one-half the amount due, all but one landowner forfeited their leases, and Jefferson College's large landholdings became worthless. The board of trustees was consequently burdened with heavy debts, which it had no means of repaying.

To make matters worse, enrollment also declined drastically in 1819. Included in Jefferson College's 1818 record enrollment were approximately thirty female students. How many, if any, of those students were enrolled in collegiate courses is not known, but most of them transferred to the Elizabeth Female Academy which opened in Natchez on November 12, 1818. This academy, founded by the Washington Circuit of the Methodist Conference, is cited by some as the first degree-granting institution of higher learning for women in the South, perhaps in the United States. But others trace the origins of higher education for women in this country to the Troy (New York) Institute, established in 1822.[21]

A comparison of the course of study at Elizabeth Female Academy with the curriculum at Sharon College does warrant the conclusion that the academy offered a collegiate course from its beginning. Students at Elizabeth Female Academy received a classical education with courses in Greek, Latin, Aesop's fables, sacred history, intellectual philosophy, Caesar's *Bella Gallica,* mythology, chemistry, and botany. Honor students were allowed to study "polite literature" and pursue other "ornamental studies." Graduates of the institution were awarded a degree entitled *Domina Scientiarum.* The fortunes of Elizabeth Female Academy, like those of other colleges in antebellum Mississippi, ebbed and flowed but mostly ebbed. The academy closed after its twenty-ninth year in 1847.[22]

While trying to deal with the drop in enrollment and the loss of revenue, the Jefferson College board of trustees came under severe attack from the religious right. At a meeting in Natchez in 1818 a convention of ministers, representing several evangelical denominations, denounced Jefferson College authorities for neglecting the religious instruction of their students and leveled several other charges against President McAllister and the board of trustees. To appease the concerns of local evangelicals, the board appointed the Reverend R. F. N. Smith to the faculty and over the next two years he vehemently defended the institution. Nonetheless, Jefferson College continued to decline in enrollment, endowment, and esteem.[23]

In an effort to alleviate its financial distress, the legislature made an additional $4,000 loan in 1820. Those funds brought only temporary relief, however, and Jefferson College's indebtedness continued to mount. Eventually the Reverend Mr. Smith was released because the board could not pay his salary, and in June 1821 President McAllister retired.[24] Following McAllister's retirement, Jefferson College was operated as a preparatory academy under several different principals.

Destitute of resources, the college and its physical facilities fell into disrepair and its public esteem declined still further.

In his 1825 annual report to the legislature B. B. Grayson, president of the Jefferson College board of trustees, expressed his "regrets that the well-intentioned efforts of the trustees have not resulted in [something] more substantial." The report detailed the succession of financial crises and legal disputes that had delayed the college's initial opening and had forced its suspension on several occasions. Grayson informed the legislature that Jefferson College was at that time without a principal, without students, and without "any active funds." The suspension of Jefferson College in 1825 left the state without a collegiate institution for boys. That situation prompted a group of citizens at Clinton to establish Hampstead Academy in 1826. The academy's curriculum was elevated to collegiate standards the following year.[25]

The dismal tone of Grayson's report caused Representative William Haile of Wilkinson County to introduce a resolution to place Jefferson College under the governance of the state legislature. During the debate over Haile's resolution some legislators questioned the board's handling of college funds, many others expressed a general disappointment that the college had not prospered, and some upstate representatives recommended the relocation of Jefferson College to a more "central situation."[26] After extensive debate Haile's proposal passed, and the reorganization of Jefferson College was implemented during the next legislative session.

On January 26, 1826, the legislature revoked Jefferson College's original charter and reorganized its board of trustees. The governor and lieutenant governor were made ex officio members, with the governor serving as president of the board. The law reduced the number of trustees to twenty-four and gave the legislature the authority to appoint board members.[27] Supporters of the 1826 law expanding the state's role in the governance of Jefferson College believed they were securing its future as the primary institution of higher learning in Mississippi. But they were soon to be disappointed.

In 1829, just three years after the reorganization of Jefferson College, Governor Gerard C. Brandon lectured the legislature on the relationship between "ignorance and despotism." A well-educated citizenry, he said, could not be deceived by "fraud or stratagem." Mississippi, however, was not providing its young men and women the kind of education he considered essential to self-government. Governor Brandon then reviewed the "troubled history" of Jefferson College and concluded that its "failure has been principally [owing] to an effort on the part of the trustees to force the institution beyond its means and a want of corresponding patronage on the part of the public."[28]

After this brief and unflattering review, Governor Brandon recommended that the Jefferson College board of trustees return the college's charter to the state. The surrender of its charter, he contended, would enable the legislature to support "a college at a [location] more likely to meet with public patronage."[29] Although Governor Brandon did not directly allude to the rivalry between the Old Natchez District and upstate counties, his recommendation to transfer Jefferson College's charter to an institution at a more central location was a recognition that sectionalism had long been a factor in legislative squabbles and had prevented the adequate funding of Jefferson College.

Governor Brandon did not recommend the establishment of a new institution. Instead, he suggested that the legislature designate Mississippi Academy as the state university. This academy, chartered in 1826 as Hampstead Academy, was a thriving institution with an enrollment of nearly one hundred; like Jefferson College, it was technically a state-supported institution.[30] The 1827 legislation granting it a collegiate charter also allocated part of the proceeds from a second federal land grant, which Mississippi had received in 1819, to the academy for a period of five years. The enormous potential of that revenue encouraged the patrons of Mississippi Academy to seek its designation as the state university.

On April 11, 1828, Isaac Caldwell, a Mississippi Academy trustee, wrote to John A. Quitman, a wealthy and prominent politician and future governor, enlisting his support for the designation of the academy as the state university. Caldwell also urged Quitman to use his influence to prevent the legislature from dividing the rents from the 1819 land grant among all the academies of the state. It should be obvious to everyone, Caldwell wrote, that if one institution received all the rents, that institution could become a "college of the first order." And if Mississippi Academy "was a child of the state, it would stand a fair chance to inherit those lands."[31]

But Governor Brandon, even with the support of Quitman and Caldwell and many others, could not convince the legislature to create one state institution of higher learning at a central location. Instead of designating Mississippi Academy as the state university, the legislature issued the academy a $5,000 loan which was used for capital construction. The academy's board continued to seek its designation as the state university and, believing that there might be something in a name, changed its title to Mississippi College in 1830. But that public relations maneuver had no effect on the legislature. Mississippi College was not designated the state university.[32]

During the maneuvering and lobbying by the Mississippi College board of trustees, Jefferson College was struggling to survive. Hoping to increase enrollment by attracting "the popular eye with the flash of brass buttons and military uniforms," the board in 1829 reorganized Jefferson College into a military academy. E. B. Williston, the author of *Eloquence in the U.S.* and *Williston's Tacitus,* was elected president, and Major John Holbrook was appointed commander of the cadet corps.[33] The young cadets—the youngest was only five years old—displayed a "sartorial splendor" in their dashing uniforms at daily parades. The state supplied Jefferson College with small arms and a cannon for instruction in the military arts. The reorganization was very successful, and enrollment rose rapidly. The collegiate department, which had been closed since 1821, reopened in 1831. The historian of Jefferson College explains this success and provides an insight into the culture and psyche of white antebellum Mississippians. "What southern boy," he wrote, "would not thrill to the crack of musket shots, the smell of burning powder, and the clash of steel?"[34]

While President Williston and Major Holbrook were attracting young cadets in ever-increasing numbers, the board of trustees was seeking additional sources of revenue. Jefferson College's original land grant along the lower Tombigbee River had provided very little income. But in the early 1830s the Choctaw and Chickasaw land cessions added millions of acres to the public domain in north Mississippi. After those land cessions had been finalized, the Jefferson College board of trustees petitioned Congress to exchange the 1803 grant for an equal amount of land in north Mississippi. Benjamin L. C. Wailes, who so often represented the interests of Jefferson College, went to

Washington to lobby for the exchange. Congress responded favorably and authorized the exchange in 1832. Wailes then went to north Mississippi to survey the new land grant. Within a year much of Jefferson College's new township had been surveyed and sold, at an average of $6.50 an acre. Unfortunately the board of trustees invested large amounts of that revenue in bank stock, most of which was lost during the banking crisis that followed the Panic of 1837.[35]

When E. B. Williston became president of Jefferson College in 1829, American higher education was engaged in a debate over the content of the college curriculum. The prescribed classical curriculum was dominant, but a parallel course that included modern languages and modern history, bookkeeping and other business courses, agriculture, and applied sciences was becoming increasingly popular. Yale College had issued a report in 1828 defending a liberal education and the classical curriculum, and Princeton officials were criticizing the practice of grafting "electives" onto the prescribed curriculum.[36] Like the United States Military Academy and many southern colleges (including the University of Virginia) which were influenced by frontier conditions, Jefferson College was broadening its curriculum in the applied sciences and allowing its students to elect a course of study.

During the first year of his administration, President Williston made several changes in the curriculum. Students were allowed, for example, to substitute French and Spanish for Greek and Latin. New subjects such as bookkeeping and civil engineering were offered, and school officials announced in the 1830 catalog that "the application of science to the useful arts [and] practical education generally" would be emphasized in the new curriculum. In 1831 the board of trustees authorized an even wider application of the elective system. The trustees announced that Jefferson College would allow "every student to pursue what studies he may select, and when his means shall be exhausted . . . he will be accredited with a certificate of proficiency he may have attained in the arts and sciences or in any branch of learning."[37] The emphasis on applied science and useful arts was influenced by the personal experiences of the trustees. Most had come to Mississippi as pioneers, and they placed a premium on practical knowledge and applied science.

This reorganization of the curriculum reflects the influence of several instructors at Jefferson College during the 1830s who were graduates of West Point, where mathematics and science constituted a basic part of the curriculum. Because Jefferson College was a military academy as well, those courses were introduced into its program of study. The towering presence of Benjamin Wailes, the state geologist and one of antebellum Mississippi's premier men of science, also had an influence. Wailes was a longtime member of the board of trustees, and it was on his recommendation that Jefferson College established a chair of topography, civil engineering, and geology in 1836.[38]

The expansion of the collegiate curriculum was of keen interest to the members of the lyceum in Washington, Mississippi, and it also provoked a lively debate among the Jefferson College faculty, as among college faculty generally. C. G. Forshey, professor of mathematics and civil engineering at Jefferson College, and J. J. Wyche, professor of ancient languages, wrote lengthy papers on the question: "Are the Claims of the Mathematics to Predominate in General Education, Greater than the Claims of the Ancient Classics?" Their essays were published in the *Southwest Journal,* a scholarly magazine published by the Washington and Jefferson College Lyceum. The lyceum at Washington was a literary and scientific society that flourished in a tiny intellectual clearing in the dense southern wilderness. Washington and its environs, which included Natchez, was for a short while the cultural center of the Old Southwest. Its residents included, at various times, William Dunbar, John James Audubon, David Ker, Joseph Holt Ingraham, Benjamin Wailes, and many other men of uncommon learning.[39]

The brief initial success enjoyed by President Williston and Major Holbrook was followed by another period of decline. President Williston became seriously ill and was forced to resign in April 1832. Major Holbrook's outside interests occupied most of his time and caused him to neglect his duties at Jefferson College. According to Joseph Holt Ingraham, who was on the Jefferson College faculty during the 1830s, Major Holbrook was "seized with the mania for cotton-planting, which infects all who reside here for any length of time." And many patrons of the college, "perhaps regarding his additional vocation as incompatible with that of instructing," withdrew their sons.[40] That alone, however, did not account for the drop in enrollment in the mid-1830s. Many students who withdrew from Jefferson College transferred to one of the new generation of colleges established in Mississippi during the "flush times" of the 1830s–1850s. During that prolonged period of prosperity, millions of new acres were brought under cultivation and colleges were founded at the rate of one a year. Most were small struggling liberal arts schools, which competed intensely for Mississippi's collegiate students.

Rather than addressing the actual problem of too few students for too many colleges, the Jefferson College board of trustees stepped up its recruiting efforts and offered free tuition to one student from every county.[41] If the program had worked, it would have provided Jefferson College with a network of alumni and friends throughout the state. But Jefferson College records indicate that only two boys attended the school under the free tuition plan. It was discontinued after only two years.

In spring 1838 the Jefferson College board of trustees announced that the collegiate department would close for the remainder of that academic year so that the college's full income could be devoted to renovating older buildings and constructing several new ones. Jefferson College reopened in 1839 under the Reverend Abednego Stephens, a disciple of Philip Lindsley, the innovative president of the University of Nashville.[42] In his inaugural address President Stephens announced his intention to modernize the Jefferson College curriculum. He had hired Professor J. A. Midderhoff, graduate of a German university, to teach modern languages and would himself teach modern philosophy, including the works of Locke, Kant, and Cousin. Jefferson College would continue to offer the prescribed classical course, but students would also be allowed to take a parallel (or English) course, also known in some schools as the "irregular" course. The English course included modern languages, modern history and literature, modern philosophy, natural sciences, mathematics, and applied sciences.[43]

Governor Alexander G. McNutt, who had been instrumental in the appointment of President Stephens, praised him for his innovative leadership and urged the legislature to use part of the seminary fund to build up Jefferson College. This fund contained the revenue derived from the second federal land grant, which Mississippi had received in 1819. A combination of two factors, however, worked against Jefferson College and its innovative president. First, the legislature in 1840 was controlled by representatives from the new counties in north Mississippi that had little interest in Jefferson College. Second, there was increasing popular support for a state university. Governor McNutt's recommendation to use the seminary fund to upgrade Jefferson College forced the legislature to make a decision. It chose to establish a state university.[44]

After the legislature's decision, the trustess of both Jefferson College and Mississippi College realized that neither institution would receive any additional state aid. Both boards also saw that competition from Mississippi's second generation of colleges would make it difficult, if not impossible, for their institutions to survive on private donations and tuition fees alone. Consequently, they turned to the only alternative: affiliation with a religious denomination. Mississippi College, after a brief association with the Clinton Presbytery, was transferred by its board of trustees to the Mississippi Baptist Convention, which assumed ownership of the institution in 1850. The Jefferson College board of trustees initially voted to sell the college to the Natchez diocese, but announcement of the sale stirred up "all the fanatical spirit of the neighborhood" and the board placed so many stipulations on the purchase that Bishop John Joseph Chanche eventually declined the board's offer. The Jefferson College board then decided to continue the school as a military academy.[45]

The troubled history of Jefferson College is a reflection of the larger society which birthed it but did not nurture it. A child of neither church nor state, it was "a stillborn child with the politicians of Natchez, Greenville, and Washington serving as muddled midwives." Demographic conditions, the state's agrarian economy, its sparse population, and public apathy are often cited as the reasons for its failure. But William B. Hamilton perceived a more fundamental cause: "All these wants and deficiencies," he wrote, "would not have sufficed to wreck Mississippi's early educational effort if one of her besetting sins had not assisted them." Jefferson College, according to Hamilton, could have succeeded "had it not run afoul of the feud" between sections and factions, a problem that has plagued its successors down through the troubled history of higher education in Mississippi.[46]

Two

Old-Time Colleges in Mississippi, 1830–1840

Our Country is a land of colleges.
—Absalom Peters

In the early years of the republic academicians, like entrepreneurs, became infected with the American ethic of growth and greatness. Frederick Rudolph has compared college-founding in that early period to "canal building, cotton ginning," and "gold mining." America's restless money-making people favored a collegiate network, Philip Lindsley said, that was as dynamic and decentralized as the far-flung country itself. The idea of a national university was just that—an idea—with little popular appeal. The effort to establish a central university under federal patronage where "the youth of all the states" would be molded "into one mass of citizens" was doomed from the beginning, because America was to become a "culture with many capitals" and many colleges.[1]

During the opening decades of the nineteenth century America's population was doubling every twenty-five years, and in that time of plenty Mississippi was a promised land. Between 1830 and 1840 nearly eight million acres of good cotton land was sold in north Mississippi. Prices skyrocketed from $1.25 to $40.00 an acre, and the state's population soared from 136,621 to 374,431. "Kentucky's coming, Tennessee's coming, Alabama's coming," Robert J. Walker proclaimed, "and they're coming to join the joyous crowds of Mississippians." During those "flush times" white Mississippians established the plantation system, linked their destiny to slave labor and racial supremacy, and founded thirty-four colleges.[2]

There were only nine colleges in America at the time of the Revolution but approximately 240 by 1850. Almost half of those were in the South, seventeen in Mississippi. One of the three colleges established in Marshall County, Mississippi, was the University of Holly Springs. Its first president, the Reverend Joseph Travis, explained that the university was the product of a "speculative mania" that had induced the people to project "vast calculations upon slender and uncertain data." After President Travis's brief tenure, the university "wobbled on for three years" and then "went down, unwept and unhonored." The history of the University of Holly Springs was not atypical of antebellum colleges. It has been estimated that perhaps as many as 700 American colleges failed between the end of the Revolution and the beginning of the Civil War.[3]

The predominant institution of higher learning in antebellum America was the residential, liberal arts college, which historians have called the "old-time college." There were no universities in the modern sense, and even the state universities were hardly more than liberal arts colleges, though some did include a medical school and a law department. Most old-time colleges, including state universities, maintained preparatory departments; some of the smaller ones, out of financial necessity, maintained primary departments as well. Clement Eaton has found the Old South's support of higher education a "bright contrast" to its neglect of common schools. The lack of primary and secondary schools was critical in both the South and the Midwest and impeded the development of higher education in both regions. Frederick Rudolph discerned in that widespread problem an unwritten law in American higher education: "Where there are no elementary or secondary schools, there you will find a college."[4]

Most of Mississippi's old-time colleges were established in a flurry of local pride. That was especially true of the ones started by private entrepreneurs and fraternal organizations like the Masons, who founded three colleges in Mississippi. Even those begun by denominations were not so much sectarian as Christian schools, with a religious orientation and underpinning—for example, the interdenominational college established in Madison County as a "community project." The by-laws of Sharon College, founded in 1837, specified that four of its five faculty members be ministers of the Old School Presbyterian, Cumberland Presbyterian, Methodist, and Baptist denominations. The fifth faculty member was to be a nonclergyman "whose want of religious profession, provided there be good scholarship and good morals," would not disqualify him. Even Centenary College, established in honor of Methodism's first century, announced that it would not teach sectarian dogma, and the Mississippi Female College catalog stated that it was a Baptist institution "but it inculcates no denominational tenets." President Jeremiah Chamberlain of Oakland College, started by the Presbyterians in 1830, took great care to dispel the notion that Oakland was sectarian and pointed to the fact that ministers of various denominations were being educated there. He also noted that most of Oakland's students were preparing themselves as planters, physicians, and lawyers rather than as ministers.[5]

Mississippi's new Christian colleges were in large measure a religious reaction to the increasing secularization of education. The Reverend Thomas C. Thornton, first president of Centenary College, warned of the dangers of secular education. The exclusion of religious instruction from our colleges, he said, "leaves our sons to be trained to infidelity and atheism," and he welcomed students of all denominations to Centenary. He even offered scholarships to the indigent, explaining that the scholarship program was designed to produce teachers for the state's common schools; "only poor young men," he added, "will endure the trial and hardship of instructing youth." After his brief tenure at Centenary, Thornton was appointed headmaster of an academy. Within a short time he elevated the academy's curriculum to collegiate standards and thus proved another of Rudolph's laws of higher education: "Offer a young man the principalship of an academy and he will try to make a college of it."[6]

The religious tolerance expressed by Thornton and Chamberlain, and exercised by Sharon College, was more pragmatic than ecumenical. The student pool was so small in Mississippi, and competition for students so keen, that no college could afford to be sectarian and thus exclude students from other denominations. Nor could colleges erect exclusive entrance requirements. Some historians trace the tradition of low academic standards in American institutions of higher learning to the early nineteenth century, when "standards were lowered so that almost any enterprise setting up a claim as a collegiate institute, seminary, college, or university was given the right to confer degrees and dispense the benefits of a liberal education."[7]

Most of Mississippi's old-time colleges, because of their Christian underpinning, valued moral character above academic excellence—a priority true of most antebellum colleges. Amherst's president stated categorically that "character is of more consequence than the intellect." The president of Denison College agreed and added a mild indictment of higher education in America: "At college we tend to exaggerate the importance of the intellectual." Collegiate authorities, and the body politic that commissioned them, were ever wary of the "ideological disruptions" and "unintended consequences" that might result from mass education, which was becoming an "ever widening circle."[8] They monitored, and moderated if necessary, the mind-altering effects of education.

The president of the state university, in a commencement address, proclaimed the need for college officials to guard their students against "the evils of unsanctified ambition," and President Charles L. Dubuisson of Jefferson College saw apocalyptic consequences from the unfettered minds of Mississippi school boys. In his 1835 inaugural address he declared: "Without moral excellence, high literary attainments seem only to increase the power of doing evil. A man of great talent without principle, like a fallen angel, throws around him an unholy atmosphere whose malignity blasts and withers all that comes within the sphere of his influence."[9] It was precisely to curtail the evils of unsanctified ambition, and to prevent young men of talent from becoming fallen angels, that presidents in the old-time colleges taught a course on moral philosophy required for seniors.

Like most of their modern offspring, Mississippi's old-time colleges were always "pressed for money and patronage." Loans, lotteries, and land grants—along with tuition, denominational subsidies, and private donations—were the primary sources of income for the state's colleges. Although the Female Collegiate Institute in Holly Springs received a $10,500 grant from the Marshall County board of police, local subsidies were extremely rare. Colleges established by denominations and fraternal organizations received subsidies from their sponsors, but they also charged tuition and sought donations from wealthy benefactors. One of the largest gifts received by any antebellum college in Mississippi was a $50,000 gift to Oakland College by David Hunt, who gave perhaps as much as $150,000 to the school during his lifetime.[10] None of the private and fraternal institutions received any public assistance, nor did Jefferson College or Mississippi College after the legislature voted to establish a state university in 1840.

Instruction in the old-time college was predicated on the theory of "faculty psychology," which held that the mind was divided into "faculties" such as will, emotion, imagination, memory, reason, and judgment. The proper development of those faculties required mental discipline and training. The unquestioned acceptance and preeminence of this psychology in old-time colleges is illustrated by a statement in President Thomas C. Thornton's 1842 commencement address at Centenary College. "Patient investigation and close observation," Thornton said, "will prove that the attributes or faculties of the mind are as distinctly marked, as are the different parts or systems which constitute the science of anatomy." The founders of Elizabeth Female Academy put it another way: "Education is the art of forming and managing the mind."[11]

President Thornton and most of his contemporaries believed that a thorough grounding in the classics was the best means of managing, training, and disciplining the mind. They agreed with the provost of Columbia College who said in 1810: "with the study of Greek and Latin languages, sound learning flourishes or declines." In most old-time colleges students took a prescribed course in Latin and Greek, ancient history and literature, logic, philosophy, and rhetoric. The commitment to the classical curriculum and its corollary, the "Genteel Tradition," was based on the belief that a liberal education would produce Christian gentlemen and that "knowledge of Latin and Greek was the key to understanding" that "grand body of history, science, and philosophy" which "together with Christianity [is] the substance of western civilization."[12]

The elective system, an American derivative of the classical tradition, was almost as old and nearly as persistent as the tradition itself; it in fact constituted a parallel, though less popular and pervasive, tradition. The University of Pennsylvania, the United States Military Academy, the University of Virginia, and many other institutions, including Jefferson College and most of Mississippi's old-time colleges, offered an elective course in addition to the prescribed classical course. By the 1820s the success of America's free enterprise system had given rise to an entrepreneurialism "that seemed life-threatening to a society shaped by republican ideology" and that blunted the college's commitment to the republican ideals of public duty and civic virtue. The merchant and the agriculturalist were demanding substitutions and alternatives and exemptions to the classical curriculum and liberal education. The American college, according to Frederick Rudolph, was fast becoming "a means of getting ahead," not just "a means of registering that one's father had."[13]

In an effort to safeguard the classics and a liberal education in the American college curriculum, Yale College published "A Report on the Course of Liberal Education" in 1828. The Yale Report was issued to dispel the notion that American colleges "must be new-modelled" to "the spirit and wants of the age," and it defined the purpose of a college education as "the discipline and furniture of the mind." According to one historian, the Yale Report was an attempt to reconcile "the new unrestrained private enterprise" with "the republican ideals of civic virtue."[14] Whatever its purpose, the report was a convincing defense of liberal education that insured the dominance of the classical tradition for the next fifty years.

The Yale Report did not, however, prevent the gradual expansion of the curriculum in Mississippi's old-time colleges. The reforms of Francis Wayland and Philip Lindsley, as well as the new applied sciences, found ready acceptance in the educational hinterlands of the Old Southwest. As early as 1821 the Natchez College of Commerce was offering commercial training in several areas and taught night courses in bookkeeping. The legislative charter establishing Oakland College in 1830 encouraged the institution to offer courses that would "prepare young men for business." Prompted by the success of Rensselaer Institute, which had been established in 1824, proponents of commercial and agricultural training increased their appeals for vocational education. In 1839, a year after a southern convention of merchants had passed a resolution calling on colleges to offer more business courses, the Mississippi legislature chartered the Chulahoma College and Commercial Institute. And nearly a decade before the Civil War, the Southern Scientific Institute was established to provide the rudiments of an agricultural education to planters in the Old Natchez District.[15]

No public institutions in antebellum Mississippi provided formal education to its slave population or to its small number of free blacks. Mississippi was in fact the only southern state that reported no free black children in school in 1850. There was a school for "children of color and others" conducted for a brief period in Natchez by Thomas Jones, but it apparently closed after Jones was arrested for furnishing a forged pass to a slave named Tom. Although a state law prohibited the education of slaves, some slaves and free blacks did acquire the rudiments of an education. William Johnson, Mississippi's wealthiest and most prominent free black resident, was literate and kept an extensive diary up to the time of his murder. Known as the Barber of Natchez, Johnson was killed by a white man who owed him a large sum of money.[16]

Although Mississippi neglected the education of blacks, who constituted over half of the state's total population, it did not neglect the education of women. Almost half of the old-time colleges in Mississippi were women's colleges or, as contemporaries preferred to call them "female colleges." The curriculum at the women's colleges combined the classics with other courses that collegiate officials considered appropriate for female students. The conventional view of women's education in antebellum Mississippi was embodied in a formal statement issued by the founders of Elizabeth Female Academy in 1818. "Female virtues," the founders wrote, "relate to domestic more than public things. The education of females, therefore, should teach them to aspire to those virtues peculiar to their sex." Other Mississippi educators, though not very many, did not accept such a limited view of women's intellectual capacity or interests. The Reverend J. P. Lee, president of Whitworth College for women in Brookhaven, believed "that the female is able to comprehend as the male" and conducted his school on that presumption.[17]

The pedagogical philosophy at most of Mississippi's old-time colleges was determined by their individual governing boards, most of which were self-perpetuating and included a combination of public officials, clergymen, and laymen. The legislative charter establishing an institution usually specified the number of trustees and their method of selection; in some cases there were specific requirements for board membership. At two of the three Masonic colleges only third-degree Masons could become trustees. Some of the church schools required denominational membership for board members, and in at least two cases, the Planters College and Madison College, faculty members were ex officio members of the board of trustees. At Semple Broaddus, which may have had one of the largest boards in America, the president was one of the sixty-two trustees. The law creating this institution also provided that a certain number of board members be residents of Tennessee, because a Baptist association just across the state line was supporting the school.[18]

For all the differences existing among Mississippi's various governing boards, there were two basic characteristics they shared: most trustees were laymen, and the trustees held ultimate authority over the institutions they governed. The 1840 catalog of Jefferson College stated that "the authority of the Board of Trustees is supreme." And the charter of Grenada College, like that of most other Mississippi schools, authorized the board of trustees to appoint a president and professors and "supersede them at pleasure." Governing boards exercised their authority through the college president, whose role was more of a surrogate than an executive. A noteworthy exception was Centenary College, where faculty members were given permanent tenure rather than annual contracts and could be dismissed only for cause. That enlightened policy was implemented upon the insistence of the Reverend William Winans, a popular Methodist minister and a member of Centenary's board of trustees and board of visitors. Winans declined the appointment as president of Centenary because he lacked the proper educational credentials and believed he would be unable to win the respect of the faculty.[19]

In addition to providing for faculty tenure, the Centenary College board of trustees also introduced a highly innovative experiment in college government: student participation. The historian of Centenary College referred to the experiment as "something new under the sun," and it may have been the first of its kind in America. The plan, designed by President David O. Shattuck and approved by a special board committee, separated the government of Centenary College into three departments or branches. The faculty was accorded executive and judicial authority. The legislative authority was shared by a senate, consisting of the board of trustees and the board of visitors, and a lower house comprised of twenty-one students who were elected by the student body. The only restrictions on the student assembly were that members had to be seventeen years old and that students had to be fifteen years old to vote. The faculty had veto power over the legislative branch, but their veto could be overridden by a simple majority of both houses. Perhaps the most significant feature of the experiment was the provision that a student could be expelled from Centenary College only "upon a fair trial by his peers, a jury of twelve students over sixteen years of age taken among the students by lot." Although the *Woodville [Mississippi] Republican* reported on January 24, 1846, that the experiment was "eminently gratifying" and was a credit to both the college and the students, President Augustus Baldwin Longstreet, who succeeded President Shattuck, persuaded the board of trustees to abandon it. President Longstreet, later president of the University of Mississippi, contended that "if there be anything in which age never confirms the views of youth, it is the direction and government of a school."[20]

Most presidents of America's old-time colleges, including Longstreet, Thornton, Chamberlain of Oakland College, Stephens of Jefferson College, and Barnard of the University of Mississippi, were ministers. One student has found only twenty-six American college presidents before the Civil War who were not ministers. All—ministers and laymen—were overworked and underpaid. A faculty member at Jefferson College explained that he was answering President Stephens's correspondence because Stephens had "collapsed last June from over exertion." The Reverend W. L. C. Hunnicutt was president of the same college three different times and once was president of two different colleges at the same time. It is not an exaggeration to say that, next to income, the college president and his reputation were the most important resources of the old-time college and that the president was often its most important booster. One proud president of a small Mississippi institute, which was eleven miles from the nearest railroad, asked: "Is there any other such school from the Potomac to the Rio Grande?"[21]

The Reverend Jeremiah Chamberlain was the preeminent old-time college president in Mississippi and Oakland College, which he served for many years, a premier example of an old-time college. After serving as president of Centre College in Kentucky and Jackson College in Louisiana, where he resigned because the board restricted his ministerial activities, Chamberlain persuaded the Mississippi Presbytery to establish Oakland College in 1830. In an early version of turning the first spade of dirt, Chamberlain's "own sturdy arm felled the first tree" where Oakland was to be built. For twenty-one years Chamberlain devoted his life to Oakland and developed it into one of the most successful colleges in the Southwest. Oakland succeeded, according to the Reverend Joel Parker of the First Presbyterian Church in New Orleans, because it was "above the jarrings of party politics, and far removed from the minglings of sectarian interests."[22]

Oakland granted the first college degree awarded by a Mississippi institution to James M. Smylie in 1833. By the mid-1850s Oakland had provided collegiate education to approximately one thousand students and awarded over a hundred degrees. Its 250-acre campus with nineteen buildings was one of the finest college campuses in the entire South. On the eve of the Civil War the Oakland College library, combined with the books owned by the school's literary societies, exceeded four thousand volumes. Perhaps the best testament to Chamberlain's success as a college president, however, was the fact that the institution he founded survived his tragic and violent death, which occurred during the political canvas of 1851. Mississippians were sharply divided in that campaign between the secessionist party of Governor John A. Quitman and the Unionist party of Senator Henry S. Foote. Chamberlain, who sided with the Unionists, was accused of expelling a student for making a secessionist speech. Chamberlain denied the charges but, on September 6, 1851, was attacked by a secessionist and fatally stabbed.[23]

President Chamberlain and most other old-time college presidents were not renowned as scholars or intellectuals. They were doers, not thinkers. Success was measurable to them in terms of enrollment figures, endowments, and brick and mortar. Reverend Joseph B. Stratton, who gave the eulogy at President Chamberlain's funeral, took kindly notice of that pragmatism. Stratton explained that Chamberlain's "intellectual endowments and acquirements [were not] brilliant or profound" because his life was too crowded with "duties" to allow him to achieve scholastic eminence.[24]

The bitter controversy over secession, which claimed the life of its president in 1851, eventually engulfed Oakland. Like so many other old-time colleges, it became a casualty of the Civil War. In the second year of the war the college division was closed. After the war it reopened briefly but with only a few students and only one professor. In 1871 the state purchased the campus and established Alcorn University, the first land-grant and among the earliest state-supported institutions of higher learning for blacks in the United States.[25]

If Jeremiah Chamberlain was the preeminent old-time college president in antebellum Mississippi, the Reverend William Carey Crane was the typical president. During his career in Mississippi, Crane served as president of Mississippi Female College (1850–58) and of Semple Broaddus College (1858–60). Three years after leaving Mississippi he became president of Baylor University, a position he held until his death in 1885. While at Mississippi Female College President Crane taught Greek, Latin, French, logic, history, mathematics, and bookkeeping. In addition to teaching six classes a day he was the college bursar, business manager, grounds keeper, dormitory supervisor, and caretaker of the college vegetable garden. Crane also pastored churches in Oxford, and Coldwater, Mississippi, and in Nonconnah, Tennessee. Somehow, he found time to write a history of Mississippi Baptists, as well as a volume of literary discourses, and to edit a magazine for women.[26]

While president of Mississippi Female College, Crane often found it necessary to draw upon "his own funds liberally to keep his institution going." In the neverending search for students, he even suggested to Headmaster M. W. Phillips that the Baptist-affiliated Central Female Institute at Clinton be closed and merged with the Mississippi Female College. Not surprisingly, Phillips declined Crane's kind offer. There "are some 20,000 girls in Miss.," Phillips noted; "are there not enough for you and I [sic.]?" Crane's brief tenure at Semple Broaddus was similar to his previous experience at Mississippi Female College—not enough students and not enough funds. After two years he resigned. When Crane left Semple Broaddus he had to sell most of his personal effects to settle his own debts and the obligations of the college. He sold almost everything except his library. Shortly after President Crane resigned, Semple Broaddus College suspended.[27]

At most old-time colleges the faculty consisted of the president and four professors. The president normally taught a course on moral philosophy, which in some cases was called "evidences of Christianity." The professors, in one combination or another, taught Greek and Latin, ancient history and literature, logic, rhetoric, natural philosophy, and mathematics. At those schools which had preparatory departments, and most did, the principal of that department was routinely listed as a member of the college faculty. Professors did not lecture regularly in old-time classrooms; instead, the students recited, by rote, the lessons assigned for each day. Because students were not normally expected to accumulate knowledge or general information, they rarely received library or collateral reading assignments. They performed mental exercises in the classics, which were believed to provide the best intellectual stimulation for developing youthful minds.[28]

Since most old-time college presidents were ministers, and their institutions were sustained by a constituency who believed that a college education should build character and produce Christian gentlemen in the "Genteel Tradition," collegiate officials were as concerned about the souls of their students as about their minds. Student deportment was monitored with a relentless and unforgiving eye. President Moses Waddel of the University of Georgia "would sweep the horizon . . . with his spy glass" in search of students who might be breaking college rules.[29]

The old-time residential college was "a large family, sleeping, eating, studying, and worshiping together under one roof." When boarders were accepted at Union Female College they became "members of our family," and Jackson College authorities promised its patrons that discipline at the school would be as "nearly parental as possible." Because discipline, or the lack of it, more often than scholarship determined the reputation of an institution, presidents and professors were sometimes hired because of their skill at crowd control. Faculty members had to live in the dormitory and police their students, and students naturally resented this espionage.[30]

Leonard D. Gale, a professor of chemistry and geology at Jefferson College, provided a lengthy critique of student behavior at southern colleges. Professor Gale attributed the failure of many southern institutions not so much to the "want of funds or able professors" as to the disruptive behavior of southern students. "Most of our institutions," he explained, "if they gain sufficient celebrity to fill them with pupils, a riot or some other outbreaking would occur and students or professors, or both, are dispersed and the institutions are to be commenced *de novo.*" "If we examine into the history of those institutions that have failed," he continued, "we shall find that bad government, or inability to support discipline at all, has been the main cause. . . . Their [southern students'] habits of roving about, being masters of their own time, and unaccustomed to study renders study or confinement a tedious and tiresome process." Gale contrasted southern students with their northern counterparts and concluded that southern boys were less easily governed because of the difference in "the manner of rearing the children in the two sections of the country." "In the north," he explained, "children are by habit taught to obey until they become of age," but southern boys are "commanders and masters at home" and they "wish to exercise the same spirit when they become inmates of the college."[31]

The Reverend William Winans basically agreed with Professor Gale and complained that too many southern institutions had "run afoul of this shoal." The experiment in student government at Centenary College may have been an effort to alleviate the tension between the faculty and students. Professor Gale's unflattering assessment of southern students was also corroborated by the Reverend John N. Waddel of the University of Mississippi, who described the university's first class as "disorderly and turbulent . . . idle, uncultivated, viciously disposed and ungovernable." Like Gale's critique, Waddel's description was probably only slightly exaggerated, inasmuch as half of the university's first class had been expelled or suspended by the end of the year. On the other hand, John Millington, a professor of natural science at the university, reported only that "a little occasional ferment" occurred that first year. Mrs. Millington, the professor's wife, said she had "never seen better behaved young men."[32]

If students in the old-time colleges were more disruptive and incorrigible than students of a later era, there were several good reasons. Like Semple Broaddus, most old-time colleges were located in "rural settings free from the haunts of dissipation"; students were required to be up at sunrise for morning prayers and in bed by ten. But unlike Semple Broaddus, which provided a gymnasium for recreational activities, not all colleges could afford to meet the social and recreational needs of their students. Most colleges were so strapped for funds that they could only provide extracurricula activities through a fee system. Jackson College students, for example, "as a recreation and relief from the dullness of study," were allowed to take music courses. But parental permission and a special fee were required. Moreover, the oral and public student examinations often provoked resentment. The young scholars were questioned by their professors and also by members of the board of trustees and the general public. For those who passed a public examination could be exhilarating, but for those who failed it could be humiliating. If a student felt that a professor had intentionally demeaned him, he would naturally seek ways to avenge himself. Also, antebellum students were much younger than today's students. Jefferson College had a five-year-old cadet, Semple Broaddus admitted students as young as eight, Oakland enrolled boys at twelve, and Centenary admitted thirteen-year-olds. The board of trustees of the University of Georgia at first admitted students at thirteen but then raised the age to sixteen, because the trustees found that young boys with "half formed judgments" were "apt to run into excesses and improprieties of almost any kind." The University of Mississippi limited general admission to sixteen-year-olds but admitted fifteen-year-olds under certain conditions.[33] Practically all of Mississippi's antebellum colleges admitted students in their early teens. Most lived in dormitories, an unnatural habitat that breeds misbehavior and allows misconduct to feed upon itself.

Students in Mississippi's old-time colleges were not really different from modern students. An early historian of higher education in America, Charles F. Thwing, has concluded that "the college student is not a class, he is a race, and he is a race which is the same, apparently, in all countries as in all climes." He might have added "in all times," because college students, whether in the old-time colleges or the modern universities, have always sought diversion from the "dullness of study." And southern students, at least before modernization, considered getting drunk and stealing chickens a part of the college experience. At Oakland a youthful laureate celebrated that tradition:

At Oakland when the sun was low
   All spotless lay the virgin snow
And rich and merry was the flow
   Of Egg-nogg in the Cottages.

But Oakland saw another sight,
   When freshmen yelled in green delight
And sophomores at dead of night
   Assailed the neighboring poultry-yards.

His brain upset with the new-made flip,
   A junior longed to grace the trip
And giving each old Prof. the slip
   Rushed on to join the revelry.[34]

This abbreviated version of "A Parody" appeared in *Oakland Maga-zine,* a student publication sponsored by the two literary societies at Oakland College. Literary societies, which sponsored campus publi-cations, discussion groups, and declamation contests, were the most popular of the extracurricular activities at Mississippi's old-time col-leges; they offered antebellum students a means of satisfying their in-tellectual interests. Many literary societies owned their own buildings and were the repositories of more books, journals, and magazines than the college libraries.[35]

Mississippi's antebellum liberal arts colleges were founded with the noblest intentions and the greatest expectations, but few survived the Civil War. The late-nineteenth century, however, saw a resurgence in the popularity of liberal arts colleges. During the 1880s and 1890s sev-eral new institutions—mostly denominational schools—were estab-lished in Mississippi. In 1839, just as Mississippi was entering the ante-bellum college boom, Governor Alexander McNutt addressed an open letter to the state's college presidents asking their counsel in the matter of establishing a state university. Some college presidents thought it was an idea whose time had finally come and some urged, even pleaded, with the governor to designate their institution as the state university. But most would have agreed with Rev. Jeremiah Chamberlain of Oak-land College who, good Presbyterian that he was, opposed the estab-lishment of a state university. In his response to the governor's in-quiry, Chamberlain asserted that "a state university never has been, or ever will be, in this *free country,* a real blessing to the community at large." A state university would produce an intellectual aristocracy, he said, which would endanger American democracy. Education must be available to all—an end best served by the decentralized, nonsectarian collegiate system that provided moral instruction as well as intellectual training. President Chamberlain then reiterated his denomination's dic-tum that education was "the legitimate business of the church, rather than the state."[36]

In spite of President Chamberlain's objections and Governor Mc-Nutt's misgivings about the establishment of only one public univer-sity, the legislature appointed a committee in 1840 to select a site for the state university. This action was a clear indication that Missis-sippi's lawmakers favored greater separation of church and state. Two years later Governor Tilghman Tucker vetoed a bill establishing a new

Methodist institution, on the grounds that the college charter was being given to the Mississippi Methodist Conference. In his veto message Tucker said that granting a state charter to an "ecclesiastical council of a religious sect" would link church and state and would bring into "our courts questions of an ecclesiastical character." "On the subject of religion," he argued, "there should be no legislation."[37]

The Grenada *Weekly Register* reported that Governor Tucker's veto "created a profound sensation throughout the state, not only among the Methodists, but also amongst other denominations."[38] During the next session, however, the legislature skirted the issue of church and state by granting the charter to a group of private citizens. Governor Tucker allowed the bill to become law, and the institution was established. But before it graduated its first class, a state university had been established and higher education in Mississippi had entered a new era.

—Three—

Founding the State University, 1840–1865

*The day that witnesses the completion of this magnificent temple
of learning will be regarded as the dawn of a new era
in the history of letters.*
—Governor Albert G. Brown

During the early stages of the antebellum college boom the feud between sections and factions prolonged and postponed the establishment of a state university. Evangelical clergymen, who regarded "the encroachment of scientific discoveries upon sacred mysteries with profound intolerance," had also kept up their opposition to secular education. Another factor delaying the establishment of a state university was the bickering between supporters of public schools and supporters of higher education. A correspondent for the *Southern Reformer* accused Mississippi's aristocracy of trying to conceal its opposition to common schools while promoting the interests of higher education. "A strict analysis of their conduct," this unnamed correspondent claimed, would expose "a desire to build up and endow splendid colleges" for "the benefit of the rich and privileged class, rather than the endowment of schools for the whole community." Alma Pauline Foerster has found that the southern gentry nurtured the notion that free schools were "a bounty to the indigent." To southern aristocrats education was a luxury, not a right, and like other luxuries education should be enjoyed by those who could pay for it.[1]

All the objections to a state university, and the obstructions that had delayed its establishment for so long, were finally overcome by a combination of two circumstances. First, the gradual depletion of the seminary fund convinced many of Mississippi's leaders that the only way to prevent a total loss of the fund was to establish a state university and allocate the remainder of the fund to that institution. Because of mismanagement and malfeasance, as well as bank failures during the Panic of 1837, the seminary fund had gradually declined from nearly $300,000 in 1833 to only $90,000 in 1845.[2] Every governor since 1819, when Mississippi received its second land grant, had urged the legislature to establish a public university and to safeguard the seminary fund.

Second, the deepening sense of urgency about educating their sons at home finally persuaded Mississippi's leadership to establish a state university. "Send your sons to other states," warned a Mississippi collegiate official, and "you estrange them from their native land [and] our institutions are endangered." His warning was an old one that had roots in Western history at least as far back as Henry II, who "forbade Englishmen from studying in France." The German principalities established their own universities "to retain the training [of] secular officials" in their own hands and "to keep the money in the country." Colonial fathers complained that American boys who went off to college at Cambridge and Oxford came back as Englishmen, and they began educating their sons at home. By the early 1830s, as the sectional crisis deepened and the agitation for abolition heightened, the Mississippi mind turned back upon itself. Mississippi took on a siege mentality, and every governor from 1830 on cited the urgency of educating Mississippi's sons at home. Governor Albert Gallatin Brown, who signed the law chartering the University of Mississippi, had long favored the founding of a state university for reasons that went beyond academics: "Those opposed to us in principle can not be entrusted with the education of our sons and daughters." Realizing that education was the "process by which a culture transmits itself across the generations," Governor Brown and the founders of the university were determined to indoctrinate Mississippi's youth as well as to educate them.[3] They presumed a society's right, indeed its obligation, to defend itself against change, and they used the society's educational institutions as the instruments of its survival.

Having at last accepted the propriety of establishing a public university in 1840, the Mississippi legislature appointed a committee to recommend a suitable location. After a prolonged and acrimonious debate, and by only one vote, the legislature selected Oxford, a tiny rural hamlet in the northeastern part of the state. Oxford was chosen over Mississippi City, a town midway between Biloxi and Gulfport on Mississippi's seacoast. The location of the state university in "a sylvan exile" was a conscious choice, in keeping with an entrenched tradition in United States higher education. The unhappy history of town and gown, which had characterized the medieval university, created an enduring antipathy between colleges and cities that Americans sought to avoid. The statute establishing the University of North Carolina, for example, prohibited its location within five miles of any seat of government or in any town where courts of law or equity met. The University of Georgia was established "as deep in the woods and as far from civilization as possible." Even Mark Hopkins favored a country setting because "fine scenery" helped build character. That theory prevailed as long as America was rural and green, but after the country became urbanized educators adopted a more pragmatic approach. Frederick A. P. Barnard, for example, president of New York's Columbia University, scorned the notion that learning could not flourish in an urban environment. That sentiment, he said, would only have merit "if study were a pursuit to be prosecuted in the open streets."[4]

In 1846, after Oxford had been selected but before the university had opened, the controversy over the institution's location resurfaced in the state legislature. Some lawmakers from south Mississippi spoke boldly of secession, and their sentiments were seconded by several south Mississippi newspapers that bitterly criticized the location of the state university. Both the *Woodville Republican* and the *Natchez Courier* wondered whether Louisiana would have south Mississippi if it could divest itself from the rest of the state.[5]

Horatio Fleming Simrall of Wilkinson County, the southwestern-most county in the state, compared the location of the University of Mississippi to the "coruscations of the north pole." The aurora borealis "are the most brilliant known," he admitted, "but are not seen or enjoyed by near one-fourth of the globe." So will it be with the state university, "this great 'northern light' of Mississippi." "The greater portion of the state," he predicted, "will never derive any benefit from it." Because Oxford was virtually inaccessible to large portions of the state in the 1840s, Simrall proposed that the state be divided into four collegiate districts and that the seminary funds be divided equally among the colleges or universities in each district. Simrall argued that his plan would permit an equitable distribution of the land-grant funds and would benefit the entire state rather than just one section. After a long, lively debate Simrall's proposal was defeated by a vote of thirty-nine to thirty-six, most legislators voting along sectional lines.[6] Simrall's proposal was the last effective challenge to the location of the University of Mississippi until the 1930s, when Governor Theodore G. Bilbo recommended its relocation to Jackson.

The law chartering the university in 1844 established a thirteen-member board of trustees appointed by the governor. Although the law did not require a geographic distribution of board membership, Governor Brown took special care to see that all sections of the state were represented. Once in place the board became self-perpetuating and virtually free from external pressure. It was given absolute authority over the university, with power to appoint the president and faculty and remove them at pleasure, to design the university curriculum, to establish rules of student conduct, to plan and lay out the campus, and to superintend the construction of university buildings. It was also given custody of the seminary fund. Before the board could make use of those funds, however, the legislature repealed that provision on the grounds that the land grant had been given in trust to the legislature of the state.[7] The trustees had the power to govern a university but not the funds to finance it. Consequently, the board of trustees and the university became supplicants before the legislature at each successive biennium.

After the board's control over the seminary fund had been revoked, Governor Brown sent a special message to the legislature requesting a large appropriation for the construction of university buildings. Along with his request for funds the governor also recommended the establishment of ten preparatory schools at various locations throughout the state. He suggested that $800 be appropriated annually to each of the ten academies and that they be placed under the governance of the university's board of trustees. "Nothing is clearer to my mind," he remarked, "than that the college will not succeed without the aid of auxiliary schools."[8] The governor had attended both Jefferson College and Mississippi College and realized the inadequacy of Mississippi's secondary school system. Nevertheless, his recommendation for establishing preparatory schools was not enacted.

On February 25, 1848, the board of trustees of the state university adopted an organizational structure and a curriculum designed primarily by the Reverend John Newton Waddel, a member of the original board of trustees. Waddel was the son of President Moses Waddel of the University of Georgia and the nephew of John C. Calhoun. The curriculum he recommended and the board adopted was the prescribed four-year classical course, based on the belief that Christianity was the basis of all learning. Under Waddel's plan the university faculty included a president and four professors. The president was also professor of mental and moral philosophy, rhetoric, evidences of Christianity, logic, and political economy. The other faculty positions were designated as the chair of ancient and modern languages, the chair of mathematics, the chair of natural philosophy (physics) and astronomy, and the chair of chemistry, geology, and mineralogy.[9]

The course on the evidences of Christianity sparked a heated exchange between the Reverend Mr. Waddel and board member E. C. Wilkerson, who objected to the introduction of such a course at a public institution. Trustee John J. McCaughan, "a pronounced infidel," also objected to the course on Christianity and the appointment of ministers to the faculty. The course was kept as a part of the university's curriculum, but both Waddel and McCaughan later resigned from the board of trustees—Waddel to become a member of the faculty and McCaughan to protest the course on Christianity and distance himself from a public university that would style itself "a Christian institution." Even though the course on Christianity remained a part of the curriculum, ministerial students paid no tuition, and four of the first five presidents were ministers, the university was still sometimes ridiculed by Mississippi's evangelical clergy as a "regularly organized infidel institution."[10]

There were nearly two hundred applicants for the faculty positions at the university and seventeen for the presidency. The leading contender for the latter position was the Reverend Augustus Baldwin Longstreet, then president of Emory College in Georgia. Longstreet, championed by Waddel, felt so certain of his selection that he prematurely resigned his post at Emory. But Judge E. C. Wilkerson and

John McCaughan blocked his election.[11] The anti-clerical faction engineered the appointment of George Frederick Holmes, a twenty-eight-year-old historian from William and Mary College. Albert Taylor Bledsoe, an 1830 graduate of West Point and one of the South's eminent teachers, was appointed to the chair of mathematics; John Millington, a scientist of international reputation, to the chair of chemistry, geology, and mineralogy; and Waddel to the chair of languages. The fourth chair was not filled until sometime later. President Holmes's inaugural address was a masterful defense of the classical curriculum and a plea for funds to equip the library and the laboratories. At the time of his inauguration the university's income had been largely consumed by the construction of campus buildings including the Lyceum, which Holmes called one of the most elegant structures in the South.[12]

President Holmes announced in his inaugural that the "inquisitional system" of discipline prevalent in old-time colleges throughout America would not be practiced at the university and that he would not allow the faculty to conduct "espionage" against the students. He asked the students to "pledge your honor as gentlemen that you will not violate" the rules of the college. But his experience with the honor system, a rare innovation in American colleges at that time, was extremely disappointing. The university's first class of eighty students proved to be ungovernable. By the end of the first session only forty-seven were still in school: five had been expelled, eight suspended, twelve allowed to withdraw, and eight were missing, their whereabouts unknown.[13]

The failure of President Holmes's honor system and the total breakdown of discipline brought scorn to the university and criticism to its youthful president. He left in less than a year. According to John D. Wade, Longstreet's biographer, Holmes could not "stand the racket." Personal and family problems, however, complicated matters for him. In January 1849 Mrs. Holmes returned to Virginia with an ill child; when the child grew worse, President Holmes took a six-weeks' leave in March to join them in Virginia. He also became ill and could not return when his leave expired. Though Holmes claimed to have written the board explaining his circumstances and asking for an extension, for some reason his letters were never received. On July 10, 1849, the board declared the office vacant and the next day elected Longstreet; it denied Holmes's request for reinstatement to the presidency. Holmes was later appointed to the chair of history at the University of Virginia, where he enjoyed a long and distinguished career.[14]

During the interval between Holmes's departure in March and Longstreet's arrival in November, the university's "reputation for infidelity increased." As a means of damage control the board adopted a new set of rules and regulations. Rule One set the date for the beginning of the academic year. Rule Two stated that "the regular exercise of each day will begin at sun rise with prayer. All the students resident in the college are required to be present, the roll will be called and absentees noted." Additional regulations required a faculty member to visit every boy's room at least once every day. Faculty members had the right to enter the room of any student "at pleasure" and to break open the door if a student did not open it. Rule Eight required a student to pay for the repair of the door if forced entry was necessary.[15]

When Longstreet arrived for the opening of the fall term in November 1849, he was greeted by seventy-six students and three faculty members. Longstreet was a towering presence at the university. A protege of President Waddel of the University of Georgia, a lawyer, a Methodist minister of considerable influence in the southern church, a famous raconteur, he had already served as president of two Methodist institutions, Emory and Centenary. Longstreet was also an extensive landowner and slaveholder and was virtually independent financially. Under his administration the university regained some of the public favor it had lost during its first year, and in Longstreet's second year the enrollment increased to 134. Called "Old Bullet" by students, President Longstreet was a stern disciplinarian who regarded the development of character as a major purpose of a college education. Student conduct improved somewhat, though not dramatically, during his administration.[16]

Although the university's curriculum was in keeping with the classical tradition, neither the state legislature nor the board of trustees was at all reluctant to add new courses. Southern state legislatures had historically been more pragmatic about higher education than their northern counterparts. James E. B. De Bow, editor of *De Bow's Review,* one of the South's most influential business journals, attributed that pragmatism to the South's "continual struggle with the forest." By the 1850s the state's practical-minded planters wanted more information about geology, soils, and the science of agriculture, and the university's science program became the beneficiary of Mississippi's agrarian economy. The legislature was unusually generous in allocating funds for agricultural research and for scientific apparatus. Frederick A. P. Barnard happily discovered the good effects of greed on the scholar's humble work:

> Even the patient and diligent collector of bugs, butterflies, and cater-pillars, though looked down upon . . . with an amusingly sublime lofti-ness of contemptuous regard, if he but intimate a belief that he is upon the sure trace of a method of exterminating the insect scourge of the cotton-field, is listened to with respectful, nay, with greedy ears, and is elevated at once to a position of comparative dignity.[17]

Throughout the 1850s the Mississippi legislature made several spe-cial appropriations to what was called in the laws of 1852 the "Agricul-tural and Zoological Science department." Actually, no such depart-ment existed, nor was much agricultural science beyond basic geology and mineralogy taught at the university. Some faculty members op-posed the introduction of any applied sciences into the curriculum, on the basis that such courses intruded upon the classical tradition and were incompatible with the primary role of the university to provide a liberal education and produce Christian gentlemen. After Barnard be-came president in 1856 the legislature wanted to establish a school of agriculture at the university. Barnard's scholarly interests tended more toward pure science, however, and he did not favor the plan, though for practical reasons he avoided openly opposing it. Although a school of agriculture did not materialize, the university did accumulate a large holding of scientific apparatus. Barnard's biographer claims that its laboratory equipment was "unsurpassed by that of any institution on the continent."[18]

While the natural sciences advanced at the university, the social sci-ences were not being neglected. Both President Longstreet and Jacob Thompson, president of the board of trustees, were advocates of the social sciences. Recognizing history and the social sciences as legiti-mate academic disciplines became one of the positive legacies of Presi-dent Holmes's brief tenure. Holmes had believed that history would eventually become a science and should have a permanent place in the college curriculum. President Longstreet taught the senior course on moral philosophy from a dogmatic and decidedly religious perspective, but the study was in essence a social science. Some historians, in fact, trace the social sciences in American colleges to those required courses on moral philosophy.[19]

Soon after President Longstreet came to the university he and Jacob Thompson, both of whom were lawyers, initiated plans to start a law department. The board had the authority to establish the department but no funds to fill the chair of law or to secure a library. In 1854 Thompson made a personal appeal to the legislature for a special appropriation to set up a school of "Governmental Science and Law," explaining that the university needed a chair of law but "not of law alone." The philosophy of government should be taught along with law, he said, because instruction "in the science of government we think of high importance to the southern youth." Though it was hardly necessary, Thompson reminded the lawmakers that "we live in a confederacy of states" and the "political relations of the states to each other are looked at in somewhat different lights according to the geographic points of view."[20] Couching his call for funds within the framework of states' rights, Thompson correctly presumed that such an appeal would not be denied by a legislature so stirred by the sectional crisis of the 1850s. His request for a special appropriation was granted, and in the fall of 1854 the university admitted its first law class. The law course did not replace the apprenticeship system, however; during its early years the law department more often trained politicians than practitioners.

When A. B. Longstreet assumed the office of president in 1849, he pledged to restore order among the students and to repair the university's reputation. His initial success convinced the supporters of the institution that "there was at the helm a Master Spirit," and the university regained much of its popular support.[21] But unlike his successor, F. A. P. Barnard, who devoted all his powers and talents to the university's improvement, Longstreet was not driven by a single commitment. His energy was divided between religion and politics, academics and business endeavors, as well as between his devoted, close-knit family and the larger community that honored him with high office.

Because President Longstreet considered his Methodist ministry the primary mission of his life, he was frequently absent from his duties at the university. When the board adopted a policy on absenteeism and threatened to dock the pay of any professor who missed class without a proper excuse, Longstreet was infuriated, saying that if he could not "attend the sick" he would resign. He did in fact tender his resignation along with a request that the board rescind that unpopular policy. The board did not accept his resignation nor did it revoke the rule on absenteeism. J. M. Henry, an Oxford resident who knew President Longstreet quite well, wrote to Governor John J. McRae that his resignation was all a bluff anyway, because "Old Longstreet is making too much money too fast for him to be induced to resign." Wade writes of Longstreet's propensity for profit while he lived in Oxford: "True to his fixed custom, Longstreet did not let slip any good chances of turning over an honest dollar."[22]

During the great tariff controversy in 1832 Longstreet came down on the side of the nullifiers, and he remained a states' rights, straight-ticket Democrat throughout his life. Both he and his son-in-law, the illustrious Lucius Quintus Cincinnatus Lamar, were among the highest counsels of the Mississippi Democratic party. As the sectional crisis intensified during the 1850s, there was a corresponding increase in the rancor between southern Democrats and southern Whigs. When the Whigs went underground in 1855 and associated themselves with the Know-Nothing party, Longstreet branded their secrecy as "fool hardy . . . unscrupulous, and cowardly" and linked the Know-Nothing movement to abolition. By this inference Longstreet impugned the "Southern manhood" of any Whig who might be in consort with the Know-Nothings. Apparently he exempted no one, neither the Whig members of the board of trustees nor Professor Barnard, an outspoken Unionist and former Whig editor. During the last two or three years of Longstreet's tenure his relationship with Barnard was strained, and some believed that Barnard undermined President Longstreet with the board of trustees, especially its Whig members.[23]

The political composition of boards of trustees had influenced the organization and management of southern state universities for several years. The preponderance of Whigs or Democrats had affected the curriculum, the selection of faculty, and university regulations.[24] Until the mid-1850s it had been a dignified contest played out in the quiet confines of the board room. But the anxiety that accompanied the sectional crisis brought that contest, and all others, out into the open where good judgment often gave way to displays of quick temper. The Whigs and Know-Nothings reponded in kind to Longstreet's scathing commentary. They called President Longstreet a "dotard" and a "clown," ridiculed his writings, questioned his moral and intellectual fitness for office, and accused him of indoctrinating the university's students. Longstreet countered that charge by accusing the Know-Nothing party of "whisper[ing] the students of my charge into midnight meetings, and there binding them by oath upon oath" to its political creed.[25]

The spectacle of the president of the state university trading epithets with a secret society was unseemly, even to Democratic governor John J. McRae. Longstreet's political entanglements, among other things, convinced Governor McRae and public officials that the state had conceded too much independence to the university's self-perpetuating board of trustees and had virtually forfeited its role in the management of the university's affairs. As a remedy the governor recommended the establishment of a board of visitors. Since the university was a state institution, he reasoned, it should be subject to the visitation of the state through regularly appointed agents. A board of visitors would have a beneficial effect on the management of the university and members' attendance at public examinations would encourage students to become better prepared. Finally, the governor said, the affairs of the university "would be brought into public notice" by the various reports that the board of visitors would publish from time to time.[26]

The university's governing board was not required to make any kind of public report or otherwise account for its actions except to the state legislature. As a consequence, news of the university was disseminated by word of mouth, editorial commentary, Sunday morning sermons, campaign speeches, gossip, rumor, and innuendo. Governor McRae felt confident that the reports issued by the board of visitors would reduce the damage from rumor and innuendo, some of which he admitted was calculated by its enemies to disparage the university. Governor McRae's proposal for a board of visitors—rejected by the legislature—was the first effort in a continuing search for a structure of governance that would protect Mississippi's institutions of higher learning from political intrusion but would also satisfy the understandable desire of public officials to make those institutions responsive and responsible to the body politic.

Governor McRae's effort to expand the role of the state in the university's affairs was followed six months later by President Longstreet's resignation, though there seems to have been no connection between the two. Longstreet, sixty-six years old and financially independent, wanted to spend his last years living the quiet life of a country gentleman. When he tendered his resignation on July 10, 1856, the board unanimously rejected it. But Longstreet declined their request to remain, and the trustees then accepted his resignation; on July 16, they awarded him the honorary Doctor of Divinity degree. His retirement was brief. The following year he became president of the University of South Carolina.[27]

It was presumed that Waddel would succeed President Longstreet. But to Waddel's mortification he was passed over in favor of Frederick Augustus Porter Barnard, a native of Massachusetts and an 1828 graduate of Yale. Barnard was also a Whig and a Unionist—neither a mainstream southern position. During the secession crisis of 1851, while he was a faculty member at the University of Alabama, Barnard had delivered an oration on the Fourth of July in support of the Union. In Mississippi that could have been dangerous, but Barnard's tact and good humor had mollified the "secesh Democrats" in Alabama. As the sectional crisis deepened, however, and as President Basil Manly's sectionalism intensified, Barnard had become an increasingly controversial figure at Tuscaloosa. President Manly was a Baptist minister and a strict adherent to the closed classical curriculum, whereas Barnard was an Episcopal minister moving gradually toward favoring a reorganization of the collegiate curriculum. In 1854, the tension with President Manly steadily getting worse, Barnard resigned to take a position at Oxford.[28]

After being elected president, Barnard devoted his considerable energies to the single purpose of making the University of Mississippi one of the major institutions of higher learning in the country. He was tireless in that effort, comparing himself to "a stick so crooked it could not lie still." Barnard attacked the university's problems with an urgency that sometimes brought criticism from his less energetic colleagues, from some board members who favored progress but not change, and from a large segment of the Mississippi press who just did not like the "Damn Yankee."[29] During his five-year tenure President Barnard faced three continuing and unrelenting problems that had plagued his predecessors and would continue to preoccupy his successors: discipline, funding, and governance.

In residential colleges where teenage students were rousted at sunrise for morning prayers, where faculty members were required to keep students under constant surveillance and invade their privacy, and where boys of disparate ages were housed in common quarters, it is no wonder that discipline was a continuing problem. President Barnard became one of the earliest critics of dormitory housing. He was especially averse to daily room inspection, doubting its utility and admitting that he often neglected to visit the rooms when it was his turn to do so. He also said he "never knew a president before who was expected to do it."[30] But the patrons of the university expected Barnard to build character in their sons and to make men of their boys.

Though Barnard did not solve the problem of student misconduct, like a growing number of other college presidents he recognized the increasingly complex, expanding interests of the American college student and offered an intelligent response. In 1857 he persuaded the board of trustees to build a gymnasium at the university, and he introduced the study of art into the curriculum as a means of awakening and developing the students' higher nature. Alma Pauline Foerster cites Barnard's 1854 report, *Art Culture: Its Relation to National Refinement and National Morality,* as the best and most complete defense of aesthetic studies by any southern educator before the war.[31]

Unlike some college presidents Barnard felt challenged rather than threatened by change, because his own ideas about what a college should be, and some day would be, were evolving. He wanted the University of Mississippi to set the pace, not just keep pace with the changes taking place in the American collegiate system on the eve of the Civil War. But Barnard found the university's board of trustees unfriendly to change and slow to act. It is a testament to his talent and zeal that he was able to achieve as much as he did and to survive what one of his biographers has called the "dreadful years" in Mississippi.[32]

More challenging than the problem of student behavior, and in the long run more important, was the university's funding problem which Barnard attacked with his characteristic zeal. He actually began working on the funding difficulties shortly after joining the faculty in 1854. President Longstreet had asked Barnard to investigate the seminary funds account to determine how much, if any, of the lost funds could be recovered. That research brought Barnard into close contact with Jacob Thompson, an influential politician and president of the board of trustees. The two men developed a close friendship, which proved

beneficial to Barnard later, but Barnard's inquiry into the seminary
fund account rubbed some old and deep wounds. In the aftermath of
the Panic of 1837 Mississippi had repudiated several million dollars'
worth of state bonds. These had been issued in 1838 to shore up the
state's banking system and to save the seminary funds, which had been
invested in some of the financially troubled banks. The banks had
failed, the funds had been lost, and a bankrupt state had repudiated its
own bonds. Repudiation, a volatile and divisive issue, had tainted the
reputation of Mississippi. Mrs. Barnard had been reluctant to come to
Mississippi in 1854 because she did not want to live in a "repudiating
state."[33] Some of the bitterness had waned by the 1850s, and few
wanted to revive the feelings of that unhappy episode.

Barnard stirred some of those old feelings by asking the legislature
to acknowledge the university's claim to the full amount of the seminary fund: $277,332.52 in 1833. Although Barnard was not imme-
diately successful in pressing the claim, nearly thirty years later the
legislature finally recognized the legitimacy of that claim and made a
special appropriation to the university. During his investigation of the
seminary fund Barnard also discovered that Mississippi had received
only one land grant in support of higher education—the one given in
1819. Under the provisions of the federal land-grant statute, Mississippi was entitled to two townships. Barnard contended correctly that
the 1803 grant to Jefferson College was a separate transaction which
occurred during the territorial period and should not affect the university's right to an additional township. Barnard informed the board of
trustees of his finding and requested that the matter be laid before the
United States Congress. He was confident that Congress would grant
Mississippi its fair share of the public domain. Barnard's presumption
was correct, but the Civil War intervened and Mississippi did not receive its second township until 1894.[34]

Although Barnard was not successful in securing either the full
amount of the seminary fund or the second land grant, he was able to
persuade the legislature to adopt a policy of annual appropriations for
the university. Barnard explained that several other southern states,
notably Virginia, South Carolina, and North Carolina, had adopted
such a policy, which proved extremely beneficial in long-range planning. The legislature acceded to Barnard's request in 1856 and appropriated $100,000, to be paid in five annual installments of $20,000.[35] As

the public image and esteem of the university ebbed and flowed, however, the legislature threatened, almost annually, to withhold the current installment. Consequently the university remained a supplicant, and its officials were forced to practice the indelicate, unacademic art of pandering to the whims of state legislators. Thus was born an unfortunate tradition of enduring strength.

During the same session in which the legislature adopted the procedure of annual appropriations, Governor McRae recommended the establishment of a state-supported college for women. In a special message to the legislature he referred to the continuing efforts of Sallie Eola Reneau, well-known advocate of a state college for women, and commended "the subject to the favorable consideration of the legislature." Two weeks later Senator James Drane of Choctaw County introduced a bill establishing the State Female College, to be located in Yalobusha County. The house concurred, the governor signed the bill, and the college was chartered on February 20, 1856. The law establishing the college empowered its board of trustees to expend whatever funds the state might appropriate. But no state funds were ever appropriated to the State Female College, and the institution never opened. As a result, the state university remained the only public institution of higher learning in antebellum Mississippi.[36]

With the problems of student conduct and funding somewhat under control, if not entirely resolved, President Barnard then focused his attention on the worrisome matter of university governance. The existing rules of governance, Barnard complained, were "so framed [as] to commit the regulation of the most minute details of administration including even such matters as the ringing of the college bell and the arrangement of the hours of recitation to the Board of Trustees." Determined to reduce the board's administrative role in university affairs, he recommended at the July meeting in 1857 a thorough revision of the rules and regulations governing the university. His recommendation, along with a memorial (resolution) from the faculty for general improvements at the university, was sent to a committee for study. Four days later Barnard and the entire faculty were summoned before the board and informed that the governance of the university would not be modified. That board meeting lasted for eight days, July 9 to July 17. Barnard confided to his friend Eugene Hilgard that during those eight days "there were three or four star chamber days." He was surprised by the board's reaction and told Hilgard: "Before I was President I was influential"; now "they treat me as they did Longstreet" and "if I hear from them at all, it is in the form of some official interrogatory, behind which lurks some contingent censure."[37]

Barnard's disappointment in the way the trustees had been treating him must have been somewhat mollified by the board's reversal on the rule changes at its next meeting. On November 9 the board agreed to practically all of Barnard's recommendations and adopted a new set of regulations that transferred most of the internal governance of the university to the president and the faculty. There are two accountings for the board's reversal. First, Barnard's power of persuasion may have eventually won over some of the trustees who had originally opposed his reforms. Second, and probably more important, the board's new president, Governor John J. McRae, endorsed the rule changes. The governor was made president of the board by an 1857 statute that amended the university's charter. The new law, which was the legislature's alternative to Governor McRae's recommendation for a board of visitors, authorized the legislature to appoint the members of the board of trustees and made the governor ex officio president of the board. Barnard soon found a friend and ally in Governor McRae. When he resigned from the university and was leaving Mississippi in September 1861, Barnard met briefly with Governor McRae at the Oxford depot. Barnard wrote of that last meeting: "After expressing his regret at my retirement, he remarked to me, 'I shall always have one source of satisfaction in the recollection that I have voted for every measure which you have ever recommended.'"[38]

Barnard's success in persuading the legislature to make annual appropriations, and the board's adoption of his new rules, encouraged him to advance a proposal that he had been working on for the past two or three years. On March 15, 1858, Barnard addressed an open letter to the board of trustees in which he recommended several changes of "considerable moment," including a radical reorganization of the university. Barnard first noted that the American collegiate system as it existed in 1858 functioned primarily for the disciplining of the mind rather than for the dissemination of information. He then asserted that a rapidly changing world, and one of increasing complexity, demanded that colleges and universities not only "diffuse knowledge among men" but by original investigation "add to the priceless mass." To meet that new imperative the University of Mississippi would have to be radically reorganized.[39]

Over the next hundred pages Barnard sketched the details of a *Universitas Scientarium,* a university that would include all the branches of science and medicine, agriculture, law, classical studies, civil and political history, and oriental learning. The new university would be divided into undergraduate and graduate levels and would require a new pedagogy. There would be no more task work, rote, and recitation. Learned professors would lecture, students would become inquisitive, and an intellectual climate would pervade the library and permeate the laboratories. His letter was a brilliant defense of pure science that time has done little to damage.

President Barnard's design for a *Universitas Scientarium* was not original, nor was he the first to seek its implementation. Columbia had already adopted a similar plan and Francis Wayland, Philip Lindsley, Bishop Leonidas K. Polk, and others had been discussing the need for reforms in the collegiate system for several years. If his plan differed from the others, the difference lay in the fact that it more closely followed the pattern of German universities—an influence no doubt of his friend Hilgard, who at the age of twenty had won a *summa cum laude* doctorate at Heidelberg University. The sweeping dimensions of Barnard's recommendations dazzled the few Mississippians who read his *Letter;* some, Barnard claimed, could not have been paid to read it.[40]

Barnard's letter, though addressed to the board of trustees, was really a letter to the people of Mississippi. It was published several months before the board's annual meeting and was widely circulated by Barnard's allies and by friends of the university. Barnard conceded that some would object to the cost of the reorganization because Mississippi was a young state, "in her infancy," and could not be expected to "undertake labors as have marked the history of other communities" that are "in the maturity of their powers." To liberate the people from their habit of thinking small and slow, Barnard first praised them and then prodded them. He reminded his readers that it was their forebears who had settled that tiny intellectual clearing in the Mississippi forest around Natchez and Washington. "It was not a class of ignorant and needy adventurers who planted themselves upon these fertile valleys," he wrote. "They were intelligent and enlightened men, many of them highly educated," and no frontier community anywhere was "more respectable in an intellectual point of view" than the community that "they themselves constituted here."[41]

Having appealed to their pride of place and past, Barnard then linked the future of Mississippi to the fortunes of the university. "Regarding the University," Barnard wrote, "as its own intellectual position is assumed at a higher or lower level, the repute in which the state itself is held abroad will also be higher or lower."[42] What was good for the university was good for Mississippi, said Barnard. But his critics said, what was good for the university was good for Barnard, and he was accused of using the university to advance his own career. Barnard was in fact an ambitious man, endowed with the spirit of an academic entrepreneur. Like most men of large talent and vision, he was impatient with lesser men who would not enlarge their vision or concede the limits of their talents.

Most of Barnard's critics, however, were associated with the other colleges in Mississippi, whose existence would be imperiled by the university's enhancement, or they were radical secessionists who doubted his "southernness." The patrons and sponsors of Mississippi's small liberal arts colleges naturally opposed Barnard's *Universitas Scientarium,* and some rallied against it. To justify the need for his new university, Barnard was thus forced to fault the existing collegiate system in Mississippi. "If we trust the testimony of our presses," he said, "we shall be slow to admit that there are anywhere to be found educational advantages superior to those which we possess." "We have no such thing as a school with its strong and weak points. All our schools are strong—they have no weak points," he continued with diminishing tact; "our system is the wisest system," our discipline "the most judicious," our "Faculties are the ablest," our "scholars are the very most proficient the world ever saw." "Who ever heard of a college" in Mississippi, he asked, "which was *not* all that is here described?"[43]

Barnard found no disposition among the state's press or public officials to test the "claims or merits of our institutions"; that, he said, had had a "pernicious" effect on the state's collegiate system. If the colleges can "so cheaply win the guerdon of superlative praise," they will not strive for that "substantial merit which nobody appreciates." The practice of "universal laudation" of the state's colleges by the Mississippi press, Barnard said, misleads the public mind by producing a contented faith in a merit that is "more imaginary than real" and exempts the institutions from "that outside pressure which is the most effectual stimulus to internal improvement."[44]

It was obvious to Barnard, and he thought it should be obvious to the university's board of trustees, that the thoughtful citizens of Mississippi were "disgusted with hyperbole" and "anxious for a little honest fact." They saw through the "universal laudation" and realized that they had to send their children out of state for an adequate education. The trustees, therefore, were obligated to provide them and the state a first-rate institution. If they would implement his proposals, he assured them, the University of Mississippi would soon rank among the finest institutions in America. Barnard concluded his lengthy letter with an impassioned plea for the enactment of his reforms and a promise to the trustees that a true university "will be your noblest monument."[45]

The letter stirred deep resentment in the college community, especially at the church schools, and among the state's journalists whom Barnard had accused of misleading the public mind. Those two influential constituencies reacted quickly and vehemently to his criticism. Both groups "gave vent to their spleen by heaping denunciatory epithets upon the University." The evangelical clergy renewed their charges that the university was a "citadel of atheism," and the press branded it "a hotbed of abolitionism."[46]

It is impossible to say what would have been the fate of Barnard's *Universitas Scientiarum* had the Civil War not intervened. The only part of his reorganization plan that the board enacted was a change in the title of president to chancellor. Whatever chances Barnard may have had of implementing his educational theories were lost amid the growing controversy over slavery and states' rights. As the impending crisis drew closer, Mississippi's political leadership became more concerned about a man's beliefs than his theories and the chancellor of the state university had to meet the acid test of southern manhood. He had to be "sound" on slavery and states' rights. Because Barnard was northern born, was known to be a Unionist, and had the college catalog printed in the North, Mississippi's radical editors denounced the university as "a nursery of Yankeeism"; "with a holy horror" they "forewarned the Southern parent of the danger of sending his son here." Barnard's severest critic was John Richardson, editor of the *Prairie News*. The best indication of Richardson's radical views on states' rights was his reference to Jefferson Davis as a "Union shrieking conservative."[47]

The situation that most distressed Barnard, however, and that finally eclipsed his fifteen-year career in Mississippi, was the Branham Affair. Henry Branham, an Oxford resident and son-in-law of A. B. Longstreet, had long harbored the suspicion that Barnard had turned the board of trustees against President Longstreet. In 1859 Branham accused Chancellor Barnard of using information given by one of his female slaves as the basis for dismissing a university student. The slave girl had been raped and beaten. Barnard dismissed the student accused of the deed and would not allow him to apply for readmission. Under state law slave testimony was not admissable as evidence against a white person. Branham continually agitated the situation until both the legislature and the board of trustees conducted an investigation. Although both inquiries exonerated the chancellor, most Mississippi "fire-eaters" remained doubtful of his "southernness." Governor John J. Pettus had serious reservations about Barnard's fitness to be chancellor. The Branham affair, which Barnard called an outrage "without parallel in the annals of civilization," disheartened the chancellor, and he concluded that the university was "a thing too far above the ruling stupidity of the day to be a success." Deciding to leave Mississippi, he sought a position at Yale in 1859; but the appointment went to someone else. His last two years in Mississippi were miserable; only "poverty glued him to Oxford."[48]

On January 9, 1861, Mississippi adopted the Ordinance of Secession, which was drafted by L. Q. C. Lamar, a mathematics professor at the university. Soon afterward the students began withdrawing from the university and "eagerly pressed to be received into the army." Chancellor Barnard and President Jefferson Davis asked Governor Pettus not to muster the student units into the Confederate military service. Sending young boys off to war, President Davis said, was like "grinding the seed corn of the republic." But the excitement of that time swept the young men away and into the army. The board thought of reorganizing the university as a military academy but decided against such a course and finally closed the institution.[49]

In the fall of 1861, after the students had gone off to war and the campus was deserted, Chancellor Barnard wrote to the board: "We are inhabitants of a solitude. Our university has ceased to have visible existence." Many feared and some despaired of its future. But the University of Mississippi was not born "to taste life and pass away," Frank Keyes wrote on the eve of the war; "it shall stand from generation to generation."[50]

—Four—

Expansion of Higher Education,
1865–1900

*It would be cheaper for Mississippi to send all of its students to
Harvard or Yale than to maintain so many colleges.*
—Frank Burkitt
Mississippi Legislature, 1886

"In a world remade by the Civil War," Frederick Rudolph writes, an ambitious and enterprising group of educational reformers "seized the initiative in higher education" in the same way that John D. Rockefeller, Andrew Carnegie, and Washington Duke did in big business. It was a gilded but dynamic age. President James B. Angell of the University of Michigan found the public mind so "plastic" and "impressionable" that almost any energetic academic could influence the development of higher education in postwar America. "Only in the desolated, abandoned Southland" was there an absence of these dynamics, Rudolph adds, and "southern colleges, like the South itself, could but hold on, hold on to romantic dreams of the Old South that never was." Joseph Stetar agrees with Rudolph; after tracing the developments in higher education that led eventually to the establishment of the modern university, he concludes: "No such development was evident in the nineteenth-century South where colleges struggled to remain alive. Left virtually destitute by the War and lacking students, buildings and assets, college leaders clung more to romantic dreams and were unable to share in the bold expansion experienced by other regions."[1]

Rudolph leaps to a conclusion that is incorrect in the main, and Stetar overlooks the sometimes heroic efforts of southern educators to recoup and reshape higher education in the postwar South. Mississippi, for example, established a public school system in 1870 and provided scholarships for college students who agreed to teach in that new system. It also established the first black land-grant college in the United States in 1871; founded a state-supported normal school for blacks in 1873; established an agricultural and mechanical college in 1878; made the state university coeducational in 1882; founded the first state-supported women's college in the United States in 1884; and reorganized the curriculum, introduced the elective system and restructured the academic departments at the University of Mississippi in 1889. As for holding on to romantic dreams of the Old South, that came later.

The first graduating class at the University of Mississippi after the war was addressed as "The Young Men of the New South." They were told that they were living in a time "a blaze in the spirit of industry, enterprise, and freedom" and were advised that their New South must have "elevated scholarship" and "extensive learning" in "all the various departments of literature, science, ancient, medieval, and modern."[2] Stetar's assertion that southern colleges were lacking in "students, buildings and assets" is also incorrect, at least as far as the University of Mississippi is concerned. The university suffered virtually no damage during the war, and when it reopened almost two hundred students enrolled.

Just three months after the surrender at Appomattox, Governor William L. Sharkey convened the University of Mississippi board of trustees for a special meeting at Oxford. At his urging the board decided to reopen the university and announced that the fall term would begin in October. John N. Waddel was named chancellor, and three faculty members were soon appointed. Governor Sharkey allocated $6,000 from a special cotton tax to fund the university for the coming academic year, but that meager amount proved to be insufficient. It was supplemented by a $50 tuition fee and later by a $5,000 lottery.[3]

Neither the board of trustees nor university officials had anticipated a large enrollment. Both were surprised by the arrival of 193 students in early October. Chancellor Waddel was impressed with the maturity of those students, most of whom were Confederate veterans, but he was distressed by their lack of academic preparation. Although few of these students could have met prewar admission requirements, Chancellor Waddel and the board of trustees agreed to admit them. Waddel later explained that he would not reject "worthy young aspirants after knowledge because they were backward and ignorant." The chancellor believed that it was his "duty to take them by the hand and raise them from the lower to the higher . . . departments of education." The university's decision to enroll students who could not meet its admission standards was criticized by some Mississippians who accused Chancellor Waddel and the university of "degrading the cause of higher education."[4]

Three weeks after the opening of the University of Mississippi, Chancellor Waddel had an opportunity to defend its admission policy in a speech before a joint session of the state legislature. Waddel outlined the deficiencies of the state's common schools and explained that under the present circumstances Mississippi's young men, especially its veterans, could not obtain adequate preparatory training. As a remedy to that dire situation Chancellor Waddel recommended the establishment of "a thorough system of public schools" to be linked with the "reorganization of the University upon an enlarged scheme." The proposed statewide system would embrace elementary, secondary, and higher education and would, Waddel said, "complete the circle of education, as concentric, not antagonistic, but mutually auxiliary." The 1865 legislature rejected Waddel's recommendation because it was too expensive and too radical. Educational development at all levels in Mississippi was put on hold for five years.[5]

The Civil War had disillusioned most white Mississippians, who were psychologically unable to accept defeat or the consequences of emancipation. After nearly five years under martial law the people of Mississippi finally accepted the "world remade by the Civil War" and installed a new political order in January 1870. It lasted until 1876. The new order, known as Reconstruction, was put in place by the state's recently established Republican Party; it included black elected officials, northern Republicans called carpetbaggers, and southern whites known as scalawags. The terms *carpetbagger* and *scalawag* were coined under the emotional stress of military defeat and during a time of great social upheaval. Mississippians who could not or would not accept the new order used the words, full of hate and bitterness, in anger against the apostles of the new order. The idea of blacks in public office was a bewildering notion to most white Mississippians; they considered the new order an abominable experiment, doomed to failure and to be endured only so long as necessary.[6]

One of the first measures passed by the new order was a law establishing a statewide public school system. Another was a bill reorganizing the university, which at that time was Mississippi's only state-supported institution of higher learning. Under the new statute the governor appointed the trustees and continued as ex officio president of the board. Governor James L. Alcorn, a wealthy planter and former slaveowner, an ex-Confederate general, a scalawag, and Mississippi's first Republican governor, appointed a combination of Democrats and Republicans to the university's new board of trustees and enjoined them to "purge its halls" of "political factions," an old "vice that has haunted them so long." The Reconstruction board took office in 1870.[7]

In spite of Governor Alcorn's admonition, and in spite of the fact that the Reconstruction board did not disturb the administration or the faculty, the Democrats railed against the governor, the board, and even the university itself. The Jackson *Clarion,* a bitter and partisan journal, proclaimed that the university "had been ruthlessly seized by the Spoilsmen who have determined to radicalize it." Instead of being radicalized, however, during the five years the Republican Party controlled the board of trustees, it was actually shielded from factional politics. When the Republican board was installed in 1870, L. Q. C. Lamar held the chair of law. Lamar had drafted Mississippi's Ordinance of Secession and was extremely critical of Reconstruction. Like Longstreet's attacks on the old Know-Nothings, Lamar's attacks on Republicans were often personal, always bitter, and sometimes even violent. In the federal court at Oxford, while defending some Ku Klux Klansmen, Lamar threatened to throw a chair at a person in the courtroom, and he actually struck the United States marshal who tried to restrain him. The Reconstruction board scrupulously avoided a confrontation with Lamar. According to the historian of Reconstruction in Mississippi, Lamar wanted "to become a martyr at the hands of the Republicans." Many Mississippi politicians through the years have reaped the benefits of martyrdom at the hands of the federal establishment, or enemies of the state, or even the criticism of the northern press. Disappointed in the board's refusal "to cooperate in his scheme," Lamar resigned.[8]

Lamar was replaced by Thomas L. Walton, a Mississippi lawyer whose theory on states' rights brought criticism to him and the university. Walton taught law students that the federal constitution, laws, and judicial decisions took precedence over the state constitution, laws, and court proceedings. In speeches, articles, and lectures Walton insisted that Mississippi was bound by the Fourteenth Amendment and had to abide by federal court orders based on that amendment. When Walton's views reached south Mississippi, the Crystal Springs *Monitor* joined many other Democratic newspapers in urging Mississippians to take their sons out of the university because "their minds were being imbued with the worst principles of scallawag and carpet-bag politics."[9]

The attacks against the university by partisan politicians and newspapers indicated that Governor Alcorn's plea had gone unheeded. Moreover, most of the criticism was unfounded and fabricated. Jonathan Tarbell, an especially despised carpetbagger board member who was often singled out for special abuse by the Democrats, claimed that "no political question or consideration has ever intruded itself into deliberations of the trustees." Judge Tarbell's statement was made during the bitter campaign of 1873, when the carpetbagger Adelbert Ames defeated James Alcorn for governor. It may have been a self-serving statement, but there was some truth to it and to Tarbell's claim that "the political bias of individual trustees" did not influence their decisions. Edward Mayes, L. Q. C. Lamar's son-in-law and a practicing attorney in Oxford during Governor Ames's administration, has described Ames's policy toward the university as "thoroughly conservative and wise." Mayes added, "he left it thoroughly alone." When Mayes later became chancellor, he would have wished for the same. One indication that the Republican board was not ruled by partisan, political, or sectional bias is the fact that when Chancellor Waddel resigned in 1874 the Reconstruction board appointed an ex-Confederate general to succeed him.[10] The University of Mississippi actually prospered under the Reconstruction government; during that volatile period whatever damage it suffered came from those who claimed to be its friends.

As Mississippi was implementing its new political order in 1870, American higher education was also entering a new era. According to Laurence Veysey, 1870 was the "Anno Domini" of higher education in the United States. Two towering figures assumed college presidencies about that time: Charles W. Eliot at Harvard in 1869 and Noah Porter at Yale in 1871. Cornell and California had recently opened, Frederick A. P. Barnard had just begun his career at Columbia, and Johns Hopkins University was on the drawing board. In his inaugural address President Porter proclaimed that American higher education was "convulsed by a revolution."[11]

In the anno domini of American higher education the University of Mississippi became, on paper at least, a true university. Its transformation from a liberal arts college began almost as soon as John N. Waddel was installed as chancellor in 1865. In his inaugural address Waddel urged the board of trustees to make the university, in his words, a "republic of letters" and to reorganize its curriculum. The board authorized Waddel to modify the curriculum, but he preferred to revamp it, explaining that the University of Mississippi was a university in name only and should be thoroughly reorganized. Persuaded by his argument, the trustees in the summer of 1869 authorized Chancellor Waddel to study the organization of America's leading institutions of higher learning. During that summer the chancellor visited Harvard, Yale, Amherst, University of the City of New York, Princeton, Massachusetts Institute of Technology, Brown, Michigan, and the University of Georgia. At the board's fall meeting Waddel recommended an organizational plan based on the best features of Harvard and Michigan. After a year-long study the trustees approved Waddel's plan and authorized him to implement as much as the university's financial condition would allow.[12]

Under Chancellor Waddel's reorganization plan, most of it implemented in the 1870 fall term, the university was divided into three departments: a preparatory department; a department of science, literature, and arts; and a department of professional studies. The preparatory department was superseded by the subfreshman class in 1883 and finally discontinued in 1893. The department of science, literature, and arts offered six different courses of study (or majors) leading to four undergraduate degrees and two graduate degrees, the Master of Arts and Doctor of Philosophy. The Bachelor of Arts, Bachelor of Science, and Bachelor of Civil Engineering degrees were prescribed courses, but the Bachelor of Philosophy was a "largely elective" course. The professional department included the School of Law and Governmental Science, School of Medicine and Surgery, which did not open until several years later, and Department of Agriculture and the Mechanic Arts.[13]

Professor Eugene Hilgard, who organized the college of agriculture, studied the curriculum at Yale's Sheffield School, which emphasized theory and laboratory instruction, and at several Midwestern state universities, which favored practical field work. Hilgard recommended a combination of the two approaches. On October 2, 1872, the four-year agricultural course was open to students, but none enrolled. A disappointed Hilgard reported to the chancellor that prejudice against scientific farming and a lack of funds for expensive equipment had stymied the agricultural program. Hilgard also criticized the tradition of trying to meet the demand for vocational education only after the demand arose. "Such is," he said, "the theory of but too many who exert influence over our institutions, both in public life and in the press." Instead of reacting to developments as they occurred, the university should conduct an educational campaign, Hilgard said, to "dispel prejudice and misunderstandings" against "bookfarming." There was strong support for agricultural education among Mississippi's agrarian leadership, especially in the Grange, but the politicians who represented the state's farming constituency favored a separate institution rather than a unit within the old aristocratic state university. The politics of agricultural education was not as volatile in Mississippi as in South Carolina, for example, "under "Pitchfork" Ben Tillman. But some politicians, most notably Frank Burkitt and James K. Vardaman, did exploit the lingering enmity between Mississippi's dirt farmers and the old aristocracy. During its brief existence, the university's school of agriculture attracted very few students.[14]

The reorganization of the university in 1870 raised the question of state-supported higher education for blacks, heretofore provided only by two private colleges, Shaw University and Tougaloo. Established by the Mississippi Conference of the Methodist Episcopal Church at Holly Springs in 1866, Shaw was an ambitious enterprise that included a commercial institute and a medical school in addition to the traditional collegiate course; it was overrun with students when it opened. In 1890 its name was changed to Rust University and subsequently to Rust College. Tougaloo University was established in 1869 at Jackson by the American Missionary Society and the Freedmen's Bureau. Both

Shaw and Tougaloo received small state subsidies to support their teacher training programs, or normal departments. The state also provided small tuition grants to students at both institutions who agreed to teach in Mississippi's new public school system. The normal department at Shaw University was later separated from that institution to become State Normal School, a coeducational state teachers college for blacks. Its enrollment eventually reached two hundred. In 1896 Governor John M. Stone praised State Normal School as one of Mississippi's best investments in education.[15]

In their first flush of freedom Mississippi's former slaves craved education, and they stormed the citadels of learning where the "stores and treasures of knowledge" had been secreted from them during their years in bondage. Their hunger to know about "the world remade by the Civil War" made many white Mississippians uneasy. Edward Mayes, a tutor at the University of Mississippi in 1870, wrote about those early anxious days of jubilee: "There was a strong undercurrent of nervous apprehension, lest at any time some aggressive negro student should . . . demand admission to the University, in which case an explosion was regarded as inevitable."[16]

That undercurrent of apprehension stirred Judge Robert S. Hudson of Yazoo City to ask in an open letter to Chancellor Waddel in 1870: "Will the faculty as now composed, receive or reject an applicant for admission as a student on account of color?" Waddel and the faculty responded that they would be "governed by consideration of race and color" and would "instantly resign should the trustees require them to receive negro students." The correspondence between Hudson and Waddel was widely published in the Mississippi press and prompted extensive comment. Former governor William L. Sharkey praised Chancellor Waddel, saying "the University was saved." The Jackson *Clarion* wrote of the faculty, "We warmly endorse their stand." But Governor Alcorn branded Hudson's letter as the "stuff of political hucksters" and chided the "obsequious faculty" for allowing "such a man as Judge Hudson" to intimidate them. He added that they were at liberty to resign at any time.[17]

Robert W. Flournoy, a former slaveowner, Confederate colonel, and scalawag editor of a newspaper called *Equal Rights,* demanded that the controversy over the university's admission policy be settled by the federal courts under the terms of the Fourteenth Amendment. Flournoy announced in his newspaper that he would encourage black students "competent to enter the University" to seek admission and "test the question whether the professor [Waddel] or the Constitution is supreme." But no black students sought admission during Reconstruction. Things take time in Mississippi. Nearly a century later a black student competent to enter the university did seek admission. The question was placed before the federal courts, which ruled that "the Constitution is supreme" and ordered that the student be admitted. When he enrolled, the explosion—"regarded as inevitable"—occurred.[18]

That deferred commitment to educational equality in Mississippi was made possible by the establishment of Alcorn University, one of the nation's earliest state-supported institutions of higher learning for blacks. It was founded in May 1871 on the old campus of Oakland College, which the state had recently purchased for $42,000. Originally the school was to be named Revels University in honor of Senator Hiram Revels, one of Mississippi's most prominent leaders during Reconstruction and the first black to serve in the United States Senate. Senator Revels deferred, however, suggesting that the university be named in honor of Governor Alcorn. There was some discussion about offering the presidency to Frederick Douglass, but the offer was made instead to Senator Revels who accepted.[19]

When the Morrill land-grant funds became available to Mississippi in the fall of 1871, Alcorn University was allocated three-fifths of those funds, the other two-fifths going to the University of Mississippi. Alcorn was also allocated $50,000 annually by the state legislature. Four-year scholarships were awarded to one student from each legislative district on the basis of competitive examinations; each scholarship recipient also received an annual stipend of $100 drawn from the common school fund. Although Alcorn University originally limited admission to male students, women were admitted unofficially in 1884 and officially in 1903. Over five hundred women students applied for admission the first year Alcorn became coeducational.[20]

Alcorn University began under auspicious conditions. Its curriculum included courses in agricultural science and industrial arts, a classical collegiate course leading to a Bachelor of Arts degree, and teacher training. Agricultural students gained practical field experience on the university's ninety-acre demonstration farm, and industrial arts students received instruction in well-equipped machine and woodworking shops. But the school's bright beginnings were soon dimmed, first by internal discord and then by the politics of race. President Revels's willingness to curry favor with the white power structure eroded his standing in the black community. By his deference to whites and his narrow vision he stifled the aspirations of Mississippi's young blacks, who lashed out at him in anger and frustration and rebelled at his leadership. Student unrest finally prompted a legislative investigation in 1874 that resulted in the removal of the board of trustees and the faculty, the dismissal of the president, and a complete reorganization of the university. When the Democrats regained control of the state legislature in 1876, however, President Revels was reinstated. Two years later, Alcorn was again reorganized.[21]

In 1878 Alcorn University's original charter was revoked, and a new charter reestablished the institution as Alcorn Agricultural and Mechanical College. Although the state's black population was significantly larger than its white population, the Democratic legislature reduced Alcorn's share of the Morrill land-grant funds from three-fifths to one-half; it also abolished the $100 stipends for scholarship students. Over the next two decades Alcorn's annual appropriations were drastically reduced. Established as a "white ploy to defuse the radical demand for the racial integration of the University of Mississippi," Alcorn was later allowed to dilapidate by the architects of white supremacy.[22]

The statute rechartering Alcorn A & M in 1878 also established Mississippi Agricultural and Mechanical College and transferred the school of agriculture from the state university at Oxford to the new college at Starkville. Mississippi A & M opened higher education to the sons of Mississippi's industrial classes, and it came to be known fondly as the "People's College." Though the supporters of an agricultural college were happy to see its establishment, many felt disappointed by its location. The Raymond *Hinds County Gazette* confessed that its worst fears had been unfounded; Mississippi A & M College would not be located in Alabama or Tennessee, the editor happily reported, but in the extreme northeast section of Mississippi, the "stomping grounds" of Governor John M. Stone. The *Gazette* accused Governor Stone of using his political influence to locate the new institution in his "neck of the woods."[23]

Political considerations may also have played a role in the selection of Mississippi A & M's first president, General Stephen D. Lee, a West

Point graduate and former Confederate general. As a member of the state senate in 1878, President Lee had supported and voted for the bill establishing the agricultural college. His support for the advancement of agricultural science may have stemmed from his own well-known failure as a farmer after the Civil War. Lee was selected over two out-of-state applicants. When President Lee resigned in 1899, former governor John M. Stone succeeded him; again, politics may have been involved in the selection.[24]

During the interval between the founding of A & M College in 1878 and its opening in 1880, President Lee and the board of trustees built a campus, assembled a faculty and designed a curriculum. Of the three, designing the curriculum was the most problematic. Senator Justin Morrill, the father of land-grant colleges, had long been admonishing college officials to "lop off a portion" of the "old, useless classics and fill the vacancy—if there is a vacancy—with less antique and more practical" courses. President Lee was certainly willing to do that. He gave botany, chemistry, biology, and other sciences priority in designing the curriculum, but he was handicapped by the legislature's failure to appropriate sufficient funds to build a demonstration farm or equip the laboratories and workshops. President Lee was also distracted by the traditionalists on the faculty, especially, G. S. Roudebush, head of the English department, Reverend W. J. T. Sullivan, a Methodist minister and head of the mathematics and civil engineering department, and J. A. Bailey, head of the department of ancient languages. All three men lobbied for the inclusion of classical studies and liberal arts in the curriculum. At their insistence, and in "deference to the wishes of a large class of citizens of the state," President Lee and the board of trustees allowed the classics and liberal arts to be taught "on demand."[25]

That concession was not a compromise on President Lee's part, because he considered the classics and the sciences "handmaidens to the agricultural and mechanical arts." Mississippi A & M's original curriculum was based on President Lee's theory that "an intelligent understanding of agriculture as a science and an art [requires] an education as broad and liberal as that needed for mastering any profession." Although Lee allowed instruction in the classics, he would not divert funds from the practical studies to pay for the liberal arts courses. Consequently, the forty students who signed up for Greek and Latin in 1880 paid Professor Bailey a special tutorial fee. President Lee and the supporters of agricultural education soon learned that there was a much greater demand for book learning than for "book farming." When Mississippi A & M opened 354 students matriculated, but few of them were farm boys. Most students in that first class were sons of well-to-do families from the surrounding counties in northeast Mississippi; they came not to study the soils or the rhythm of the seasons but to prepare themselves for the learned professions. It should have embarrassed President Lee that his own son, a graduate of A & M's first class, took a collegiate course and then went off to Harvard to study law.[26]

Frank Burkitt, a member of A & M's first board of trustees, a Grange activist, a populist editor, and a member of the state legislature, was highly critical of the school's curriculum, its faculty, and President Lee. He once said that if the people of Mississippi listened to the "Michigan professor who runs the college farm" they would all starve to death. Burkitt's criticism prompted a public debate over the role of the classics in the agricultural college. Only two years after A & M opened, the legislature appointed a special committee to "inquire into the present condition" and "adaptation to the end for which [the school was] created." During the investigation that took place on the campus in February 1882, the committee interrogated President Lee as well as several professors and trustees. Lee explained that Mississippi A & M was "in a period, when if its technical stamp is not put upon it, it will [fail] as most other agricultural colleges have." The existing academic and literary courses were not the problem, he said; A & M was lacking the "equipment and surroundings to make it an industrial college." When agricultural schools were not provided adequate laboratories and equipment, he went on to explain, they became liberal arts colleges in fact and agricultural colleges in name only.[27]

Following the committee's investigation, the A & M faculty was thoroughly reorganized. By the fall session of 1882 the "traditionalists had been routed from the faculty." Only two of the original faculty members remained, and President Lee announced that the new professors "believe in industrial education." More significantly, the legislature appropriated $120,000 for new buildings, laboratories, and equipment at A & M. To prevent the institution from becoming a local liberal arts college for northeast Mississippi, the legislature established an enrollment quota for each county and prohibited the admission of out-of-state students.[28]

In spite of everything that the legislature could or would do to put a "technical stamp" on Mississippi A & M, the nontechnical and liberal arts courses proliferated. Just as the old-time college began its transition to the modern American university with the founding of Harvard in 1636, so did Mississippi Agricultural and Mechanical College begin evolving into a comprehensive multipurpose university in the year of its founding. By its third year, notwithstanding President Lee's proclamation that his faculty believed in industrial education, the number of English courses had increased from seven to twelve. History, both ancient and modern, was soon added along with philosophy, logic, economics, and political science. A few years later the school established a department of psychology and ethics.[29]

Even though the literary departments were expanding, the professors of agricultural science did not abandon their mission to Mississippi farmers, despite the ridicule heaped upon book farming by "the man in the furrow." After years of battling the "prejudice and misunderstandings" about scientific agriculture, agricultural scientists finally realized that the field rather than the classroom, demonstrations rather than lectures, and future farmers rather than the man already mired in the furrow should be the focus of agricultural education. A major step toward a more pragmatic pedagogy was taken in 1884 when the faculty recommended that Mississippi A & M set aside $1,000 of its annual income for agricultural experimentation and that "farmers institutes" be conducted on a regular basis throughout the state. The Hatch Act of 1887 augmented and greatly expanded the work of agricultural experimentation and extension work at A & M.[30] One of the pioneers of that early extension work in Mississippi was Professor D. L. Phares, whose contributions to the improvement of the state's agriculture have yet to be fully recognized or appreciated.

Given the state's limited resources and the prejudice against scientific farming, which arose as much from apathy as from conscious opposition, A & M's contributions to the improvement of the state's agriculture during its first two decades were not insignificant. In terms of industrial and mechanical progress, however, the land-grant college had virtually no impact on Mississippi's economy. President Lee's re-

quests for funds to establish programs in the mechanic arts went unheeded, and the institution's instructional emphasis remained literary
and agricultural.[31]

In the post-Reconstruction era, a time of severe retrenchment under
Democratic leadership, Mississippi was struggling to meet the meager
needs of its four existing institutions of higher learning: the University of Mississippi, the State Normal School at Holly Springs, Alcorn
A & M, and Mississippi A & M College. Nevertheless, in 1884 the
legislature yielded to public pressure and established a fifth state institution at Columbus—the Industrial Institute and College, a multipurpose school for white females. During the early years of Reconstruction, there had been some public desire for a state-supported
college for women. At the behest of Sally Eola Reneau, an elaborate
amendment establishing the Reneau Female University of Mississippi
at Oxford had been added to the university's charter in 1872. The
legislature had named Reneau principal of the female university and
ex officio vice-president of the University of Mississippi but had not
made any state funds available to the new institution. Reneau renewed
her earlier request for a federal land grant, but Congress turned it
down. The law establishing the Reneau Female University was repealed the following year. After a second attempt to establish a state
university for women failed, Reneau abandoned her effort and left
Mississippi. About a decade later, the state university began admitting
women students. But because most of these students took the classical
course, popular support for an industrial and vocational school for
women continued. Orchestrated by Annie Coleman Peyton, this show
of support culminated in the founding of the Industrial Institute and
College.[32]

The institute's multiple mission was to provide industrial education,
teacher training, and a collegiate course leading to a bachelor's degree.
To prevent the school from becoming just another local liberal arts
college for northeast Mississippi, the law establishing it fixed an enrollment quota for each county in the state. Although the Industrial Institute was intended to emphasize vocational and industrial training, its
first president, R. H. Jones, announced that the young ladies who attended his institute would receive an education as "thorough and extensive as that conferred by our best colleges for young men." The
same debate over curriculum that had taken place four years earlier at

Starkville was repeated in nearby Columbus. The collegiate faculty insisted that the girls in the industrial and normal departments be required to take a certain number of academic courses. They found a convincing ally in President Jones. Over the objection of the vocational instructors, literary courses were required of all students enrolled at the institute. Enlargement of the academic curriculum at the expense of industrial and vocational departments brought criticism to the institution and its president. The board of trustees constantly interfered with the management of the school, and President Jones finally resigned in protest of their interference.[33]

Following a succession of short-term presidents and years of internal discord and nepotism, a legislative committee found the Industrial Institute and College in utter disarray in 1896. After hearing the committee's report, the legislature threatened to withhold future appropriations unless the board of trustees could arrest the decline of the institution. This legislative action, of course, would have guaranteed the school's continued decline, if not its demise. At that point the board of trustees made a special appeal to Andrew Kincannon, the state superintendent of education, to accept the presidency. In their initial contact with Kincannon the trustees promised not to interfere with his administration and to seek additional funding for the school. Kincannon accepted the appointment, and the board honored its pledge of noninterference.[34] Kincannon's administration was highly successful. After a ten-year term at Industrial Institute and College, he was appointed chancellor of the University of Mississippi.

Although Mississippi was supporting five institutions of higher learning by the mid-1880s, public school officials still claimed, with some justification, that teacher training was being neglected. The state had funded teacher training for blacks with some success since 1870, but there was no state-supported normal school for whites. Mississippi was in fact the only state without a training school for its white teachers. In 1884 the state superintendent of education cited the lack of well-trained and competent teachers as the number-one problem of public education in Mississippi. He pleaded with the legislature to create a normal college for white teachers. Though several bills establishing a state normal school for whites were introduced in 1884, none were enacted. Instead, teacher training was included in the mission statement of the Industrial Institute and College, and both the state university and the agricultural college also expanded their teacher training programs over the next few years. Even those additional programs failed to meet the demand for competent public school teachers, and the furtive plea for teacher training continued.[35]

During the late nineteenth century, Mississippi's system of higher education included the five state-supported institutions, several privately owned and short-lived normal schools, and several denominational colleges. Some church schools such as Whitworth College in Brookhaven and Chickasaw College at Pontotoc survived the Civil War and continued to operate for several years thereafter. But Mississippi College at Clinton was the only antebellum church school that emerged from the war with a strong financial base and a stable enrollment. Denominational support for higher education remained very strong in Mississippi, however, and several new church schools were established after the Civil War. In addition to Rust and Tougaloo, and several junior colleges, the new generation of four-year church schools included Natchez College, Campbell College, and Carrollton Female College. Only four of them—Blue Mountain (Baptist, founded in 1873), Belhaven (Presbyterian, 1883), Millsaps (Methodist, 1890), and Jackson College—are still in operation. Jackson College was established in Natchez by the Baptist Home Mission Society in 1877 but was moved to Jackson in 1883. It became a state institution in 1940 and is now Jackson State University.[36]

Most of Mississippi's private liberal arts colleges maintained their own preparatory departments. Even the state schools had either preparatory divisions or subfreshman classes. Mississippi's public school officials complained that the existence of so many college preparatory departments had prevented the development of a strong system of state high schools. It was a perplexing problem with no quick or simple remedy. College authorities could not disband their preparatory divisions until they were convinced that the secondary system could furnish a continuous flow of admissable students, but public high schools could not develop if their most likely students were enrolled in college preparatory departments.

A major step in the process of weaning preparatory education from the colleges was taken in 1893 when the University of Mississippi discontinued its subfreshman class and began admitting students who had accumulated ten prescribed high school credits. The practice of admitting students to college on the basis of high school credits had begun in Michigan in 1870 and had initiated the American high school movement. The practice also proved to be very successful in Mississippi. By 1917, 140 high schools had entered into an arrangement with Mississippi institutions of higher learning to accept standardized high school credits for college admission. Although the arrangement seemed to be working well in Mississippi, some public school officials expressed strong misgivings. They believed that it gave the colleges too much control over the high school curriculum and caused some high schools to cater to precollege students while neglecting those whose education would end with high school.[37]

The discontinuation of the subfreshman class at the University of Mississippi in 1893 was only one feature of a major reorganization that had begun in 1889 under Chancellor Edward Mayes. Under Mayes's reorganization plan the number of schools (or majors) in the department of science, literature, and arts had increased from ten to twenty-one. Several new schools such as history, belles lettres, and elocution had been created; the school of natural history had been divided into the separate schools of zoology, botany, and geology; and the school of modern languages had become the schools of French and German. Chancellor Mayes had also established a philosophy department, a highly innovative move in 1889, by separating logic from the department of moral science which was the offspring of the old "evidences of Christianity" course. Chancellor Mayes's emphasis on belles lettres (particularly English literature) as an academic discipline placed him in the company of John Bascom and James Russell Lowell who pioneered the study of literature at Harvard.[38]

In his effort to modernize the university, Chancellor Mayes focused much of his energy on the development of the university's library. As he was installing the new curriculum he began construction of a new library building, which he located in the center of the campus. Although the university's library could hardly match those of other state universities, even in the South, its holdings were reclassified in accordance with the methods then in use in the nation's best academic libraries.[39]

One of the most popular features of Chancellor Mayes's reorganization was the extent to which elective courses were allowed. The elective system, which was spreading rapidly throughout American colleges, provoked strong opposition and ridicule from many traditionalists. In a memorable academic put-down, Professor Carey Thomas of Bryn Mawr asked incredulously: if college credit is given for ladder exercises in gym classes, why not give students credit for walking up stairs; or if credit is given for swimming, why not give partial credit for one's morning bath? President James McCosh of Princeton dismissed the whole elective system as little more than a bid for popularity. In spite of such contemptuous attitudes the elective system was gaining headway even at Yale by the mid-1880s.[40]

Frederick Rudolph's statement that the "least elective institutions of all were the state universities of the South, which were in the grasp of poverty" is only half right. Most southern state universities were grappled in penury, but they were not hostile to the elective system. The contrary was closer to the truth. H. E. Shepard, writing in the *Sewanee Review* in 1893, lists "the introduction of the elective system" as one of "the fundamental evils which mark the higher forms of academic life in the Southern states." The University of Mississippi could have been a prime target for Shepard's scorn. The Bachelor of Philosophy degree was made "wholly elective" under Chancellor Mayes's reorganization plan in 1889, and the other undergraduate degrees also permitted a large number of elective courses.[41]

Chancellor Edward Mayes was a man of large vision, who promoted the development of the university with a zeal reminiscent of Chancellor Barnard. "It was inevitable," according to James Allen Cabaniss, that Mayes' vigor and tireless energy would sooner or later provoke dissatisfaction just as Barnard's had." And like Barnard before him, Mayes was unable to make Mississippi a first-rate university. His efforts were frustrated by the twin maladies of penury and politics, and he resigned in 1891.[42]

In spite of the Industrial Revolution and the urbanization of America in the late nineteenth century, the South—Mississippi in particular—remained rural and agrarian. The state's cotton economy was subject to a capricious market and dominated by sharecropping. Almost two-thirds of its farmers, 62.27 percent, were tenants in 1890. Mississippi's official policy of racial discrimination and exploitation prevented over half of its population from becoming productive citizens. Industrialization and urbanization were stymied, and economic stagnation produced years of retrenchment.[43]

Because of the limited state resources, as well as the social and class dynamics during the late nineteenth century, a sometimes acrimonious rivalry developed among the state's institutions of higher learning, especially between the state university and the agricultural college. In 1880, the year Mississippi A & M opened, the legislature voted to compensate the university for the loss of the seminary funds. The board of trustees had told the legislature that the recovery of those lost funds was absolutely necessary if the University of Mississippi was to become "a seat of learning whose renown shall attract crowds from all parts of the earth, as did Cambridge, Bologna, and Oxford of old." It is doubtful that the legislature expected the university to attain such renown. Still, it acknowledged the institution's right to compensation and thereafter made an annual special appropriation of $32,000, an amount equal to the interest the university would have received had the seminary funds not been lost.[44]

The validity of that special appropriation, and especially its fairness, was challenged by the trustees of Mississippi A & M, who claimed that the original funds had not been designated to one particular "seminary of learning" and that A & M should also receive a share of the interest on the lost funds. Senator James Z. George, a member of the Mississippi A & M board of trustees, called the special appropriation a fraud on the people of the State and accused the University of Mississippi of making "forays on the treasury whenever it suits its convenience or its tastes to do so." In a rejoinder, Chancellor Mayes accused the senator of viewing the matter with "a jealous eye" and of being "anxious to find offense." A nasty public debate over the fairness of that special appropriation developed between Senator George and Chancellor Mayes. The debate, conducted in the press and in pamphlets, went on for several months.[45]

The ugly exchanges between Senator George and Chancellor Mayes reveal much about the origins of the rivalry between State and Ole Miss. The dispute was about more than just money. Senator George personified the People's College. A son of the industrial classes, he was called "Commoner" by his admirers with the same pride that the Populists felt in hailing William Jennings Bryan as "The Great Commoner." But his aristocratic detractors often chided him for his country manners and unkemptness. Traces of chewing tobacco often showed at the edge of his mouth or on his shirtfront and vest. Without the benefit of a college connection, Senator George was a self-made man in a time and place where lineage was prized above self-reliance. He was often taunted for his lack of ancestry; his congressional biography did not give the name of his father or any forebears and stated only that he "moved to Mississippi with his mother when a lad." Chancellor Mayes, with his distinguished Virginia ancestry, was a striking contrast to Senator George. His father served in two branches of government and held the chair of law at Transylvania University. Mayes began his college education in Virginia, then earned two degrees from the University of Mississippi. Through marriage to the daughter of L. Q. C. Lamar, he entered the lineage of the Longstreets.[46] In his dialogue with Senator George, Chancellor Mayes betrayed a contempt for his adversary and a condescension that smacked of class. That contempt was directed not just at George but also at the institution whose interests he defended.

Chancellor Mayes referred to the University of Mississippi as the state's "most precious possession"; as such, he believed, it warranted the special appropriation. The chancellor's logic was simple and unassailable. If the university was the state's most precious possession, then the agricultural college was less valuable and therefore would have to occupy a lower level in Mississippi's educational hierarchy. In the minds of the alumni and friends of Mississippi A & M, that special appropriation to the university in 1880 was incontrovertible evidence that an educational hierarchy did exist. They were incensed by it—by the insinuation that the university and the rich kids, the sons of the old aristocracy, still came first because they were better than everybody else. The University, which educated the lawyers, doctors, and politicians, was superior to the "cow college," Mississippi A & M. This prevailing notion that the university was the preeminent institution of higher learning and that other state schools should look up to it was articulated by a legislative committee in 1886: "Nothing is better calculated to detract from the merits of the [university] than unfriendly remarks. . . . It should not be regarded by other schools or colleges as a rival, but looked up to as affording superior advantages not attainable elsewhere, as pre-eminently superior to all others, and to which all others should be tributary."[47] The legislature's recognition of the University of Mississippi as the state's superior institution and its call for an end to criticism confirmed the belief of the industrial classes that the university was the last standing bastion of the old aristocracy.

The bitter and wasteful rivalry between the university and other state institutions of higher learning was paralleled by a similar rivalry between the emerging common school system and the expanding system of higher education. In 1886 Representative Frank Burkitt, in one of his angry outbursts, accused Mississippi's aristocracy of maintaining several colleges for the favored elite while ignoring the needs of the common people. Burkitt claimed that Mississippi was spending $150.00 dollars a year per college student but only $1.50 for students in the common schools, which he called the "poor man's only university." The state's educational priorities, he said, should be turned bottom side up. The legislature's response to Burkitt's outburst was the enactment of a comprehensive school law that enlarged and upgraded the common school system and created yet another claimant against the state's resources. Two years later Burkitt became chairman of the house appropriations committee and forced a drastic reduction in the appropriations for higher education. Mississippi A & M, which Burkitt singled out for special punishment, lost almost $15,000.[48]

The history of higher education in Mississippi in the late nineteenth century was shaped by the dynamics between a social order in transition and a power structure resistant to change. Because that power structure controlled the purse, the courts, the law, the pulpit, the press, and the classroom, Mississippi was not unlike a totalitarian state. Nevertheless, the status of the common man and of blacks and women had been forever altered by the Civil War and the Industrial Revolution, and even in Mississippi the Gilded Age was a time of rising expectations. Mississippi's power structure felt threatened, unsure whether it could control the consequences of mass education. On the eve of the new century, Mississippi's leadership "circled the wagons," began to hold on to dreams of an Old South that never was, and tightened its grip on the public institutions of higher education. In 1886 President W. B. Highgate of State Normal School was accused of encouraging his black students, by his own example, to be uppity and ambitious; he was fired and the school was eventually closed. President Jones of the woman's college at Columbus had to reassure the board of trustees in 1887 that he was not teaching his female students "to demand the rights of men nor to invade the sphere of men" but instead was teaching each woman "those beautiful Christian graces that constitute her the charm of social life, and the queen of the home." In 1888 a verbal attack in the state legislature on Mississippi A & M's "imported scholars," which was followed by a reduction of their salaries, led to an "epidemic of resignations." In 1889, shortly after requiring Chancellor Mayes and his faculty to sign a statement acknowledging that they served at the "wish" of the board and could be dismissed at its "will," the University of Mississippi's board of trustees fired five of the eight professors and allowed two others to resign. In 1896 the all-white Alcorn A & M board of trustees appointed the Reverend Edward H. Triplett president of the college. Triplett, who lacked a college degree, was not well received by the Alcorn faculty. The board of trustees was so angered by the reaction to its authority that it dismissed virtually the entire Alcorn faculty.[49]

Each of Mississippi's five public institutions of higher learning was autonomous and governed by a separate board of trustees. The governor appointed the members of all five boards; as ex officio chairman of each board, he was the only link between them. Many board members were politicians, and the institutions they governed felt the fury of factional politics. In 1896, for example, the University of Mississippi board of trustees included the governor, the state superintendent of education, the state treasurer, a state supreme court judge, two ex-governors, a congressman, one former state senator, and one future United States senator. College presidents were inevitably drawn into political contests; if they were not on the winning side they were subject to dismissal. Reprisals sometimes extended even to the faculty.

The mischief of factional politics, and its intrusion into academia, peaked during the first decade of the twentieth century. Stirred by the election of Governor James K. Vardaman, the industrial classes and the dirt farmers, who came to be known as "rednecks," were determined to democratize higher education. That determination climaxed in the undignified dismissal of Chancellor Robert Fulton, an episode that eventually led to the consolidation of the individual governing boards. The creation of one consolidated board of trustees for all the state's institutions of higher learning signaled the beginning of a new era of higher education in Mississippi.

Five

A State System of Higher Education, 1900–1928

In establishing a state system of higher education the new
consolidated board of trustees promised to "make haste slowly."
—Board of Trustees, 1910

When Governor Andrew H. Longino was inaugurated on January 16, 1900, Mississippi had a population 92.3 percent rural, the highest rate of illiteracy in the nation, and the lowest per capita income. Governor Longino linked those three conditions with the state's languishing school system, its traditional hostility toward outside corporations, and its tolerance of mob violence. Longino, a pivotal figure in Mississippi's political history, was the first governor elected after the Civil War who was not a Confederate veteran and the last governor to be picked by the ruling elite that controlled the Democratic Party. In his inaugural message he predicted a tidal wave of industrial development and called on the legislature to change Mississippi's antibusiness reputation "so that capital hunting investment" will not "pass Mississippi and go to other states offering wise legitimate inducements." On mob violence, Governor Longino predicted that businessmen would not locate in a state where life and property are not "respected by the people and protected by the courts." He admitted that "the work of the mob" was an unpopular subject but said it was "a fact about which, for the public good, every law abiding citizen should be bold to speak in condemnation."[1]

Governor Longino hailed education—but not traditional or classical education—as the sure remedy for what ailed Mississippi. Because higher education in the South had focused on mental discipline and statecraft, he complained, the sons of the South had followed "political rather than mechanical callings." He challenged the state's educational leadership "to test and prove the wisdom" of industrial education, and he asked the legislature to establish a school of technology at "the Agricultural College." The new school could promote the development of industry, he said, and could provide skilled managers for the cotton mills established in Mississippi during the 1880s.[2]

Governor Longino's reference to Mississippi A & M as the "Agricultural College" is significant. Mississippi's land-grant institution had become for all intents and purposes a liberal arts college that provided agricultural instruction but only minimal training in the mechanic arts. It acquired this image and character partly because the legislature did not appropriate sufficient funds to equip its mechanical shops and laboratories. But more important, President Stephen Lee did not promote industrial education because he feared "the mechanical course would sabotage the agricultural feature of the institution."[3]

Industrial education at Mississippi A & M was virtually nonexistent until 1894 when A. J. Wiechardt established the Department of Mechanic Arts and Electricity. Professor Wiechardt also offered a course in "the art of cotton manufacture" and persuaded President Lee to seek legislative funding for a textile school. In 1896 and again in 1898 Lee and the board of trustees unsuccessfully petitioned the legislature for the necessary funds. By 1900, however, the legislature was much more amenable to industrial development. During the first session in the new century it passed several bills designed to make Mississippi more attractive to industry, including a measure establishing a textile school.[4]

The original appropriation of $40,000 proved to be so inadequate, however, that school officials had to go to the North "to beg equipment for the new department." Fortunately, "manufacturers proved to be exceedingly generous," and the textile school opened in June 1901. When the old argument about academic courses in an industrial curriculum was repeated, the classicists won again. By 1907 the director of the textile school complained that over half of its curriculum consisted of liberal arts courses emphasizing "the development of the man" and "leaving as secondary the training of the machinist." The initial popularity of the school was not sustained, and by 1911 enrollment began a precipitous decline. In 1914 the textile department was closed.[5]

The decline in the popularity of the textile course was paralleled by an unprecedented expansion and proliferation of liberal arts courses. During the first decade of the twentieth century, A & M College achieved astonishing academic breadth under President John C. Hardy. A department of pedagogy, a summer normal school, four departments of modern languages, a school of general science, and several new humanities courses were added during his administration. In 1911, the year that marked the beginning of the enrollment decline in the textile school, Mississippi A & M's enrollment exceeded one thousand—1,090. But more than half of those students were enrolled in nontechnical courses.[6]

The academic proliferation at A & M drew considerable criticism from Frank Burkitt and from James K. Vardaman. Burkitt, now in the state senate, renewed his complaint about wasteful duplication at the state's institutions of higher learning and claimed that Mississippi was not getting a good return on its educational investment. Burkitt cited figures indicating that the state was spending eight times more than private schools per college student and forty times more than it was spending per student in the public schools. Governor Vardaman also criticized the agricultural college for expanding its academic curriculum and accused it of "catering to the elite." But "the White Chief" reserved his bitterest diatribes for black educational institutions. "There is no need multiplying words about it," he said; "the negro will not be permitted to rise above the station which he now fills," and education "renders him unfit for the work which the white man prescribed." The state's only obligation to blacks, according to Governor Vardaman, was to provide vocational and moral training.[7] The legislature did not accept Vardaman's extreme view and left the black public school system intact.

Although Governor Vardaman could not persuade the legislature to dismantle the black school system, he did use his executive authority to weaken it in two instances. He vetoed the appropriation for the State Normal School at Holly Springs, and in 1904 the institution that had trained two thousand public school teachers since its opening in 1873 was forced to close. In his veto message Governor Vardaman reiterated his claim that knowledge "inspires aspirations" in blacks that endanger white supremacy. The hunger of Richard Wright, who was born near Natchez during Governor Vardaman's last year in office and who later became one of white supremacy's severest critics, verifies Vardaman's claim. Wright's early education is a testament to Mississippi's intention to keep blacks in "their place." Of his childhood experience in Mississippi Wright remembered, "I was building up in me a dream that the entire educational system . . . had been rigged to stifle."[8]

Vardaman further weakened the black school system through tampering with salaries at Alcorn A & M College. After becoming chairman of the Alcorn board of trustees, he forced a reduction in the salaries of the school's academic faculty and raised those of its vocational teachers. The governor's action had the "salutary effect of discouraging higher education among Negroes and of insuring that the blacks remained agricultural laborers."[9]

James K. Vardaman was elected in 1903 largely by Mississippi's dirt farmers and day laborers, whom he promised that he would drive the wealthy elite from their positions of power and privilege. Like the common people he championed, Governor Vardaman considered the state university the last bastion of the old aristocracy, and he was determined to democratize it. The "need" to do so was dramatized in 1905 when seven Ole Miss fraternity students who had been suspended for violating the rules governing Greek societies were readmitted and allowed to graduate. The readmission of those students angered Dean Garvin Shands of the law school and Duncan H. Chamberlain, an ardent antifraternity law student. In January 1906, Chamberlain published a pamphlet to inform the "common people" of Mississippi that their university was still catering to "the so-called upper classes"; moreover, he accused Chancellor Robert Fulton of being partial to fraternity boys.[10]

To clear away rumor from fact, Chancellor Fulton asked the legislature to investigate the charges. Acting on his request, the university and colleges committee conducted an investigation that completely exonerated Fulton. Three committee members, however, presented a minority report that was very critical of the chancellor and asked the board of trustees to conduct its own investigation. After the publication of Chamberlain's pamphlet and the legislature's investigation, which some said was stacked in Fulton's favor, Governor Vardaman was convinced that the university needed new leadership. It would not be easy to remove Fulton. He had been at the University of Mississippi for nearly forty years and was the brother-in-law of Congressman John Sharp Williams, Vardaman's opponent in the upcoming senate race. Vardaman's political enemies could claim that Fulton's dismissal was the result of factional politics. Nevertheless, when Vardaman appointed new board members in 1906, he made certain that they would vote to dismiss Chancellor Fulton.[11]

For several weeks before the June board meeting there was widespread speculation that Chancellor Fulton would be dismissed if he did not voluntarily resign. The chancellor vowed not to resign; but a few days before the meeting Fulton was convinced by his supporters on the board that he did not have enough votes to survive, and he tendered his resignation. Saying that he would not continue to serve a board "swayed by the will of their master, Vardaman," he declined the board's offer of the chair of astronomy. Chancellor Fulton was not the only casualty of that June 1906 meeting. Dean Garvin Shands was also forced to resign, largely at the insistence of Judge Robert Powell, a new Vardaman appointee. Judge Powell's son was one of the seven students originally expelled in 1905. The judge personally blamed Dean Shands and was determined to "drive" him from the University. The board reduced Dean Shands's salary by $400 in a move calculated to induce his resignation.[12]

The removal of Chancellor Fulton and Dean Shands, and the long delay in finding a replacement for Fulton, convinced a large segment of Mississippi's leadership that some way had to be found to shield the institutions of higher learning from factional politics. Simultaneously there was increasing popular support for greater coordination among the state schools and for the elimination of costly duplication. In view of this popular consensus and the nearly unanimous consent of the state's educational leadership, the legislature abolished the four existing boards in 1910 and established a single board of trustees. To keep the colleges out of politics and politics out of the colleges, elected officials were prohibited from serving on the new board of trustees. The consolidated board was given authority over the state university, Alcorn A & M, Mississippi A & M, and the Industrial Institute and College. The central board, as it was sometimes called, did not govern the state's two teachers colleges, however. Mississippi Normal School, established in 1910 at Hattiesburg, and Delta State Teachers College, which opened at Cleveland in 1924, were governed by separate boards until 1932 when the legislature consolidated the three boards.[13]

The new consolidated board, composed primarily of businessmen, met for the first time in July 1910 and pledged to meet its responsibility with an "openness of mind." Its actions would be based on its assessment of Mississippi's immediate and long-range educational needs. The board did announce, however, that it would reorganize the four separate institutions into a coordinated state system of higher education. There would be many changes, some that might appear radical, but the board reassured the people of Mississippi that it would "make haste slowly."[14]

The link between Mississippi's economic progress and the quality of its educational system was recognized by the businessmen who governed Mississippi's institutions of higher learning. That relationship was the subject of the first speech given by James Sexton, the central board's first and only president. Sexton heralded the creation of the consolidated board as a "mile post in the educational history of our state" and made an impassioned plea for a coordinated system of public education that extended from the elementary school all the way up to the state university. An improved, coordinated system, he asserted, was essential for the development of Mississippi's economic resources. Because duplication and wasteful rivalry among the institutions of higher learning had impaired the state's economic development, he called on college officials and alumni to "banish forever the puerile idea" that there is "any sort of rivalry" between the university and other higher educational institutions. "But," he quickly added, "it is pre-eminently the mission of the University to set the pace for all our educational institutions." Though all the state's colleges claimed to be overcrowded and all were lobbying for larger appropriations, that overcrowding appeared more pressing than it actually was, Sexton claimed. He cautioned college officials against playing the numbers game. Some schools, he understood, counted students taking only one course, correspondence courses, or off-campus courses; students in the subfreshman class; and even those taking elementary mathematics. Sexton likened that system of counting to the Kansas farmer who advertised an auction of thirty-two head of stock: "When the stock came to be sold, the thirty-two head were found to embrace two horses one mule, one cow, and twenty-eight hens." Sexton warned college officials that if they played the numbers game with the legislature, they could not "reasonably object when the politicians [sought] to play the same game with the colleges."[15]

The reorganization of Mississippi's governing boards and the effort to coordinate the state's several colleges into a system of higher education was in keeping with a national trend which Laurence Veysey calls "a season of reassessment." Veysey explains: "The years 1908, 1909, and 1910 witnessed the widest flurry of debate about the aims of higher education ever to occur so far in the United States. The existence of the debate, which soon became widely spread throughout the general magazines, provided one of the signs that an era of academic pioneering had come to an end. This was a season when men drew back and took stock." That season of reassessment was prompted, according to a University of Chicago professor, by widespread "dissatisfaction among the people, among ourselves as college men, with the results of education . . . from the bottom up."[16] It can only be wondered if Mississippi's new board of trustees, which came into being during that season of reassessment, could have achieved the great promise that its first efforts presaged. But after only two years the nonpolitical board was superseded.

In January 1912 Frank Burkitt introduced a bill to repeal the statute that prohibited elected officials from serving on the central board of trustees. He and other public officials asserted that the state's institutions should not be controlled by "designing school men" who were not responsible to the taxpayer or subject to the popular will. Two weeks later, another measure, which superseded Burkitt's bill, completely reorganized the board and reinstated the governor as ex officio president.[17]

While the legislature was debating the various bills to reorganize the governing board in 1912, William A. Ellis of Carthage introduced a resolution to study the feasibility of consolidating the University of Mississippi and the agricultural college. It was clear to Ellis that Mississippi's long-term interests would be better served by a system of higher education rather than by several separate and autonomous institutions. Although the resolution would not have required a consolidation, only a consideration of that possibility, it was defeated.[18]

Of the factors that contributed to the 1912 law reorganizing the board and reinstating the governor as ex officio president, the most important was the long-standing presumption, especially among members of the legislature, that the governor was the head of the state's educational institutions in the same way that he was head of the state militia. A house resolution, for example, authorizing a special visitation of the state colleges stated that "Governor Edmund F. Noel, as chairman of the state's educational institutions," would head the delegation. The senate held the same presumption. A resolution to abolish coeducation at the university was ruled out of order by the chairman of the senate because "the Governor had not recommended the subject matter."[19]

Another important factor in the 1912 reorganization was the lingering controversy involving Chancellor Andrew Kincannon. There had been a range of accusations against university officials including fiscal mismanagement, football recruiting violations, and sexual improprieties. The controversy concerning the Kincannon administration was cited by some of the state's leading politicians as a justification for reasserting the state's authority over its institutions of higher learning. Although a legislative committee exonerated Chancellor Kincannon and other university officials, rumors and innuendos continued to plague his administration. Kincannon finally resigned in 1914 because he "was unwilling for the school to become a political chattel."[20]

Two years after Chancellor Kincannon's resignation a similar but less sensational situation occurred at Mississippi A & M. President George R. Hightower, a Governor Brewer appointee, had become very unpopular after only four years in office. The movement to oust Hightower found favor with Governor Theodore G. Bilbo who was in his first term as governor. As ex officio president of the board Governor Bilbo acceded to the call for new leadership at A & M, and with the nearly unanimous consent of the trustees he removed President Hightower. Editor Fred Sullens of the *Jackson Daily News* wrote that President Hightower's removal was unfortunate but necessary.[21]

President Hightower's dismissal and Chancellor Kincannon's resignation sparked another public outcry about politics and public education. The *Itta Bena Times* declared: "It is time to quit playing politics in the management of institutions of higher learning. We must get a better faculty, provide them with a sense of security and stability in order that the University may provide the kind of educational instruction necessary." Walter Clark of Clarksdale agreed that it was time to quit playing politics at both Ole Miss and State and issued a challenge to friends of both schools:

> It seems to me that the time is ripe for those men who have attended the University of Mississippi and the Agricultural and Mechanical College at Starkville to end the reign of politics in these two institutions. . . . There are enough Oxford and Starkville men in Mississippi with sufficient brains and influence forcibly to tear these schools out of the grasp of the politician.[22]

Although Walter Clark made no reference to the Industrial Institute and College in his appeal for an end to the "reign of politics" in higher education, he should have. When Lee Russell ran for governor in 1919 he sought the endorsement of its president, Henry L. Whitfield. President Whitfield not only declined to support Russell but actively campaigned for his opponent. Russell was elected in 1919. He fired Whitfield in 1920.[23]

The effort to end the reign of politics in Mississippi's institutions of higher learning seemed to be a lost cause, as did the effort to consolidate the colleges. But Mississippians love lost causes. Both efforts were taken up in the legislative session of 1920. Of several bills introduced to restructure higher education, the most ambitious was proposed by George L. Sheldon, a representative from Washington County. His bill would have consolidated the University of Mississippi, the Agricultural College, and the Industrial Institute into one institution named the University of Mississippi and located in Jackson. The Industrial Institute and College would have remained in Columbus as a junior college for women. Senator Julius C. Zeller of Yazoo County was the floor leader in the senate for the measure which the press termed the Sheldon-Zeller Bill. The legislature received petitions from alumni of all three institutions opposing the consolidation plan, but there were many who favored it—most significantly, Governor Bilbo, whose first term was just ending; the new governor, Lee Russell; and House Speaker Mike Conner.[24]

Senator Zeller met with a group of Jackson citizens on January 21, 1920, to discuss the advantages of consolidating the three institutions in their city. Zeller explained that the physical plant at the university was in deplorable condition and that university officials had requested

$700,000 for emergency repair and expansion. Similar urgent requests had been made by the other institutions, and the legislature was considering a special $2 million appropriation. It would be better to spend that money on a new university, Zeller said, than to repair old, worn-out buildings. But he quickly added that consolidation should not be based on considerations of brick and mortar alone: "This is the psychological moment for the legislature to realize that if we are ever to have a great university, an institution that will compare favorably with universities in other states, we must build anew, locate the institution at a center of population, broaden the scope of its work, and make it a University in something more than a name."[25]

As convincing as Zeller's argument was, little popular support for consolidation existed outside Jackson. After the defeat of the Sheldon-Zeller bill, several other options were considered. Some legislators opposed consolidation but favored moving the university to Jackson. To get that option before the legislature, Lamar Quintus Cincinnatus Williams of Newton County introduced "an Act to move the University of Mississippi from its present location near the town of Oxford to the city of Jackson." When Williams's bill got to the floor for debate, Representative Buz M. Walker, Jr., the son of Buz M. Walker, Sr., who was dean of the School of Engineering and future president of Mississippi A & M, offered an amendment to abolish the school of engineering at the university and transfer all engineering courses to Mississippi A & M College. Walker's amendment was tabled. The bill to move the university to Jackson was defeated by a vote of eighty-two to thirty-seven.[26]

Ironically, the one change that emerged from all the maneuvering was a change in name only. During the debate on the consolidation bill, President Henry Whitfield invited the legislature to visit the Industrial Institute and College. After their visit the lawmakers voted to keep the school independent and autonomous and changed its name to Mississippi State College for Women.[27]

Although thwarted at every turn in 1920, proponents of reform did not abandon their efforts to end the reign of politics or to establish a state system of higher education. In 1922 the joint legislative committee on the university and colleges visited each state institution of higher learning and found the campuses in varying stages of ill repair. After expressing its concern about the physical condition of the campuses, the committee spoke to the issue of politics and inveighed against its disruptive effects: "If the Czar of Russia and the Kaiser of Germany could pursue a policy of hands off when it came to their university professors, then surely we can observe this rule. . . . Otherwise, we shall never develop an esprit d'corps for learning and culture in our state."[28] What the Czar and the Kaiser could do, Mississippi governors could not or would not. During every campaign, gubernatorial candidates invariably solicited the support of college presidents and faculty.

The 1923 governor's race illustrates the close connection between politics and academics in Mississippi and documents its consequences. When Henry L. Whitfield, the former president of Mississippi State College for Women, ran for governor against Bilbo in 1923, the board of trustees made a special effort to keep the colleges out of that election and believed it had succeeded. Ambrose B. Schauber, the board secretary, wrote to Governor Russell on July 23, 1923:

> I am glad to advise you, as you know, that these schools are not in politics. The Board of Trustees adopted a policy some time ago of keeping the schools out of politics and we have requested that everyone connected with these institutions refrain from taking any part in any political campaign. It is their right to vote as they please but we think it serves the best interest of the institutions for them not to get involved in any political campaign and I am glad to be able to report that this policy of the Board of Trustees has been adhered to by everyone connected with these institutions.

Secretary Schauber's statement is incredible, given the fact that from the outset of the campaign the institutions of higher learning were deeply entangled in the contest. Whitfield sought and secured a public endorsement from President Joseph Cook of the Mississippi State Teachers College at Hattiesburg and appointed Harry Bryan, the son-in-law of Vice-chancellor Alfred Hume of the university, as his state campaign manager. Whitfield also had the active support of the Mississippi State College for Women alumni association. Like Whitfield, Bilbo sought and received the public endorsement of several college officials, including university chancellor Joseph Neely Powers.[29]

The election of Henry Whitfield in 1923 meant that Joseph Neely Powers would probably be dismissed as chancellor. Powers and Whitfield had been adversaries since the early 1900s, when both men had served as the elected state superintendent of education. At the June 1924 board meeting a motion was made to reelect Chancellor Powers. Governor Whitfield's three appointees, along with Willard F. Bond, the superintendent of education and an old ally of Whitfield, voted no. The four carry-over board members voted yes. Governor Whitfield broke the tie by voting to dismiss Chancellor Powers. A motion was then made to elect Alfred Hume chancellor. That motion also produced a tie vote, which Whitfield again decided by voting in favor of Hume, the father-in-law of his state campaign manager. Six years later, when Bilbo gained control of the board of trustees, Hume was removed and Powers reinstated.[30]

His own political entanglements notwithstanding, Whitfield was an enlightened governor whose progressive leadership was cut short by his death in 1927. During the 1923 campaign he had addressed the problems of rural unemployment and the alarming increase of racial violence. Once in office he embraced a broad legislative program that included better mental health care, tax reform, industrial development, expanded vocational training, and improved quality of life for Mississippi's black citizens. Whitfield's moderate position on race received a generally favorable response, even praise, from some of the state press. In commenting on Whitfield's pledge to be the governor of all the people, including blacks, the *Jackson Daily News* admitted: "We all know . . . that we have not given the negro a square deal, and it is gratifying to know that we have a governor endowed with the courage to speak out and tell the truth about it." The Committee of One Hundred, an organization of leading black citizens, also praised the governor for his courageous stand.[31]

Governor Whitfield's efforts to mollify race relations were only one part of his larger plan to reorder the state's priorities. Whitfield realized that Mississippi's economic development was linked to its educational system, which needed fundamental reform. The governor was especially concerned that the state university had not broadened its service role or directed its research efforts toward solving some of the state's most pressing problems. Governor Whitfield went to Oxford and personally appealed to university officials to form an alliance with the state of Mississippi akin to the University of Wisconsin's association with its state. The "Wisconsin Idea" epitomized the pragmatic, problem-solving relationship between a state and a state university.[32]

Governor Whitfield envisioned the same kind of relationship between Mississippi and its public institutions. Soon after his inauguration he moved toward making that goal a reality.

In the fall of 1924 Governor Whitfield took a delegation of farmers, bankers, businessmen, and educators on a two-week trip to Wisconsin to study the Wisconsin Idea. That trip convinced the state's business leaders that a similar program could be implemented in Mississippi, and they returned with a new-found faith in the state's economic future. While the business community, in cooperation with the legislature, was designing a strategy for industrial development, Governor Whitfield arranged for a University of Wisconsin consulting team to conduct a comprehensive study of Mississippi's entire educational system. The study, conducted under the supervision of Professor Michael V. O'Shea, was the first professional appraisal of Mississippi's institutions of higher learning. A lengthy report, known as the O'Shea study, was published in 1927.[33]

In a preamble to the report O'Shea acknowledged that Mississippi was just "emerging from the period of depression and discouragement" following the Civil War, and he applauded the state's leadership for at last "coming to see that their prosperity individually and as a state depends upon universal education." But Mississippi's institutions of higher learning, O'Shea found, had resisted modernization and were clinging to the "Genteel Tradition" that "was in vogue throughout our country fifty years ago." "In Mississippi," the report said, "one frequently hears the phrase, 'We plan our courses so as to develop character in our young people,'" but one rarely finds a curriculum designed to "train young people to develop the agricultural, industrial, economic, and human resources of Mississippi." That assessment was followed by a warning: "If the higher institutions do not modify their program in view of the special needs of Mississippi, it may easily happen that the state will be seriously drained of its superior young men and women, educating them for other states where they stand a chance of finding employment."[34]

Consequently, O'Shea recommended that Mississippi's system of higher education be thoroughly restructured. He recommended the establishment of a single state board of education with authority over the public schools and higher education, the appointment of a commissioner of higher education, and the merger of the three white institutions of higher learning into one University of Mississippi. Although the three separate campuses would be maintained, each would be assigned and limited to specific degree programs. The two teachers colleges, which had greatly expanded their liberal arts curricula, would also be continued, but their degree programs would be limited to teacher education. O'Shea stated that he had spent little time studying Alcorn A & M; the report consequently included few recommendations about higher education for blacks.[35]

The O'Shea study singled out the University of Mississippi for special criticism and several specific recommendations: significant curriculum revision, more research activity directed toward solving Mississippi's social and economic problems, and a stronger faculty. Of the three, faculty development should be the university's top priority. "The University of Mississippi can render service to the state much more effectively," the report stated, "by building up its faculty than by expanding its physical plant."[36]

In 1927, the year the O'Shea report was published, Theordore G. Bilbo was elected governor for a second term. In his second inaugural Bilbo referred to the O'Shea study and pledged to implement its basic recommendations. Ironically, Governor Bilbo's effort to reform and improve the state's institutions of higher learning lingers in Mississippi's historical memory as a great myth that is at variance with historical fact.

—*Six*—

The Bilbo Purge, 1928–1932

But I was looking fifty years ahead for Mississippi.
    —Governor Theodore G. Bilbo

When the O'Shea report was published in June 1927 Mississippi was in the midst of a hotly contested political campaign between Theodore Bilbo and Dennis Murphree, the lieutenant governor who had succeeded at Governor Henry Whitfield's death in 1927. The state's institutions of higher learning, as usual, were in the thick of the fray. As the campaign progressed, Bilbo became increasingly upset by the political involvement of college officials and board members.

President J. C. Fant of Mississippi State College for Women (MSCW), for example, gave a glowing introduction of Dennis Murphree to a special student assembly that left little doubt about his personal preference for governor. And MSCW alumni made no effort to conceal their support for Murphree. Various alumni groups bought newspaper advertisements and established committees on correspondence to write letters on his behalf. Two members of the college board, Mrs. Daisy McLaurin Stevens and Mrs. Robert Ralston, and the wife of a former board member, Mrs. O. F. Lawrence, all of whom had ties to MSCW, were members of Murphree's state campaign committee. The opposition to Bilbo among MSCW supporters stemmed in large measure from his support of the Sheldon-Zeller bill in 1920. Bilbo was also aware of open opposition to him at Mississippi A & M College and State Teachers College at Hattiesburg.[1]

It was the opposition of Ole Miss officials in particular, however, that most upset the seasoned veteran of six campaigns. Robert Farley, a young law professor, wrote letters to friends and alumni urging them to work for Bilbo's defeat. "A vote for Bilbo is a vote against Chancellor Hume," Farley explained. Farley's conjecture was based on rumors that Bilbo, if elected, would fire Hume and reinstate his old friend Joseph Neely Powers, who had been fired four years earlier by Governor Whitfield. The fact that Powers was campaigning for Bilbo and had endorsed his populist promise of free textbooks lent credence to Farley's assumption. When he learned of the letters, Bilbo asked Chancellor Hume to reprimand Farley and instruct him to quit the letter campaign. Hume refused to do so, telling Bilbo that Farley's private political opinions did not come under his jurisdiction and he would not intervene.[2]

Several other university officials campaigned against Bilbo, including William Hemingway, the former mayor of Jackson and a professor of law, who in his classes openly ridiculed Bilbo and his redneck politics. Thomas Turner and others kept records on university personnel who campaigned against Bilbo and passed that information on to the governor. Turner later served on the board of trustees of state institutions of higher learning from 1964 to 1976.[3]

Embittered by the politics of Ole Miss officials, Bilbo saw their opposition to his populist platform as proof that the university was still catering to Mississippi's old aristocracy. Like his predecessor Henry Whitfield and some other southern governors, Huey Long of Louisiana in particular, Bilbo looked to the state university as a catalyst in solving the state's social and economic problems. But as Governor Whitfield and Michael O'Shea had found, the institution was still under the sway of the "Genteel Tradition" and the old notion that a university should train the mind and build character. Although the success of his populist platform would depend upon a progressive, problem-solving state university, Bilbo was convinced that Ole Miss as it existed in 1927—an isolated liberal arts college in poor repair—could contribute little to Mississippi's "progress and future glory."[4] He now had the findings of the O'Shea study and not just the complaints of the university's old enemies as he began, during the political canvas of 1927, to formulate his plan for reorganizing Mississippi's system of higher education.

As the reorganization plan was being formulated, bits and pieces of it leaked to the press. One version called for sweeping changes in the system's leadership, and rumors ran amok about who would be dismissed. Another feature of Bilbo's plan, which became the subject of increasing speculation and many resolutions, was the relocation of the university to Jackson. The possibility of moving Ole Miss to Jackson first surfaced around 1900, then again soon after the creation of the consolidated board in 1910, and once more in 1920. Some legislative leaders had for several years considered the university's relocation such a likely possibility that they were reluctant to build up the Oxford campus. In 1927, for whatever reason, "the University was slowly dying of neglect, and drastic measures were necessary if the institution was to be revitalized."[5]

On October 8, 1927, the Ole Miss student newspaper reported that a bill would be introduced in January 1928 to move the law school and the medical school from Oxford to Jackson. The *Mississippian* endorsed the move and also favored upgrading the two-year medical course to a four-year degree program. The student editor, W. A. Lomax, was even more emphatic about moving the law school. Lomax claimed that the Ole Miss law school consisted of one classroom, a totally inadequate library, one office for our professors, and a class schedule that "resembles an Egyptian hieroglyphic puzzle."[6] Since large expenditures would be necessary to upgrade both schools, it seemed preferable to Lomax to move them and build anew in Jackson where students in both schools would have opportunities for laboratory experiences that Oxford did not afford.

As the question of moving the university to Jackson became the subject of public discourse, the tone of the discourse became increasingly emotional and sentimental. In December 1927 Chancellor Alfred Hume issued a public statement opposing the relocation of the university. Many Mississippians of that era, as Charles Wilson has explained, were baptized in the blood of the "Lost Cause," and Chancellor Hume played upon their precious memories with great rhetorical skill:

> The University of Mississippi is rich in memories and memorials and a noble history. . . . The memorial window in the old library erected in loving memory of the University Grays, the Confederate monument

nearby, and the Confederate soldiers' cemetery a little farther removed are as sacred as any ancient shrine, altar, or temple. Instead of moving the University away that it might be a little easier to reach, ought not the people of Mississippi to look upon a visit here as a holy pilgrimage.[7]

The chancellor's statement was reported by the Mississippi press in a way that implied the Ole Miss students endorsed his position. The *Mississippian* denied one report in particular which claimed that Ole Miss students were "bitterly opposed" to moving the university. To measure opinion the paper conducted a poll in which students were asked to vote for or against the removal of the university and for or against removal of only the medical and law schools. On the question of moving the entire institution to Jackson, 410 students voted for and 219 against. But on the question of relocating only the professional schools, 152 students voted for and 350 against. The students clearly preferred to move all or none of the university.[8]

On the day Lomax reported the results of the poll, he published a perceptive editorial entitled, "What Will You Do With Your State University?" Lomax admonished the lawmakers to move it or leave it "but do something" about the university. If they left it at Oxford they should "make it a real university," though that was not his preference. Lomax saw the coming decade as a time of "great destiny" and predicted that the advent of electrical power would inaugurate a new era of industrialization in Mississippi. The future of Mississippi, he said, was linked to the future of the state university: "We advocate a great University of Mississippi at Jackson for the good of Mississippi." But Lomax predicted that the rivalry and jealousy of other state institutions "who wish to see Ole Miss remain in a secondary position" would once again prevent the relocation of the state university. Still, he could not resist one last admonition to the lawmakers: "Gentlemen of the Legislature . . . give us a University worthy of the name."[9]

Four days after Lomax's editorial was published Governor Theodore G. Bilbo was inaugurated for a second term. His inaugural address was a well-crafted statement. Even editor Fred Sullens of the *Jackson Daily News,* his bitterest critic, grudgingly acknowledged that Bilbo's inaugural was one of "the ablest messages . . . in the memory of this writer." Other newspapers, even some that had opposed him, praised his address, though many expressed reservations about the cost of his agenda, estimated at between $60 million and $100 million. The high cost of Bilbo's legislative program triggered a conditioned response from the "low pressure" faction of the Democratic Party, a powerful coalition composed of fiscal conservatives dedicated to low taxes and economy in government. Bilbo represented the populist or redneck faction which, even though it outnumbered the low pressure group, enjoyed little legislative success because it was outmaneuvered by the crafty conservatives who controlled the administrative machinery and committee structure of both houses of the legislature. The low pressure faction was stunned by the visionary, costly proposals in Governor Bilbo's inaugural and they, with help from the Great Depression, ultimately defeated his legislative program.[10]

Bilbo's inaugural address embraced a wide range of reforms and other programs which he considered essential to Mississippi's social and economic advancement. He reiterated his campaign proposal for free textbooks, a $2.5 million mental hospital, two charity hospitals, a separate correctional facility for young inmates, and a $53 million highway program. To these Bilbo added another costly and controversial proposal:

> If I were called upon to name the one thing that would do more to develop Mississippi and bring to her the highest degree of progress and future glory than anything else, I would not hesitate in saying that the moving of the University of Mississippi to the capital city of Jackson and the building and equipment of a twelve or fifteen million dollar institution would be that thing.

But there was even more that could and should be done. Bilbo reminded the legislature of Governor Whitfield's effort to modernize the state's school system and cited O'Shea's call for radical changes in higher education. "We are spending too much money," he said, "to longer delay this reform." Governor Bilbo then outlined his reorganization plan that had been the subject of so much speculation during the summer and fall of 1927.[11]

In addition to his proposal to relocate the university, Bilbo recommended a new eight-member state board of education that would replace both the three existing college boards and the state board of education, which consisted of the governor, secretary of state, attorney general, and superintendent of education. The new eight-member board of education would govern the public schools and the state institutions of higher learning. It would appoint the state supervisor of public schools and the commissioner of higher education and would assign a role and scope function to each of the public colleges, including the teachers college. With that authority, and with a unified administrative structure, the new board of education could coordinate the state's entire educational system from kindergarten through graduate school; it could also correlate curriculum development to the social and economic needs of Mississippi.[12]

The members of the new state board of education would be appointed by the governor to serve eight-year terms, one member rotating off the board each year. That cycle would preclude any governor from appointing a majority of the board. Bilbo conceded, "It may be charged that the present administration will have the right to appoint the full board, this is true, but after the system is once inaugurated the future will be safe." Governor Bilbo promised that he would not play politics with the new system "because the education of our young men and women is too sacred to permit the blight of partisan politics to mar its record."[13] Although Bilbo's reorganization plan was well conceived and based largely on O'Shea's recommendations, it was overwhelmed by the emotional reaction to his proposal to move the university. Consequently, the plan itself was never considered on its merits.

The day after Bilbo's inauguration, Senator Linton Glover North introduced a resolution to relocate the University of Mississippi to Jackson. Senator North was a native of Vicksburg, a graduate of Mississippi A & M College and, according to the *Jackson Daily News,* "an upstanding, progressive young man" motivated by "the sole hope of building a bigger and better University." The *Daily News* reminded its readers that Senator Julius Zeller had recommended the establishment of one consolidated university in Jackson eight years earlier. "But the legislature," said the *Daily News,* "lacked the largeness of vision to see it." Jackson business leaders heartily endorsed the relocation of the state university, but they had some reservation about the $12- to $15-million cost of the new institution. Governor Bilbo's response to their concern is an indication of just how committed he was to the establishment of a first-rate university:

I fully understand that the proposal suggested in my inaugural address is a big one, but I was looking fifty years ahead for Mississippi. . . . It is my dream to make this the outstanding University in the entire South; one that will attract students from beyond the borders of the Southland. . . . I do not insist upon a fifteen million dollar program to begin with; the start could be made in a smaller way, but the plans must be made for the distant future.[14]

While the populist governor and the Jackson plutocrats were forming what some must have considered an unholy alliance, Chancellor Alfred Hume and Mayor Taylor McElroy of Oxford were plotting a strategy to keep Ole Miss at Oxford. Their strategy, based on emotion and sentiment, appealed to the state's well-known sense of place and even evoked the memory of the "Lost Cause." Chancellor Hume's most eloquent expression of that sentiment came in his special plea to the legislature: "Gentlemen, you may move the University of Mississippi. You may move it to Jackson or anywhere else. You may uproot it from the hallowed ground on which it has stood for eighty years. You may take it from these surroundings that have become dear to the thousands who have gone from its doors. But, gentlemen, don't call it Ole Miss."[15]

The legislature was stirred by the chancellor's rhetoric and voted 109 to 9 to leave Ole Miss at Oxford. Two weeks later Governor Bilbo addressed a joint session and conceded that the university would not be relocated. He then entreated the lawmakers to build a great university at Oxford and asked for a special appropriation of $5 million for new buildings. He also urged the legislature to build hard-surface roads from various points in the state to Oxford to make the institution more accessible. Bilbo's entreaties went unheeded, however, and the legislature appropriated only $1.5 million. The governor was irked by that paltry appropriation but was more upset with the board of trustees and Chancellor Hume for not requesting more. In 1927 Hume had asked for $165,000 for capital improvements; in spite of the dire needs of the university, he requested only $265,000 in 1928.[16]

As concerned as Governor Bilbo was about the university's physical condition, he was even more concerned about its academic programs that had come under heavy criticism. In 1927 the Ole Miss law school lost its accreditation and the university's medical school was placed on probation. Two years later the Southern Association of Colleges and Schools found that the university's general academic program did not meet several of its standards. SACS singled out the faculty for special criticism and noted that a "large proportion" of the faculty had taken their degrees at the university. Though it did not rescind the university's accreditation, SACS urged Chancellor Hume to eliminate the deficiencies as soon as possible.[17]

The $1.5 million appropriation which Bilbo had secured in 1928 enabled Chancellor Hume to remedy some of the most glaring deficiencies and infused the university with new vigor. Hume reported that a "transformation is being wrought." Hoping to capitalize on the expansive spirit of that transformation, a department chairman went to the chancellor with a request to buy "the back issues of an important professional journal" at a cost of $125. According to procedures then in effect all library purchases had to be approved by the chancellor. Even though part of the special appropriation was slated for library improvements, Chancellor Hume turned down that request, telling the department chairman that he "found it difficult to persuade the students to read the textbook, much less outside reading assignments . . . [and] saw no reason why $125 should be spent on old periodicals."[18]

When Chancellor Hume announced that the university would use some of the 1928 appropriation for the purchase of new steel library shelves, the *Mississippian* proclaimed, "Let's first get a Library." W. A. Lomax, the student editor, ridiculed the library's holdings in philosophy, science, and mathematics, most of which, he said, had either been "donated" or "bought at auctions." If a book "even hints at disturbing the established political, social, or religious questions of the day, it is not on the University Library shelves." That, Lomax asserted, should "not be the case in a great University, the alleged home of free thought."[19]

It was obvious to Governor Bilbo that Ole Miss was not a great university in 1928, nor was it even a good university, and he was convinced that under Chancellor Hume it never would become one. Known fondly as "Little Allie," Hume was perhaps the most popular and beloved chancellor in the institution's history. At the time of his dismissal in 1930 he was sixty-four years old and had been at the university forty years. When Hume, a devout and staunch Presbyterian, assumed the office of chancellor in 1924 he had announced the singular goal of his administration:

My greatest aspiration for the present administration is not that we may put on a big building program, though we certainly need badly a number of new buildings; not that we grow rapidly in enrollment of students and size of faculty, however necessary and desirable both may be; not that we excel in scholarship and athletics, however much I want these too; but when the historian makes record of what this administration stood for pre-eminently, I am hoping that it may be truthfully said that it was characterized by the exalting of character, by putting the emphasis on things moral, by stressing religious and spiritual values.[20]

Chancellor Hume's administrative policies were an extension of his personal faith, and he cloaked the university in a religious atmosphere. Students were not allowed to smoke, drink, dance, wear shorts on campus, or play tennis on Sunday and were required to attend daily chapel services. Ole Miss was often called, in jest, "Hume's Presbyterian University." Michael O'Shea's pointed criticism that Mississippi institutions of higher learning planned their "courses so as to develop character" was probably aimed at the university. Chancellor Hume, according to Hardy Poindexter Graham, also embraced "the University's traditional role as the institution devoted primarily to the needs of the upper classes of Mississippi society" and the "outdated concept of the University as an isolated liberal arts academy."[21] But Governor Bilbo was determined that the University of Mississippi would not remain a liberal arts academy or a provincial university hidden away in the hills of northeast Mississippi. He would transform the university if he could not relocate it.

In June 1928 Bilbo announced his intention to replace Chancellor Hume if he could persuade the board of trustees to do so. But the board, as constituted in 1928, refused, and Hume was reelected on an annual contract like other college presidents. Governor Bilbo did succeed, however, in persuading the board that governed the State Teachers College at Hattiesburg to dismiss Joseph Anderson Cook, the school's first and only president. Cook had come under heavy fire from former students, alumni, and public school teachers who believed that his administrative philosophy was hopelessly antiquated. He routinely locked the gates to the campus at twilight and restricted movement on and off the campus after dark. Many professional and business leaders in Mississippi's rapidly growing coastal region envisioned a much broader role and scope for the State Teachers College, and they were doubtful that Cook, then sixty-five years old, had either the vision or the vigor to develop its enormous potential. Governor Bilbo agreed with that assessment and recommended that the board replace Cook with a younger, more progressive administrator. The trustees initially refused to dismiss President Cook, but when R. E. L. Sutherland voluntarily resigned from the board, his replacement voted not to renew Cook's contract. Claude Bennett, the superintendent of Biloxi city schools, replaced Cook as president in October 1928.[22]

In 1929 Governor Bilbo, more convinced than ever that Alfred Hume was "temperamentally unfit" to be chancellor of a modern comprehensive state university, renewed the effort to remove him. The incident that strengthened his resolve was Chancellor Hume's dismissal of the editors of the college yearbook. Decreeing that some of the yearbook's poetry and puns were "libelous slurs at girlhood and womanhood," Hume impounded the annual, expelled the two editors, and established a board of control to censor future student publications.[23] The expulsion received extensive press coverage, and Hume came under heavy criticism for the arbitrary manner in which he had handled the entire affair. Under intense pressure to reinstate the students, he did eventually readmit one of them but denied that he had done so under pressure from the board or anyone else. Hume explained that his was an "act of free grace," that he had meted out "mercy not justice" because the student had come to him as a "penitent child or sinner." Hume proclaimed that he would never compromise a principle because, in an obvious reference to Bilbo's characterization of him, he was "temperamentally unfit" for that sort of thing.[24]

In his 1929 report to the board of trustees Chancellor Hume explained the expulsion of the two students and addressed the larger issue of freedom of thought at a university. In most cases, he conceded, faculty members should be given the right to express their opinions. "[But] occasionally freaks are found," he said, "who prove exceptions to the rule." Academic freedom might sometimes be academic nonsense, the chancellor added, offering two illustrations in which a college president or a board of trustees would be at liberty to dismiss a faculty member or otherwise restrict his right of expression. The first example was a teacher who taught that the world is flat and square; the second was a professor of history who might teach that secession was treason and that Robert E. Lee was a traitor. If an Ole Miss professor made such a claim, Hume said, his chair of history should become "instantly vacant." And if the professor should claim that his academic freedom had been abridged, "the emphatic answer, coming quick and hot," should be, according to Chancellor Hume: "Sir, . . . you may not trample under foot what we regard as sacred as long as you hold a position in our institution."[25]

As ex officio chairman of the board of trustees Governor Bilbo received Chancellor Hume's report, but he was not swayed by it. Shortly before the summer meeting of the board in 1929 he announced that he would again recommend the replacement of Hume. The board again rejected Bilbo's recommendation and reelected Hume for another year. After this second setback Fred Sullens, in an editorial entitled "Forget It, Theodore," advised Bilbo to give up the effort. Sullens warned that Hume's removal would provoke "bitter resentment among hundreds of 'Ole Miss' graduates, many of them prominent in public life." "It would mean," Sullens said, "that these men will . . . throw every possible obstacle in the path of your administration."[26]

Nevertheless, Bilbo would not abandon his reorganization plan or his effort to remove Chancellor Hume. In his third annual message to the legislature on January 6, 1930, the governor repeated his recommendations for a new state board of education and a commissioner of higher education. He also requested an additional $1 million bond issue for capital construction at the university. To those requests he added a rather startling addendum. Bilbo announced that he would recommend sweeping personnel changes, including presidents and faculty, at all of the state's institutions of higher learning when the boards of trustees met in June of that year.[27] Time was running out. He had only two years left of his four-year term, and at that point he had achieved virtually none of his major goals.

Governor Bilbo decided to act on his own in those areas, including higher education, that were subject to executive authority. He was determined to improve Mississippi's collegiate institutions and to do so not from the bottom up but from the top down. By January 1930 Bilbo had decided to reorganize the entire system of higher education. The *Jackson Daily News* reported the governor's annual message under the caption, "Bilbo promises Clean Sweep of College Presidents," and quoted the governor as saying that younger men were needed to lead the state's institutions of higher learning.[28]

Over the next few months the subject of age and length of service figured prominently in any discussion of the impending shake-up at the state institutions. It was frequently noted by the press, for example, that President Buz M. Walker of Mississippi A & M was approaching seventy and that he had been associated with the college in one capacity or another for nearly fifty years. Robert E. Lee Sutherland, who was rumored to be the next president of Mississippi State College for Women, refused to tell reporters his age. "If it is necessary to say anything about my age," he remarked, "you might say that I would pass for 48, perhaps younger." Sutherland was fifty-two at the time of his appointment.[29]

Age and energy were not the only considerations in Bilbo's determination to bring new leadership to the state institutions. There was more to it, especially in Chancellor Hume's case. Bilbo had stated publicly several times that Hume's educational philosophy was outmoded and that he lacked the vision to transform Ole Miss into the Greater University of Mississippi—a transformation Bilbo regarded as essential for the state's economic and social development. The governor also wanted to increase the chancellor's salary from $4,800 to $25,000, a whopping 500 percent increase, to enable the board of trustees to recruit an educator of national reputation. Governor Bilbo cited the University of Wisconsin and the University of Chicago as examples that Mississippi might emulate. Wisconsin had recently named Glenn Frank president, and Chicago had just appointed Robert Maynard Hutchins, then only thirty years of age.[30]

The board had rebuffed Bilbo in 1928 and 1929, but in 1930, when he decided to extend his purge to the faculty level, he operated from a much stronger advantage. Because of several additional appointments Bilbo controlled a majority of the central board that governed the University of Mississippi, Mississippi A & M, Mississippi State College for Women, and Alcorn A & M. He did not, however, control the board governing Delta State Teachers College, and his effort to replace its president, William Kethley, was unsuccessful. Bilbo had already replaced the president of State Teachers College. He made no effort to remove President Levi Rowen at Alcorn College or to reorganize its faculty in 1930.[31]

For several weeks before the June 1930 meeting of the central board of trustees, some MSCW alumni had lobbied for the appointment of Dean Nellie Keirn, who had been acting president since the death of John C. Fant in 1929. But Keirn "did not desire the presidency on a permanent basis," advising the board that she preferred to remain as dean of the college. The alumni effort on behalf of Dean Keirn was linked to the broader effort to secure the appointment of a woman president. Even though MSCW was the first state-supported women's college in the country, it had never had a female president. In fact, not until 1988, after the school had become coeducational, did Clyda Rent become its first woman president. Once Nellie Keirn declined to be considerd, the two most serious candidates for the MSCW presidency were Claude Bennett, president of State Teachers College, and R. E. L. Sutherland, the former president of Hinds Junior College. After Bennett announced that he intended to stay at Hattiesburg, Sutherland was assured of the position and on June 13 was elected unanimously.[32]

The speculation over who would get the presidency at Mississippi A & M obscured the circumstances under which President Buz M. Walker was vacating that position. Walker was known to be a Bilbo partisan who had helped raise funds for the governor's 1927 campaign. Because of his alliance with Bilbo the *Clarion-Ledger* assumed that Walker's position was safe and predicted that he would be reappointed. Walker had been the subject of widening criticism for several months before the June 13 board meeting, however, and he was personally blamed by some alumni for college's lack of growth. Anticipating the worst, he secured a position in North Carolina and announced his intention to leave Mississippi A & M when his current contract expired in June. Despite his announcement, on the day of the board meeting a group of A & M alumni informed the trustees that they had persuaded President Walker to reconsider, that he had done so, and that he wished to remain as president. Their eleventh hour maneuver was not successful, though, because Bilbo and the board of trustees had already decided not to reelect Walker. His removal is an indication that Bilbo's effort to reform higher education was not a mere purge of political enemies, nor a petty political maneuver to reward friends.[33]

There had been much speculation that Alfred Butts, a popular professor of education at the agricultural college, might be elected president of either Mississippi A & M or Ole Miss. That possibility prompted backroom maneuvering by Ole Miss forces, who wanted to get Butts elected to the A & M position. Their strategy was simple: secure the A & M presidency for Butts, which would take him out of the running for the job at Ole Miss and would save Chancellor Hume. They believed that Bilbo lacked the votes to have Joseph Powers elected chancellor of the university. Butts was so complacent about either position, however, that he was eventually eliminated from both. His elimination virtually guaranteed that Hugh Critz would get the A & M presidency. Critz was an alumnus and former dean of the school of agriculture at Mississippi A & M, as well as a former president of one of the regional agricultural colleges in Arkansas. According to Fred Sullens, Critz was not aligned with any Mississippi political faction and his appointment would elicit "no complaint from any quarter."[34] At the time of his appointment, he was on retainer by the Mississippi Power and Light Company in its public relations department.

At the June 13 board meeting Hugh Critz was nominated. As a gesture in defiance of Governor Bilbo, A. B. Kelly, who had not been appointed by Bilbo, nominated President Walker. Critz was elected by a seven to two vote. Willard Bond, the state superintendent of education, joined Kelly in voting to retain Walker. Kelly then moved that Critz's election be made unanimous, and the motion carried. The board next took up the election of the chancellor. A. B. Schauber, a member of the board of trustees when Powers was fired in 1924, nominated the former chancellor; Paul Bowdre, a Bilbo appointee, nominated Alfred Hume. Powers was elected by a vote of six to four.[35]

It is probable that the shake-up of the college presidents would have provoked no more than the customary gust of outrage, which would soon have faded. But at a meeting on June 27, and a subsequent meeting on July 5, the board of trustees reorganized the faculty and staff at MSCW, Mississippi A & M, and the university. At Mississippi State College for Women ten faculty members out of a total of fifty-three and at least four staff members were dismissed. At Mississippi A & M, in addition to President Walker, R. S. Wilson, the director of extension, and J. R. Ricks, the director of experiment stations, were also replaced. Athletic Director W. D. Chadwick was relieved of his duties but retained as "Professor unassigned, outside of athletics, at the same salary." It is difficult to determine how many support personnel were fired or reassigned, but there were slightly more than one hundred changes—a figure that includes county agents, home demonstration agents, experiment station workers, and clerical personnel but not faculty members. The best estimate of the number of teaching faculty who were relieved or reassigned is twenty, certainly no more than twenty-five, out of a total of ninety-one.[36]

The turnover at Ole Miss is much easier to document, because the Bilbo purge at the university has been researched by Hardy P. Graham and it involved a relatively small number of people. Also, the board minutes contain much more information about the personnel changes at the university than about those at A & M and MSCW. On the same day that Joseph Powers was elected chancellor, Julius Christian Zeller was elected vice-chancellor. Zeller, a state senator at the time of his appointment, listed farming as his occupation in the biographical section of the senate journal. Though the appointment of Senator Zeller is sometimes cited as evidence that Governor Bilbo put hacks in high places because they were his friends and that he took no accounting of their qualifications, Senator Zeller is the worst possible example. His academic credentials were impressive: B.A. and B.D. from the University of Chicago; M.A. and B.O. from Grant University in Athens, Tennessee; M.A. and D.D. from the University of Chattanooga; Doctor of Civil Law from Illinois Wesleyan University. He had held the chair of philosophy and education at Illinois Wesleyan and had served as president of the University of Puget Sound. In 1930 the *Jackson Daily News* wrote that "there is not an abler member in either branch of the lawmaking body than Senator Zeller. He is both a scholar and a statesman." For several years Zeller had been opposed to Bilbo but had found common agreement with him in the proposal to move the university to Jackson. Both men, after failing in this effort, joined in a common cause to improve, enlarge, enhance, and upgrade the university.[37]

Two weeks after Zeller's appointment Chancellor Powers presented his faculty nominations to the board of trustees. The board declined to reelect eighteen of them. The minutes of that meeting list the ages and credentials of those eighteen faculty members and, in most cases, also list the credentials of their replacements. Each was replaced by a professor with bona fide academic credentials at least equal to his own; in most cases the credentials of the new faculty members were superior to those removed. The dean of the graduate school, for example, did not have a Ph.D. and had been at the university for thirty-seven years.

Bilbo insisted that he be replaced by a younger man, Nathaniel Bond, with a doctorate from Tulane. Most of the dismissed professors were in their late sixties or early seventies. Governor Bilbo recommended that faculty members in their mid-sixties who were not retained be given emeritus status with compensation, but the legislature did not appropriate the necessary funds. Very few of those dismissed held graduate degrees and several had only a baccalaureate, which they had taken at the University of Mississippi. Although most departments were affected by the purge, Bilbo and the board did not disturb the history department, chaired by Professor Charles Sydnor, who held a doctorate. Sydnor later enjoyed a distinguished career at Duke University.[38]

In addition to the eighteen faculty members, at least thirteen clerical and staff personnel were also replaced. One of those was J. C. Eskridge, the director of buildings and grounds. When Eskridge was informed of his dismissal he fired off a letter to Governor Bilbo demanding an explanation. "Everyone in Lafayette County knows that I have championed your cause from your entry into Mississippi politics until the present time," he wrote. "So come clean. . . . I want to know why." Several days later Eskridge received a reply from Governor Bilbo explaining the cause of his dismissal:

> The chief cause of complaint seems to be that you were lazy or in other words, not as alert on the job as you might have been. You know in this day and time when there is so much unemployment and so many people are waiting for a chance, it behooves us all to be constantly on the job. I am very sorry that it was necessary to dismiss you, but there were others who felt that they could be on the job at any and all times and one of them is being given this chance.[39]

The final tally of the Bilbo purge of 1930, or at least the best estimate, included one college president (Hume at Ole Miss), eighteen faculty members at the university, ten at MSCW, and twenty or twenty-five at Mississippi A & M. The number of clerical, staff, and support personnel who were fired was probably 125. The reaction to the purge was swift, severe, and subject to the most partisan interpretation. Both Bilbo and the board were powerless to hold back the torrents of criticism that their action precipitated. The criticism came from two different fronts: the opposition press, whose reaction was hardly more than a nuisance, and professional and educational associations, whose decisions to revoke accreditation repudiated Bilbo's effort to reform and reorganize Mississippi's system of higher education.

One of the first and fiercest condemnations of the purge came from Bilbo's old nemesis, Fred Sullens. Because of the "whirligig game we call politics," Sullens wrote, "with each succeeding governor we have seen competent men voted out, able faculties torn to pieces, and new regimes established." It was not just this latest incursion but its epic sweep that shocked Sullens. He reported that the college faculties had not been "revised"; they had been "ravished." Almost lost amid his outrage was a grudging concession: "The men who succeed [Hume and Walker] will carry on with more energy and efficiency than the two pale, slender, gray haired scholars. . . . They are younger and probably more progressive in purpose than the men they are soon to succeed." Also among Sullens's lamentations was a prediction that political intrusion into higher education would continue "until some clever brain devises a plan to remove our colleges wholly beyond the realm of political influence."[40] He took no notice that Governor Bilbo had recently recommended such a plan to the state legislature.

John Hudson, a freelance writer who kept up a running feud with Governor Bilbo, described the purge in an article for the *New Republic* entitled "The Spoils System Enters College." According to Hardy P. Graham, Hudson's article was an "extreme example of distortion and falsification." Hudson reported that Bilbo had fired 50 professors at Ole Miss and 129 at other colleges and that 233 more were in jeopardy. His estimate of faculty members fired or in jeopardy totaled 412, when in fact there were only about 300 faculty members in the entire system. Hudson also identified the new president of Mississippi A & M as the director of public relations for the Mississippi Power and Light Company, but he did not list any of Critz's academic credentials or positions. He also incorrectly identified the new chancellor of the university as a real-estate salesman who had never earned a college degree.[41]

John Hudson's article was the primary source for many of the early and erroneous accounts of the "Bilbo Imbroglio." The Mississippi Education Association, for example, reported in *Advance*, its official journal, that fifty faculty members had been dismissed at the university and claimed that Bilbo's only motivation was "to punish enemies and to reward friends." In a follow-up article published a month later, the editor reported that he had received a letter from Chancellor Powers correcting his figures. The editor admitted that he had used the figures in John Hudson's article and had presumed that they were accurate. The editor apologized and then surmised, "After all, ultimate good will probably come from the evils herein discussed."[42]

The Bilbo purge gained national attention, and headlines, and prompted several investigations by accrediting agencies. The university's law school was expelled from the American Association of Law Schools, and the medical school was placed on probation by the two medical accrediting agencies. But the director of one medical association wrote to Chancellor Powers: "great good will no doubt came out of the whole mess. The school has had a good jolt which should shake it into life and give it a more wholesome aspect and more activity. Maybe the new dean can and will do what is needed . . . to build up the school." The Society of Civil Engineers, the American Association of University Professors, the American Association of University Women, and the Association for American Universities either dismissed, expelled, or placed the university on probation. But none of those associations, according to Graham, "conducted a thorough investigation." The Society of Civil Engineers, for example, did not even contact university officials before dismissing the university and knew nothing of the conditions there.[43]

Two professional associations, both of which conducted on-site investigations, did not censure the university. The American Pharmaceutical Association, in fact, commended the new dean and allowed the school of pharmacy to retain its "A" rating. The American Association of State Universities conducted a two-day investigation by W. O. Thompson, president emeritus of Ohio State University and chairman of the association's committee on university control. Thompson's report offered some justification for the faculty dismissals and exonerated the university of "many criticisms levied against it." It also stated that popular accounts of the situation, specifically John Hudson's *New Republic* article, contained many exaggerations and distortions. On the basis of Thompson's report, the Association of State Universities at its annual meeting in 1931 declined to censure the University of Mississippi and expressed its disagreement with the accrediting agencies that had done so.[44]

The action that most seriously damaged Mississippi's institutions of higher learning was the loss of accreditation by the Southern Association of Colleges and Schools. At its annual meeting in December 1930, the association suspended the University of Mississippi, Mississippi A & M, Mississippi State College for Women, and State Teachers College at Hattiesburg. Alcorn A & M College was not accredited by the Southern Association at that time and was therefore not affected by the suspension. SACS did not cite the institutions for violating any of its standards but based its suspension instead on what it called "the tone of an institution" and "the spirit of administration." Perhaps in a move calculated further to embarrass Bilbo and the Mississippi board of trustees, SACS admitted Delta State Teachers College to membership, even though it did not meet all the association's standards.[45]

Some members of the board of trustees believed that the Southern Association's action was punitive and not entirely free of political taint. The executive committee of the association, for example, refused to allow a statement from Governor Bilbo to be read to the organization's general assembly. Moreover, the O'Shea study, which formed the basis of Governor Bilbo's reorganization plan, had been critical of some of the Southern Association standards. O'Shea had intimated that Mississippi's fulfillment of those standards was not so important as meeting the more immediate educational needs of its people. Whatever may have been the motive that caused SACS to suspend Mississippi's institutions of higher learning, Fred Sullens did not like it. Sullens wrote that the suspension was "cruel, wanton, brutal, unnecessary, and devoid of any semblance of constructive thought."[46] Many Mississippians shared Sullens's anger at both the Southern Association and Bilbo. But some others saw an opportunity to "devise a plan to remove our colleges wholly beyond the realm of political influence," and they determined to use the Bilbo purge as proof that some dramatic reforms were necessary.

Theodore Bilbo might have been "Governor Inglorious" as Wigfall Green called him, or "a slick little bastard" as William Alexander Percy described him. But Chester Morgan, in his recent reappraisal of Bilbo's senate career, has shown that he was not all bad. Bilbo did try to do right, so the evidence suggests, in reorganizing Mississippi's system of higher education. That is not to deny that he wreaked revenge upon some of his enemies in higher education. It is to say that he tried to do what needed to be done. The Brookings Institution studied higher education in Mississippi in 1931 and repeated with only slight modifications most of Bilbo's recommendations.[47] As the Brookings study was being conducted, Mississippi was in the process of choosing a successor to Governor Bilbo, and the plight of the state's colleges was a prominent issue in that campaign.

—Seven—

A Constitutional Board of Trustees, 1932–1944

To attempt to keep politics out of [college] boards is just as vain as
the pursuit of a wraith across a meadow in the moonlight.
                                        —David E. Crawley
                                         State Senate, 1940

During the 1931 campaign all the gubernatorial candidates, and several legislative candidates, promised the people of Mississippi that they would end the reign of politics at the state's colleges and pledged to the various accrediting agencies that they would not only take politics out of the colleges but also take the colleges out of politics. For a variety of reasons, the voters found Martin Sennett Conner most convincing and elected him governor. Conner was a former speaker of the house of representatives, a member of the low pressure faction, and an implacable foe of Governor Bilbo.

One of the successful legislative candidates in the 1931 campaign was Joseph Anderson Cook, the former president of State Teachers College who had been fired by Bilbo in 1928. Cook was elected to the state senate from Lowndes County. Soon after the legislature convened in January 1932 he introduced Senate Bill 59, a lengthy and detailed measure designed by a wily old veteran of the school wars to place the institutions of higher learning "beyond the realm of political influence." Senator Cook's bill was based largely on the O'Shea and Brookings Institution studies and included many of their recommendations. The measure passed with little opposition.[1]

The 1932 statute consolidated the three boards of trustees into one ten-member board with governance over all the state institutions of higher learning, including the two teachers colleges. Trustees served twelve-year staggered terms, with one-third of the members rotating off the board every four years; members could not succeed themselves. The governor remained ex officio president of the board, but the law did not make the superintendent of education a member.[2] Instead of establishing a commissioner of higher education, the statute authorized the board to appoint an executive secretary and to employ whatever additional clerical staff it deemed necessary. The executive secretary of the board of trustees would never exercise the authority that O'Shea or Bilbo or the Brookings study had envisioned for the commissioner of higher education. College presidents would not yield their authority or their institution's autonomy to the new executive secretary, and this role as it evolved over the years became more administrative than executive.

Under Senate Bill 59, which also established a new funding procedure, college presidents were required to prepare detailed budgets estimating the expenditures at their institutions for the next biennium. A combined budget for all institutions would then be prepared by the executive secretary and submitted to the legislature thirty days before the opening of each session. The board was also required to submit a biennial report to the legislature accounting for the expenditure of public funds and detailing the condition of campus buildings, enrollment, and faculty workloads. On the basis of those institutional budgets and the board's biennial report, the legislature would make a single appropriation to the board of trustees for higher education. The trustees in turn would allocate a portion of the total appropriation to each school. Before the enactment of that statute, the legislature had made separate and individual appropriations directly to each institution.[3]

Section seven of the 1932 statute mandated a mission for each institution of higher learning and required the board of trustees to make academic program adjustments at the various schools in conformity with the role and scope function they were assigned. Although that provision ordered the board to coordinate the state's system of higher education, the law did not consolidate the junior college system with the senior institutions, as the Brookings study had recommended.[4]

The new law included two provisions in particular that were designed to protect the institutions of higher learning from political interference and to keep them out of entangling political alliances. First, the statute gave college presidents the sole authority to nominate the faculty and staff at their institutions. Although faculty tenure was not established, there was a general understanding that politics would not be a consideration in personnel matters and that faculty members would be reappointed, in the words of the statute, "during the period of satisfactory service." It was the protection provided by that clause that Senator Cook, Governor Conner, and others hoped would at last end the reign of politics at the state's institutions of higher learning. The other provision prohibited college officials and influential alumni from lobbying the legislature in the interest of their favored school. The law was very specific in that regard: "All relationships and negotiations between the state legislature and its various committees and the institutions named in this act shall be carried on through the Board of Trustees. No official, employee, or agent representing any of the separate institutions shall appear before the legislature or any committee thereof except upon the written order of the Board or upon the request of the legislature or a committee thereof."[5]

Following the enactment of this law, Governor Conner appointed ten new trustees whose first and most pressing duty was to regain the accreditation of Mississippi's institutions of higher learning. At its first meeting on March 1, 1932, the board of trustees appointed a committee to open negotiations with the Southern Association, and in July the board requested a formal review of the Mississippi situation. The trustees received a favorable response from the association's executive secretary, who advised them to proceed with reorganizing the state institutions under Senate Bill 59.[6]

At its annual meeting in December 1932 the Southern Association restored provisional accreditation to Mississippi's institutions of higher learning and advised the board of trustees that all restrictions would be lifted when certain conditions were met—specifically, an increase in faculty salaries and an increase in general academic support funds. The Great Depression, however, precluded that possibility. Even though salaries and support funds were not raised, and in fact were reduced, the Southern Association of Colleges and other professional accrediting agencies restored full accreditation and membership to Mississippi institutions over the next two years.[7]

One condition that the Southern Association required for reaccreditation was the reinstatement of the administrators and faculty members who had been dismissed during the Bilbo purge of 1930. To meet that condition the new board of trustees dismissed Chancellor Powers in June 1932 and reappointed Alfred Hume. This was the second time Joseph Powers had been dismissed as chancellor of the University of Mississippi—a double dismissal unique in the history of higher education in Mississippi. President Robert E. Lee Sutherland of MSCW was also fired in 1932 and replaced by Burney L. Parkinson. In April 1933 President Claude Bennett was dismissed at State Teachers College in Hattiesburg and replaced by Jennings Burton George. The following July President Hugh Critz of Mississippi State College (formerly Mississippi A & M) was replaced by George Duke Humphrey.[8]

Many faculty members and support personnel were also reinstated, but for a number their reprieve was short lived. Among the promises Martin Conner made during the 1931 governor's race was a pledge to balance the state's budget. As governor he achieved that astounding feat during a period of depression by slashing state expenditures and initiating a 2 percent sales tax. The first biennial appropriation under Governor Conner was 48 percent below the last appropriation of the Bilbo administration, and the institutions of higher learning were especially hard hit. In June 1932 more than 160 employees at the six institutions were discharged. In order to balance the institutions' budgets for the following year, faculty salaries were reduced by 25 percent.[9]

In addition to financial exigencies Mississippi's new, consolidated board of trustees also wrestled with the problem of institutional autonomy and program coordination. One of the board's top priorities was the establishment of a role and scope function for each institution. As an initial step in that direction the board abolished the engineering program at Ole Miss, because it was considered an unnecessary and costly duplication of the engineering program at Mississippi State College. But before venturing too far afield, the board of trustees asked the Division of Surveys and Field Studies at George Peabody College to study higher education in Mississippi and to formulate a role and scope function for each of the state's six public institutions.[10]

At the time of the Peabody study Mississippi was supporting more institutions of higher learning per capita than any other southern state, and a larger percentage of its white students attended college than any other state in the region. According to the O'Shea study, Mississippi's unusually high collegiate enrollment, especially for an impoverished rural state, was caused by the "eagerness" of white Mississippians "to have their children acquire a degree from a college or university, largely for the social value which it is presumed to possess." To capitalize on that "eagerness," and to garner their share of the student market, Mississippi's institutions of higher learning engaged in an unseemly competition. More significantly, they were forced to lower their admission standards and were induced to expand their course offerings and popular degree programs to attract greater numbers. Such conditions made coordination increasingly difficult, but increasingly necessary.[11]

The need for statewide coordination was apparent to the Peabody study team. It reiterated the major recommendations made by O'Shea, Bilbo, and the Brookings Institution, in particular the assignment of specific missions to each institution and the establishment of a commissioner of higher education. The Peabody study also cautioned the board of trustees against expanding graduate education and repeated the Brookings recommendation that the junior and senior colleges be consolidated into a single state system of higher education. The study team did not include Alcorn College in its survey and made practically no recommendations regarding higher education for blacks in Mississippi.

The board of trustees made a good faith response to the Peabody survey group's recommendations. Instead of establishing a single administrative officer for higher education, however, it created the Presidents Council and directed the presidents to "stimulate thoughtful cooperation on the part of the colleges." Within two years after the Peabody study, the board advised the legislature that it had met the mandate of the 1932 law requiring the board to adjust and correlate the curriculum of each institution in accordance with its historical mission. The trustees listed the role and scope functions of the white institutions as follows:

> University of Mississippi: liberal arts, literature, humanities, social sciences, and professional schools resting essentially on the liberal arts; fine arts, law, medicine, pharmacy, economics, education, civil engineering, commerce, business, and graduate education.
>
> Mississippi State College: professional schools and departments resting essentially on the natural sciences; agriculture, engineering,

mechanic arts, business and vocational education, graduate courses and such general courses as are necessary to supplement its technical training.

Mississippi State College for Women: a combination of undergraduate courses in fine arts, industrial arts, literature, languages, home economics, civics, social and natural sciences, teacher training, and courses suited for a well rounded cultural and practical education for girls.

State Teachers College and Delta State Teachers College: professional courses for the training of teachers and allied subjects.[12]

The board admitted that it had followed "a safe course" in assigning exclusive functions to certain institutions. Courses or departments or schools, it announced, would be eliminated only on the grounds of strict economy and then only after the long-term needs of each institution had been fully considered. The board also authorized the Presidents Council and the executive secretary to study the feasibility of reactivating courses or departments that had been discontinued and of adding new programs if there was sufficient demand.[13]

That concession proved to be unfortunate because, as David Levine has found, "the free market had not proved efficient enough in education." Unlike the California board of regents, which created a single statewide system of colleges based on California's "genuine educational needs," Mississippi's board of trustees—in spite of the Peabody study's admonition—sustained the tradition of institutional autonomy and invited college presidents and other clever academics to ply them with arguments for keeping old programs and for adding new ones. The lay board of trustees proved to be no match for the rhetoricians and mathematicians. Chancellor Hume calmly and convincingly cautioned the board of trustees against taking the Peabody study too seriously. He told them to be especially wary of statistics, which, "while having the appearance of reliable accuracy," are often misleading. That was especially true, Chancellor Hume continued, when dealing with "questions of education."[14]

The members of Mississippi's board of trustees deferred to the presidents of the colleges they governed on "questions of education." The board was persuaded by Chancellor Hume to reestablish the school of engineering at the university just four years after it had been abolished. President Humphrey of Mississippi State persuaded the trustees to expand State's school of business, even though the Peabody study had recommended its discontinuation, and to allow the institution to establish a graduate school in 1935, again in spite of a specific recommendation not to do so.

There was general dissatisfaction, especially in the legislature, with the board's unsuccessful effort to coordinate the state colleges into a unified system. And the board's failure to reduce the duplication of degree programs prompted two or three bills in almost every legislative session during the 1930s to either consolidate or abolish some of the state institutions. In the 1934 session, for example, House Bills 344 and 345—sponsored by thirty-five members of the house—would have abolished State Teachers College at Hattiesburg and Delta State Teachers College at Cleveland. Neither bill reached a vote on the house floor because each was withdrawn in favor of House Bill 555, which would have consolidated all the state's institutions of higher learning into a university system. That bill was also defeated.[15]

By 1934 the rivalry—even jealousy—among the white institutions was so entrenched, and their supporters so territorial, that closing or consolidating any of the colleges was a political impossibility. In its effort to be fair, the new board of trustees actually became indulgent and allowed the institutions, including both teachers colleges and Alcorn A & M, to add new programs and expand existing ones without regard to the state's genuine educational needs. Eventually the six institutions became eight, and each became a comprehensive university offering a wide range of academic programs. Some of the comprehensive universities even became multicampus institutions with several degree-granting branches.

If the new, consolidated board of trustees gets low marks for its effort to coordinate the state's system of higher education, it probably deserves a failing grade in its attempt to shield the institutions of higher learning from politics. There was evidence of that failure in the very first general election following the board's establishment. The 1935 governor's campaign was a bitter contest in which a millionaire businessman, Hugh White, defeated the "runt hog" populist, Paul B. Johnson, Sr. Those veteran campaigners headed the two factions of Mississippi's Democratic Party, and the campaign was ugly and acrimonious, even by Mississippi standards. In a one-party system elections rarely turn on principles; they turn on personalities. Where there is no clash of political issues, there is almost certain to be a collision of personal ambitions in which everyone is forced to take sides. College officials and faculties lined up on one side or the other in 1935.

In a press release issued shortly after his election, Governor White accused several college officials and board members of playing politics during the 1935 campaign. What he actually meant was not that they took part in the election but that they campaigned for his opponent. He specifically accused President Parkinson of MSCW; President George of the State Teachers College at Hattiesburg; John Lee Gainey, business manager at the University of Mississippi; and William H. Smith, executive secretary of the board of trustees. He also accused B. H. Hazard and J. H. Currie, two board members, of openly campaigning against him. Governor White announced that he would soon hold a press conference to expose the political activity of those individuals. After his inauguration on January 21, 1936, rumors circulated throughout the capitol that there would be several changes at the institutions of higher learning as well as a complete reorganization of the board of trustees.[16]

At a press conference on February 18, 1936, which he called to announce his plans concerning the board of trustees, Governor White dramatically waved a letter above his head. If the people knew what was in that letter, he said, they would understand why he could not work harmoniously with the existing board of trustees and why he needed a strong voice in the affairs of the state's educational institutions. Governor White declined to reveal the contents of the letter, but he did say that it was from a board member to a private citizen—implying that the letter was an appeal to support Paul Johnson and that many other citizens had received similar letters. During the press conference Governor White announced his intention to dismiss President Parkinson of MSCW.[17]

For several weeks before the press conference, it had been generally known that President Parkinson was in jeopardy. MSCW students and alumni had written several letters to the editor pleading with the governor and the board not to dismiss him. Fred Sullens of the *Jackson Daily News*, who had endorsed Hugh White in his losing campaign in 1931 and again in 1935, responded to a letter from an MSCW student: "President Parkinson is going to do a fadeout in the political picture and all the letters he persuades members of the student body to write can't save him. Listen little lady, listen softly with both ears open. A few weeks hence there will be no parking place for President Parkinson on the campus at MSCW. In rude words it is this: President Parkinson is going to pass out. So are some other people."[18] That cavalier commentary on the dismissal of President Parkinson and the intimation that others would soon follow is in stark contrast to Sullens's moral outrage at the Bilbo purge five years earlier.

During his February 18 press conference, Governor White indicated that he would ask the legislature to reorganize the board of trustees, although he did not specifically endorse House Bill 242. That recently introduced bill, which proposed an increase in the number of board members from ten to thirteen, had provoked a great deal of comment, especially the provision that the three new members would serve four-year terms and after their terms expired the number of trustees would revert to ten. House Bill 242 would allow Governor White to appoint seven new board members, giving him control of the board. White said that he did not particularly want a larger board and that, if the trustees who had opposed him in 1935 would resign, he would be content to let the board remain at ten members.[19]

There was divided and diverse reaction to Governor White's effort to reorganize the board. The Columbus *Commercial Dispatch* supported the governor's plan and endorsed the removal of four of the six college presidents. Those radical steps were necessary, the *Dispatch* said, because "certain members of the Board have brazenly abused their trust, prostituted their authority, and used their office for political purposes. The officials took their chances with politics and they should take the consequences of politics." The *Dispatch* accused the board of trustees of depositing large amounts of money in certain banks and invoking sanctions against other banks on the basis of partisan politics. The newspaper suggested that the League of Nations could advantageously study the board's use of sanctions and concluded: "The Colleges are under partisan political control and have been during the regime of the present Board. Therefore, Governor White ought to have the power and the authority to add members to the Board." The *Commercial Dispatch* reassured its readers that Governor White did not intend to inject politics into the affairs of the colleges; he only wanted a voice in the administration of the institutions for which he would be responsible during the next four years. It was still presumed, by that editor at least, that the governor by virtue of his office was the head of the state's educational institutions.[20]

While the debate on Governor White's bill was in progress, a resolution was introduced to reorganize and consolidate the Mississippi system of higher education. Like several of its predecessors, it got lost in the legislative shuffle and never came to a vote. Hilton Waites, the chairman of the house university and colleges committee, opposed the resolution consolidating the state institutions but supported House Bill 242 because he believed all state-supported institutions should be subject to the will of the people. During the debate on the bill Waites made a few critical remarks about the university, and some Ole Miss students hanged him in effigy in early February 1936. A house resolution was hastily introduced and passed to "condemn the unseemly conduct" of the Ole Miss students. Theodore Smith, a young representative from Corinth, opposed the resolution on the grounds that the legislature had more pressing problems to address and should not waste its time reacting to college pranks.[21]

Thomas Bailey, Walter Sillers, Sam Lumpkin, and several others opposed House Bill 242, because they feared that any tampering with the college board might be considered political interference by the Southern Association and might again jeopardize the accreditation of the state institutions. Walter Sillers introduced an amendment to the bill that would have prevented any person associated with an institution of higher learning from participating in politics "even to the extent of keeping them from voting." It is not absolutely clear whether Sillers's amendment was an effort to kill House Bill 242 or Sillers actually intended for his amendment to become law.[22]

On the senate side of the capitol Joseph Cook, who had authored the 1932 bill establishing the consolidated board, reminded his colleagues that his bill had been designed to remove the colleges from politics. But, he was sorry to say, it had not done so, and he favored increasing the number of trustees to give Governor White control of the board. Other senators supporting the house bill argued that the existing board had been permeated by politics from its beginning and that Governor White had promised to dismiss only those educational officials who had campaigned against him. In a rather strange logic, supporters of the bill advanced the theory that Governor White would have to fire several college presidents as a means of keeping politics out of the institutions of higher learning. Senator Frank Harper stated for the record his reason for voting for House Bill 242—a reason based on the tradition that the governor was head of the state's institutions of higher learning: "I believe that the governor as the head of the affairs of the state ought to have full authority over the institutions of the state and then hold him strictly responsible for the outcome of the management of the state institutions. . . . I voted to turn the affairs of the state over to Governor Conner and I am now voting to turn it over to Governor White."[23]

House Bill 242 passed on February 21, 1936. The *Clarion-Ledger* reported its enactment in blazing headlines: CONTROL OF COLLEGES GOES TO WHITE. Although its passage bode ill for the state's institutions of higher learning, they did not suffer from any significant political intrusion during Governor White's administration. President Parkinson, President George, and the board's executive secretary were not removed, but there was continuing support during Governor White's administration for the consolidation of some institutions and for the closing of others. In 1937 Senator Bill Burgin introduced a bill to "disestablish" State Teachers College at Hattiesburg and make it the "Southern Branch of the University of Mississippi." The following year representative Joseph May of Simpson County introduced a bill to suspend indefinitely the operation of State Teachers College, but neither bill passed.[24]

College officials and board members apparently did not learn from their unhappy experience of 1935 and again became involved in the 1939 governor's race. After Paul Johnson, Sr., defeated former Governor Mike Conner in August, Johnson announced that he would reorganize the board of trustees and remove at least one college president, possibly more. Within a few days following his inauguration, on January 16, 1940, a bill was introduced to increase the board of trustees to fifteen members. That increase would allow Governor Johnson to appoint nine new members and give him control of the board.[25]

Both houses debated the bill extensively, in much the same spirit that they had debated Governor White's bill four years earlier. Senator David Crawley of Attala County opposed the bill but admitted that any "attempt to keep politics out of [college] boards is just as vain as the pursuit of a wraith across a meadow in the moonlight." Senator

James C. Rice of Natchez objected to the "politicalizing" of the board and the constant flux of its membership. But supporters of the bill argued that the increase in the size of the board was merely an extension of the same courtesy they had accorded to past governors and that it was only fair to give Governor Johnson a majority on the board. The bill increasing the board to fifteen members passed in early March 1940. Fred Sullens, who had opposed Governor Johnson in both 1935 and 1939, reported the passage of the bill with a shout of "hooray for ignorance!" and announced that "all persons who voted for him and are able to read and write should now apply for positions on faculties of our institutions of higher learning." Those who are not able to read and write, he continued, might get in if they could positively prove their support of the governor.[26]

Shortly after Governor Johnson's new appointees joined the board of trustees, a new college was added to the number of institutions under the governance of that expanded board. On May 6, 1940, the legislature authorized the transfer of Jackson College to the state and changed its name to Mississippi Negro Training School. Mississippi's newest state institution of higher learning, and its second state-supported college for blacks, was partially funded by the Rosenwald Fund from which it received a $30,000 annual grant. After Mississippi Negro Training School became a state institution, the legislature appropriated $10,000 to it annually. The school is now Jackson State University.[27]

The second reorganization of the board of trustees in a period of four years convinced many supporters of higher education that Mississippi's institutions of higher learning had not been removed from politics, and some were fearful that Governor Johnson would again jeopardize their accreditation. Those fears were not unfounded. Shortly after his appointees took control of the board of trustees Governor Johnson dismissed several administrators and faculty members at State Teachers College in Hattiesburg.[28] The Southern Association of Colleges and Schools reacted quickly. It placed the teachers college on probation, threatened to withdraw accreditation from the state's other institutions of higher learning, and warned the board that the association would monitor the situation very closely for any additional signs of political interference. The Southern Association's action rallied a small and dedicated group of men who were determined to find some way of shielding the institutions of higher learning from continued political intrusion.[29]

That small group of men included H. B. Watkins, O. B. Taylor, Oliver Emmerich, John C. Stennis, and Means Johnston. They met with Governor Johnson to discuss the possibility that Mississippi's institutions of higher learning might again lose their accreditation and to explain the long-term damage that would cause. As an alternative to the existing statutory board, and as a permanent solution to the recurring problem of political interference, they proposed a constitutional amendment creating a politically independent board of trustees. The advantage of a constitutional board over a statutory board would be that any change in its organization or any modification of its authority would require an amendment to the state constitution, a much longer and more involved process than statutory revision. A constitutional board had been under consideration for several years but had been delayed primarily because no one wanted to give any governor the power to appoint an entire board. It became increasingly evident, however, that if Mississippi's institutions were ever to be governed by a board free of politics such a risk would have to be taken.[30]

In the first few days of the 1942 legislative session a constitutional amendment creating a new board of trustees was introduced. With Governor Johnson's support it passed both houses in early March. The amendment was ratified during the general election in 1943 and became Article 8, Section 213A of the Mississippi Constitution. In the next legislative session a bill implementing the amendment was introduced and quickly passed. The law created a thirteen-member board of trustees, all of whom were appointed by the governor. Twelve of the trustees would serve twelve-year, staggered terms, with four members rotating off the board every four years. Those twelve trustees were appointed from the seven congressional districts, the three supreme court districts, and two from the state at large. The thirteenth member was the LaBauve Trustee of De Soto County, who served a four-year term and could vote only on matters pertaining to the University of Mississippi.[31]

On March 30, 1944, Governor Thomas Bailey submitted his nominations to the state senate, and they were quickly confirmed. The new constitutional board of trustees met for the first time on May 18, 1944.

Given the great effort that went into the establishment of a politically independent board, it is an ironic commentary on the state's priorities that the *Jackson Daily News* heralded the new board's first meeting with the caption: FOOTBALL IS ASSURED FOR STATE COLLEGES. At this first meeting the board reinstated intercollegiate athletics, which had been cancelled in 1942 because of the war.[32]

The board was trying to get the colleges ready for the return of peace. But along with peace came the college boom, the dimensions of which few American colleges adequately anticipated. Set off by rising expectations and sustained by the GI Bill, the postwar enrollment explosion changed the American collegiate system. After the Civil War the American college had been secularized; after World War II it was democratized. Perhaps the classic response to the democratization of higher education was the action taken by the New York board of regents. In the immediate aftermath of World War II the regents established a statewide university system with the motto, "Let Each Become All He Is Capable Of Becoming."[33] In postwar America, the college gates were opened wide.

—Eight—

The College Boom, 1944–1954

I took a small college and made it a big university.
—President William D. McCain
University of Southern Mississippi

After all the talk about taking politics out of the colleges, politics intruded upon the very first meeting of the new constitutional board of trustees. For several weeks before the meeting on May 18, 1944, there were rumors that a professor at Delta State Teachers College and the executive secretary of the board of trustees would be fired. Theodore Bilbo, who was then a United States senator, had accused the Delta State professor of openly espousing racial equality. J. A. Ellard, the executive secretary, was supposed to be fired because he had campaigned for Governor Thomas L. Bailey's opponent in the 1943 election. The charges against the Delta State egalitarian were not brought before the board nor was his fate discussed, but a motion was made to fire the executive secretary. Oliver Emmerich, a McComb newspaperman, offered an amendment to the motion stipulating that, if the motion to fire Ellard passed, he would resign. Emmerich explained: "I've worked too hard and too long to get a constitutional Board to take this thing out of politics. We have got to view this thing, the man that you are talking about, he served under a political Board and he had to cater accordingly. If he would show any signs of playing politics next week or the week after, I'd be willing to fire him. Therefore, if your motion passes I will resign."[1]

Emmerich's forceful assertion was convincing, and the motion to dismiss Ellard was withdrawn. That unheralded incident marked a turning point in the history of higher education in Mississippi—the transition of the college board from a political instrument to a public institution. That change made it possible for Chancellor John D. Williams to fend off an effort by Governor Fielding Wright to dictate appointments at the university. Shortly after he became chancellor in 1946, Williams received a telephone call from Governor Wright "instruct[ing] him to appoint a certain person head of the university laundry." The next day Chancellor Williams drove to Jackson to discuss the matter with the governor, who informed him that during the telephone conversation he had had a state senator in his office. The governor then explained to Chancellor Williams, who had only recently come to Mississippi, "You have your row to hoe, and I have mine." The meeting ended amicably, the appointment was not made, and the state's institutions of higher learning were at last free of political patronage.[2]

It was fortunate for Mississippi's collegiate officials that they were not distracted by petty politics, because they were soon in the midst of an enrollment explosion that created enormous, immediate problems for their institutions. On August 20, 1945, just five days after the Japanese empire had signed a treaty of peace, Acting President Clarence Dorman of Mississippi State College wrote to the board of trustees expressing his great relief that the war was at last over but admitting it was difficult "to realize that this is the post-war era." President Dorman predicted that the GI Bill would make it possible for "thousands" of students to go to school who "would not have attended college under ordinary circumstances." He added, "we can not turn them away."[3]

The postwar enrollment explosion revived a debate over the nature and function of higher education in American society that had been ebbing and flowing for two or three decades before World War II. The proliferation of colleges and universities, and the dominance of the elective system had created academic disorder, according to Robert Maynard Hutchins, and had left the American collegiate system without identity and clarity of purpose. Hutchins, along with Abraham Flexner, was among the nation's severest critics of the elective system and academic specialization. At the University of Chicago President Hutchins had designed a curriculum that was divided into "fields of knowledge" rather than an "assortment of courses" to be selected by the student. Under the Chicago Plan students were admitted to the university by examination rather than by the accumulation of high school credits. To Hutchins the development of intellect rather than of functional skills should be the primary aim of a liberal education. According to Frederick Rudolph, Hutchins and his Chicago Plan were "a kind of strange and wonderful throwback to Jeremiah Day and the Yale Report of 1828."[4]

Some of President Hutchins's disciples established at St. John's College in Maryland a curriculum "built around the one hundred greatest books of the ages." At this "ideal college" faculty members were "intermediaries between the books and the students." Critics of the St. John's curriculum and the Chicago Plan claimed that they were "a retreat into western classicism." According to Benjamin Fine, the educational editor of the *New York Times,* President Hutchins and his followers were the right-wingers of American higher learning by whose positions on major educational issues other educators measured their own. In *Democratic Education,* published in 1945, Fine analyzed the debate over the nature and function of higher education and divided American institutions of higher learning into four classifications. The "extreme aristocratic wing" included the University of Chicago, St. John's, and other institutions that promoted what he called an intellectual aristocracy. The far left wing of higher education was represented by several experimental liberal arts colleges such as Bennington, Sarah Lawrence, Antioch, and Bard. The other two groups occupied the middle ground and included the more traditional private colleges, such as Harvard and Stanford, and the public institutions, especially the land-grant colleges and state universities.[5]

American higher education, according to Fine's assessment, faced two distinct if not diametric alternatives as it entered the postwar period of growth and expansion. The country could follow Hutchins, who believed that higher education should not be concerned "with relative ends and immediate adaptation of the individual to existing surroundings but with values independent of time and particular environment." Or the country could follow the lead of Chancellor Deane W. Malott of the University of Kansas, who believed that the function of higher education "is to give a broad understanding of life and to prepare men and women . . . as self-respecting members of our economic society."[6]

As the United States emerged from the world war, it was evident that the role of the college and university was changing. Some resisted the change and others encouraged it, but almost everyone discussed and studied it. The most important and probably the most influential of the numerous studies of higher education conducted just after the war was the President's Commission on Higher Education. In his letter of appointment President Harry Truman specifically directed the commissioners to examine higher education "in light of the social role it has to play." The President's Commission, which produced a six-volume report entitled *Higher Education for American Democracy,* rejected President Hutchins's notion that higher learning should be concerned only with timeless ideals: "American colleges and universities must envision a much larger role for higher education in the national life. They can no longer consider themselves merely the instrument for producing an intellectual elite; they must become the means by which every citizen, youth, and adult is enabled and encouraged to carry his education, formal and informal, as far as his native capacities permit." The commission added that higher education must be "better adapted to contemporary needs" and must encourage American isolationists to shape a new and wiser world view in recognition of the "oneness of the modern world."[7]

Oliver Carmichael, a member of the President's Commission, went even further in attributing a social function to higher learning. In *The Changing Role of Higher Education,* published in 1949, Carmichael asserted that higher education must accept its new role as "society's Number One agency for promoting fundamental social progress" and argued that relevancy should be the "chief criterion in judging the value of courses or programs." Higher education must therefore, he said, "go down into the marketplace, into the homes and communities [and] cooperate with government, business, and industry."[8]

In the end, however, it was not the commissions or the faculties or the governing boards that determined the character of higher education in postwar America. It was, as Frederick Rudolph has said, the students who "took charge of change" and by their sheer numbers redefined the American college and university. In 1870 only 1.7 percent of the 18- to 21-year age group was in college; in 1900, 4.01 percent; by 1948, 20 percent. A collegiate curriculum designed for 1.7 percent or even 4.01 percent of the college-age population would certainly not satisfy the demands of 20 percent, and colleges began adding elective courses.[9] Once the prescribed curriculum was abandoned, collegiate education was destined to be shaped by student demand. As enrollment expanded, the curriculum expanded—each reacting upon the other. In the postwar years the readiness of a college to respond to student demand, and the ability of its officials to anticipate those demands, influenced the growth and success of institutions of higher learning more than any factor other than location. That was especially true in Mississippi.

Higher education in Mississippi experienced the same kind of enrollment patterns and curriculum expansion that characterized American higher education as a whole. In 1900 college enrollment in Mississippi was 2,727, with 2 percent of the 18- to 21-year age group in college. By 1950 the total student population was 21,716, with 14.67 percent of the college-age group enrolled. As with colleges nationally, Mississippi's enrollment growth was gradual until the college boom, and then it soared.[10]

In the last year of the war, enrollment at Mississippi State College was 761. In the first full academic year after the war it jumped to 3,391; almost 75 percent, or 2,458, were veterans. At Ole Miss during the spring semester of 1945 enrollment was 657; in the fall semester, 1,271; a year later, 3,213. At Mississippi Southern College the fall 1944 enrollment was 264; in 1946, 1,189. At Jackson College for Negro Teachers 195 students were enrolled in 1944; 633 in 1946, and over 500 veterans were turned away. President Jacob Reddix told the board of trustees that Jackson College, if it had the facilities, could enroll 1,000 students during the regular academic session and over 2,500 in the summer session. Delta State Teachers College had 205 students in 1945 and 891 three years later. Alcorn and Mississippi State College for Women experienced less dramatic gains largely because Alcorn was in a remote location and dormitory facilities at MSCW limited enrollment to approximately 1,250.[11]

Mississippi's private colleges experienced similar though less dramatic enrollment growth during the years following World War II. Some of the smaller schools, like Whitworth, Campbell, and Pontotoc College did not benefit from the postwar college boom and eventually suspended operation or merged with other institutions. Others, however, like Millsaps, Mississippi College, Belhaven, Blue Mountain, and William Carey College at Hattiesburg have continued to provide liberal arts education into the 1990s and are an integral part of the system of higher education in Mississippi.

As Mississippi entered the postwar college boom, the board of trustees of state institutions of higher learning realized that it must act quickly if expansion was to be ordered, controlled, and directed. To provide a data base for some quick and difficult decisions, the board retained Joseph E. Gibson, director of higher education in Louisiana, to conduct a general study of higher learning in Mississippi and asked W. T. Sanger to survey the state's need for medical education.[12]

While Gibson and Sanger were conducting their studies, the board was trying to govern the institutions of higher learning under circumstances far less than ideal. Several college presidents were embroiled in public controversies, and agitated alumni groups were calling for new leadership. The board of trustees realized that the changing role of higher education would require a new philosophy of management. In spite of its promise not to make wholesale changes, the board replaced four of the seven college presidents during its first two years.

The first president to be dismissed, at the board's second meeting on June 14, 1944, was William H. Bell of Alcorn A & M. Fifty years of neglect and paltry appropriations had left Alcorn in shambles. One official in the state department of education claimed that the Alcorn campus was virtually uninhabitable and recommended that it be closed. There were also complaints from some state officials that President Bell, who had been in office since 1934, "leaned altogether towards arts and sciences" rather than vocational training at Alcorn. Bell was replaced by William H. Pipes, who had an undergraduate degree from Tuskegee and a doctorate from the University of Michigan. President Pipes was committed to making Alcorn an agricultural college in the best land-grant tradition, but he told the board of trustees that to fulfill its mission Alcorn either had to be moved to a more central location or had to be made accessible by hard-surface roads. President Pipes's administration, and his considerable efforts to gain accreditation for Alcorn, were frustrated by the fact that Jackson College was assigned the role of providing general education courses for Mississippi's burgeoning black college enrollment. President Pipes served only four years and was succeeded by Jesse R. Otis in 1949.[13]

At its next meeting, in January 1946, the board of trustees dismissed President Jennings B. George of Mississippi Southern College. President George, who "stood like a rock against loose living," was a throwback to the old-time college president. He had been "horrified to discover that faculty members and students did their shopping uptown on Saturday afternoon." He "felt it was undignified for scholars to shop at that time, for that day was reserved for the common people to shop." Many southern alumni clamored for his removal on the grounds that time had passed him by. After spurning the board's request that he resign, George was finally voted out of office and succeeded by Robert Cecil Cook.[14] Six months later President George D. Humphrey of Mississippi State failed to win a vote of confidence. Following that defeat, which produced seven negative votes, President Humphrey resigned and was succeeded by Fred Tom Mitchell. At its next meeting the board of trustees declared vacant the office of chancellor of the University of Mississippi. The board then voted not to reelect Chancellor Alfred Butts because "it was best for the university that a change be made." On July 15, 1946, John Davis Williams was appointed to succeed Butts.[15]

President Burney L. Parkinson of MSCW escaped this first wave of change, although many alumni were complaining that the "college had stagnated" under his leadership. When President Parkinson could not be persuaded to resign of his own accord, the board passed an automatic retirement policy and thus induced him to retire in 1952. Parkinson was succeeded by Charles Pinckney Hogarth. President William M. Kethley of Delta State Teachers College, and President Jacob Reddix of Jackson College continued in office for several more years.[16]

In the early fall of 1946 Joseph E. Gibson and the study group he chaired published its report, the most comprehensive survey of higher education in Mississippi since the O'Shea study. Gibson chastised the board for not having implemented more of O'Shea's recommendations. He stated bluntly that the board of trustees had to design a role and scope for each of Mississippi's institutions and see that the schools remained within the parameters of that design. But, he warned, "the price of allocation of functions is eternal vigilance by the coordinating authority." Before discussing the particulars of role and scope, Gibson flirted momentarily with a pipe dream. He wondered about the wisdom of consolidating all the state's white institutions of higher learning into one Greater University of Mississippi at Jackson. Gibson acknowledged that consolidation was not popular, but he said the study committee "felt compelled" to recommend this "excellent way of achieving most of the things the Board and the people of Mississippi so earnestly desire." He asked rhetorically, "What greater monument could the first constitutional board bequeath its state than this greater University of Mississippi?"[17]

Unlike most of the previous studies, Gibson's assessed the needs of black higher education at some length and concluded that those needs were not being met. Gibson recommended that a new vocational school for blacks be located near the center of the state's black population. Though he did not recommend the closing of Alcorn, he did question the wisdom of maintaining the school in its remote location and suggested that the board at least consider merging it with Jackson College.[18]

Although it had the best of intentions, the board of trustees implemented very few of the Gibson recommendations. Ironically, it actually did one of the things the study recommended against. W. T. Sanger, who made the study of medical education, recommended that the board maintain the two-year medical school at Oxford rather than establish a four-year program at Jackson. In spite of that recommendation, however, the board of trustees decided to establish a new medical center with a full complement of medical degrees and health-related graduate programs. In 1950, after several years of intensive lobbying, the legislature created the University Medical Center in Jackson.[19]

During the three or four years immediately following the Gibson study, the board assigned role and scope functions to each institution of higher learning and accepted the assurances of college presidents and deans that they would thoughtfully expand their degree programs with a minimum of duplication. But the board failed to see that the dynamics of growth required more, not less, governance and that institutional autonomy was incompatible with a coordinated state system of higher education. Mississippi's institutions of higher learning were simply overwhelmed in the postwar years, and curriculum expansion was dictated by student demand rather than by board policy. College enrollment statewide zoomed from 4,000 in 1920 to 10,000 in 1940, to 20,000 in 1950, to 35,000 in 1960, to 55,000 in 1965, and to 70,000 in 1970.[20]

At the very time the board was assigning role and scope functions to each institution, circumstances were already in motion that would eventually force it to abandon those assignments and would alter the traditional hierarchy of higher education in Mississippi. On July 21, 1948, an ambitious group of one hundred alumni met in Hattiesburg, according to a newspaper account, TO BOOST MISSISSIPPI SOUTHERN. That group included mayors, legislators, and businessmen who agreed that Mississippi Southern College should become a comprehensive institution, one that could meet all the educational needs of the state's most rapidly growing region.[21]

When Robert C. Cook became its president in 1945, Mississippi Southern College was a small normal school located deep in the Piney Woods of south Mississippi. But its alumni and area businessmen in particular had long envisioned Mississippi Southern as a liberal arts college, perhaps even a university some day. To the hearty approval of its faculty, students, and alumni, President Cook pledged to use his office to promote the expansion of Mississippi Southern College and prophesied that its enrollment would "skyrocket" under his leadership. His prediction came true sooner than even he had expected. During the first three years of Cook's administration enrollment quadrupled, with over half of those students in liberal arts and business courses. Southern billed itself as the "Cinderella" of Mississippi's institutions of higher learning.[22]

A member of the faculty at the University of Mississippi before the war, Cook understood the traditional roles of the state's institutions of higher learning. The 1932 consolidated board of trustees, with the tacit approval of the state's political and educational leadership, had established a priority pyramid with the university as the "capstone of public education in Mississippi." Mississippi State came next, then Mississippi State College for Women, then Delta State and Mississippi Southern, and finally Alcorn A & M. That "pecking order," as Cook called it, was never voiced by the state's public officials and certainly not by members of the board of trustees. But it was a reality that Cook and other college presidents had to live with.[23]

President Cook claimed that the new constitutional board was not only aware of the pecking order but actually sustained it. According to Cook, H. M. Ivy, who headed the Ole Miss faction on the board of trustees from 1944 to 1956, wanted Mississippi Southern and the other state schools to remain small specialized institutions. President Cook realized early in his administration that the only way he could bring about the transition of Mississippi Southern from a small normal college to a university was to gain the support of influential board members. "My only hope at that time," he recalled many years later, "was to gain the friendship of two Board members who had helped me over a period of years." With the aid of those two trustees, John W. Backstrom and R. B. Smith, Jr., Cook was able to expand Mississippi Southern's academic program and reorganize its curriculum during his first few years in office. According to one historian of the college, that early reorganization was a major step in transforming Mississippi Southern from a small single-purpose teachers college to a large multipurpose university.[24]

At the request of President Cook, and under pressure from its growing south Mississippi constituency, the state legislature amended Mississippi Southern's charter in 1948 and allowed the college to grant undergraduate degrees in academic areas other than teaching. That amendment effectively repealed the mission of Mississippi Southern and made it a liberal arts college. But the amendment simply gave legislative sanction to a process that was already well underway and had been observed as early as 1927 by Michael O'Shea. After its charter was changed, Mississippi Southern quickly added new undergraduate departments and expanded its graduate division. One of the most popular additions was the department of commerce, which offered five new undergraduate majors and attracted record enrollments. President Cook boasted that Mississippi Southern's growth was the result of its improved academic standing rather than its location and announced in 1951 that Southern's enrollment included students from seventy-eight of the state's eighty-two counties, twenty-four states, and eight foreign countries.[25] While Mississippi Southern College was expanding under President Cook, and even more dramatically under President William D. McCain who succeeded him in 1956, a similar expansion was taking place at Mississippi State and at Mississippi State College for Women.

According to John K. Bettersworth, the appointment of Fred Tom Mitchell as president of Mississippi State College in 1945 joined "the time and the man." President Mitchell launched an expansion at State that was reminiscent of the growth under John C. Hardy during the first decade of the twentieth century. President Mitchell came to Mississippi from Michigan State, which had doubled its enrollment in the previous decade, and he was determined to create those same dynamics at Mississippi State. To the sheer delight of State's faculty, students, and alumni, President Mitchell promised that he would not rest until Mississippi State was "literally the academic equal of its peers." He disdained the "academic penury" that State's historical mission had imposed on it and directed his faculty to design a curriculum that would meet Mississippi's "ever changing demands." With enrollment soaring from 761 in 1945 to nearly 4,000 in 1949, the temptation to design a curriculum by student demand was too compelling to resist. In those boom years President Mitchell created a new image for the institution and brought a new sense of self-esteem to Mississippi State.[26]

President Mitchell was disappointed with Mississippi State's offerings in the social sciences and was downright "embarrassed" that it did not have a library building. In 1945 the library, located on the third floor of the biology building, had a seating capacity of 140 for an enrollment of 3,391. Mitchell quickly remedied both situations by acquiring funds to build a new library and by expanding the social sciences, in particular the sociology department. The expansion of the social sciences, humanities, and business courses during his administration was nothing short of spectacular. From 1945 to 1953, 417 new courses were added to State's curriculum—one-third of them in the school of business and 82 in the social sciences. The growth of the graduate program was even more impressive. In 1945 only 262 graduate students were enrolled, and only four graduate degrees were awarded. By the time Mitchell retired in 1953, graduate enrollment had climbed to 1,041 and 136 degrees were conferred. Mitchell was determined to see the agricultural college become a comprehensive university, but his untimely retirement for health reasons prevented his achieving that goal. Mississippi State did not gain university status until 1958.[27]

In many ways the expansion at Mississippi State College for Women best illustrates the postwar changes in higher education in Mississippi and symbolizes the interaction between the college campus and the larger society that sustains it. Shortly after the war MSCW officials abandoned the old school uniforms and permitted students to keep automobiles on the campus. With the uniforms went the traditional role of women in Mississippi society, and with the cars came a new sense of freedom and mobility. It was also at MSCW that the first signs of racial discord appeared on a Mississippi campus. For several years the YWCA had maintained a local chapter at MSCW; but when its board of directors voted to admit black members, MSCW officials disaffiliated with the national organization and disbanded the campus chapter.[28]

Under President Charles P. Hogarth, MSCW initiated an aggressive recruiting policy and experienced "the most phenomenal growth in its history." The shortest route to a record enrollment was a curriculum that offered students what they needed, or wanted. During President Hogarth's administration MSCW added five new degree programs and, in one year alone, fifty-five new courses. Most of those new courses were in liberal arts and business and other academic areas not traditionally associated with women's colleges.[29] Mississippi State College for Women, though it had denied for fifty years any intention of doing so, seemed to be "invading the sphere of men."

Although most of the curriculum expansion at the white institutions occurred in contravention of official board policy, or while the board was looking the other way and not exercising "eternal vigilance," the changes at Mississippi's black colleges were carried out according to a plan carefully designed by the board of trustees. Unlike their white counterparts, however, black alumni had little input or influence on board decisions. In 1945 almost half of the state's black population but only one black institution of higher learning, Coahoma Junior College, was located in the Delta. The board of trustees considered relocating Alcorn to that area but decided instead to recommend a new institution, and in 1946 the legislature established Mississippi Vocational College at Itta Bena. It opened during the summer session of 1950 with an enrollment of 300.[30]

Most board members realized that higher educational facilities for blacks, even after the establishment of Mississippi Vocational College, were still unequal to those for whites. In the hope of postponing the day when black students would seek "the same opportunities" that were available to whites, the board established an out-of-state scholarship program. Under that plan the state of Mississippi would pay the tuition, and in some cases other expenses, for blacks who went out of state to obtain graduate and professional degrees which were not available at Mississippi's black institutions. When it announced the new program, the board of trustees explained that "competent [Negro] leaders" have "requested the board to promote this program" rather than establish "professional or graduate programs at Alcorn A & M or Jackson College." The board did not quote by name any college president or other black leaders who preferred to send their sons and daughters away to school rather than upgrade their own institutions. In Mississippi, as in other southern states on the eve of the civil rights movement, the role of black college presidents was extremely difficult. They had to maintain a delicate equilibrium between an increasingly militant black student population and an increasingly nervous white power structure.[31]

Although the board of trustees was reluctant to establish new graduate and professional programs at the black institutions, it was forced by postwar circumstances to restructure the curriculum at Jackson College. In 1940, the enrollment at the college was 131; in 1949, 2,500 students enrolled in its summer session and hundreds more were turned away. Mississippi's new teacher certification program, which stressed advanced training and college degrees, ignited a demand for higher education among Mississippi blacks that was reminiscent of their desire for education after the Civil War. It became imperative that Mississippi's black colleges be reorganized.[32]

In 1951 the board of trustees issued a new mission statement for the state's three black institutions of higher learning. Alcorn was to continue to offer teacher training in vocational agriculture and home economics, but it would emphasize mechanical arts, agriculture, and allied sciences. Mississippi Vocational College would also offer some teacher education but would stress vocational training. Under the new mission statement the function of Jackson College was significantly altered; it would become a liberal arts college offering a broad range of undergraduate degrees in the arts and sciences and in education, as well as graduate degrees in a few selected fields.[33]

The historical roles of Mississippi's public institutions of higher learning were permanently altered during the postwar college boom, by numbers to be sure but also by changes in the world at large. At the inauguration of President Cook in 1945, N. L. Englehardt, the associate superintendent of the New York City school system, spoke of a new role for the American college. "Whether willingly or not," he said, "the college has become a seat of learning for world situations. It must train constructive citizens for the largest community in which they live, namely the world itself in which all men are neighbors."[34] That new role rendered obsolete the single-purpose institution with its specialized curriculum, and a new multipurpose college with a broad curriculum superseded it. That development destroyed the old pecking order and altered the traditional relationships between Mississippi's institutions of higher learning.

As early as 1949 Chancellor Williams sensed that a "pattern of higher education in Mississippi has emerged and taken shape since the close of the war" that undermined the role of the University of Mississippi "as the capstone of public education in the state." Seeing other collegiate institutions broaden their mission and expand into academic areas that had long been the exclusive domain of the university, Williams warned the board of trustees that the "dispersal or duplication of those special functions" would lead to a "general mediocrity which is the inevitable consequence of an over-extended operation." Because the board of trustees, the legislature, and the general public attached increasing importance to enrollment figures, university officials found themselves arguing that "the size of the on-campus student body is by no means an adequate basis for judging the expense of operating an institution of higher learning." The original missions, and the traditional roles of institutions of higher learning, according to Chancellor Williams, "are the most reliable standards" for the allocation of state funds.[35]

Chancellor Williams and his administration held to the traditional role of the American university, sided with President Hutchins, and rejected relevancy as the best measure of an institution's effectiveness. But the "question of whether Mississippi is to have a great University in addition to its system of junior and senior colleges," Chancellor Williams wrote in 1951, would be decided not by the Ole Miss faculty and administration but by the people of the state, the legislature, the building commission, and the college board.[36] The admission that it could not control its own destiny created a laissez-faire attitude, a lull of mind, at Ole Miss that Chancellors Barnard or Mayes would never have allowed to develop.

In the aftermath of World War II the faculty, friends, and alumni of the other institutions—Mississippi State and Mississippi Southern in particular—decided that it was not the university's prerogative to be "the capstone of public education in Mississippi." And while the university was waiting for others to decide its fate, Mississippi State and Mississippi Southern outstripped it in enrollment, broadened their course offerings, upgraded their academic programs, and established themselves as peers, not rivals, of the state university.

In the aftermath of the war, the 1960s, Mississippi's collegiate system continued to change as the society that sustained it changed. And when that society experienced upheaval, as it did in the 1960s, the colleges and universities also experienced upheaval.

—*Nine*—

Race, Rights, Riots, Role and Scope, 1954–1962

We don't give a damn if you burn it down.
—Alcorn A & M student, 1957

Shortly after the Supreme Court issued the Brown decision, the Mississippi legislature passed a resolution directing all public officials and state agencies to "prohibit, by any lawful, peaceful, and constitutional means, the implementation or the compliance with the Integration Decisions of the United States Supreme Court."[1] The board of trustees, which was subject to that resolution, hoped to respond to the Brown decision in a peaceful, unpublicized way, but board members were bound by history and heritage to resist it. Most trustees were emotionally and intellectually unprepared for the changes that would soon engulf them, and college presidents were too timid to tell them that Mississippi would have to accept those changes.

To blacks in postwar Mississippi higher education was the avenue of upward mobility, the "yellow brick road" to the American dream. Very few white Mississippians understood the hold that dream had on blacks, or their determination to reach it. One of the few whites who did understand was Hodding Carter, the Pulitzer Prize–winning editor of the Greenville *Delta-Democrat Times*. In 1948 he delivered the commencement address at Alcorn College. When later asked by the *Atlanta Journal* to summarize his speech Carter remarked, "I felt that what I said to them was not needed, for I had advised them not to be content with the manifold inequalities experienced by their race. . . . I know that they are identical in their aspirations and their good citizenship with college graduates anywhere [and] there can be no good reason for fearing or longer subjugating any American who dreams our common, sturdy dream of a fair chance and a place, our place, in the sun." "That's all those Alcorn graduates want," Carter concluded, "and it's the least that they deserve."[2]

To say that the college board was emotionally and intellectually unprepared for the impending civil rights revolution is not to say that it had no warning of what was to come. On July 11, 1939, Chancellor Alfred Butts wrote to Calvin Wells, the chairman of the board, advising him that blacks were seeking admission to the professional schools in other southern states and that Mississippi could soon expect some black applicants. The board's response to that warning was not only an expression of public policy, it was also an intimation of the measures that a closed society might take to keep itself intact. Chairman Wells replied to Chancellor Butts: "We will litigate until the cows come home before we permit any such thing as that [integration]. I sincerely trust that no effort will be made by any negroes to enter [our] institutions. I believe they have too much sense to do so. . . . I would feel sorry about what would happen to them in 24 hours after they got there. However, we will not anticipate any trouble along that line until we meet it."[3]

The trouble started sooner than Wells had anticipated. Almost immediately after World War II, black veterans began to challenge Mississippi's closed society. There was an "undercurrent of nervous apprehension," not unlike the feeling after the Civil War, that some aggressive black student might seek admission to one of the state's white institutions, the medical school in particular. That ominous prospect was often discussed among the state's white leadership. On July 22, 1949, Walter Sillers, speaker of the house of representatives, wrote to Governor Fielding L. Wright to express his concern that Mississippi might soon face the problem. Sillers considered the admission of blacks to the medical school "unthinkable" and vowed to close the school if necessary to avoid "the tragic consequences" of integration. A year later, in August 1950, the board of trustees armed the presidents of Mississippi's white colleges with the power to avoid those "tragic consequences." In an incredibly naive act, the board gave them the authority to "accept or reject any applicants according to the best interest of everyone."[4]

Three years after the board adopted that policy, and one year before the Brown decision, Charles Dubra, a black minister from Gulfport, applied for admission to the Ole Miss law school. Dubra had an undergraduate degree from Claflin College in Orangeburg, South Carolina, and a master's degree from Boston University. Dubra told Robert Farley, dean of the law school, that he did not want any trouble or publicity connected with his admission. He said that he was not an activist, not even an integrationist, and would live quietly off campus in the Oxford black community.[5]

Dean Farley brought Dubra's application to the attention of Chancellor John D. Williams. At the next board meeting, Williams asked Farley to give a full report on the situation. After explaining the details and evaluating the application, Dean Farley recommended that Dubra be admitted. The trustees discussed the question intensely. H. M. Ivy, president of the board, favored admitting Dubra, but R. D. Morrow and others strongly opposed it. As Dean Farley remembered, Morrow "got almost violent over the idea of it."[6] The board rejected Dubra's application on the grounds that Claflin College was unaccredited, even though Dubra's graduate work at Boston University would have made him eligible for admission. Significantly, published board minutes give no indication that the matter was ever discussed. Dubra accepted the board's decision and did not seek legal redress. His acceptance of his rejection seemed to confirm the board's belief that "it"—integration—would never happen in Mississippi.

In the summer after Dubra's rejection the U.S. Supreme Court ruled in *Brown* v. *Board of Education* that racial segregation in public schools was a violation of the rights guaranteed to all Americans under the Fourteenth Amendment. Shortly after that decision, Medgar Evers, a graduate of Alcorn A & M College who was currently employed by the NAACP, applied for admission to the Ole Miss law school. His application was forwarded to the board of trustees and rejected because Evers had failed to include two letters of recommendation from alumni attesting to his good moral character—at that time a requirement for admission to any state-supported college in Mississippi. A short time later Evers submitted two letters from Ole Miss alumni in his home county recommending his admission. Somewhat surprised that he had been able to obtain the letters, the board reinterpreted the requirement and advised Evers that those letters did not satisfy the admission standards. He would have to secure two letters from alumni in

Bolivar County where he was then living, not his home county. While he was responding to that interpretation, the board increased the number of letters required from two to five. About that time Evers was offered the position of state field secretary of the NAACP, which he decided to accept rather than pursue admission to Ole Miss.[7] The Medgar Evers case reinforced the notion that, by delay and duplicity, the board could prevent integration from happening in Mississippi.

Although the board of trustees made no public disclosure of his application, a Jackson newspaper reported that Evers had applied to the law school and had been rejected. Euclid R. Jobe, the board's executive secretary, scolded the press for breaking the story: "Why don't the newspapers wait until a suit is filed before reporting these cases. We don't think application of negroes for entrance at state schools is any news at all." In a reply to Jobe's criticism, the *Jackson Daily News* defended its decision to print the story and advised Jobe to "give full attention to his nice salaried job with the educational Board and not try to set himself up as a censor of newspapers."[8] The most significant aspect of this repartee is not the question of censorship or secrecy, as important as that might be, but Jobe's implication that any black applicant to a white institution would be forced to file suit in order to gain admission.

The publicity surrounding the Evers case contributed to the mounting agitation over the issue of integration and opened the floodgates of popular diagnosis. Almost every Mississippian ventured a solution to the "nigra problem." One of the simplest and most astounding was offered by former governor Fielding Wright, an unsuccessful candidate for reelection in 1955. Wright's solution was printed on the front page of the *Jackson Daily News* on February 17, 1955: "I propose that legislative action be taken setting up a committee to go into every section of the state to determine what the situation would be if children of both races were forced into the same school. . . . The legislative study would unquestionably show that any attempt to mix the white and colored races in our public schools would inevitably result in violence and bloodshed. To avoid violence Mississippi could order the maintenance of segregated schools." The editor was relieved that "a practical and common sense plan for handling the segregation problem" had at last been found. It was so simple and so logical. Since whites would resort to violence to prevent integration, Mississippi should be exempt from the Supreme Court's decision. Fielding Wright was neither sinister nor stupid, but like most other white Mississippians he was imbued with a belief in white supremacy and segregation. To hold such beliefs in the postwar world was, to William Faulkner, "like living in Alaska and being against snow."⁹ Yet, fidelity to another lost cause would again skew the world view of Mississippi's white leadership.

The militant phase of the civil rights movement began in Mississippi, as it did elsewhere, on the college campus in the springtime. In March 1957 a group of Alcorn students began boycotting the classes of Professor Clennon King, who had recently come to Alcorn College from Georgia. King, a minister, had been an organizer for the NAACP. But after a disagreement with its leadership, he had disassociated himself from the NAACP and, while teaching at Alcorn, had written several articles for a Jackson newspaper criticizing the organization and endorsing segregation. He became something of a celebrity among whites, but he riled the black community in Mississippi. The Alcorn students were protesting not only King's criticism of the NAACP but also his derogatory, demeaning attitude toward women in his classes. The students were dissatisfied with President J. R. Otis's response to their complaints, and the boycott eventually spread to other classes.¹⁰

As the boycott spread, a board committee composed of E. R. Jobe, H. G. Carpenter, chairman of the Committee on Negro Education, and Verner Smith Holmes went to the Alcorn campus to investigate the situation. After discussing the strike with President Otis and the Alcorn faculty, the committee assembled the student leaders, scolding and ordering them to return to class. The students were told that the board might even close the college if they did not return to class immediately. The delegation from the board was startled when a young woman student responded: "We don't give a damn if you burn it down."¹¹ It was an announcement that a new era in race relations had dawned in Mississippi—an announcement that virtually went unheard because the white people of Mississippi were not listening. One of the few leaders who did hear her was Verner Holmes, a McComb physician who had been on the board for only about a year. Holmes heard the black voices of the 1950s and listened to them.

President Otis, who had already been replaced by the board of trustees, was scheduled to leave office on July 1. Empowered by the board to act in its behalf, the three-member delegation removed Otis immediately and closed the college. The board committee then asked his successor, J. D. Boyd of Utica Institute, to assume the presidency as soon as possible. After Boyd took office the situation began to ease, and the board announced that any students who wished to return to Alcorn would be reinstated without penalty. Students were required to sign a written statement, however, that they would not continue the boycott or support it in any way. If they refused to sign, they would not be readmitted. The trustees would not grant the students' demands while the boycott was in progress, but after Alcorn had reopened and classes had resumed the board directed President Boyd to relieve Professor King of his classes. In July 1957, the board terminated King's contract and presumed that the King affair was at last resolved.[12]

But in May 1958 Clennon King called E. R. Jobe at the board office and told him that he wanted to pursue a doctorate in history at Ole Miss. Jobe advised King to write for an application, to fill it out and provide all the documents required in the application, and to submit his papers to the registrar at the university. King did not want to seek admission under the normal procedure, however, because he believed university officials would find some technicality on which to deny him entry. He told Jobe that he was going to Oxford to make a personal application for admission. Jobe informed Governor James P. Coleman and the Mississippi Highway Patrol that King would apply for admission at the university on May 16.[13]

Governor Coleman, in consultation with Attorney General Joe Patterson, decided that they would have to take steps to prevent any violence that might result from King's attempt to register. Instead of going to Oxford, where his presence would attract the attention of the press, the governor went to Batesville, a town about twenty miles west of Oxford, to coordinate the actions of the highway patrol and other state officials, including the university registrar. When King arrived at the Lyceum, the administration building, he was led into a room and left alone for quite some time. Fearing that he was in physical danger, King began shouting for help and pleading for someone to save him. Governor Coleman explained what followed:

> And then there came over the radio, "Governor, this fellow is in the registrar's office and he is hollering Help! Help!, they are going to kill me! He's hollering loud enough for the press out in front of the Lyceum

to hear him. What am I going to do?" Well, I said, I think we have
fooled with Reverend King about as long as we need to. I said just go
in there and get him . . . and take him off the campus and turn him
loose. . . . In a little bit, the radio came on: "This fellow says he is going
to come back on the campus. . . ." I said, We have just had enough of
this. I was thinking about Alcorn and all his other erratic behavior. I
said I really think he is crazy. . . . You take him down to Jackson and
have two doctors examine him. . . . don't commit him without a hearing. And Judge [Stokes V.] Robertson gave him a hearing and sent him
to Whitfield [the state mental institution in Jackson]. . . . Now a lot of
folks thought it was a gimmick, but it wasn't any gimmick.[14]

While Clennon King was serving his brief term in Whitfield, a small
group of citizens was drafting a list of charges against Chancellor
Williams and several Ole Miss faculty members, accusing them of sub-
verting the Mississippi way of life. The charges were first presented
orally to the board of trustees on September 18, 1958. After hearing
the charges, the board directed the two most prominent accusers,
Wilburn Hooker and Edwin White (a member and former member of
the state legislature), to submit their allegations in writing. On November 18, 1958, Hooker filed a thirty-six-page letter with the board
office. He explained that he had been accumulating the information
contained in his letter since 1952, when he first learned that some university professors were attempting to subvert "our civilization here in
Mississippi." White's letter explained in some detail how serious he
thought the situation was at Ole Miss and added, "Since my name is
not for publication, I would like to name some of the pinkos on the
faculty." White then listed several faculty members he considered to
be subversive.[15]

    Among the specific charges made by Hooker and White were the
following: Will Campbell, a religious counselor, had played ping-pong
with a Negro in the YMCA building; Robert Farley, the dean of the
law school, had stated publicly, as Thomas L. Walton had a century
earlier, that Mississippi must obey the U.S. Supreme Court; Roscoe
Boyer, a faculty member in the school of education, had poked fun at
the southern drawl and bragged that he was born in the North. James
Wesley Silver, who had been at the university twenty-two years and
served as chairman of the history department, was singled out for special criticism. He was accused of denigrating the conduct of Confeder-

ate authorities. As evidence, his accusers cited a master's thesis written by an Ole Miss student that was critical of Confederate officials; "this thesis" they declared, "could well be the fruit of Dr. Silver's lectures."[16] At the time those accusations were made Silver was a visiting professor at Harvard University, teaching courses in Civil War and southern history.

Perhaps the most sensational charges were leveled against Professor Quinton Lyon of the philosophy department. He was accused of apostasy. Professor Lyon's popular, widely used college textbook, *The Great Religions,* was condemned because it did not declare Christianity as the only true religion and did not brand all others as false. Supporting the charges of apostasy against Professor Lyon was this remarkable statement: "At a high school press institute, Lyon gave the invocation and a high school student, who is an informed Christian, stated that the invocation was odd and strange and that she was unable to understand it."

Professor Lyon was an ordained minister and an eminent scholar with two earned doctorates. A local Oxford newspaper referred to Professor and Mrs. Lyon as "active members of the Methodist church." At the time the accusations were made, Lyon was preparing a series of lectures to be delivered in Spanish at the University of Panama, where he would be a visiting Fulbright scholar during the 1960 academic year.[17]

In addition to these and many other charges against specific individuals, the accusers claimed that there was a communist cell and possibly an NAACP chapter on the university campus. After the formal allegations had been submitted, the board directed all university personnel who had been accused to respond in writing to the charges against them. A board committee, called the Special Committee on Charges of Apostasy at the University of Mississippi, studied those responses. Following what it called a "thorough investigation," the committee filed its report at the August meeting.

According to the *Jackson Daily News,* Chancellor Williams was asked to sign an oath attesting to his belief in one omnipotent God, in the literal truth of the Bible and the Tenth Amendment, in the doctrines that Mississippi was a sovereign state, that the U.S. Supreme Court is not above the Constitution, and that racial integration often leads to intermarriage. The minutes of that meeting do not include any discussion of what took place, nor do they indicate whether Chancellor Williams was asked to sign an oath. The minutes state only that the board adopted the committee's report, cleared Chancellor Williams and all faculty members of the charges against them, and considered the case of apostasy and subversion at the university closed. A board statement released to the press after the meeting expressed unanimous and unreserved confidence in Chancellor Williams and his administration. The statement also disclosed that after an intense investigation, the committee found no communist cell or NAACP chapter at the University of Mississippi.[18]

Just as the furor over apostasy and subversion at Ole Miss was winding down, an even more volatile situation was developing at Hattiesburg. In September 1959, Clyde Kennard filed his second application for admission to Mississippi Southern College. The Clyde Kennard story is long and involved, and it is a dark, sorry episode in Mississippi history.

Clyde Kennard was a thirty-one-year-old black man who owned a small poultry farm in rural Forrest County near Hattiesburg. He had been honorably discharged from the United States Army in 1952 with the rank of sergeant. While in the army, he had received the Korean Service Medal, the United Nations Service Medal, and a Good Conduct Medal. Kennard had completed his high school equivalency while in the army and, after his discharge, had enrolled at Fayetteville State College in North Carolina. He had also attended the University of Chicago.[19]

Clyde Kennard was not a civil rights activist, but he was a member of the NAACP chapter in his small community of Eatonville. He was intelligent, perceptive, thoughtful, soft-spoken, and obsessed with a desire to improve the lives of black Mississippians. He wrote several letters to the *Hattiesburg American* explaining his actions, letters that were well crafted and often profound. In a December 6, 1958, letter he wrote:

> Although I am an integrationist by choice, I am a segregationist by nature and I think most Negroes are. We prefer to be alone, but experience has taught us that if we are ever to attain the goal of first class citizenship we must do it through a closer association with the dominant (white) group. We believe that there is more to going to school than to listening to the teacher and reciting lessons. In schools, one learns to appreciate and respect the abilities of others. We say that if a

man is a good doctor, though his face be white as light or black as darkness, let him practice his art. We believe that the best engineer should build the bridge or run the train. We believe that the most efficient secretary should get the best paying job and the greatest scholar the professorship. We believe in the dignity and brotherhood of man and the integrity and fatherhood of God and as such men should work for the upbuilding of each other in mutual love and respect. We believe when merit replaces race as a factor in character evaluation, the most heckling social problem of modern times will have been solved. Thus we believe in integration on all levels from kindergarten to graduate school, in every area of education, in government—federal, state, and local—, in industry from the floor sweeper to the superintendent's office, in science from the laboratory to the testing ground. This I believe is our creed and though it is not perfect, still I had rather meet my God with this creed than with any other yet devised by human society.[20]

In that letter Kennard indicated that he would apply for admission to Mississippi Southern College for the semester beginning in January 1959.

Following several news stories about Kennard's intention to enroll at Southern, the State Sovereignty Commission directed its chief field investigator, Zack J. Van Landingham, to conduct an investigation of Clyde Kennard. The Sovereignty Commission was a state agency created in the aftermath of the Brown decision to "prevent encroachment upon the rights of this and other states by the Federal Government" and "to resist the usurpation of the rights and powers reserved to the state." Some of the funds appropriated to the Sovereignty Commission were channeled into the Citizens' Council, an organization dedicated to the perpetuation of racial segregation.[21]

On December 17, 1958, Van Landingham filed a preliminary report with the Sovereignty Commission. Although he referred to Kennard as an "integration agitator," he found that Kennard was not being sponsored by any civil rights group. Van Landingham also reported that a local committee of black citizens had been asked to persuade Kennard to withdraw his application. The local black leaders, who saw an opportunity to bargain with the state's power structure, agreed to talk to the applicant if the state's leadership would agree to establish a junior college at Hattiesburg.[22]

Kennard had first inquired about admission to Mississippi Southern

College in 1955. Since that time a lengthy dossier had been compiled, but Van Landingham could not locate the file in 1958. Officials at Mississippi Southern told him that the missing dossier contained practically no derogatory information about Kennard, and the Sovereignty Commission's own investigation found no direct communication between Kennard and the NAACP or any other civil rights organization. Van Landingham did pass on to the commission a rumor that had been passed on to him by a Hattiesburg attorney. The lawyer told Van Landingham that his maid had told him there were some white people from "the outside" who were stirring up the Negroes.[23]

On December 16, 1958, Van Landingham met with President James White of Mississippi Vocational College at Itta Bena. President White told Van Landingham that he had been in Hattiesburg the day before and had talked with local black leaders who were trying to persuade Kennard to withdraw his application. White told Van Landingham that he had also gone to Hattiesburg in 1955 and had helped persuade Kennard to give up his efforts at that time to gain admission to Mississippi Southern. But this time President White believed that a new approach was necessary. He suggested that President McCain of Mississippi Southern ask Kennard to drive up to Jackson with him to confer with E. R. Jobe. While Kennard was in Jobe's office, Governor Coleman could "accidentally" drop in on the meeting and talk to Kennard, telling him that he was causing ill will between the races and could be responsible for the closing of Southern as well as some of the black colleges. White offered the opinion that Kennard wanted recognition from those in authority and could be persuaded by a conference with President McCain and Governor Coleman to withdraw his application.[24]

When Van Landingham forwarded President White's suggestion, he noted that White had also mentioned the Hattiesburg black leaders' interest in getting a junior college for that area. Undoubtedly, said Van Landingham, McCain, Jobe, and Coleman might use that as a bargaining point with Kennard if a conference was arranged. But Governor Coleman rejected the idea of an accidental meeting in Jobe's office, preferring to meet with Kennard in his own office. A conference was soon arranged. Coleman remembered Kennard as "very mannerly and polite"; he "was extremely and favorably impressed with him":

> We sat there and talked about the situation and about his application for admission and all that for I guess two hours. And I told him that under

the circumstances then prevailing in the state that I didn't believe that he was really going to promote the best interests of black people by stirring that situation up, that it was not the appropriate time, that it was going to take time to change, and that while he could [legally] force his way into the institution, I wondered whether or not in the long run he would be doing himself and black people in the state any good. And I said you just go back home and you think about this and if you decide that you just have to, go ahead and apply for admission, and go through the courts, because obviously you are going to be forced through the courts. If you decide though to delay it for a while and see how things go and so forth, well then so far as I am concerned I would think it was the wise decision. I know it would relieve me because I am trying to keep down all the strife I possibly can.[25]

During that meeting, which President McCain also attended, Kennard agreed to withdraw his application. There was some speculation at the time that Kennard consented only to hold off submitting his application until after the governor's election in the summer of 1959. In that campaign Ross Barnett was running against Carroll Gartin, and it was generally presumed that Governor Coleman favored the more moderate Gartin. The conventional wisdom was that a racial flare-up at Mississippi Southern would work to the benefit of Barnett. Governor Coleman has stated emphatically, however, that his effort to persuade Kennard to postpone his application was not influenced by the governor's race.[26]

Nevertheless, shortly after the Democratic primary in August 1959, in which Ross Barnett defeated Carroll Gartin, Clyde Kennard resubmitted his application for the semester beginning on September 15. When his application was received, President McCain telephoned Van Landingham who, in turn, informed Governor Coleman. Van Landingham told the governor that Mississippi Southern officials would pursue a policy of delay and inaction in an effort to prevent Kennard from completing his application by September 15. On September 8, McCain and Van Landingham met with Governor Coleman in Jackson. The three men examined Kennard's application papers and determined that Kennard had resubmitted the form that he had withdrawn after his meeting with Governor Coleman. He had merely updated the application and the medical examination and had resubmitted the original papers. By updating his medical exam, Kennard had practiced a fraud. Upon that basis, his application would be rejected.[27]

To his notes taken at that meeting, Van Landingham added a chilling postscript. If the people knew that Kennard had reapplied, he wrote, "public opinion might have swayed Kennard from going through with his plans." President McCain seconded Van Landingham's presumption. "I had a group in the state," he recalled years later, "I don't know whether to say it was threatening me or promising me that they would put twenty thousand people around this campus to prevent it." McCain added, "I would not have had a job the next day if I had admitted him." The board of trustees would have fired any college president, he claimed, who voluntarily admitted a black student.[28]

As the application deadline neared, economic pressure was brought to bear on Kennard. In early September the Forrest County Cooperative foreclosed on his poultry farm and confiscated his stock. The Southern Farm Bureau Insurance Company canceled its liability coverage on his private automobile. The Sovereignty Commission attempted to secure his banking records, but the local bank refused its request. Clyde Kennard was not deterred, however, by any of those maneuvers.[29]

At 9:20 A.M. on September 15, Clyde Kennard arrived at President McCain's office. Zack Van Landingham and the press had come earlier. Both Van Landingham and McCain tried one last time to persuade him to withdraw his application. Kennard said that he had "thought this thing out thoroughly"; "he believed what he was doing was right and that he was doing it for both the white and colored race." Following a brief discussion of the reasons why his application was denied, Kennard was escorted out a side door unattended by reporters and photographers.[30]

About twenty minutes later President McCain and Van Landingham were told that Kennard had been arrested on the campus by two Forrest County constables. Van Landingham called the county jail. A constable explained that he and another officer had observed Kennard's car earlier that morning driving at an excessive rate of speed; they had chased but lost the car. In his report to the Sovereignty Commission Van Landingham described what followed:

> They claimed that they came on the campus and spotted the car, and found whiskey in it and waited at the car until Kennard reappeared. . . . They had charged Kennard with reckless driving and illegal possession of whiskey. . . . I immediately telephoned Governor Coleman's office

to advise him that in my opinion it appeared to be a frame-up with the planting of the evidence in Kennard's car.[31]

Eventually, the Mississippi Supreme Court dismissed those charges and remanded the case to the files.

But in the meantime, more serious charges were filed against Kennard. Early on Sunday morning, September 25, 1960, the Forrest County Cooperative was burglarized, and $25 worth of chicken feed was stolen. It was the same cooperative that had foreclosed on Kennard's poultry farm. Later that day Kennard was arrested and charged with accessory to burglary, a felony under Mississippi law. Johnny Roberts, a nineteen-year-old black youth, testified that he had sold the feed to Kennard who knew it was stolen property. In Forrest County Circuit Court Johnny Roberts was convicted but received a suspended sentence. On the basis of Roberts's testimony, Kennard was convicted by an all-white jury which deliberated ten minutes before returning its verdict. Kennard was given the maximum sentence of seven years in the state penitentiary—one year in prison for each $3.57. The Mississippi Supreme Court affirmed the lower court's ruling. An appeal to the U.S. Supreme Court was denied.[32]

The sentence was carried out, and Kennard was sent to Parchman prison. A northern journalist interviewed him after two years in prison and was astounded to learn that Kennard was not bitter. He assured the interviewer that there were still some "good people" at Mississippi Southern. Within a year or so after being sent to Parchman, Kennard developed intestinal cancer. Under the best of circumstances his chances for survival would not have been good, but under prison conditions he deteriorated rapidly. John Howard Griffin (author of *Black Like Me*), Martin Luther King, Jr., and Dick Gregory accused prison officials of denying Kennard proper medical care and began to put pressure on Governor Barnett to release him. Kennard weighed less than a hundred pounds at the time and was near death. When advised of his condition, and told that he might soon die in Parchman, Governor Barnett gave him an early release. Kennard was taken to Chicago for emergency surgery, but he was beyond recovery. He died on July 4, 1963.[33]

One of the most remarkable aspects of the Clyde Kennard episode is that his name—which appeared in newspaper headlines, in the secret files of the State Sovereignty Commission, in legal documents of both state and federal courts, and in the records of Parchman prison—

never appeared in the minutes of the board of trustees of state institutions of higher learning. Members of the board who served during
those troubled years, when interviewed two decades later, could not
recall that his name was ever brought before them or that they ever
made any decision concerning his application. There was such need
for unity, unanimity, and conformity in Mississippi's closed society
that the college board and college officials deferred to the state's power
structure on matters that threatened the "Mississippi Way of Life."

While the state's power structure was dealing with race and rights
and riots, the board of trustees was still groping with role and scope.
Neither group enjoyed much success. At about the time Governor
Coleman was trying to persuade Clyde Kennard to withdraw his application, Chancellor Williams was trying to convince the college
board that Mississippi could not support more than one comprehensive university. He stripped the issue of role and scope of its academic
folderol and asked the board in October 1959, "Shall Mississippi develop one great university recognized nationally and regionally," or
shall we have two universities or three universities "of lesser stature?"
"I do not recommend combining any of the present institutions," he
said. "My proposal is to allocate further appropriations for highly specialized doctoral programs to one specific place." In stating the obvious
Chancellor Williams concluded, "It is too expensive and impractical for
the state to permit duplication by institutions in these areas."[34]

However obvious or wise Chancellor Williams's proposal may have
been, it had come too late. Mississippi State College had already been
given university status. The legislature had already expanded the mission of Mississippi Southern, and it too would become a university
within a decade. Delta State Teachers College in Cleveland was renamed Delta State College in 1955, and its curriculum, course offerings, and degree programs were expanded. In 1956 Jackson College
for Negro Teachers was renamed Jackson State College, and both its
graduate and undergraduate divisions were enlarged. Two decades
later Mississippi would be supporting not one, or two, or three, but
eight universities.

Although the board may have preferred to devote its attention to
academic issues such as role and scope, the election of Ross Barnett in
1959 signaled a return of politics to the board's deliberations and decisions. Governor Barnett's five new appointees were M. M. Roberts,

Ira "Shine" Morgan, Ray Izard, William O. Stone, and Leon Lowry (the LaBauve Trustee). The new trustees joined Verner Holmes, Charles Fair, Thomas Tubb, S. R. Evans, R. B. Smith, Tally Riddell, J. N. Lipscomb, and H. G. Carpenter.[35] This was clearly the most politically oriented membership since the establishment of the constitutional board. In less than a year after his appointees joined the board, there was evidence that Governor Barnett and his counselors would become deeply involved in academic affairs.

In the spring of 1961, Bill Barton ran for editor of the student newspaper at the University of Mississippi. Barton had worked as an intern for the *Atlanta Constitution* and had covered the sit-in demonstrations in Atlanta during the summer of 1960. On the basis of information supplied by the Georgia Bureau of Investigation, the Mississippi State Sovereignty Commission had mistakenly identified Barton as a participant in the demonstrations and had compiled a confidential dossier on him. He was officially classified in the Sovereignty Commission records as an "agitator." While Barton was campaigning for editor that spring, the Sovereignty Commission—with Governor Barnett's approval—leaked the erroneous information and Barton was defeated.[36] Governor Barnett's acquiescence in the Sovereignty Commission's effort to influence a student election was a mere prologue to his involvement in the James Meredith crisis.

—Ten—

The Meredith Crisis: NEVER

We must either submit to the unlawful dictates of the federal government, or stand like men and tell them NEVER.
—Governor Ross Barnett

In a speech on July 5, 1962, Chancellor John D. Williams asked an Ole Miss alumni chapter in Greenwood to help him protect the "spirit of free enquiry" at the university. The U.S. Court of Appeals for the Fifth Circuit had just ordered the admission of James Howard Meredith. Within months Chancellor Williams would be asking Ole Miss alumni everywhere to help him save the university itself.[1] Few people anticipated the violent confrontation that Meredith's admission provoked, and fewer still understood the sweeping import of one lone black man's admission to Ole Miss. But James Meredith understood; he knew precisely what he was doing and what its consequences would be: "I returned to my home state . . . to accomplish my divine mission. . . . I had returned to Mississippi because I had developed a master plan to replace . . . the doctrines and principles of white supremacy. . . . I intend to build a better system and to replace the old unsuitable customs with more desirable ones."[2] Important though they were, gaining admission to Ole Miss and breaking the color barrier there were only part of Meredith's "divine mission." He wanted to change the system itself, to open up the closed society that had shut out blacks for so long.

The Meredith crisis was one of the crucial events in the American civil rights revolution, as well as a turning point in Mississippi history. It was a test of the federal government's resolve and a state's will to resist. Meredith manipulated events in such a way as to pit President

John Kennedy and the federal government against Governor Ross Barnett and the state of Mississippi. The Kennedy administration's willingness to use as many as thirty thousand troops dissolved massive resistance in Mississippi and removed any doubt about the federal government's resolve. Although that resoluteness would be tested several times again, the issue was settled in Oxford in October 1962.

James Meredith chose to integrate the University of Mississippi rather than Mississippi State or Delta State because Ole Miss was a symbol; it was still a bastion. To many Mississippians Ole Miss was "a lonely outpost amid the quiet splendors of the old regime," and it "whispered the last enchantments" of the Old South. Meredith correctly presumed that if the racial barrier fell there, it would come down everywhere. His enrollment at Ole Miss was soon followed by the peaceful admission of blacks to Mississippi's other state institutions, including the junior colleges, high schools, and grammar schools, and then to the lunch counters, the public parks, and the polling places.

The desegregation of the state institutions of higher learning also accelerated the restructuring of Mississippi's educational hierarchy, which had begun early in the postwar era. As increasing numbers of black students were attracted to traditionally white institutions, by popular degree programs not available at black colleges and by better facilities, black colleges sought means to expand their own degree programs and to upgrade their faculties and physical plants. After desegregation, competition and duplication eventually engulfed the entire state system; as a result, coordination became educationally and financially imperative.

Although not felt immediately, the Meredith crisis did influence the governance of higher education in the long term. Governor Barnett's direct involvement in academic affairs revived the memories of the Bilbo imbroglio and the fear that the Southern Association of Colleges and Schools might again suspend Mississippi's institutions. That did not happen, however. After the crisis subsided, and after Governor Barnett's appointees left the board, the new trustees were determined to exercise the autonomy that the board's constitutional status provided them. And over the next two decades the Mississippi board of trustees gained a degree of political independence that some authorities in higher education have cited as a example for other states to emulate.

Meredith began his assault on the closed society in September 1960 shortly after his discharge from the air force. He enrolled at Jackson State College and was befriended by a small group of students who bolstered his resolve. The election of President John Kennedy triggered that determination. On January 21, 1961, the day after Kennedy was inaugurated, Meredith wrote his first letter to the University of Mississippi requesting a catalog and application forms. On January 26 he received a letter from the registrar, Robert B. Ellis, saying, "We are very pleased to know of your interest in becoming a member of our student body. . . . If we can be of further help to you in making your enrollment plans, please let us know." Before returning his application Meredith wrote the NAACP Legal Defense Fund to request legal and financial assistance in the event a costly court case was necessary. Without waiting for a reply, Meredith returned his application and added a historic postscript: "I sincerely hope that your attitude toward me as a potential member of your student body [will] not change upon learning that I am not a white applicant. I am an American-Mississippi-Negro citizen."[3]

At the time Meredith wrote that letter, South Carolina and Mississippi had the only two state universities in the South that had not been desegregated. Most other southern universities had been integrated without disruption and violence. James Meredith hoped his admission to Ole Miss could be achieved without the kind of violence Autherine Lucy's enrollment had caused at Alabama in 1956. In a letter accompanying his application, he wrote: "I feel certain that this application does not come as a surprise to you. I certainly hope that this matter will be handled in a manner that will be complimentary to the University and the state of Mississippi. . . . I am very hopeful that the complications will be as few as possible." In the same letter Meredith informed the registrar that he did not comply with the requirement of five letters of recommendation from alumni, because all the university alumni in his home county were white and he did not know any of them personally. Instead Meredith included five letters from black citizens in his community who attested to his good moral character. In the meantime he had asked the various colleges he had attended while in the air force to forward copies of his transcripts to the University of Mississippi.[4]

Meredith's application triggered a mechanism that had been in place since 1954. One copy of his application and other correspondence was sent to the executive secretary of the board of trustees, and six copies to the state attorney general's office. (The number sent to the attorney general was later reduced, because University officials were concerned that some copies might fall into the wrong hands.)[5] Mississippi's white power structure, in consort with the board of trustees and university officials, employed a strategy of delay, deception, and duplicity in the hope of dissuading James Meredith from breaking the barrier of race and color at Mississippi's first, oldest, and proudest university. Their strategy was based in part on their past experience with Charles Dubra and Medgar Evers but mainly on the hope that Meredith might just go away if they did not let him in. A few days after receiving his application, the registrar sent him a telegram, dated February 4, 1961:

FOR YOUR INFORMATION AND GUIDANCE IT HAS BEEN FOUND NECESSARY TO DISCONTINUE CONSIDERATION OF ALL APPLICATIONS FOR ADMISSION . . . RE-CEIVED AFTER JANUARY 25, 1962. YOUR APPLICATION WAS RECEIVED SUBSE-QUENT TO SUCH DATE AND THUS WE MUST ADVISE YOU NOT TO APPEAR FOR REGISTRATION.[6]

After receiving that initial rejection, Meredith wrote the Justice Department on February 7, 1961, to inform the civil rights division of his intention to seek admission to the University of Mississippi. The opening sentence of that letter reveals the anguish that he and "his people" experienced as second-class citizens: "Whenever I attempt to reason logically about this matter, it grieves me keenly to realize that an individual, especially an American, the citizen of a free democratic nation, has to clamor with such procedures in order to try to gain just a small amount of his civil and human rights."[7]

On the day Meredith wrote to the Justice Department, he received a letter from Thurgood Marshall, director of the NAACP Legal Defense Fund. Marshall asked Meredith for a copy of his transcripts and the latest catalog of the University of Mississippi. He closed with the statement, "I think it should go without saying that we are vitally interested in what you propose." Neither Meredith nor Marshall knew, however, that the admission requirements listed in the catalog Marshall had requested were being revised on the very day of his request. At a special called meeting in the Woolfolk state office building in

Jackson, the board of trustees was constructing a new set of entrance requirements designed to make it impossible for Meredith to gain immediate and untroubled admission to Ole Miss.[8]

At that called meeting on February 7, 1961, the board of trustees adopted a policy that would allow an institution to reject transfer students from unaccredited colleges. Two other measures prompted by Meredith's application were also adopted. First, the board declared that "all applications which present false, contradictory, questionable, or uncertain data" will "be rejected or referred to the Board of Trustees." Second, the trustees adopted a measure that would keep Meredith from coming to the campus to register. The new policy stated that all applicants "must receive a certificate of admission before presenting themselves for registration."[9] The board misjudged Meredith's determination to negotiate those minor hurdles. To an even greater extent, they miscalculated the effectiveness of the stop-gap measures.

After examining Meredith's transcript and other credentials, Thurgood Marshall and the NAACP offered their legal assistance and assigned Constance Baker Motley to his case. On February 16 Meredith received a letter from Mrs. Motley advising him to make certain that all his transcripts and other papers were in order and to apply for the summer term beginning on June 8. As he was preparing his application for the summer term, Meredith received a letter dated February 21 from the university registrar that read, "Since we are unable to accept your application for admission, I am returning your check in the amount of $10 which was submitted as a room deposit."[10]

Meredith immediately returned the deposit with an application for the June 8 summer term. After hearing nothing from the registrar concerning his summer application, he inquired about its status in a letter on March 18. In the meantime he maintained an active correspondence with Constance Motley. After almost two weeks had passed without hearing from the registrar, Meredith again wrote Ellis and asked whether there was anything else he needed to do to complete his application. His March 26 letter commented in closing: "However realizing that I am not a usual applicant to the University of Mississippi, and that some timely items might need to be considered, I certainly hope that the entire matter will be handled in a manner complimentary to the University of Mississippi." When Meredith heard nothing from the university for almost two more weeks, he wrote the dean of the college of liberal arts asking him to evaluate his transcript, to review his application with the registrar, and then to advise him if he had met all admission requirements.[11]

On May 9 Meredith finally received a letter from Ellis. The registrar advised him that only forty-eight of the ninety hours he had earned could be accepted by the university. None of the credit taken at Jackson State College, which was not accredited by the Southern Association of Colleges and Schools, would transfer. The presumption, or perhaps the hope, was that Meredith would be so discouraged by the loss of almost half his college credits that he would abandon his effort to gain admission to the university. The registrar emphasized that the evaluation of his transcript did not in any way indicate approval or disapproval of his application. Ellis closed by saying, "In view of the foregoing [the loss of forty-two hours' credit] please advise if you desire your application to be treated as a pending application." After conferring with Mrs. Motley, Meredith advised the university on May 15 that he would accept the evaluation of his transcript and wanted his application to be considered for the summer term. He also applied for married student housing for the summer.[12]

On May 15, the day Meredith advised Ellis that he wanted to keep his application active, the university committee on admissions revised the admission standards in accordance with the board's action of February 7. The new policy stated that students could not transfer to the university from colleges that were not accredited by a regional accrediting agency. Furthermore, a student who was attending a college or university would not be eligible for admission to the university if he or she withdrew from the previous institution "in the midst of a quarter, or tri-semester" in order to enter the university. These new standards were prompted specifically by Meredith's application. Since Jackson State College was not accredited by the Southern Association at that time, Meredith would not be eligible to transfer from that institution. Also, Jackson State was on the quarter system and Ole Miss on the semester system. Because the academic calendars of the two institutions did not coincide, it would be virtually impossible for Meredith to transfer to the University of Mississippi from Jackson State without withdrawing "in the midst of a quarter." Moreover, the admissions committee incorporated into university regulations the new board policy that would reject applications "containing false, contradictory,

questionable, or uncertain data." These three new admission requirements appeared for the first time in the 1962 University Bulletin, along
with a notation of unbelievable candor: "Changes or revisions [in admission requirements] are sometimes made without prior notice in
order to cope with changing conditions."[13]

Ten days after adopting these new admission standards the university formally rejected Meredith's application. In a letter dated May 25,
1961, Robert Ellis advised Meredith that his application was rejected
because the University of Mississippi did not admit transfer students
from nonaccredited institutions and because he did not present the five
letters of recommendation from university alumni as required. The
registrar concluded: "I see no need for mentioning any other deficiencies. Your application file has been closed."[14]

Until Meredith received this letter of formal rejection he had maintained a low profile. University authorities, board members, state officials, and those who knew about his application maintained strict secrecy in planning a strategy to preserve segregation at the university.
After his formal, written rejection, however, James Meredith filed a
class action suit on May 31, 1961, in the federal district court. Mrs.
Motley wanted to appeal directly to the board rather than file suit. But
Meredith preferred a lawsuit because he believed the courts would decide the issue swiftly and painlessly. He sought, first, a preliminary injunction ordering his immediate admission to the university and, second, a permanent injunction barring the university from discriminating
against any blacks in its admission policies. The board of trustees, university officials, and several state officials were named in the suit.[15]

Judge Sidney Mize, the district judge, set the hearing on the preliminary injunction for June 12 at Biloxi. After much wrangling and many
objections, the hearing was rescheduled and moved to Jackson. Finally, on December 12, six months after the hearing on the preliminary
injunction had begun, the district court ruled in favor of the University
of Mississippi. Judge Mize stated that James Meredith had not established by evidence that he was denied admission solely on the basis of
race. The judge based his ruling on the registrar's testimony which
"shows conclusively that he gave no consideration whatsoever to the
race or the color of the plaintiff." He further ruled that the admission
policies adopted by the board of trustees, even those enacted after
Meredith filed his application, were not designed "in any attempt di-

rect or indirect, to discriminate against anyone solely on the grounds of race and color." Judge Mize concluded: "The testimony shows, and I find as a fact, that there was no discrimination against any student . . . solely because of his race or color."[16]

Meredith appealed Judge Mize's ruling and asked the fifth circuit court to grant his request for a preliminary injunction so that he could enroll for the semester beginning on February 8, 1962. A three-judge panel consisting of Elbert Tuttle, Richard T. Rives, and John Minor Wisdom denied Meredith's request on January 13, 1962. In unusually pointed language, however, the panel overruled Judge Mize on several points and admonished him for his conduct of the hearing. Judge Wisdom was baffled by the record of the hearing which he said had been argued "in the eerie atmosphere of never-never land." Judge Wisdom also took judicial notice that Mississippi "maintains a policy of segregation" and that this is "a plain fact known to everyone." The panel did strike down the requirement of five alumni recommendations, because that requirement was "a denial of equal protection of the laws in its application to Negro candidates."[17]

The fifth circuit's response was clearly favorable to Meredith's contention that he was denied admission because of race, but the court stated that Meredith had not conclusively proven his case. The panel could not determine from the record of the hearing if there were other valid nondiscriminatory grounds for the university's rejection of Meredith's application. Judge Wisdom therefore sent the case back to the district court and ordered a full trial on Meredith's request for a permanent injunction.[18]

On Wednesday, January 24, 1962, the trial opened. Meredith called several university officials to the stand, all of whom testified that as far as they knew his application had been handled the same as any other application. Constance Motley asked the registrar why he had rejected Meredith's application. Ellis responded: "It struck me . . . that he was trying . . . to make trouble at the University." Ellis also testified that he had found discrepancies on Meredith's application—for example, the fact that Meredith claimed to be a resident of Mississippi whereas Ellis considered him an out-of-state student. Dean Lewis, Chancellor Williams, E. R. Jobe, and most of the board of trustees were then called by the plaintiff. The board members testified under oath that they had not held any "formal" discussions with university officials or among themselves regarding the application of James Meredith and that the board had no policy excluding blacks from any of the state's institutions of higher learning. E. R. Jobe testified that he, as executive secretary, could say unequivocally that the board had adopted no such policy since the Brown decision in 1954.[19]

Mrs. Motley asked Tally D. Riddell and other trustees whether they had ever seen any Negro students on the Ole Miss campus. Riddell replied, "I'm not able to answer that question. If you'll tell me what you mean by Negro I'll try to answer it. . . . I know people whose color is darker than yours and I don't know." When Verner Holmes was called to the stand Mrs. Motley asked him the same question, and he replied that he had never seen or heard of any Negro students at the University of Mississippi since 1954. Years later he remarked to the author that he had been astounded by the testimony of his colleagues and university officials who claimed that they could not identify a Negro when they saw one. He had also become uneasy about the legal advice the board was getting. As a practicing surgeon he was schooled in the use of specialists, and it was sensible to him to rely on lawyers in legal disputations. But, as the trial proceeded, he had begun to notice that his instincts were at variance with the legal strategy employed by the lawyers on the board and in the state attorney general's office. Holmes refused to lie under oath.[20]

After the plaintiff had called his last witness, Constance Motley attempted to put into the record several articles that had recently appeared in Jackson newspapers. The articles included references to James Meredith's attempt to enroll at the "all white University" and his effort "to break the color barrier" in Mississippi. But Judge Mize refused to allow the news stories to be admitted as evidence. The plaintiff then rested his case, and court was adjourned in the late afternoon on Thursday.[21]

When court resumed on Friday, January 26, the defense presented its case. The only witness called by the state was Robert Ellis. In a surprise move Ellis produced five affidavits and entered them as evidence to demonstrate the lack of good moral character of James Meredith. Four of the five had been signed by the Attala County residents who had originally provided Meredith with letters of recommendation. Assistant Attorney General Edward L. Cates had secured the affidavits on January 15 at the Kosciusko law offices of state senator John Clark

Love. Four of the affiants stated that, when they wrote the original letters of recommendation, they did not understand that Meredith would use them to gain admission to the University of Mississippi. An unsigned affidavit from the other person who had originally recommended Meredith—his cousin Larry Meredith—was also introduced; it stated: "At the time of the signing of this [recommendation] I knew full well and was aware of the purpose for which such certificate was to be executed." Larry Meredith's affidavit was the only one of the five that included the statement, "I am not now nor have I ever been in any serious trouble or convicted of any crime or misdemeanor." Ellis testified that he knew nothing about the affidavits other than the fact that he had received them in the mail from Edward Cates with this explanation: "In order to assist you in determination of the good moral character and background of James H. Meredith . . . we enclose the executed affidavits. . . . We know you want these affidavits for your file on James H. Meredith." Ellis added that he placed the documents in "the Negro's inactive admission file."[22]

Ellis introduced the affidavits while being questioned about Meredith's character by Charles Clark, a special counsel to the state attorney general. The registrar testified that he was convinced Meredith was not just trying to get an education but that he had a mission in life. In a final question Clark asked Ellis:

Q. What did the race or color of James Meredith have to do with any action you have ever taken . . . with regard to his application?
A. Meredith's race or color has had no influence on the decisions which I have taken.

On cross examination Mrs. Motley asked Ellis whether he knew how the affidavits from the Attala County citizens were obtained and by whom. Ellis replied that he only knew he had received them in the mail from Cates about a week before the trial started. When asked if he knew whether the people had "freely signed" the affidavits, Ellis said he had "asked Mr. Cates that specific question" and had been assured that the documents were signed freely. He admitted under further questioning that he was taking Cates at his word and that he had not checked further.[23]

In the closing oral arguments on Saturday morning, January 27, the state argued at length that James Meredith was a troublemaker who lacked good moral character and for that reason, rather than race, the university had denied him admission. After both sides rested, Judge Mize took the case under advisement and announced that he would rule on or before February 8, the start of the spring semester. On February 3, the judge found as fact that Meredith had not been denied admission because of race. In his ruling Judge Mize stated:

> The plaintiff. . . . called as adverse witnesses nearly every member of the Board of Trustees, who testified unequivocally and definitely that at no time had the question of the race of a party ever been discussed at a meeting of the Board of Trustees . . . and that so far as the members of the Board of Trustees were concerned, all policies and regulations were adopted without regard to race . . . and that at no time was the application of James Meredith . . . ever discussed by any members of the Board of Trustees.
> The registrar . . . testified . . . that the question of race of the Plaintiff was not discussed or considered in any way whatsoever when his application for admission to the University was being considered. All of the other officials of the University testified to substantially the same thing.
> The proof shows on this trial, and I find as a fact that there is no custom or policy now, nor was there any at the time Plaintiff's application was rejected, which excluded qualified Negroes from entering the University. The proof shows, and I find as a fact, that the University is not a racially segregated institution.[24]

Meredith appealed Judge Mize's ruling and asked the fifth circuit to order his immediate admission while his appeal was under review. Judge Elbert Tuttle, a member of the panel that heard Meredith's appeal, urged the fifth circuit not to wait but to grant the injunction while the appeal was pending. Judge Tuttle argued that the probability of the court's final relief to Meredith was so overwhelming that any further postponement would be unfair to the plaintiff. More important, Tuttle predicted that a delay would encourage the "rise of massive resistance" to Meredith's admission in Mississippi. In spite of Judge Tuttle's rather strong argument, the three-judge panel denied Meredith's plea for an injunction. Jack Bass has aptly called the judges of the fifth circuit "unlikely heroes"; nonetheless, they missed an opportunity to prevent the violence that occurred at Ole Miss in the fall of 1962 when they did not order Meredith's admission in February. The resisters were given time to organize.[25]

On June 25, the fifth circuit finally reversed the district court and directed Judge Mize to order Meredith's admission. The circuit court's order stipulated that all institutions of higher learning under the governance of the board of trustees were covered by the ruling. Judge Wisdom's sharply worded opinion criticized the procedural and legal delays of the university and the board of trustees and cited numerous errors in Judge Mize's conduct of the trial. Judge Wisdom wrote:

> A full review of the record leads the court inescapably to the conclusion that from the moment the defendants discovered that Meredith was a Negro they engaged in a carefully calculated campaign of delay, harassment, and masterful inactivity. It was a defense designed to discourage and defeat by evasive tactics which would have been a credit to Quintus Fabius Maximus.[26]

At the insistence of Judge Tuttle the fifth circuit court enjoined the board of trustees and "all persons in active concert" with them, including university and state officials, to "act expeditiously" on the application of James Howard Meredith. Anyone acting to thwart, obstruct, or otherwise prevent the implementation of the court order would be held in contempt of the fifth circuit court. Tuttle and his fellow "heroes" had not enjoined the University of Alabama authorities or Alabama state officials in the Autherine Lucy case in 1956, and their order admitting her to the University of Alabama was eventually frustrated. They were determined to prevent a similar situation in the Meredith case. James Meredith had finally won his case in court. "In every other state but Mississippi that would have solved the matter," wrote Professor Russell Barrett. "Instead, it soon became clear that he had reached but one more detour of the many that remained."[27]

In an effort to shield Chancellor Williams from the enormous political pressure and emotion generated by the court's order to admit Meredith, the board of trustees divested university officials of all authority to act on his application:

> Authority in anywise connected with or relating to action on the application of James Howard Meredith . . . is hereby withdrawn from every official of the University of Mississippi. . . . The entire power, author-

168 MAKING HASTE SLOWLY

ity, duty, responsibility, and prerogative with regard to action on the application and/or admission of said James Howard Meredith should be and the same is hereby expressly reserved exclusively unto this Board of Trustees of Institutions of Higher Learning, effective immediately.[28]

The board then directed E. R. Jobe to obtain Meredith's application papers and to keep them in his possession until the board made a "final disposition of this matter." But before the matter was settled, the thirteen members of the board of trustees, most of whom had lived quiet, uneventful lives, would become the dramatis personae of a historic event chronicled on every continent in the world. Few trustees realized that they would soon be in the eye of history.

A week after the board assumed authority over the Meredith application, Justice Hugo Black vacated all remaining legal obstructions and on September 10 directed the district court to carry out the fifth circuit's decree. On September 13 Judge Mize acted on Justice Black's directive and ordered the University of Mississippi to admit James Meredith.[29] On the evening of Judge Mize's order, Governor Ross Barnett addressed the people of Mississippi on a statewide television network. He said that Mississippi had only one of two choices: "We must either submit to the unlawful dictates of the federal government, or stand like men and tell them NEVER!" Governor Barnett pledged to go to jail if necessary and called upon all other public officials to make a similar commitment; he promised that no school would be integrated as long as he was governor. Under a 1954 constitutional amendment Governor Barnett had the authority to close any or all of the state's public schools to prevent integration, and his oblique reference to that authority startled many Ole Miss alumni who feared that Barnett's counselors might actually persuade him to close the university. Within a few days after the governor's speech, a secret committee of Ole Miss alumni organized. Its singular purpose was to keep the university open, even if that meant admitting Meredith.[30]

The day after Governor Barnett's televised address, the board of trustees held a called meeting at the Woolfolk state office building in Jackson. All members were present for that "stormy" three-hour session. E. R. Jobe presented a review of the various injunctions pending against the trustees and university officials. There were two significant features. First, the board of trustees and university officials were specifically named in the fifth circuit's injunction and would therefore be in contempt if the decree was not implemented. Second, the injunction against the trustees would apply to their successors should the existing board resign or be impeached.[31]

After Jobe's review of the injunctions, Attorney General Joe Patterson and special counsel Charles Clark met with the board members to discuss their options. It was evident early in that discussion that they had only two choices: defiance or compliance. Patterson and Clark advised the trustees that the state's legal limits of resistance had been reached, they were under injunction to admit Meredith, and failure to do so would certainly result in contempt citations. Six board members, responding to the legal circumstances, assumed a position which few holders of public trust had ever held in the state's long and troubled history. Those six trustees were willing, however reluctantly, to admit James Meredith to Ole Miss and thus to end racial segregation as a public policy in Mississippi. Board members who accepted compliance as the alternative to contempt at that early date were Thomas Tubb, Charles Fair, and Tally Riddell (all three lawyers), R. B. Smith, J. N. Lipscomb, and Verner Holmes. All five of Governor Barnett's appointees—M. M. Roberts, Ira "Shine" Morgan, W. O. Stone, Ray Izard, and Leon Lowry—stood firmly against compliance. The two other board members, H. G. Carpenter and S. R. Evans, had not assumed an identifiable position as of September 14. Board members had made a pact among themselves that any action on Meredith's application would be recorded, and thus made official, only if the vote were unanimous. That pact prevented an official vote on a motion to admit Meredith on September 14 and on several later occasions.[32]

Following Attorney General Joe Patterson's dismal assessment of the situation, Governor Barnett's executive assistant assured the board of trustees that the governor was formulating a new legal strategy to keep Meredith out of the university. He pleaded with the board to take no action until it heard from Governor Barnett. Not a single board member, as an act of free choice, favored the integration of Ole Miss. All were therefore willing to listen to Governor Barnett, though some doubted the existence of any other legal options.[33] The trustees' discombobulation began at the called meeting on Friday, September 14, and continued through the following fortnight and on into that fateful fall. The board did not adjourn on Friday but recessed until Monday. Over the weekend, while members were anxiously, and perhaps against their own better judgment, awaiting an explanation of his new strategy, Governor Barnett opened a secret telephone contact with Attorney General Robert Kennedy and other officials at the Justice Department.[34]

On Monday, September 17, board members returned to Jackson for their meeting with Governor Barnett. Attorney General Patterson and Charles Clark also attended the meeting. To the surprise of everyone, except those few who were privy to his plan, board president Thomas Tubb invited the press to the meeting. Although trustees were convinced that any further resistance was futile, they had agreed not to make any public statements. Opening that meeting to the press was the only way they could make it known that some of them were willing to comply with the court order. Tally Riddell moved to open the meeting, but Ray Izard, a Barnett appointee, finally persuaded the board to meet in executive session.[35]

During the closed meeting Governor Barnett briefly outlined the options open to him in his legal battle against James Meredith. A special session of the legislature, which had been called several weeks earlier, would convene the next day; Barnett anticipated legislation that would give him new options in dealing with the crisis. The governor also told the board that Meredith had been charged with false voter registration, and it might be possible, he suggested, to arrest and jail him on those charges. When Meredith enrolled at Jackson State College he registered to vote in Hinds County. State officials later claimed that he was a resident of Attala County, where he owned property, and charges were filed against him. Governor Barnett also mentioned two other options that shocked some board members. First, he raised the possibility of closing the university. Then, he asked the board members whether they would be willing to accept contempt citations and go to jail.[36]

After Governor Barnett left the meeting, the trustees held a lively discussion about the meaning of contempt of court. Registration for the fall term was scheduled for the next week; if Meredith was not registered, university officials and the board of trustees would be in contempt of court. Tubb, Fair, Riddell, Smith, and Holmes stated bluntly that they were not going to let this happen. Their statements, unequivocal and unamendable, prompted a bizarre haggle among the lawyers on the board over the nature of contempt. M. M. Roberts—a lawyer, a

Barnett appointee, and the governor's most stalwart supporter—argued that "contempt of court means nothing" and that the federal court would not send board members to jail for contempt. Roberts's impassioned plea to defy the court and stand with the governor strengthened the resolve of Barnett's appointees, but other board members were unnerved by the talk of contempt citations and jail sentences.[37]

After the meeting adjourned, E. R. Jobe read a brief statement to the press saying that no action had been taken and that, unless called into a special meeting by the president, the board would convene for its regular monthly meeting on Thursday, September 20. In answer to a reporter's question about closing the university, Thomas Tubb explained that the board did not have the authority to do so but that the governor did.[38] Tubb's intimation that the university could possibly be closed, subtle though as it was, sounded an alarm; for the first time the rank-and-file alumni realized that their university might be in jeopardy. They finally realized that there were some, even in high places, who would sacrifice the University of Mississippi for the cause of white supremacy and segregation.

If President Tubb's intimation required careful reading, a statement issued by Verner Holmes after that Monday meeting needed no interpretation at all. Board members had agreed not to make any public statements, but Holmes thought that "was a great mistake" and decided that "somebody from the board should say something." His opportunity came when a reporter stopped him as he was leaving the September 17 meeting with Governor Barnett and asked him if he was willing to go to jail. Holmes, an Ole Miss alumnus and vice-president of the board, responded: "I am not willing to go to jail. . . . This would be ridiculous and ineffective. . . . I will not vote to close the University."[39] Verner Holmes was the first individual directly involved in the Meredith crisis who publicly denounced Governor Barnett's pledge of defiance. Moreover, his statement was the first indication that there was strong support within the board of trustees for keeping the university open, even if it had to be integrated. Holmes's statement was encouraging to Ole Miss students who wanted to keep the university open at almost any cost, and Jackson newspapers were soon complaining that the student body was more concerned about keeping the university open than keeping Meredith out.[40]

As tension and speculation mounted, and as the date of registration neared, Governor Barnett and Attorney General Robert Kennedy continued their telephone conversations on an almost daily basis. Neither the board of trustees nor university officials participated in those conversations; they were not privy to them except by rumor. A memorandum written by Robert Kennedy of a conversation on September 17 indicates that university officials were not even consulted about when or where Meredith would be registered: "[Governor Barnett] made the point that he felt that Meredith should register at Jackson at the State House at 3 o'clock on Thursday, September 20. . . . He indicated the Board of Trustees was meeting at that moment in another part of the building; that if I decide that Meredith should register at Oxford rather than Jackson, that he would get them back again tomorrow and tell them of our decision." On the following day Chancellor Williams, unaware that this conversation had taken place, announced that James Meredith would come to the campus to register on September 20 and would be treated as any other student. The chancellor also warned students against conducting any kind of demonstration. Williams's statement was a severe blow to the hard-line segregationists' long-standing claim that Governor Barnett had the unanimous support of university officials.[41]

As it became increasingly apparent that the unthinkable might actually happen at Ole Miss on Thursday, September 20, a Jones County judge issued an injunction prohibiting Meredith's admission to the university. The intent of the injunction, which cited the board of trustees, university officials, and federal authorities, was to set aside the decree of the U.S. Supreme Court. On the same day the trustees also received a telegram from Attorney General Kennedy, stating in the plainest language possible that the federal government would enforce the Supreme Court's order to admit Meredith. The telegram advised the board and university officials that Meredith would arrive on the campus the next day, September 20, to register.[42]

On September 19, the same day that the Jones County judge issued his injunction, the legislature enacted a law (Senate Bill 1501) prohibiting the admission of any person to a Mississippi institution of higher learning who had been convicted of a certain class of offenses including, specifically, false voter registration. The plan, which required the cooperation, consent, and complicity of a large number of public officials, was that Meredith would be charged, tried, and convicted of false voter registration. His conviction would then trigger the provisions of Senate Bill 1501, referred to on the day of its passage as the "Meredith law."[43]

While the legislature was drafting the Meredith law, a Jackson television and radio station was editorializing:

> This is a WLBT-WJDX Editorial, an expression of opinion by the management of these stations:
>
> The members of the Board of Trustees of Institutions of Higher Learning have a privilege this week that few men will ever have.
>
> Never have men in the history of Mississippi had such unity behind them. Never have men been confronted with a decision on which so much depends—the sovereignty of not only the State of Mississippi, but possibly the Sovereignty of all of our States.
>
> They do not need legal maneuvers to enable them to make their decisions. They are men of honor, conviction, and fortitude. Their names will go down in history for the decision that they will make.
>
> These men are to be envied by all—for the heroic opportunity that comes to a man only once in his lifetime whereby he can, if necessary, sacrifice his life for his State and, in turn, save his country. There are very few men of stature anywhere in our State who would not gladly change places with these Trustees. Their decision is one of not just preventing a negro from entering the University. It will be one to set the precedent that Mississippi is a State of integrity.
>
> These men will not succumb to threats from outside our State. These are men who have been especially selected by the past three Governors of our State to serve in a way that few men are ever called upon to do.
>
> We must depend on our Trustees to take the only honorable stand open to them. Many of them are reaching the twilight of their lives. We pray for their guidance and their strength. May God be with them as they make this crucial decision![44]

On the day this editorial was aired Ira Harkey wrote, "In a madhouse's din, Mississippi waits. God help Mississippi."[45] Harkey was the Pulitzer Prize–winning editor of the Pascagoula *Chronicle* and one of the very few editors who criticized Governor Barnett's policy of defiance.

While all Mississippi was waiting, the board met in a late-night secret session to give Governor Barnett one last chance to convince them that he had a legal way "to keep him out." Verner Holmes remembers that five-hour meeting at the medical center "as the worst experience of the whole thing." The governor was accompanied by "two big strapping" bodyguards who remained in the room the entire time. Thomas Tubb, president of the board, opened the meeting: "Governor, we are meeting here at the request of Mr. Izard and he has some questions he wants to ask you. We are 'out of soap' in court so the Attorney General tells us." Tubb then turned to Mr. Izard and said, "Ray, you take charge." Izard reassured Governor Barnett that the board wanted to keep Meredith out of the university if it could be done legally and without closing the institution. He then asked the governor to tell the board how he planned to keep Meredith from registering the next day.[46]

Years later President Tubb recalled the governor's reply: "And Ross went into this . . . speech, you know, about the Tenth Amendment and never did touch on the question or the answer to it. I reckon he went on for fifteen or twenty minutes." Mr. Izard finally interrupted the governor, asking him to be more specific. Barnett resumed his speech about the First Amendment, the Tenth Amendment, and the usurpation of states' rights by the Supreme Court. Izard again interrupted the governor and again he resumed his oration. Realizing that Barnett's opponents were growing restless, Izard—also beginning to show signs of frustration—shouted: "We've got to know what is the legal way to keep him out, that's all we want to know." The governor's exasperated reply shocked his supporters and confirmed the worst suspicions of his detractors: "The only way I know to keep him out is just don't let him in." It was apparent to Verner Holmes and others that "he actually had no plan, no way of doing it."[47] Governor Barnett's only strategy was to delay as long as possible—a strategy based partly on the recommendation of a Hattiesburg attorney who informed the governor that someone in the Justice Department had said the federal government would back down at the last minute to avoid a violent confrontation with Mississippi.

When board members realized that Governor Barnett actually had no plan at all, tempers began to flare. Angry words and threats were exchanged. The governor was "like a lion in a cage" and became abusive of individual board members. M. M. Roberts had to calm him down more than once, and one trustee had to be physically restrained from advancing toward the governor during a particularly acrimonious exchange. Another board member became so distraught that he had to be given emergency medical attention and had to spend the night in the hospital. When the discussion turned to the possibility of contempt citations, both Governor Barnett and M. M. Roberts again downplayed the significance of the charge. "Forget it, contempt means nothing!" said Barnett. "They won't do anything to you, just don't let the word 'contempt' worry you."[48]

During that frantic session the trustees searched for and found an alternative to compliance or contempt. On September 4, the board had assumed the sole authority to act on the application of James Meredith to shield Chancellor Williams and other university officials from the repercussions they might suffer if they integrated the school. At that medical center meeting the board members considered extending the shield to protect themselves from contempt. If the board had the power to dispossess the registrar of his authority to register James Meredith, it had the power, they reasoned, to confer that authority upon someone else. The board could designate the governor registrar of the university and invest in him the sole and exclusive authority to act on Meredith's application. That stratagem had already been considered among Barnett's advisers. It was brought before the board inadvertently when Ray Izard said to Governor Barnett in frustration, "We'll let you do it. We'll let you reject him."[49]

Some board members were ready to vote for Meredith's admission Wednesday night when they realized that Governor Barnett had no legal or logical plan for keeping him out. But because it was late and everyone was so distraught, they decided to wait until the next day. When the board convened the following morning, September 20, President Tubb announced that Meredith would be on the campus later that day to register. A motion was made to admit him. In anticipation of such a motion Tally Riddell, who was in the university hospital, had drafted a statement explaining why he was voting to enroll Meredith and authorized Tubb to cast his vote. Riddell also authorized Jobe to read his statement and release it to the press. When M. M. Roberts saw Riddell's statement, he became angry and agitated and tried to persuade Jobe to destroy it. Jobe refused to do so. After reading the statement to the board, he released it to the press. But the motion to admit Meredith was still defeated, by one vote. After conducting some routine business, the board recessed for lunch.[50]

Shortly after the noon break began, Governor Barnett called the board office and told Jobe that he was going to meet Meredith on the campus later that afternoon. He wanted the board to name him registrar with the authority to act on Meredith's application. The board hurriedly reconvened to act upon Governor Barnett's request. Board members were also advised that Meredith had been tried and convicted, in absentia, of false voter registration earlier that morning and might be arrested in Oxford.[51]

The trustees talked about flying up to Oxford to see that Meredith was allowed to register. Instead they adopted by a vote of nine to one, with Verner Holmes casting the dissenting vote, M. M. Roberts's motion to transfer to "Honorable Ross Barnett, the Governor of the State of Mississippi," the "authority, right, and discretion of this Board to act upon all matters pertaining" to James Meredith and the University of Mississippi. As that motion was being debated, Governor Barnett was already on his way to Oxford. He carried with him a Hinds County arrest warrant for Meredith on the false voter registration charges. He also had another injunction, issued earlier that morning by a Hinds County justice of the peace, barring Meredith's admission: "It is against the public policy of the state of Mississippi as well as its laws for a colored person to be admitted as a student at said institution and his enrollment and entry therein would be in violation of the laws of the state of Mississippi."[52]

That injunction ordered the board of trustees to carry out a public policy which they and university officials had sworn under oath did not exist. It no longer mattered, however, because by mid-afternoon on September 20, 1962, the board of trustees had transferred its authority over the University of Mississippi to the state's political power structure. To keep it, the board would have had to defy Governor Barnett in a public confrontation.

—Eleven—

The Meredith Crisis: ЯƎVƎN

Yes I said NEVER, *but not to myself, never to myself.*
—Thomas Tubb
President, Board of Trustees

On Thursday afternoon, September 20, 1962, James Meredith and a small escort of federal marshals arrived on the Ole Miss campus and were led through a noisy but not unruly crowd of students to a small auditorium where Governor Barnett and Robert Ellis sat at a table. Following an exchange of friendly greetings Governor Barnett asked, "Which of you gentlemen is Mr. Meredith?" Meredith identified himself. Barnett then read a declaration of interposition which, he claimed, allowed him to interpose himself as governor between an unlawful dictate of the federal government and the implementation of that dictate in the sovereign state of Mississippi. Then, on the basis of the authority vested in him by the board of trustees, Governor Barnett denied James Meredith admission to the University of Mississippi. Following another brief but polite exchange, Meredith and his escort left the campus and returned to Memphis.[1]

After what appeared to be a victorious confrontation, Governor Barnett and a few insiders who had accompanied him to Oxford held a celebration in the Alumni House. One of those celebrants was Thomas Turner. As he and the governor were enjoying the moment of triumph Turner asked, "Ross, how far are you going to go with this thing?" The governor asked how far Turner would go, and Turner responded, "I'd make them point a gun at me and tell me to move over. Then I'd move over and say come on in." The governor said, "That's exactly how far I'm going." Everybody laughed.[2] Though spoken in jest during an unguarded moment, Governor Barnett unwittingly scripted the scenario he would later suggest in seriousness as a peaceful resolution to a deepening crisis.

Because Meredith had now officially been denied admission, Chancellor John D. Williams, Dean A. B. Lewis, and Robert Ellis were technically in contempt; they were ordered to appear in federal court in Meridian the next day to show cause why they should not be found in contempt. The three university officials were represented by attorney Fred Smith, a brother of board member R. B. Smith. On Friday morning they stopped at Jackson on their way to the hearing in Meridian. While Chancellor Williams, Fred Smith, and several other lawyers were preparing their defense in a downtown Jackson law office, Governor Barnett appeared. He pleaded with the chancellor to stand firm and if necessary to go to jail. Barnett told Williams that he would double his salary if he would defy the court order. Chancellor Williams declined even to discuss any further resistance, and the matter was dropped.[3]

Later that afternoon Judge Sidney Mize dismissed the contempt charges against university officials, because they had been divested of the authority to act on Meredith's application. Still later in the day, a three-judge panel in Hattiesburg issued contempt citations against the board of trustees and ordered the board to appear in New Orleans on September 24 to show cause why they should not be held in contempt. University officials were also ordered to appear with the board in New Orleans.[4]

The news that the board had been cited for contempt raised the anxiety level among Governor Barnett's counselors. Some had already advised the governor to vacate the existing board and appoint a more stalwart group. On Saturday, September 22, the day after the trustees had been ordered to New Orleans, Governor Barnett huddled with his advisors at the Governor's Mansion for a strategy session. Since E. R. Jobe wanted the board to be represented at the conference, he called S. R. Evans in Greenwood and asked him to attend the meeting. Evans had already been invited but had declined. Jobe told Evans, "I've got to have someone at that meeting." It was essential for the board to know what Governor Barnett was planning, but there were few lines of communication open between them. When Evans finally agreed to go, a highway patrol car was dispatched to drive him to Jackson. Fifteen or twenty people attended the meeting, including William Simmons, executive secretary of the Citizens' Council. There was no focus to the meeting, only a wide-ranging, free-wheeling review of circumstances and options. The various constituencies agreed only that compliance and capitulation were "unthinkable."[5] A statement on the front page of the *Jackson Daily News* published later that afternoon may have captured the mood of the meeting. An unidentified board member, in jest perhaps, had pledged his fealty to Governor Barnett: "I am prepared to be cited for contempt, I am prepared to go to jail, I am prepared to die. And I'm even prepared to go to hell."[6]

On Sunday afternoon, the day after the strategy session in the Governor's Mansion, another very different kind of meeting was held in Jackson. William Mounger, president of Lamar Life Insurance Company, Baxter Wilson, an executive in the Mississippi Power and Light Company, Tom Hederman, publisher of the *Clarion-Ledger* and *Jackson Daily News,* and Calvin Wells, chief counsel for Lamar Life, met in Wilson's office to discuss the general state of affairs. Convinced that Mississippi's business leadership should do something, they agreed to talk to their associates and colleagues and get back together as soon as possible.[7]

On that Sunday night most of the board members were in New Orleans preparing for their Monday morning contempt hearing. There was much lobby talk in the Roosevelt Hotel. In small groups and informal discussions, board members contemplated their fate. As late as Sunday night a few trustees remained adamant and vowed to go to jail before they would vote to admit Meredith. The next morning in federal court the trustees were told the plain facts: if they did not direct the University of Mississippi to enroll Meredith, they would be removed from office, fined, imprisoned, and replaced by court-appointed members who would order Meredith's admission. The court allowed a fifteen-minute recess for consultation between clients and attorneys.[8]

Board members delight in telling the story that during that brief recess Ira "Shine" Morgan, who had a slight hearing impairment, asked his counsel to verify what he thought he had heard: "Did I hear that Judge say that if we didn't let Meredith in Ole Miss that he was going to fine us?"

"That's right, Shine."

"And that he would send us to jail?"

"Yes."

"And that he would kick us off the Board and put people on who would let him in."

"That's right, Shine."

"Now, let me get this straight. That judge said he was going to kick us off the Board and put people on who would let Meredith in, if we didn't vote to let him go to Ole Miss, and that he was going to fine us and put us in jail!"

"That's right, Shine, and he gave you fifteen minutes to make up your mind."

Said Shine, "Wonder why he gave us so much time!"[9]

After the recess, board president Thomas Tubb informed the court that the board had voted unanimously to register Meredith at 2:00 P.M. the next day in Jackson. The board was polled in the court room, and each member present voted yes. The one absent member, polled by telephone, also agreed.[10]

Realizing that the board's decision would excite the public, William Mounger and Calvin Wells directed the management of WLBT and WJDX, which were owned by Lamar Life, to "tone down" their editorials. At a meeting at the medical center Monday night, Mounger, Wilson, and Wells were joined by Ed Brunini, Bob Herrin, Joe Latham, and one or two other Jackson businessmen. All the men agreed that the board had no other choice, but all were concerned about the repercussions. They decided to call other businessmen across the state and invite them to a private meeting in Jackson to discuss the crisis they feared would lead to massive violence. They also made plans to meet again the next night.[11]

Just before eight o'clock Monday night, Robert Kennedy called Governor Barnett to arrange for Meredith's registration the next day. The governor was astounded that the board had voted unanimously. He told Kennedy, "That's really shocking to me, I heard it a little while ago. . . . I'm surprised at that really. They were so firm about it two days ago. They changed their minds mighty quick."[12]

If Governor Barnett was surprised by the quick capitulation of certain board members, Verner Holmes was incensed by it. "I was tempted," he said, "to get up in court and say this is a vote of the Board that I will not go along with. . . . I'm glad I didn't, but I was really mad at the way that [those] who got us in trouble about-faced so easily and so fast." "You know," he bemused, "had I been a politician, and was going to run for something, I would have gotten up right then and let them put me in jail for a few days. . . . And I'd have probably beat Paul Johnson for governor [in 1963]."[13]

Governor Barnett was so upset by the board's action that he could not carry on a coherent conversation with Kennedy and frequently interrupted their talk to confer with his advisors. Meredith's safety was uppermost in Kennedy's mind, and he pressed the governor for assurance that state authorities would maintain order. The governor finally ended the conversation: "I am in a big hurry here now. I appreciate your calling. I will let you know tomorrow whether or not I can advise you of our proceeding and . . ." Kennedy interrupted, "And work out his protection?" Barnett answered, "I will let you know what our proceedings will be." Kennedy closed, "Thank you, Governor."[14]

Robert Kennedy's fabled skill for problem solving failed him in the Meredith crisis. Both President Kennedy and the attorney general were extremely reluctant to use federal troops to force integration. But, "as smart as they were," J. P. Coleman observed, "they let Ross Barnett drive them . . . into a corner where they finally had to [use troops] anyway."[15] Robert Kennedy agreed with that assessment but used another metaphor:

> What I was trying to avoid, basically, was having to send troops and trying to avoid having a federal presence in Mississippi. In my judgement, what [Barnett] was trying to accomplish was the avoidance of integration at the University of Mississippi, number one. And if he couldn't do that, to be forced to do it by our heavy hand; and his preference was with troops. . . . He had people pulling and pushing him from so many different directions that I think he just got himself into a bigger and bigger box. He eventually pulled me in with him.[16]

If the use of troops was to be avoided and if Kennedy was to prevent Barnett from pulling him into the box, it had to be done by Tuesday, September 25. After that, the drama had to be played out to its conclusion.

Tuesday was a busy day for the board of trustees, Governor Barnett, James Meredith, the Justice Department, and the legislature. A resolution calling for the board to resign was drafted that day in the legislature, but it was not actually introduced. One representative had to be forcibly restrained from proposing a resolution of secession. The legislature did, however, summon Robert Ellis to a committee hearing at 2:00 P.M., the hour that had been set for the registration of Meredith in the Woolfolk state office building.[17]

On Tuesday morning as board members were returning to Jackson from their New Orleans court appearance, they saw that a large crowd had gathered at the Woolfolk building and were informed that Governor Barnett's emissaries occupied the board office. When Thomas Tubb learned that the board office had been commandeered, he instructed E. R. Jobe to tell the board members to meet him in the restaurant at the Sun-N-Sand, a motel across the street from the Woolfolk building. Back on Mississippi soil, under threat of imprisonment, meeting in a motel coffee shop and with two members absent, the board of trustees reaffirmed its unanimous vote to admit James Meredith to the University of Mississippi. But the board missed its last chance to prevent a riot. Tubb explained: "The worst mistake that was made was made by me that day. . . . John Doar [of the Justice Department] called me and wanted to know if we could bring the registrar to the . . . federal building so Meredith could be admitted there. . . . That's unusual, I said. We've got enough pressure and cussing now, and I don't think the Board ought to be imposed with doing any irregular thing, they would condemn us all over Mississippi for doing that." Doar answered, "Well, I was just trying to make it easy."[18]

After they reaffirmed their vote to admit Meredith, the board members walked across Lamar Street, through the parking lot, to the south entrance of the Woolfolk building. As they crossed Lamar Street the taunting began. The crowd knew who they were, because their names and pictures had been in all the papers. For a week the press had speculated about their vote, and all of Mississippi had awaited it. The waiting was over, and the board had voted to integrate Ole Miss. The unthinkable, the "it won't ever happen in Mississippi," was going to happen because these men walking across this street, through this crowd had voted to let it happen.

Verner Holmes still remembers that historic stroll. As he and the others walked through the crowd, one or two at a time (they were afraid to walk in one group), several people cursed him. Others kicked dirt on him as he passed by. He remembers that some in the crowd spit on him—a mean, surly gesture, intended not to soil him but to insult him. Even more unnerving were those who stood silent and leered at him and the others as they walked by. That crowd was only a few words and gestures away from being a mob. There would be several such assemblies in Mississippi over the next five days.[19]

When the trustees finally reached the board office they found it overrun with legislators, politicians who had been close to Barnett from the beginning of the Meredith crisis, a few of the governor's counselors, highway patrolmen, and the media. When Jobe walked into his private office he found Governor Barnett sitting at his desk, talking on the telephone.[20] By then it was 1:25 P.M. and the governor was talking to Robert Kennedy, who had just informed him that Meredith was on his way to the Woolfolk building to register. Governor Barnett was evasive about what could happen when Meredith arrived. He told the attorney general that a large crowd had gathered around the building. That made Kennedy uneasy. He would not let Meredith be put at risk.[21]

Burke Marshall then talked to Thomas Tubb and Charles Clark. Tubb told Marshall that the registrar was being detained in a legislative hearing and that the committee "would use police if necessary to prevent him from leaving the room where he was being questioned." Charles Clark advised Marshall that Meredith would have to be at the board office within the next half hour or so because the board would "stick to the letter of the court's order," which required that Meredith be at the board office by 2:00 P.M. to register. If Meredith was not there by that time, Clark said, he would have to "be registered during regular office hours at Oxford at some time in the future." Marshall then asked Judge Elbert Tuttle to extend the time for Meredith's registration. Tuttle did so, but the attorney general was still concerned for Meredith's safety. At four o'clock Kennedy called Barnett back and again pressed him for assurance that Meredith would be protected and that state police would maintain order. Governor Barnett gave his assurance that everything was under control.[22]

After those assurances, Kennedy directed John Doar and Chief U.S. Marshal James McShane to escort Meredith to the Woolfolk building. When they arrived about 4:30 P.M., they were led through the crowd to the board office. A Barnett aide rapped sharply on the closed door. The governor appeared and again asked, this time for the television cameras, "Which of you gentlemen is Mr. Meredith?" After Meredith identified himself, the governor again read a proclamation denying him admission to the university. He added that he did so politely. The federal officials, mocking the governor, agreed to leave politely. As they walked down the corridor Governor Barnett called out, in a practiced afterword, "You'll come see me at the Mansion." He turned back into the crowded board room amid cheers, rebel yells, shouts of "Yea Ross," and the popular strains of his theme song, "Roll with Ross."[23]

Most people in that milling crowd of two thousand were lost in the emotion of the moment. Most had come to boo the board, or to cry for another cause that was lost. A few had come to see history in the making. Emma Holmes had defied the sternest admonition of her board-member husband not to come, so determined was she to stand once in the eye of history. James Meredith also recognized the significance of that moment. As he and his federal escort were leaving the Woolfolk building their car stopped at a traffic light, and Meredith saw the impact of his challenge to the closed society.

> Just as the light was about to change, Marshal McShane asked me if those were some of my friends, indicating a group of six or seven Negroes standing on the corner. I suppose they had been waving at us, but I hadn't seen them. I waved at them as we pulled away from the light. They were all common folk, my people, maids still in uniform and common laborers, but . . . the pride they displayed [was] overwhelming. This is what I was fighting for, and I had my reward in the brief seconds that I saw my unknown friends on that corner.[24]

Early the next morning, September 26, Burke Marshall called Tom Watkins, one of Governor Barnett's most trusted advisors, for help with some resolution to the crisis. Watkins agreed that the "matter had gone too far" and told Marshall that "if there is to be any school integration in Mississippi it would have to be done forcibly." Watkins suggested that on the "next effort to escort Meredith into the University," federal officials "should 'gently' attempt to push the Governor aside" but "should use 'the mildest kind of force.'" "This would make the Governor's point," Watkins explained, "and give him an out because the federal government would have forcibly brought about desegregation." Marshall passed that information on to McShane and Doar, who put the thesis to a quick test.[25]

When Meredith and his escort arrived at the university later that morning, they were blocked by Lieutenant Governor Paul Johnson and a phalanx of highway patrolmen. Barnett had remained in Jackson in case Meredith tried to register at the board office. Doar and McShane had been instructed to "gently" muscle their way through; not privy to the plan, Johnson jostled both men. That celebrated confrontation was a ridiculous pantomime. The Ole Miss student newspaper seemed puzzled by the "comic elbowing and shoving." James Meredith enjoyed the scene and later admitted, "I could not pass up this golden opportunity to get in a little elbowing." After a few minutes McShane doubled up his fist, shook it in the face of the lieutenant governor, and said (or perhaps asked), "You understand that we have got to break through." Apparently Johnson did not understand or, more likely, did not want to be remembered as the "one who stepped aside." "The Little General," as Meredith called him, balled up his fist and shook it at McShane. When all the fist-shaking and shoving were over, Doar, McShane, and Meredith left Oxford and returned to Memphis. Then the telephones started ringing.[26]

Burke Marshall called Watkins and asked him what went wrong. Watkins explained that the federal authorities "had not used enough force." How much is enough force, Marshall asked? Watkins suggested that the next escort should include "25 marshals with side arms." Marshall agreed to send Meredith back to the campus the next day with an escort of twenty-five armed marshals, "if it were clearly understood that the resistance to this amount of force would be token." Watkins told Marshall that he would talk to the governor and get back with him.[27]

Over the next several hours a most bizarre haggle ensued. It was first agreed that the lead marshal would draw his gun, but Governor Barnett later decided that show of force was not sufficient. Under the next plan, the lead marshal would draw his gun and the other marshals would slap their holsters as if ready to draw. That was acceptable, at first. But Governor Barnett began to have second thoughts, which he explained to the attorney general: "General, I was under the impression that they were all going to draw their guns. This could be very embarrassing. We got a big crowd here and if one pulls his gun and we all turn it would be very embarrassing. Isn't it possible to have them all pull their guns? . . . They must all pull their guns. Then they should point their guns at us and then we could step aside." As this haggling continued, Robert Kennedy pressed the governor for a guarantee that he would keep the peace and protect Meredith and the marshals. When Barnett wavered, Kennedy called the whole deal off and directed McShane and Doar not to take Meredith to the campus Thursday afternoon. He told Governor Barnett that they would try again the following week, maybe Monday or Tuesday.[28]

After this impasse developed, President John Kennedy decided to call Governor Barnett on Saturday morning in an effort to resolve the Meredith crisis peacefully. The affable young president from Massachusetts and the wily old governor of Mississippi had a pleasant talk. But Kennedy assured Barnett that he would use all the resources of his office to carry out the court order. The governor explained to the president that Tom Watkins was at that very moment trying to work out a plan to resolve the situation. Just as the conversation ended without any agreement except to keep talking, Barnett added, "Appreciate your interest in our poultry program."[29]

Within less than an hour the president and the governor were back on the telephone. Kennedy called Barnett back to discuss a proposal—a "hidden ball trick"—that Tom Watkins had just made to the attorney general. The president put Robert Kennedy on the line to explain the plan. Federal authorities would announce that Meredith was going to the university campus on Monday, October 1. On the basis of that information, both Governor Barnett and Lieutenant Governor Johnson would be at Oxford to block his admission. In the meantime Meredith would actually go to Jackson, where he would be registered in the board office. Governor Barnett could claim that the Kennedys had misled him. President Kennedy even agreed to let Barnett scold him in the sternest language if that would serve his political interest in Mississippi. With Meredith registered, Barnett would then declare that the battle was lost and would allow Meredith to attend the university. Governor Barnett was enthusiastic about the proposal and saw it as a solution to the impasse.[30]

To President Kennedy the one remaining but most important consideration was Meredith's safety. He pressed Governor Barnett for a commitment that Mississippi law enforcement officers would keep the peace at the time of Meredith's enrollment and during his continued attendance, or at least as long as it was considered necessary. Barnett equivocated. The president pressed harder. Barnett began backing off, and again asked for a cooling-off period:

> *President:* Now as I understand it, Governor, you will do everything you can to maintain law and order.
> *Governor:* I'll do everything in my power to maintain order.
> *President:* Right.
> *Governor:* We don't want any shooting.
> *President:* I understand. Now, Governor, what about . . . can you maintain this order?
> *Governor:* Well, I don't know. That's what I am worried about. I don't know whether I can or not. I couldn't have [Thursday] afternoon. . . . There were men in there with trucks and shot guns. . . . They were just enraged. You don't understand the situation down here. . . . Will you be willing to wait a while and let the people cool off on the whole thing?
> *President:* How long?
> *Governor:* Would you make a statement to the effect, Mr. President, that under the circumstances existing in Mississippi that there will be bloodshed . . . you want to protect the life of James Meredith and all other people and under the circumstances at this [time?] it just wouldn't be fair to him and others to try to register him.
> *President:* At what time would it be fair?
> *Governor:* I don't know . . . we could wait . . . it might be in two or three weeks . . . it might cool off a little.
> *President:* Would you undertake to register him in two weeks?
> *Governor:* Well, you know I can't undertake to register him myself.
> *President:* I see.[31]

That conversation again left the president uneasy. He now doubted the governor's commitment to a civilian solution and, more important, his ability to maintain order. At 5:00 P.M. Mississippi time, Governor Barnett called the president back to assure him that the diversion plan was the best possible solution to the situation and that he and Lieutenant Governor Johnson would see that the highway patrol maintained law and order. Governor Barnett convinced President Kennedy of his resolve to keep his end of the deal. Satisfied and relieved, the president halted the contingency plan for calling up the National Guard and federal troops. But Assistant Attorney General Norbert A. Schlei kept working on the mobilization orders and took the papers home with him. He had a feeling they might be needed later that night or the next day.[32]

While President Kennedy and Governor Barnett were working out the details of the "hidden ball trick," about one hundred businessmen and women were meeting informally and secretly in Jackson on Saturday morning. They had come to that clandestine meeting in response to telegrams and calls from William Mounger, Ed Brunini, and the small group of Jackson businessmen who had met several times over the past week or ten days. Those men and women represented the power structure in Mississippi, but they had waited too long to influence the course of events and prevent a violent confrontation between federal and state authorities. A few of them knew of the secret talks between federal and state officials, but they kept that information within the smallest circle. Some had sent telegrams to Governor Barnett urging him to comply with the court order and assuring him that they would publicly support his decision. Their advice was prefaced by the disclaimer that they too believed in segregation and praised the governor for his heroic stand in its defense. The telegrams were so delicately worded that their impact might have been lost, and probably was.[33]

Throughout Saturday afternoon and into the early evening, Governor Barnett spent most of his time trying to persuade his counselors to accept the agreement he had made with the president. By game time, however, he had lost his own resolve to honor it. At the Ole Miss–Kentucky football game that night, Governor Barnett was called to speak at halftime. As the governor spoke, the world's largest rebel flag unfurled to the stirring strains of "Dixie." The stands were washed in a sea of red and blue rebel flags. On that haunting night those flags were more than a symbol of college spirit; they were a political statement.

Governor Barnett, known fondly as Ole Ross, was one of Mississippi's last great stump speakers. His right fist clinched, rising and falling, circling in rhythm with the words, Ole Ross proclaimed in his raspy, throaty voice as he stood at the fifty yard line:

I love Mississippi . . . .
I love her people . . . .
I love her customs . . . .[34]

The words ricocheted through Mississippi's Memorial Stadium as forty thousand people in thunderous ovation hailed their leader and lofted their flags into a night sky. Some have said they heard a "heil" here and there among the crowd. Verner Holmes "was ashamed of that demonstration and frightened by it." Several other people who were in the crowd, but not a part of it, have admitted that images of the Nuremberg rallies flashed through their minds.[35]

While Governor Barnett's halftime speech was thrilling to many, it was puzzling to those who had inside information. After the game J. P. Coleman talked briefly with former governor Hugh White as they were leaving the stadium. White asked, "J. P. do you know what's going on about this Meredith business?" Coleman replied that he did not know what the situation was at that point. Governor White surprised Coleman by saying, "I don't understand Ross making that speech because I know that he has already agreed to admit Meredith."[36]

After the ballgame Governor Barnett called the Justice Department. His call was forwarded to the attorney general, who had gone home. Governor Barnett told Kennedy that he wanted to call off the deal. Kennedy was angered by that unexpected turn of events and accused the governor of breaking his word to the president. The two men ended the conversation amicably, Barnett agreeing to keep working on the situation. The governor also promised to call Kennedy early Sunday morning to let him know if the situation changed during the night. President Kennedy was called at the White House and told that the deal was off. He reluctantly signed the documents federalizing the Mississippi National Guard and authorized Cyrus Vance, secretary of the army, to send troops to Oxford and the university if necessary.[37]

Almost twenty years later, in 1979, J. P. Coleman and Verner Holmes spent two days and a night at Ole Miss for a joint interview to discuss those troubled times. Coleman had become chief judge of the U.S. Court of Appeals for the Fifth Circuit, and Verner Holmes was just beginning his twenty-fourth year on the board of trustees. They were on the campus of the university where they had met almost fifty years earlier. At that time, Coleman had told Holmes that he was going to run for governor some day, and Holmes had given his solemn pledge of support. Elected governor in 1955, Coleman had appointed Holmes to the board of trustees of institutions of higher learning in 1956.

As the recollections proceeded step by step through the Meredith crisis to Saturday night, September 29, 1962, Judge Coleman paused, leaned his massive frame back in an easy chair, sighed and said, as if it were the first time it had occurred to him, "Verner, you know, had I been Secretary of the Army [President Kennedy had offered him that appointment], I would have had to sign the orders to send troops to Ole Miss, and although they had to be sent, there wasn't any question about that, I couldn't have signed it."[38]

On Sunday morning, September 30, Governor Barnett called Attorney General Kennedy. That disjointed conversation dragged on for thirty minutes, during which Governor Barnett made one last desperate effort to postpone the whole affair. Failing at postponement, he and Tom Watkins proposed another mock confrontation between federal and state authorities. Their suggestion was fraught with such potential for calamity that Robert Kennedy finally rejected it. The tone of that conversation also reflects a deepening distrust between the principle negotiators:

> *Governor:* We will have about 175 or 180 highway patrolmen in there—unarmed; no guns, no sticks of any kind. We will have quite a number of sheriffs unarmed—probably 75 or 100 deputy sheriffs. Then they will form this second line. The highway patrolmen will form the first line; the sheriffs the next. The sheriffs will have probably 200 or 300 soldiers behind them. No one will be armed. I will be in the front line and when Meredith presents himself, I'll do like I did before. I will read a proclamation denying him entrance. I will tell the people of Mississippi now that I want peace and we must have no violence, no bloodshed. When you draw the guns, I will then tell the people. In other words, we will step aside and you can walk in.
>
> *Kennedy:* I think it is silly going through this whole facade of your standing there; our people drawing guns; your stepping aside; to me it is dangerous and I think this has gone beyond the stage of politics, and you have a responsibility to the people of that State and to the people of the United States. This is a real disservice. . . .
>
> *Governor:* I have said so many times—we couldn't have integration and I have got to do something. I can't just walk back.
>
> *Kennedy:* You can say the National Guard has been called up and you don't want to have the people from the state of Mississippi responsible for placing Mr. Meredith in the institution and therefore you are going to step aside on this.

Governor: I'll say words to that effect. But I have to be confronted with your troops.

. . . .

Kennedy: The President is going on TV tonight [Sunday]. He is going through the statement he had with you last night. He will have to say he called up the National Guard; that you had an agreement to permit Meredith to go to Jackson to register, and your lawyer, Mr. Watkins, said this was satisfactory. . . .

Governor: That won't do at all.

Kennedy: You broke your word to him.

Governor: You don't mean the President is going to say that tonight?

Kennedy: Of course he is; you broke your word; now you suggest we send in troops, fighting their way through a barricade.

Governor: Don't say that. Please don't mention it.

Kennedy: The President has to say that. You said we would fly him to Jackson and register him while you had everyone in Oxford. . . .

Governor: Why don't you fly in this afternoon; please let us treat what we say as confidential?

Kennedy: You talk to Watkins and call me back this afternoon. I have discussed this with you before; I want to know specifically the plan you have and how it is going to work. I want to maintain law and order.[39]

Governor Barnett was startled that his conversation with federal authorities had been taped and that President Kennedy would reveal those negotiations on national television. Bobby Kennedy realized that he had finally found the governor's weak spot, and he took advantage of Barnett's fear of exposure. Tom Watkins and Burke Marshall quickly worked out a plan to bring Meredith to the campus later that afternoon.

Colonel T. B. Birdsong, chief of the Mississippi highway patrol, then talked with Edwin Guthman from the attorney general's office to arrange for Meredith's arrival. Since university officials were not expecting Meredith to return to the campus until Monday or Tuesday, Tom Watkins asked Burke Marshall to inform Ole Miss officials that Meredith was coming in that afternoon. Anxious to get one more assurance that state authorities would maintain order, Marshall replied, "We are not going to put Meredith in until the situation is physically stabilized." Watkins told Marshall that Birdsong had already been sent to Oxford and he assumed the situation was stable. Marshall then agreed to call university officials and tell them that Meredith would be on the campus within an hour or two.[40]

A few minutes after three o'clock on Sunday afternoon, Hugh Clegg answered the downstairs telephone in the chancellor's residence at the university. It was Burke Marshall. Chancellor Williams, Dean of Students L. L. Love, and Clegg, Williams's administrative assistant, were making preparations for Meredith's arrival which they thought would be on Monday or Tuesday. The three men were startled when Marshall told them that federal marshals would bring Meredith to the campus within the hour. Clegg pleaded for a delay, saying that the university could not get ready for Meredith's arrival on such short notice, but Marshall insisted, "They are coming this afternoon." A short time later he called back to announce, "Mr. Clegg, the highway patrolmen have just admitted the U.S. marshals on to your campus." After a brief discussion with Chancellor Williams, Clegg went to his office in the Lyceum. Unaware of the deal between Barnett and Kennedy, Clegg called Governor Barnett to tell him that federal marshals were already on the campus and that Meredith was on his way. A secretary in the governor's office told Clegg that Barnett had gone fishing and would not be back until Monday.[41]

Through the late afternoon and early evening a milling crowd of students gathered in front of the Lyceum building, which had been cordoned off by marshals and other federal officials. Meredith was to register in the Lyceum the next morning. The crowd, gradually augmented by "outsiders," had grown larger and more restive by nightfall. At 7:30 P.M. Governor Barnett announced on a statewide radio and television network that Meredith was on the campus. He explained that he had been forced to yield to the "armed forces and oppressive power" of the United States and that he had conceded to Meredith's admission in order to prevent violence and bloodshed. His speech was brilliantly crafted. He surrendered without saying so.[42]

After the governor's remarks, federal officials became increasingly uneasy about the potential for a large-scale riot. The crowd was no longer hurling epithets; they were throwing brickbats, lead pipes, and Molotov cocktails. A bulldozer headed toward the line of marshals around the Lyceum. Tires on army trucks were slashed and canvas truck tops set afire. In the wake of sporadic gunfire, rumors circulated through the mob that a highway patrolman had been killed. At approximately eight o'clock, just moments before President Kennedy went on national television to announce that Meredith was safely on the campus and would register the next morning, the crowd surged toward the marshals who immediately gave the order to fire tear gas. As the marshals fired the gas into the surging mob, several people— including some highway patrolmen—were hit by the canisters and suffered fractures and broken bones. The pep rally atmosphere was gone. Most of the college kids, who had just come to see what was happening, left with it. Only the real resisters, the true believers, remained to fight what Willie Morris has called an echo of the last battle of the Civil War.[43]

As the battle raged on the Ole Miss campus, Hugh Clegg left the Lyceum and drove to his residence to telephone several people: members of the secret alumni committee that had been formed to help keep the university open; the university attorney; other staff members; the student infirmary; and the governor, who had not gone fishing after all. Colonel Birdsong had already told Barnett about the riot. After his conversation with the governor, Clegg went to the chancellor's home. The veranda on the south side of the residence overlooked the grove where the riot was concentrated. Clegg and Williams stood there and watched the rioters deface and defame the university. Clegg stayed about thirty minutes before going home.[44]

As the rioting continued into the night, Chancellor Williams called his friend Charles Fair, a board member who lived at Louisville. Fair in turn called Thomas Tubb at West Point. Both men responded out of their esteem for Chancellor Williams and their love for Ole Miss. Tubb recalled years later: "Charlie called me and said they've got a riot at the University, and the Chancellor needs us, let's go. We asked no further questions, I got in my car and we met at Eupora. We were up there by midnight." Before leaving West Point Tubb telephoned Verner Holmes at McComb. Holmes told Tubb he would catch the next northbound train and would be at Oxford early the next morning.[45]

After Tubb talked to Holmes he called S. R. Evans, a board member who lived in Greenwood. Evans already knew about the riot. His son, a student at the university medical center in Jackson, had called moments earlier to tell his father of the situation at Ole Miss and to admonish him not to go to the university. The senior Evans had agreed that he would not. When Tubb's call came, Evans was reluctant to go to Oxford. The conversation, as Evans recalled it, was pointed and poignant: "Tubb said the Chancellor just called and said this thing is out of hand up there and he wanted some Board members, will you go? I said, I'll go." Evans got up out of bed, dressed, arranged for his wife to stay with friends, and drove to Oxford.[46]

Tubb, Fair, and Evans arrived at the chancellor's residence about midnight, and Chancellor Williams called Hugh Clegg to join them. Evans remembered that "we spent the night there. Never closed our eyes." Clegg wrote of that long night's vigil: "We all [sat] on the Chancellor's porch watching the sickening scene from a hundred yards away. Automobiles were afire. We feared the Lyceum Building would be burned." One of the gloomy men on the chancellor's porch said, "I'm afraid that there goes the University." But "just when things seemed the gloomiest," the first contingent of soldiers moved onto the campus. Clegg remembered that "we almost shouted with joy." The situation stabilized gradually, and at 6:15 A.M. General Charles Billingsly reported that the campus was secure. Some of the rioters drifted off the campus and into the business district of Oxford, where they continued the insurrection.[47]

As the officials at the chancellor's residence talked of the causes and consequences of the Ole Miss riot, Thomas Tubb suggested that Chancellor Williams make a full report to Mississippi's congressional delegation. He particularly wanted the chancellor to talk with Senator John Stennis. Williams asked Clegg to call the delegation and invite them to the campus for a firsthand view of what had happened. After trying unsuccessfully to reach Senator Stennis, Clegg reminded Williams that James Eastland was chairman of the Senate Judiciary Committee and could personally order an investigation. At Williams's request Clegg called Senator Eastland and talked with his administrative assistant, who promised to contact the senator early the next morning.[48]

Just as day was breaking on Monday, October 1, Verner Holmes arrived on the campus. As he was walking into the Lyceum building, Holmes saw several marshals escort General Edwin Walker into the building. General Walker, a retired army officer who had commanded the federal troops during the integration of Central High School in Little Rock, had just been arrested for participating in the riot. About an hour later James Meredith, also in the company of federal marshals, came to the Lyceum. He completed a registration form, paid his fees, became the first black student admitted to Ole Miss, and hurried off to an eight o'clock history class taught by Clare Marquette.[49]

While Meredith was attending his morning classes, Hugh Clegg was holding a conference call with Mississippi's congressional delegation who had assembled in Senator Eastland's office to hear Clegg's report of the riot. University officials, and Clegg in particular, claimed that the marshals had provoked the riot. After listening to Clegg's report, Senator Eastland moved with dispatch; within forty-eight hours he had arranged for Senator Sam Ervin of North Carolina to chair a subcommittee investigation. Clegg "anxiously awaited the beginning of the full investigation" but was soon disappointed. He learned a short time later, "from an unimpeachable source," that Governor Barnett had asked Senator Eastland not to conduct an investigation. The Mississippi legislature did conduct one, however. It placed the entire blame for the Meredith crisis and the Ole Miss riot on the Kennedys and the "trigger happy marshals."[50]

Before James Meredith enrolled at Ole Miss, no other public school in Mississippi—grammar school, high school, or college—had been integrated. Everything was segregated: public parks, playgrounds, libraries, beaches, theaters, doctors' offices, lunch counters, cafes, water fountains, hospitals, hotels, motels, and even cemeteries. But the color barrier was now broken. James Meredith went on to complete his degree requirements and graduate from the University of Mississippi in August 1963. On the last day of final examinations Meredith wore a lapel pin that had been popular during the weeks before his admission. On the pin, against a black background, was one word printed in white: NEVER. Meredith wore the pin upside down.[51]

Twelve

In Defense of Yesterday, 1962–1972

It looks like we are about to lose our Southern way of life.
—M. M. Roberts
President, Board of Trustees

While James Meredith was studying for his final exams in the summer of 1963, Mississippi was in the midst of a tense Democratic primary between Lieutenant Governor Paul Johnson and former Governor J. P. Coleman. The classic slogan of that campaign, "Stand Tall with Paul," was a reminder that Paul Johnson had stood up against the federal marshals at Oxford. It was presumed that since Johnson had stood up for the white people of Mississippi, they should now "Stand Tall with Paul."[1]

Meredith, who was scheduled to graduate about the time of the Democratic primary, became something of an issue in the campaign. Earlier in the year he had made a speech that some board members considered inflammatory, and they had pressured Chancellor John D. Williams to expel him. When this effort failed, they then tried to withhold his diploma. But the board voted six to five in favor of granting Meredith his degree.[2] The Mississippi press, especially those supporting Paul Johnson, reported that all four of Coleman's appointees had voted in favor of granting Meredith his degree. It was also widely rumored during the 1963 campaign that former governor Coleman had met with Governor Barnett during the Meredith crisis and had advised Barnett to "let the 'nigger' in." Coleman's long-standing friendship with John F. Kennedy was also an issue in the Democratic primary. "Little Paul," as Johnson was affectionately known among his supporters, defeated Coleman in the primary and then faced Republican Rubel Phillips in the November general election.[3]

During the general election Phillips published transcripts of the conversations between Ross Barnett, Paul Johnson, and Robert Kennedy revealing for the first time that Barnett and Johnson had made a secret deal with Kennedy to admit Meredith, while promising publicly never to surrender. Nevertheless, the people of Mississippi believed that Paul Johnson had remained faithful to "our way of life" and elected him to the state's highest office.[4]

Few Mississippians realized, however, that the 1963 election would be the last of its kind. It was Mississippi's final lily-white campaign and the final one in which politicians would use the term "nigger" in public speeches. Four years later blacks were voting in large numbers, and seventeen blacks were elected to public office. Paul Johnson's administration marked a turning point in Mississippi's resistance to change. Like a terrible swift sword, change came to Mississippi in the 1960s, and Governor Johnson wisely, often courageously, counseled Mississippians to accept that change: "While I am governor, hate, prejudice, and ignorance will not lead Mississippi. If we must fight it will not be a rear guard defense of yesterday. It will be an all out assault on our share of tomorrow."[5]

He concluded that remarkable address by saying, "God bless everyone of you, all Mississippians, black and white, here and away from home." Governor Johnson's inaugural received high praise, but his powers of expression were greater than his powers of persuasion and many Mississippians would not give up their defense of yesterday. That was especially true of some members on the college board, which played a major role in shaping Mississippi's response to change in the 1960s. It was inevitable that Mississippi would bleed in the wake of the terrible swift sword, and the second Reconstruction. But it perhaps bled more than it had to, in part because of the policies and procedures of the board of trustees. There was a clear indication that the board would fight "a rear guard defense of yesterday" even before the governor had formed the phrase.[6]

In February 1963 Mississippi State University, which ranked seventh in the nation with a record of 21–5, won the Southeastern Conference basketball championship and a berth in the NCAA postseason tournament. In the early pairings State was scheduled to play Loyola

University of Chicago, a team with several black players. If Mississippi State played Loyola, the "unwritten law" would be broken. This "law," which prohibited Mississippi's white institutions from playing integrated teams, had been formulated after Jones County Junior College played an integrated football team in the Little Rose Bowl of 1955. It had first been invoked in 1959 to keep the Ole Miss baseball team from advancing to the NCAA tournament after it had won the SEC title. One college board member declared that athletic competition with integrated teams presented the "greatest threat" to Mississippi's way of life since Reconstruction.[7]

Mississippi State had won the SEC basketball championship in 1962 but, because of the unwritten law, did not advance to the NCAA tournament. When Mississippi State again won the championship in 1963, President Dean W. Colvard and Coach James "Babe" McCarthy announced that State would play in the post-season tournament.[8] Following Colvard's announcement, the board of trustees held a special called meeting on March 9, 1963. At that Saturday meeting M. M. Roberts offered a resolution forbidding State to play in the tournament. The motion failed. Roberts then introduced a motion to dismiss President Colvard. Following a brief and bitter exchange between several members, especially between M. M. Roberts and Verner Holmes, the board gave President Colvard a vote of confidence. Roberts and Ray Izard voted against this vote of confidence.[9]

After the meeting a disconsolate Roberts told the press, "It looks like we are about to lose our Southern way of life," and confessed that he had prayed for State to lose its last two games "because I knew we would be faced with this problem." In a last desperate effort to save "our way of life," a judge in Jones County issued an injunction prohibiting the Mississippi State basketball team from leaving the state. It was the same judge who had set aside the Supreme Court's order admitting James Meredith to Ole Miss. As soon as President Colvard was advised of the court's action, both he and Coach McCarthy left the state to prevent the injunction from being served. With President Colvard in Alabama and "Babe" McCarthy in Tennessee, both safely beyond the reach of the injunction, the team left Starkville on schedule without incident.[10]

Verner Holmes's vote to allow Mississippi State to participate in the tournament, and his spirited defense of President Colvard, became well known. Soon after the vote was taken, a cross was burned at his lodge on the Bogue Chitta River where it was believed he and his family were spending the weekend. A few weeks after the cross burning, two FBI agents informed Holmes that they had the names of the men who had burned the cross. But Holmes told the agents he did not want their names. He knew that times were changing and people would change with them.[11]

But most board members were unable or unwilling to accept the changes taking place all around them. At the beginning of that now-famous "long hot summer" of 1964, when college students from all over America came to Mississippi to conduct freedom schools and registration drives in the state's black communities, the board directed college presidents to report any suspicious-looking characters on their campuses to the governor's office. After learning that a group of civil rights workers had visited the University of Mississippi at the request of some faculty members, the board adopted a lengthy and rambling resolution drafted by M. M. Roberts which read in part:

WHEREAS, among those identified with [the] "invasion," there have appeared many individuals who have a national reputation for membership in the communist party and/or other affiliates with avowed purpose to change and overthrow the Government of the United States; and a concerted effort should be made by all Americans everywhere and especially by institutions of higher learning to avoid these dangerous movements and to support conservative constitutional government and to preserve and protect the United States of America and the State of Mississippi; and the foregoing constitutes the reason for this resolution.

NOW, THEREFORE, BE IT RESOLVED that the heads of each state institution of higher learning in Mississippi shall do everything reasonably possible . . . to protect student life from undue pressure by those engaged in activities contrary to the laws of the State of Mississippi and to the image of the citizenship of the state; and that all things be had and done which may be considered proper to eliminate development of socialistic and communistic trends among the college or university youth [and] prohibit as far as possible invasions of state institutions of higher learning by outside influence contrary to the established and well-known policies of the State of Mississippi relating to good government.[12]

The "exploding tension" of that summer also prompted the board to adopt new rules restricting the use of college facilities by the general public. Under the new regulations, which were invoked for the first time at the Ole Miss–Memphis State football game at Oxford on September 19, 1964, the parents of black football players from Memphis State were not allowed to eat in the Ole Miss commons and white cafeteria workers, who had been deputized, were directed to arrest any blacks if they attempted to use the dining facilities on the day of the game.[13]

Two days before the game, board member W. D. Guest introduced two resolutions to deal with what he deemed "a serious situation." In his first resolution Guest recommended that no new contracts be made with integrated teams unless they agreed to leave all black players, students, employees, and faculty members at home when the games were played in Mississippi. His second resolution directed Chancellor Williams not to admit any "agitators" to the Memphis State game and further directed him to tell the president of Memphis State to exclude "agitators and troublemakers" from MSU's section of the stadium also. After both resolutions were tabled, George Yarbrough, who voted against tabling the motions, then suggested that black Memphis State fans could be stopped by the highway patrol at the city limits and not allowed to enter Oxford to attend the game. No action was taken on Yarbrough's proposal, and the game was played on schedule without any problems. The parents of the black players who were turned away from the university cafeteria also left without incident.[14]

The board's resistance to change and its defense of yesterday inevitably entangled it in personnel matters. The doctrinaire members of the board were determined to prevent the appointment of professors they believed to be a threat to Mississippi's way of life. The board's antipathy for subversive professors was heightened in the fall of 1963 when James W. Silver of Ole Miss delivered his presidential address to the Southern Historical Association. Professor Silver's speech, entitled "Mississippi: The Closed Society," angered several members of the board, especially M. M. Roberts, and many other state officials. Mississippi's power structure was in nearly unanimous agreement that Silver was a threat and that he should be dismissed from the university. Following his speech the board appointed a committee, chaired by M. M. Roberts, to gather evidence that could be used to dismiss Silver from his tenured position as professor of history, a position he had held since 1936.[15]

While the board of trustees was conducting its investigation of Professor Silver—even hiring private detectives to follow him to speaking engagements throughout the country—the Mississippi legislature also took up the Silver issue. On March 25, 1964, a state representative introduced a resolution demanding Silver's dismissal and pledged himself to any course of action short of violence to oust the professor. Another legislator introduced a bill to restrict Professor Silver from speaking on certain topics and to stifle his "degrading activities." He realized that dismissal would enhance Silver's reputation in the North but avowed that should no longer be a consideration, because "it is better that he get national fame than for us to receive social death." The senator added that if the university would not fire Silver the legislature should.[16]

While the legislature was fulminating, the board considered its options in regard to Professor Silver. E. R. Jobe drafted a memorandum which included several alternatives. The board could ignore "all provocation in the hopes that all will blow over." It could place Professor Silver on involuntary retirement or relieve him of all teaching duties and assign him to other work at the university. But Jobe knew the mind of the board and the mood of the legislature, and he realized that only the dismissal of Professor Silver would satisfy either group. Consequently, he recommended that the board formally charge Silver with making provocative and inflammatory speeches calculated to increase racial tension and provoke racial violence.[17]

The board accepted his recommendation, and Jobe prepared a set of formal charges that he mailed to Professor Silver on April 27, 1964. Silver informed Jobe that his counsel would respond to the charges. On May 30, 1964, Landman Teller of Teller, Biedenharn, and Rogers, a Vicksburg law firm, wrote to inform Jobe that he had been retained by Professor Silver. Teller asked for clarification of certain matters of procedure and asked for a copy of all board policies applicable to the Silver case, together with a specification of the particular charges concerning Silver's fitness as a professor.[18]

While Teller was preparing the defense, a great deal of notoriety became attached to the board's charges against Professor Silver. On the day after Silver responded to Jobe's first letter, two student honor societies at the University of Mississippi passed a joint resolution defending academic freedom at the university. The Mortar Board and the

Omicron Delta Kappa chapters resolved: "We consider reprehensible any attempt to deny the time-honored privilege of academic freedom to any member of our faculty." And John Emmerich, the son of Oliver Emmerich, wrote to his old friend Verner Holmes from Baltimore on April 29, 1964:

> I am reading about the wolves howling after Dr. Jim Silver at Ole Miss. And if I haven't told you before, I want to tell you now that Jim Silver did more for my education at Ole Miss than all the other professors combined. He was and is one of those rare men who make a college education worth all the time and expense. We have built a closed society—if anybody needs any evidence, or should I say more evidence, of it, consider this effort to "get" Jim. . . . If we're so all-fired afraid of ideas, then it would have been just as well for Ross Barnett to have closed the University. If all we want is a glorified grammar school who can produce good football teams, the state may as well save the money.[19]

Before any final resolution was made of the charges against him, Professor Silver asked for and received a leave of absence to accept a visiting professorship at Notre Dame University. Following that year at Notre Dame, Silver did not return to the university although he wanted to very much. University officials let him know that it would be best if he did not come back to Oxford, his home for the past thirty years. Silver remained at Notre Dame for another year and then moved to the University of South Florida, where he retired in 1978. Years later, he recalled those troubled times: "I don't blame Roberts or the Board. They thought they were defending their heritage, and hell, they were." When asked how he would like to be remembered, Silver said, "I just want to be remembered as someone who helped change Mississippi."[20]

Although Professor Silver's case is the most celebrated, it is only one of many similar cases involving academic freedom at Mississippi's institutions of higher learning in the 1960s and 1970s. Among those who became the subjects of such disputes were Corrine T. Carpenter of Alcorn College; Kenneth Rainey of Jackson State; Michael Trister, George Strickler, and Russell Barrett of the University of Mississippi; W. D. Norwood, Monte Piliawsky, and Sanford Wood of the University of Southern Mississippi.[21]

The underlying cause of the difficulty between the board of trustees and liberal college professors was the board's domination in the 1960s by two or three men of extremely conservative ideology. Those board members did not just resist change; they used and manipulated board policy to promote their own ideology. In 1957, for example, the trustees adopted a policy requiring faculty members to resign if they ran for public office; that policy was reaffirmed on August 19, 1971. But on April 20, 1972, the board exempted Carl Butler from the well-established policy and allowed him to complete the spring semester while running as a candidate for Congress. Professor Butler was a conservative political science professor at Mississippi State University who was campaigning as a Republican against the Democratic incumbent, David Bowen.[22]

Perhaps an even more significant example of the manipulation of policy in defense of yesterday was the board's infamous speaker ban. Following the controversial appearance of the Reverend Henry Hitt Crane at Mississippi Southern in 1955 and the celebrated case of the Reverend Alvin Kershaw at Ole Miss the next year, the college board adopted a speaker policy that required college presidents personally to approve all outside speakers. Crane was a renowned pacifist who told the students at Southern that they could, out of conscience, refuse to go to war. Kershaw had won a large amount of money on a popular televison quiz show and had donated some of it to the NAACP. Both cases remained the topic of public discussion for several years afterward. As the college board and the state legislature became increasingly sensitive to campus speakers in the 1960s, college presidents became more and more selective in approving them. But the board did not become directly involved in approving speakers until 1966.[23]

When the board was informed that Bobby Kennedy had been invited to speak at Ole Miss on March 20, 1966, M. M. Roberts introduced a resolution declaring his appearance "an affront" to the board of trustees and demanded that the invitation be withdrawn. Though the board did not rescind Kennedy's invitation, it was prompted to adopt a more restrictive speaker policy by the appearance of Aaron Henry, state president of the NAACP, at Mississippi State University in November 1966. Henry had been invited by the Young Democrats. President William Giles initially denied the request; but after the campus newspaper denounced the ban and several faculty members expressed their displeasure, Giles reversed his decision and approved Henry's appearance. At the board meeting on November 17, President

Giles informed the trustees that he had allowed Aaron Henry to speak at Mississippi State and that Henry had also spoken at the Ole Miss law school earlier that morning. Henry's appearance at State and Ole Miss infuriated several trustees. The board adopted a policy requiring that the names of all speakers be furnished to each trustee before an invitation was extended. Individual board members would then have time to persuade, or pressure, college presidents not to approve any speakers they might personally consider undesirable. Ostensibly, the new policy was established to ensure that persons convicted of certain crimes would not be allowed to speak on college campuses in Mississippi.[24]

The new policy was first invoked by Chancellor John D. Williams when the Young Democrats invited Aaron Henry to speak at Ole Miss in May 1967. Williams announced that Henry would not be allowed to speak because he had been charged with a crime some time earlier. Following the chancellor's ruling, the Young Democrats, the Ole Miss chapter of the AAUP, and Aaron Henry filed a federal suit asking that the speaker ban be set aside as a violation of first amendment rights. The federal district court ruled that the existing policy was unconstitutional and ordered the board of trustees to draft a new speaker policy that would not inhibit the right of free speech. Following that decision the board formulated a new set of regulations, which it submitted to the court for approval.[25]

While a three-judge panel was reviewing the new speaker regulations, Earl Reynolds, a well-known Quaker pacifist, was invited to speak at the University of Mississippi. Chancellor Williams had approved his appearance. On the day that Reynolds was scheduled to speak, however, M. M. Roberts petitioned Judge J. P. Coleman of the fifth circuit for an injunction preventing the speech on campus. Coleman granted the injunction. On March 14, 1969, an armed federal marshal entered a classroom at the University of Mississippi and served Reynolds an injunction prohibiting his lecture. Reynolds and the class were startled by the intrusion of the federal marshal, but Reynolds honored the injunction and quit his speech. The Ole Miss chapter of the AAUP condemned the Reynolds incident as an intolerable breach of academic freedom which would severely and permanently damage the reputation of the university.[26]

Nine months after Reynolds was prevented from lecturing at Ole Miss, the three-judge panel rejected the board's new speaker policy, which was actually more restrictive than the policy it superseded, and promulgated its own policy. The court gave the board the option of either accepting the regulations drafted by the three-judge panel or having no regulations at all. The board accepted the court's regulations. Under the new speaker policy the college president, with the advice and consent of a campus review committee, was given the final authority to approve or disapprove outside speakers.[27] Perhaps in any other state the court's final decree would have ended the controversy over the speaker ban. Unfortunately, that was not the case in Mississippi.

On February 7, 1970, the Mississippi State University Young Democrats invited Charles Evers, the black mayor of Fayette, to speak on the campus later in the spring. President William Giles approved the request. But on March 4, Executive Secretary E. E. Thrash wrote Giles informing him that the board, by a vote of twelve to one, had directed him to withdraw the invitation to Evers. Verner Holmes cast the lone vote against overruling Giles. The board cited Evers's involvement in a student demonstration at Alcorn in 1966 as the reason for its decision. President Giles, with the approval of the Mississippi State Speakers Review Committee, disregarded the board's directive and approved the request to bring Evers to the campus. Two days later the board of trustees, acting on the insistence of M. M. Roberts, invoked its power as the governing authority of Mississippi State University and ordered Giles to disallow Mayor Evers from speaking on his campus. President Giles obeyed the order and withdrew his approval of Evers's speech. The next day, claiming that Roberts and the board of trustees had acted "in open and complete contempt of the dignity and authority" of the federal district court, the Young Democrats filed a motion asking for injunctive relief and a contempt citation against the board of trustees and certain university officials. On March 9 Judge William Keady granted a restraining order permitting Evers to speak but declined to issue contempt citations against Roberts or the board of trustees.[28]

During this heated controversy President Giles received a telephone call from M. M. Roberts, who was extremely angry at Giles and distraught over the prospect that Charles Evers was going to speak at Mississippi State. Roberts became increasingly upset as the conversation proceeded. He eventually lost his composure and cursed the president, threatening to see that Giles was fired. On the day after Mayor Evers's speech at the Starkville campus, Roberts wrote a now-famous letter to the members of the board of trustees. After making very disparaging remarks about the administration at Mississippi State, Roberts noted that a luncheon for Charles Evers was scheduled and added, "I hope he smelled like Negroes usually do." In conclusion he wrote: "Somehow I wish it were so that we could clean house for those who do not understand Mississippi and its way of life, but I guess this is expecting too much of this Board. . . . Somehow, I cannot believe that Mississippi State is no longer a cow college. It is controlled by the influx of foreign ideologies, maybe city slickers." Roberts added a handwritten postscript which read: "The letter was written after some thought and registers my sincere views. We are in troubled times."[29]

About ten days after this letter was written, the board met for its regular monthly meeting, and Roberts attempted to carry out his threat against President Giles. He repeated some of the statements he had made in his letter and asked the board to dismiss Giles. In a bitter rebuttal Verner Holmes defended President Giles, arguing that the approval or disapproval of campus speakers was a decision for college presidents and not the board of trustees. Holmes reminded board members that Giles was under court order and had no alternative but to obey the law. Holmes's reasoned but impassioned assessment convinced the trustees that any further intercession was unwise. The board then distanced itself from the speaker ban controversy. It took no action on Roberts's proposal to dismiss President Giles.[30]

Long after the speaker ban controversy had subsided, President Giles remembered the students—the Young Democrats—who had sued him and the board of trustees: "I had a lot fonder feeling for those young people who sued me than they ever guessed I did. [I] would have been part of a conspiracy had I called them in and said, Look, fellows, you can go to court and do this and that. But you could stand by and approve of what they were doing silently. But you see, they never could know this."[31] They do now, if they have read this far.

The speaker ban and indeed many of the board's other policies during the 1960s and 1970s were shaped to a great extent by the board's obsessive fear of campus violence and its presumption that integration would lead inevitably to chaos and disorder. That presumption was confirmed, in the minds of some trustees at least, by the violence that occurred at Ole Miss during the Southern Literary Festival in the spring of 1965. When a biracial group of students from Tougaloo College arrived on the university campus, they were jeered and taunted by Ole Miss students. Eventually, their car was overturned and damaged extensively. The whole affair lasted only a few minutes, but it prompted extensive commentary in the state press. A Ku Klux Klan official condemned the Ole Miss English department for sponsoring the integrated festival and claimed to have in his personal possession conclusive evidence that there was "a conspiracy to liberalize the University of Oxford [sic]."[32]

The disturbance at Ole Miss during the literary festival was followed by student unrest at Alcorn College in the spring of 1966. President John D. Boyd, who had replaced J. R. Otis during the student boycott in 1957, eventually became the focus of student complaints as well. Alcorn students asked Charles Evers, who had succeeded his brother, Medgar Evers, as the NAACP field secretary for Mississippi, to organize a demonstration against President Boyd. Although the demonstration was small and peaceful, highway patrolmen were rushed to the campus to keep order. Evers was eventually given a hearing before the board to voice the student complaints. Rather than acknowledging the legitimacy of the grievances, however, the board commended President Boyd for his handling of the demonstration and the "grave danger" it presented.[33]

There were also minor demonstrations at Mississippi Southern and Delta State in opposition to the Vietnam War, but no violence occurred on either campus. The board of trustees commended the presidents, W. D. McCain and James Ewing, for their handling of those protests. Student unrest at Ole Miss, Mississippi Valley, and Jackson State, however, was much more serious. At these institutions, the unrest was a response, indirectly at least, to the board's stubborn resistance to change, particularly M. M. Roberts's refusal to give up the defense of white supremacy and racial segregation.[34] On December 8, 1969, while serving as president of the board of trustees, Roberts made a speech at the University of Southern Mississippi that acknowledged but did not apologize for his attitudes:

But as I've gone back through the years and look back, I've said to myself really that I am a racist. Every time I read a definition I say, well,

that's me. I have no apologies for it, though. It's me. And maybe that's
the reason why we have some of the problems that we have because of
how I feel about certain things that have come out of my childhood long
ago. But it's my philosophy. Many of you don't share that philosophy
and it doesn't bother me. . . . I don't share yours.[35]

About a month after Roberts's speech, Jessie Dent, an Ole Miss student from Hattiesburg, told the *Daily Mississippian* that he was tired
of trying to establish communication between the black students and
the administration. The newly established Black Student Union, Dent
said, would soon announce a set of demands expressing the goals and
aims of black students at the university. Within a month those demands were formulated, and on February 25, 1970, forty-five black
students marched to the chancellor's residence and chanted their demands. While those demands were being made known to the chancellor, another group of black students burned a rebel flag and danced on
cafeteria tables to the music of•B. B. King and Eldridge Cleaver. The
next night a group of black students were arrested and taken to the
county jail when they disrupted a concert by the touring musical group
"Up With People." Later that night, twenty-eight other blacks were
arrested on the campus and also taken to jail. The disruption of the
concert climaxed almost two years of increasing unrest on the part of
Ole Miss's two hundred black students.[36]

The racial flare-up at Ole Miss paralleled student unrest at Mississippi Valley State College. Students at Valley State were demanding, among other changes, the removal of President James H. White,
the school's only president since its opening in 1950. There were several Mississippi Valley alumni in law school at Ole Miss who sym-
pathized with the grievances of the Valley protesters. In many ways,
the unrest at Ole Miss was an extension of the disturbances at Mississippi Valley. The Ole Miss student senate considered several resolutions expressing support for the students at Valley, though none were
passed.[37]

On March 17 eight of the Ole Miss black students who had been
arrested on the night of the concert were expelled. Forty-five other
black students were also expelled but received suspended sentences.
The eight dismissed students appealed to the board and were given a
hearing at a special meeting in Oxford on April 23 and 24, 1970. None-

theless, the board upheld Chancellor Porter L. Fortune's decision to dismiss the students and commended him for the way he handled the entire situation.[38]

The kind of campus violence that the board had most feared and thus far escaped finally occurred in May 1970 at Jackson State College, Mississippi's largest black institution of higher learning. Here the unrest stemmed not from discontent with academic policies or dissatisfaction with President John A. Peoples but from a much deeper cause—what a member of the President's Commission on Campus Unrest termed the "historic pattern of racism." The school's location in downtown Jackson increased the potential for violent confrontation. Lynch Street, then a major thoroughfare connecting a white residential section in west Jackson to the downtown business district, ran through the Jackson State campus. Sometimes in the spring Jackson State students would gather along Lynch Street and taunt whites as they drove through the campus. In 1965 and 1966 there had been minor incidents of rock-throwing, and in 1967 a melee between Jackson State students and passing motorists had resulted in the death of a young black, Benjamin Brown, as well as injuries to several others. In the spring of 1968 Martin Luther King, Jr.'s assassination had provoked an even more serious demonstration in which Jackson police had arrested fifteen people and used tear gas to restore order. There had also been a minor demonstration in 1969.[39]

On May 13, 1970, a small group of Jackson State students began pelting passing cars with rocks in the late afternoon and early evening. As the crowd grew, the Jackson police department established a roadblock on Lynch Street. Mayor Russell Davis requested Governor John Bell Williams to mobilize a local National Guard unit and to place the Mississippi highway patrol on standby alert in case the patrolmen were needed. The night before, a trash trailer had been burned and a small fire set at the ROTC building. Despite reports of gunfire during the night of May 13, no serious injuries were reported.[40]

The next night, however, a larger and more restive group of students congregated along Lynch Street. Jackson police sealed off the street. While the students were milling about but doing nothing in particular, a rumor began to spread among the growing crowd that Charles Evers and his wife had been killed. That rumor greatly excited the already restless students and a truck was set afire. Students began to hurl rocks and bricks at white policemen and highway patrolmen who were stationed along Lynch Street. Shortly after midnight, the crashing sound of a bursting bottle, which coincided with the arrival of an armored riot-control vehicle, provoked a twenty-eight-second fusillade toward Alexander Hall, a woman's dormitory. Two students were killed and twelve others wounded. The deaths of James Earl Green and Phillip L. Gibbs prompted shock and anger in the black community of Jackson and throughout Mississippi. President John Peoples of Jackson State charged that the students had been slain "wantonly and determinedly." The *Blue and White Flash,* the Jackson State student newspaper, called the shooting "pure slaughter."[41]

The board of trustees lamented the incident and closed Jackson State for the rest of the spring semester. Mayor Davis, in an unprecedented move, appointed a biracial committee to investigate the killings. But Governor Williams, although he issued a formal statement deploring the tragic deaths, refused to cooperate with Mayor Davis's investigation. Jackson policemen and the city's newspapers claimed that snipers had provoked the burst of gunfire and blamed the deaths of the two students on the "toll of [student] misconduct." Student representatives from several Mississippi colleges issued statements criticizing local public officials and especially the Jackson press for justifying the shooting of college students.[42]

Following the riots at Jackson State and at Kent State in Ohio, President Richard M. Nixon appointed a presidential commission to study the unrest that had occurred on college campuses throughout the country during the 1960s. The President's Commission on Campus Unrest visited Jackson State and conducted a thorough investigation. The Commission concluded that "the stark fact underlying all other causes of student unrest [at Jackson State College] is the historic pattern of racism that substantially affects daily life in Mississippi." According to Steven Lesher, a member of the President's Commission, the academic deficiencies of Mississippi's black colleges had had a devastating effect on blacks in Mississippi: "a recycling of unsophisticated rural blacks through underfinanced colleges where they are taught, by people from similar circumstances, to teach yet another generation of the disadvantaged is like the hamster on an exercise wheel who races to escape but gets nowhere." Lesher found that black college presidents were intimidated by the white power structure, who viewed their efforts to upgrade black schools with suspicion if not hostility. Black college presidents were thus forced to serve two masters—their black constituency, who would no longer accept things as they were, and the white power structure, who would not allow black colleges to become engines of change.[43]

When the President's Commission published its findings, Governor Williams and Attorney General A. F. Summer dismissed the report as the work of a "kangaroo court." Echoing their sentiment was Congressman G. V. Montgomery, who also claimed that the report was prejudiced against Mississippi. Few white Mississippians, especially members of the board of trustees, were willing to accept any responsibility or blame for the deaths that occurred at Jackson State College.[44]

One white Mississippian, Oliver Emmerich, stood almost alone in his assessment of the origins of the Jackson State riot. A former member of the board of trustees and editor of the *McComb Enterprise,* Emmerich identified a complex set of circumstances that, in culmination, triggered the violence at Jackson State: the board's long-standing policy of banning speakers from Mississippi's institutions of higher learning, the racial dimension of almost every official public policy, the continued refusal of the state's political leadership to appoint blacks to governmental agencies that affected their daily lives, and the fact that white policemen feared no recrimination for killing blacks. Emmerich also reported that Governor Williams and Mayor Davis were at loggerheads over what had happened at Jackson State and who had been responsible for it. The two officials disagreed in particular over whether the highway patrol or city police had fired the shots that killed the two students, a question which remains unanswered.[45]

While there were serious racial disturbances on college campuses in the spring of 1970, Mississippi's public school system was peacefully implementing the most sweeping racial integration in the state's educational history. During the 1970 spring semester the state's dual, segregated school system was superseded by a unified, integrated system, and Mississippi's black and white children went to school together with unexpected success.[46] It is no mystery that public school integration was achieved more peacefully than almost anyone believed possible, because Mississippi's classroom teachers and school officials—

unlike the board of trustees of institutions of higher learning—focused their energies on acceptance of rather than resistance to integration. It had to work, and they made it work. They too were "unlikely heroes."

At no time in its troubled history has higher education been more directly influenced by the personal philosophy of a few individual board members than it was in the decade of the 1960s. The most doctrinaire member of the board of trustees in that decade, and in many ways its most influential, was M. M. Roberts of Hattiesburg. He was a true believer in states' rights, white supremacy, racial segregation, and the southern way of life. Owing in large measure to the force of his will and his obstinacy, many of Roberts's prejudices and preferences were translated into public policy. As the acknowledged "Mississippi Southern board member," he was the driving force behind the realignment of the traditional pecking order among the state's institutions of higher learning that culminated in the 1960s. Two years after he joined the board of trustees Mississippi Southern College was accorded university status, and under his influence a new funding formula was adopted in 1964. That numerically driven formula almost immediately elevated Mississippi Southern to a funding level equal to the level for Mississippi State and Ole Miss; it also paved the way for Southern's designation as a comprehensive university and its authorization to grant doctoral degrees.[47]

Roberts exercised his enormous influence on board policy through a strategy he devised shortly after becoming a member of the board: "Let me tell you, I always tied in with either State or Ole Miss, because with [one of] them, and what votes I could get outside of it, I could do something . . . if I made up my mind what I wanted to do. I had to get that crowd, I'm telling you about the manipulations . . . and that's the reason you have so many 7-6 votes, because it would be that way."[48] Like so many other board members over the years Roberts did not have a sense of humor or a sense of history, and it was difficult for him to keep things in perspective. In the springtime high jinks of college students Roberts saw a dark conspiracy; in the naive idealism of youth he saw a creeping socialism. He did not understand that those college kids who came to Mississippi in the summer of 1964 brought with them a belief in freedom that is this nation's surest safeguard against communism, fascism, or atheism. Nor did he realize that those young people were not unlike the young men and women of Mississippi, except that they had been awakened to injustice, prejudice, and racial discrimination.

Some of the most interesting confrontations in Mississippi during the 1960s occurred in the closed meetings of the college board between Malcomb Metts Roberts and Verner Smith Holmes. Unlike Roberts, Holmes had a great sense of humor, an innate sense of fairness, and a keen sense of history. His perspective on history enabled him to say years later: "I look back now, and I am ashamed of the way I voted sometimes, you know you make so many mistakes. I think back in those days we all, in our hearts, were a little racist."[49]

In those troubled times Holmes was not a militant, not even a liberal, but a realist who recognized that Mississippi and the board and the institutions it governed could not escape the changes taking place everywhere else in America. He was also a pragmatist who preferred the most direct and least painful route to change. When the federal court ordered the desegregation of the university hospital, Holmes and Robert Marston, dean of the medical center, were discussing the removal of the WHITE and COLORED signs from the hospital's main entrances. Dean Marston asked Holmes, "Should I bring it to the Board?" Holmes replied, "My God, no!" The two men took the signs down at midnight on the day before the court order was to go into effect. Holmes later said, "We were kind of disappointed that nobody even noticed it. . . . You know, a lot of times if you just do things people would accept them and not create a great controversy over them."[50]

People may not have noticed that those signs were gone, but there were two changes during the 1960s and early 1970s that could not go unnoticed. The first and most significant was the fact that Mississippi's public institutions of higher learning were integrated. Before Meredith graduated Cleve McDowell was admitted to the law school, and in 1964 Cleveland Donald was admitted to Ole Miss as an undergraduate—both by court order. After Donald's admission, the board allowed black students to enroll at the traditionally white institutions without resistance. Mississippi State University was desegregated without any disturbance in 1965; Mississippi University for Women and Delta State, in 1966; and the University of Southern Mississippi, in 1967. Alcorn admitted white students in 1966, Jackson State in 1969, and Mississippi Valley in 1970. University faculties were integrated first at Alcorn State in the academic year 1966–67; then at Jackson State in

1967–68; Mississippi Valley in 1968–69; Ole Miss, MUW, and USM in 1970–71; Delta State in 1973–74; and Mississippi State in 1974–75.[51]

The second major change was that the old pecking order had been fundamentally altered. As the old pecking order was giving way to a new hierarchy, there was also a changing of the old guard. President Colvard, who followed Ben Hilbun at Mississippi State in 1960, resigned in 1966 and was succeeded by William Giles. President Jacob L. Reddix, who was in office when Jackson State became a public institution in 1940, retired in 1967 and was replaced by John A. Peoples. Both Euclid R. Jobe, the executive secretary of the board of trustees since 1945, and Chancellor Williams, who came to Ole Miss in 1946, retired in 1968. E. E. Thrash was appointed executive secretary of the board, and Porter L. Fortune, Jr., followed Williams as chancellor. President John D. Boyd of Alcorn College, who had been there since 1957, retired in 1969 to be succeeded by Walter Washington. President James Ewing, who went to Delta State in 1956, and President James H. White, who had been at Mississippi Valley since 1950, retired in 1971. Ewing was replaced by Aubrey Lucas and White by Ernest Boykins.[52]

As significant as those changes were, there was an even more dramatic changing of the guard on the board of trustees. In 1972 Ross Barnett's five appointees, including M. M. Roberts, rotated off the board. For the first time ever a black man—Robert Harrison, a dentist from Yazoo City—was appointed to the college board. Harrison was appointed by Governor William Waller in 1972 and later served as president of the board. Governor Waller also appointed Miriam Simmons, the first woman to serve on the board of trustees in many years.[53] Those appointments were a tacit announcement that Mississippi's closed society at last was open.

Thirteen

A System of Universities, 1972–1990

*There can and will be coordination among the eight state
institutions, because we now have a system of universities and a
commissioner of higher education.*

—Will Hickman
Board of Trustees

Even after Mississippi had emerged from the crisis of integration and the days of dissent, its institutions of higher learning continued to be the focus of controversy and criticism. The primary criticism was that duplication of expensive degree programs was a waste of Mississippi's resources and made a coordinated statewide system of higher education impossible. Legislative critics and other public officials claimed that Mississippi's institutions of higher learning were trying to do too much with too little, with the predictable result that its colleges and universities were mediocre if not marginal. The call for stricter coordination of degree programs, which had gone unheeded for over three decades, eventually gave way to a public demand for the consolidation or elimination of some of Mississippi's public institutions of higher learning.

The growing support for a coordinated state system of universities in Mississippi was encouraged by an increasing national awareness that the proliferation of colleges and universities since World War II had created a "basic and inescapable need" for some kind of coordination in American higher education. In 1971 Robert Berdahl, author of *Statewide Coordination of Higher Education,* argued that academic freedom did not depend necessarily on institutional autonomy and "that the state's funding and interest in higher education legitimately permitted it some substantial voice in such major decisions as approving new campuses and new degree programs." Berdahl considered coordination inevitable; the only matter to be decided, then, was how it would be carried out. He preferred that it be done by a state coordinating or governing board; otherwise "it would occur by default at the less educationally informed and more politicized level of the governor's office or legislative staff."[1]

Governor William Waller, who took office in 1972, appointed a blue-ribbon committee to study higher education, specifically the need to coordinate degree programs and the feasibility of consolidating or closing some of the state's institutions of higher learning. When the committee published its report that was somewhat critical of higher education, the president of the board of trustees, Thomas Turner, disavowed it: "This is the governor's report." One of the committee's strongest criticisms of the state's public universities was that they did not train their graduates for jobs available in Mississippi. Turner discounted that claim altogether. "I think it's the state of Mississippi's obligation," he said, "to put jobs here for the people we turn out."[2]

The board of trustees was offended by the criticism of Governor Waller's committee. Rather than conceding the need to reevaluate its policies and priorities during a period of retrenchment, however, the board "circled the wagons" and refused to cooperate with Governor Waller and his committee on higher education. Because of that intransigence the board of trustees and its staff, according to Eugene Hickock, "became more vulnerable to institutional, governmental, and public criticism."[3]

The first indication that the board would be forced to reorder its priorities came in February 1974, when Governor Waller vetoed a special catch-up appropriation for university libraries. Waller explained that he vetoed the library bill to force the board of trustees to divert money from capital outlays to operational expenses. Because college enrollment had leveled off, the governor argued, making huge expenditures for capital construction was not a judicious use of the state's financial resources. He insisted that his veto would not damage higher education because the $65.1 million regular appropriation was sufficient to meet the actual needs of higher education. In his veto message Governor Waller also criticized the allocation formula. He claimed that the enrollment-driven formula had encouraged the duplication of popular programs by the smaller schools in order to attract students.[4]

Eight months after Governor Waller's veto of the library bill, there was additional evidence that the growth cycle had peaked. In October 1974 the state building commission imposed a moratorium on construction preplanning at the state's institutions of higher learning. During the moratorium the building commission staff would review the construction priorities as established by higher education officials. The board of trustees reacted angrily to the building commission's action, claiming it was an infringement upon the board's constitutional authority, and over the next several months relations between the board of trustees and the building commission deteriorated. But even the board, in spite of its reaction to the building commission's moratorium, had become convinced that capital construction had to be curtailed. The trustees instructed the board staff to study the requests for new buildings carefully to determine whether the requests were justified.[5] That directive was a prelude to retrenchment. It was the first indication that the board realized the postwar college boom had run its course.

While the board of trustees and university officials were schooling themselves in the management of decline, they were also formulating a compliance plan to satisfy the desegregation requirements of the 1964 Civil Rights Act. In March 1969 the Office of Civil Rights at the Department of Health, Education, and Welfare notified the board of trustees that Mississippi had to show that it was in compliance or risk the cutoff of federal funds.[6] During the early stages of that initial compliance review, M. M. Roberts, who was then president of the board, recommended that Mississippi make no response to HEW's inquiries and do nothing in the way of modifying the recruitment, admission, or hiring practices at the state's public universities. Roberts said that the civil rights law included a lengthy due process procedure that the board could use to keep the case tied up in the courts for years and thus forestall the cutoff of federal funds. The board did not accept Roberts's recommendation.[7]

The Office of Civil Rights did not follow up on its initial review of 1969, and the matter of compliance was in abeyance for several years. Eventually a suit was filed to require HEW to cut off federal funds from those states not in compliance. On February 16, 1973, the U.S.

district court in Washington ordered HEW to initiate enforcement proceedings. Following that decision HEW advised Mississippi on March 27, 1973, that it was not in compliance and directed the board to file an acceptable compliance plan within 120 days.[8]

The board of trustees, with the aid of M. M. Roberts, hastily drafted a compliance plan, which HEW just as quickly rejected. Although Roberts's term on the board had expired, he was retained as legal counsel. The rejection of Mississippi's original plan prompted sharp criticism from Governor Waller, who chastised the board for not consulting other state officials. Waller had offered his assistance but had been unable to penetrate the "air of autonomy" that, he said, isolated the board of trustees from the rest of state government. The governor also questioned M. M. Roberts's participation in formulating the compliance plan. "It would seem," said the governor, that "someone with a better record of neutrality would be better."[9]

On January 28, 1974, an ad hoc committee appointed by the board of trustees submitted to the board a draft proposal for a new plan of compliance. At the urging of Verner Holmes, the trustees discussed the draft at length with Governor Waller and other state officials before finalizing a new plan. After the plan had been completed and mailed, Thomas Turner predicted that federal authorities would give Mississippi "a big A." But in response to a reporter's question about HEW's demand for timely compliance, Turner began to hedge: "Rome wasn't built in a day . . . we've got to look fifty, one hundred, one million years ahead. . . . Mississippi's gone so far that it does irk me at times . . . well . . . they're picking on Mississippi."[10]

The Black Mississippi Council on Higher Education, claiming that blacks had been denied any substantive input in the formulation of the compliance plan, distributed a highly critical twenty-six-page review of the plan. When it later became apparent that HEW would give conditional approval, the BMCHE submitted an alternative plan which it asked HEW to accept in place of the board's plan. While HEW was reviewing both plans, a class-action suit was filed on behalf of twenty-one students at Jackson State and Alcorn State universities. That suit, which is still in litigation and is known as the Ayers case, asked the court basically to restructure Mississippi's system of higher education.[11]

On February 2, 1976, after two years of suits and countersuits, pleadings and legal maneuverings, and the separation of the junior colleges from the senior institutions in matters of compliance, federal authorities finally approved the board's compliance plan as "a framework within which the institutions of higher learning could satisfy the Civil Rights Law of 1964." Mississippi's reluctant acceptance of the desegregation provisions of the 1964 Civil Rights Act—in the classroom, at the lunch counter, and even in the church house—indicated that the power elite was losing its control over public policy and that the crack in the closed society was widening.[12]

The board of trustees had been a part of that power elite since the end of Reconstruction. It had traditionally conducted the affairs of higher education in secret, closed-door sessions far removed from the scrutiny of public opinion. Aided by the secrecy that cloaked its actions and by its constitutional independence, the board of trustees, as Governor Waller claimed, had for many years mistaken arrogance for authority. Having come of age in the closed society, most board members who served during the 1970s were uncomfortable with the direction the open society was taking.

When the Mississippi State University student newspaper asked board president Boswell Stevens if he would support interdormitory visitation, Stevens responded with an arrogance that must have amused more than it offended: "I think all of them [boys and girls] should just live together." Stevens then exclaimed that he was against dormitory visitation and would never vote for it as long as he was on the board. He criticized the *Reflector* for using a university telephone to conduct such a frivolous interview. Saying he was "tired of all this bullshit," he hung up the telephone.[13]

Boswell Stevens, who was president of the powerful Mississippi Farm Bureau Federation, was one of three presidents of the college board during the 1970s who did not hold a college degree. The other two were Tommy Turner and Milton Brister. Stevens's disdain for student opinion and his obstinacy in the face of a changing society were more or less shared by most other trustees. Their attitudes generated anger and cynicism among Mississippi's student constituency. One of the most amusing expressions of that cynicism was a cartoon in the University of Southern Mississippi's *Student Printz* showing two board members playing high-stakes poker. One said to the other: "I see your vet school . . . and raise you a sci tech building."[14]

The cynicism evident in the student press was shared by many university faculty members who believed that the board of trustees routinely played favorites with both individuals and institutions. One glaring example involved the dean of the College of Fine Arts at the University of Southern Mississippi who was indicted by a Forrest County grand jury for embezzlement of university funds. Under a plea bargaining arrangement, the dean pleaded guilty to a reduced charge. After the guilty plea had been entered and the case was settled, the board of trustees reinstated the former dean to another position at the university. The effective period of reinstatement was December 8, 1976 through June 30, 1978, at a salary of $500 per month for a total of seventeen months ($9,500). The special treatment given this dean contrasts with the dismissal of several faculty members at Mississippi Southern because of their sponsorship of a student chapter of the ACLU and their support of other unpopular causes.[15]

Another example of preferential treatment involved an Ole Miss coach. The board minutes indicate that a former coach was given a bonus at the time he left the university: "In view of [his] service to the university and his contribution as . . . coach, approve the payment of a bonus in the amount of $2,010.55."[16] The board's generosity to that former coach contrasts with the treatment of Professor Russell Barrett, a longtime member of the political science department and president of the Ole Miss chapter of the AAUP. After Barrett published *Integration at Ole Miss* in 1965, his salary was frozen. The freeze on Professor Barrett's salary was the subject of several investigations and was one of the factors that eventually led to the censure of the university by the AAUP.[17]

During the 1970s the board also had an unflattering record of partiality toward certain institutions. The most striking example involves Jackson State University's request to build a $100,000 memorial garden to its past presidents. That request, made on May 18, 1978, provoked an acrimonious and protracted debate. Even though the legislature had already appropriated the funds and the state building commission had authorized the expenditure, and even after President John Peoples had announced that construction on the project would soon begin, several board members insisted on canceling or at least scaling down the project. They claimed that such a large expenditure was not a justifiable use of Mississippi's educational resources during a period of retrenchment. As the debate intensified Verner Holmes questioned a colleague, "Don't you know that if the president of the University of Mississippi or Mississippi State was asking for something, we wouldn't do this to them?" The colleague responded, "Well, maybe not." But the board members opposing the memorial garden, according to Holmes, "were hell bent" against it.[18]

Verner Holmes's claim that similar requests from Ole Miss or Mississippi State did not trigger such rigid scrutiny was documented on January 17, 1980, when the board authorized the renovation of a dean's office at the University of Mississippi. The request to renovate that one office at a cost of $26,000, which was more than one-fourth of the total Jackson State expenditure, did not elicit even a passing comment when it was approved unanimously by the board. The board of trustees later spent over $250,000 to build a residence for the director of the Gulf Coast Research Laboratory and authorized the University of Southern Mississippi to lease a $1 million residence for its president's home.[19]

The board's special preferences and predilections often produced headlines, and the Mississippi media accused the trustees of being utterly indifferent to public opinion. For years the press had assailed the board for conducting public business behind closed doors. In the 1970s the news media stepped up the campaign to gain admission to board meetings. The board held steadfast, however, and kept its meetings closed. In doing so, it undermined its credibility and sometimes damaged its dignity. On Thursday, May 17, 1974, a comic encounter in a stalled elevator between the president of the board and several members of the press was reported with three-column photographs and full details on the front page of the *Clarion-Ledger:*

> A brief game of hide-and-seek at Thursday morning's college board meeting ended with newsmen and the new board president trapped inside a jammed elevator at the R & D Center. . . .
>
> This unlikely scenario began when new board president Milton Brister, a banker from Kilmichael, opted to forego the customary press conferences following the monthly college board meetings. . . .
>
> To avoid some 15 newsmen waiting for the conference Mr. Brister, who had indicated he would not talk to newsmen, waited in the office of Dr. E. E. Thrash, executive secretary of the college board.
>
> Meanwhile, Dr. Thrash invited newsmen into the conference room and closed the door, giving Brister an opportunity to slip out the back door of Dr. Thrash's office, and move down the hall to the elevators.

Brister, however, was spotted by some newsmen as he headed for
the exit and these newsmen boarded the elevator with him.

Brister pushed the "down" button at the same time a newsman
pushed an "open door" button, causing the elevator to jam with the
doors about 8 inches apart.

Inside the elevator, newsmen asked Brister questions—but got no
answers—and shot pictures. Newsmen locked outside the elevator
pushed microphones through the 8-inch opening and television cameras tried to shoot inside the elevator.

After a newsman pried the doors open, Brister crossed the hall and
pushed the button to summon another elevator.

However, Dr. Verner Holmes, a college board member from Mc-
Comb, counseled with Brister and asked him to issue a brief statement.[20]

After being persuaded by Holmes to meet briefly with the press,
Brister agreed to issue news releases summarizing board actions but
stated categorically, "As president of the Board, I do not plan to participate in a press conference . . . and good day to all of you." Holmes told
the group before it dispersed that he had long favored opening the
meetings to newsmen and asked them to "bear with us, we'll do better."[21] Eventually the legislature passed an open meetings law, which
required the board of trustees and all other state agencies to conduct
their meetings in public sessions.

By the end of the 1970s not only was the business of higher education in Mississippi being conducted in meetings open to the public but
higher education itself had become a vast, complex public enterprise.
The modern twentieth-century institutions of higher learning bore
little resemblance to their nineteenth-century predecessors. The new
universities were local industries with huge payrolls, and university
presidents functioned as chief executive officers. Deans and department heads were mid-level management. The newest and best equipment first found its way to the business office and physical plant and
then to the laboratory and classroom. The hub of the campus shifted
subtly from the library to the admissions office. College officials, most
of whom had never heard of James Sexton's admonition to the contrary, began playing the numbers game. The public at large and the
legislature in particular had come to expect the new CEOs of higher
education to make decisions on the basis of economics, as well as aca-

demics. And the legislature was more determined than ever to hold Mississippi's governing board accountable for those decisions.

The relationship between the board of trustees and the legislature had rarely ever been harmonious, even during the decades of growth and expansion. But during the retrenchment of the 1970s that relationship soured, and the legislature became increasingly critical of what it considered to be wasteful duplication. While the legislature was mandating the elimination of unnecessary duplication, however, the lawmakers themselves yielded to local interests in 1974 and upgraded the regional colleges to universities; they also ignored their own mandate against proliferation by establishing two new professional schools in the early 1970s. By its own action the legislature postponed the day of reckoning for Mississippi's institutions of higher learning.

Nevertheless, as the state entered the decade of the 1970s, the board of trustees was forced to respond to the mounting criticism that academic entrepreneurs were squandering Mississippi's educational resources. As a first step to curtail the proliferation and duplication of new degree programs, the board directed the eight institutions to conduct an academic inventory in April 1973 in order to identify all unaccredited degree programs. It also directed university officials to initiate long-range planning studies that would assess the future needs and goals of Mississippi's institutions of higher learning. Finally, in an effort to hold down the number of new degree programs, the board required an institution to file its intent to establish a new program ninety days before it was to start, and to explain how the new program was related to the "stated purposes" of that institution.[22] But as Joseph Gibson said so aptly in 1945, "eternal vigilance" is the price the board must pay if it means to restrict the proliferation of new programs. Board members met only once every thirty days, but scheming academics could meet thirty times every day, if necessary, to plan and plot a strategy to justify new programs.

After the academic inventories and the long-range studies had been completed, the board of trustees began consolidating and eliminating marginal programs. On February 20, 1975, the board reported to the legislature that the universities were having "surprising success in reducing duplication" and that one hundred unaccredited or unproductive programs had been discontinued. Some legislators, however, saw the board's "surprising success" as too little and too late. Senator Theodore Smith of Corinth called for even more paring of degree programs, noting that the University of Mississippi still offered more graduate programs than Harvard University.[23]

About six months after this report was made to the legislature, the board of trustees denied a request by Jackson State to begin a doctoral program in education. The board's action brought a sharp and somewhat surprising response. The *Clarion-Ledger* reported that the board denied the request because there were already similar programs at State, Southern, and Ole Miss and quoted the deans at those institutions as saying that all three of the existing programs were necessary but that one more program was not needed. E. E. Thrash, executive secretary of the board of trustees, explained that new degree programs were approved only after the board staff had thoroughly studied the request and had determined that the new program was not an "unnecessary duplication" of an existing one. But the *Clarion-Ledger* was not impressed with Thrash's explanation and accused certain board members of serving as "cheerleaders" for their favored institutions. Senator Jim Noblin of Jackson claimed that the board had denied Jackson State's request because its program would draw students from the other three institutions. He too took note that the deans of the schools with doctoral programs in education had said that three is not too many but that four was one too many.[24]

The controversy over Jackson State's proposed doctorate was only a skirmish in the impending battle over doctoral consolidation. The larger question of doctoral programs and consolidation was brought before the board in January 1976 when the board staff proposed a consolidation plan that assigned doctoral programs exclusively to Mississippi State, Mississippi Southern, and Ole Miss. This plan was primarily the work of the board staff and came as a complete surprise to university presidents, even to some members of the board of trustees. In presenting the proposal to the board, Thrash reported that nineteen doctoral programs had only one student enrolled, fourteen had only two, and ten had only three. Under the original plan the number of doctorates was to be reduced from 103 to 77.[25] After a lengthy discussion the board postponed any action for thirty days, in order to allow the university presidents to study the impact of doctoral consolidation and report their findings and recommendations to the board. Robert

Harrison, who voted in favor of postponement because he and several other board members had not been told about the consolidation plan until it was brought to the board for a vote, insisted that "any proposal this serious should be given to the Board in writing seven days prior to the meeting at which it is formally presented."[26] Thus occurred the first of a series of delays. Over the next several months the doctoral consolidation program was drastically modified.

Verner Holmes, who voted against postponement, argued that the "legislature has been after us for years to do something about this" and predicted that "if we delay, we can just kiss the whole thing good-bye." Ross Franks, the LaBauve Trustee, agreed. A thirty-day delay, he said, would "leave us open to pressure groups." Holmes and Franks were correct in their presumption that a delay would give the university presidents time to organize opposition to the proposal. On January 21, 1976, President Aubrey Lucas spoke out publicly against the consolidation plan, claiming that the University of Southern Mississippi was the big loser. According to President Lucas, USM would lose over half of its doctoral programs, more than either the University of Mississippi or Mississippi State.[27] Mississippi Southern partisans claimed that the educational power structure in the state was conspiring to return their university to a teachers college and reestablish the old pecking order. Mississippi State alumni also claimed that doctoral consolidation was the first step in restamping the old "cow college" image on their alma mater.

The board's effort to consolidate existing doctoral programs and correlate new programs to the "stated purposes" of each institution presupposed a clear statement of the role and scope of Mississippi's eight institutions of higher learning. But the board had no such instrument. Consequently, on July 15, 1976, the board of trustees began formulating a comprehensive long-range role and scope plan for each of the universities under its governance. Those role and scope statements would be nearly five years in the making.[28]

While formulating the role and scope study, and while the doctoral programs were under review, the board of trustees transferred the associate degree nursing program at the USM-Natchez branch to Alcorn University on February 17, 1977. The board also authorized Alcorn to upgrade the program to a baccalaureate degree as soon as funds and faculty could be secured.[29] The only member of the board to vote against this transfer was Bobby Chain of Hattiesburg. Chain told the Natchez newspaper that he was "mad as hell" and insinuated that the decision was a result of "horse-trading" between the small universities and their supporters on the board. Delta State had recently been awarded a new baccalaureate degree and, according to Chain, someone said "'Let's give Alcorn something,' so what do we do? We give them the Natchez nursing program. It's one hell of a thing."[30]

But Verner Holmes, chairman of the Medical Affairs Committee, explained to the *Natchez-Democrat* that transferring the associate degree program to Alcorn and upgrading it to a baccalaureate program would "be good for the patients, good for everybody." Holmes added, "It's not fair for Mississippi Southern, which is 180 miles away, to run a nursing school in Natchez with Alcorn on the front doorsteps." He intimated that the entire Natchez branch might be transferred to Alcorn University under the new role and scope plan which was being formulated. In response, board member Robert C. Cook, the former president of Mississippi Southern College, said that the proposed role and scope plan was merely "a projection we've gotten up about things that might happen in the future" and then accused Verner Holmes of "thinking twenty years ahead." The board of trustees reaffirmed the transfer of the nursing program on March 23, 1977, and the furor eventually subsided.[31]

The role and scope study mentioned several times during the controversy over transferring the Natchez nursing program was, as President Lucas said, only a working document and not board policy. Probably no other document in the board's history has undergone such close scrutiny, amendment, modification, and revision. On March 15, 1979, board president Bobby Chain reviewed a proposed draft of the statement but informed the trustees that it would undergo further revision before being presented for a final vote.[32] A week after President Chain's oral presentation, the Academy for Educational Development, a Washington consulting firm retained by the state legislature to study higher education in Mississippi, published an eleven-volume report that was highly critical of program duplication at Mississippi's eight institutions. Based on its assessment of impending budget constraints and declining enrollment, the academy issued a stern warning to the board of trustees.

To date, the philosophy of the Board of Trustees has been to delegate almost all planning and management responsibilities to the institutions. . . .

The Board of Trustees must exert a will to lead and to manage. Institutions cannot legitimately be expected to reduce or alter program scope to promote the overall good of the state without positive leadership and guidance from the Board of Trustees. . . . In light of the new constraints facing higher education in the state, the Board must define the mission of each institution and focus institutional attention on providing the programs needed to respond to their unique mission.[33]

Armed with the findings of the academy study, the legislature prodded the board to reduce unnecessary duplication and mandated role and scope assignments to the eight universities. The board, however, was already moving in that direction. Over the next few months the term "role and scope" gave way to the more cosmetic term "mission statement." The mission statements for each institution were finally completed and adopted by the board on November 18, 1981. They were drafted by a special committee chaired by Miriam Simmons and published in spring 1982 along with an accompanying document entitled "Official Explanation."[34] At the time the mission statements were announced, the board mandated a review of all degree programs and indicated that the role and scope assignments might be modified after those reviews had been completed. A continuation of an earlier policy, this new round of program reviews eventually resulted in the deletion or suspension of a large number of degree programs and a significant reduction of doctoral programs.

The mission statements divided the eight universities into three categories. The University of Mississippi, Mississippi State University, and the University of Southern Mississippi were designated as comprehensive universities. Though all three would continue to offer doctoral programs, each institution was assigned leadership roles in specific disciplines. Jackson State was classified as an urban university, whose primary mission was to "enhance the overall quality of the institution" and "to engage in more organized research that is directly related to the urban area of Jackson." The other four institutions—Alcorn, Delta State, Mississippi Valley, and Mississippi University for Women— were termed regional universities. Those institutions would continue to offer their existing baccalaureate programs and some graduate programs, at least until the results of the impending program reviews were finalized.[35]

In 1983, while the latest round of program reviews was underway, the board of trustees adopted a plan to promote "excellence" in a number of carefully selected and limited academic disciplines at the three comprehensive universities. The "Centers of Academic Excellence" were correlated to the leadership roles assigned to each university:

Mississippi State University
    Biological Sciences, Engineering, Food Science, Technology
University of Mississippi
    Chemistry, History, Physics, English
University of Southern Mississippi
    Communications (Journalism), Computer Science, Marine Science[36]

Shortly after the second phase of the comprehensive program review had been completed in 1984, the board of trustees transferred the leadership role in journalism from the University of Southern Mississippi to the University of Mississippi. That action was blasted by former board member Bobby Chain, who claimed that "a stacked board" dominated by Ole Miss and State people had aborted the leadership plan without giving it a chance to work.[37] This reassignment of the leadership role in journalism was part of a broader effort by the board to respond to the latest round of program reviews and to continue the process of eliminating marginal programs. Overall the reviews were very discouraging, and the board grappled with decisions about which programs to cut and which to keep or to consolidate. A total of 671 baccalaureate and master's degree programs were reviewed and rated as follows: 13 "commended"; 514 "approved"; 81 with "approval pending"; 3 given "conditional approval"; 59 termed "marginal"; 1 "to be phased out."[38]

In an editorial entitled, "Marginal, at Best," the *Jackson Daily News–Clarion-Ledger* was generally critical of higher education. It challenged the board to make the hard decisions necessary to eliminate marginal programs and to concentrate the state's resources on developing a few areas of excellence. Board president Denton Rogers's response to that disparaging editorial was neither defensive nor critical. Rogers simply explained that the board had already eliminated several marginal programs and had upgraded others; he also predicted that some very good programs might have to be eliminated because of recent budget cuts. With some dejection, he noted that additional and even more severe cuts were projected for the next fiscal year.[39]

Shortly after President Rogers's gloomy letter appeared in the Jackson press, the Mississippi legislature convened for the 1986 session. Among the most quarrelsome issues to be faced during that session was the funding of both the public school system and the state's institutions of higher learning. The old rivalry between the common schools and higher education resurfaced on the eve of that session. The potentially divisive issue was muted, however, when a few key legislators, including Glenn Endris of Gulfport and Ed Perry of Oxford, agreed to push the public school bill during the first two or three days of the session. Their strategy proved successful, and the school bill passed very early. Higher education officials were displeased by that maneuver, because they realized that less money would be available once the public school appropriation had been made. Their fears were not unfounded. Both the junior colleges and the universities experienced deep cuts in their 1986–87 appropriations—cuts that were severe but not surprising. In fact, they were only the latest and harshest of a series of cuts dating back to 1981.[40]

In every fiscal year since 1981–82, except the year 1984–85, the higher education budget had been reduced. In 1984 a special session of the legislature actually added $6 million. That special appropriation carried with it a recommendation that the board of trustees study the feasibility of consolidating or closing some of the eight universities and authorized $100,000 for a study. The board accepted the legislature's suggestion and retained Jack D. Foster, head of a Kentucky educational consulting firm, to conduct the study. His report, known as the Foster study, was published in January 1985.[41]

The Foster study found that closing Mississippi University for Women and Mississippi Valley State would not be very economical, because their students would likely transfer to other state schools which in turn would have to be expanded. Furthermore, the state would have to maintain the unused buildings at MUW and Mississippi Valley and pay off the bonded indebtedness on those buildings. Foster also studied the feasibility of consolidating some state institutions, but he was not enthusiastic about such an option. He concluded that public support for closing or consolidating institutions was in reality a call for retrenchment. "To some extent," Foster wrote, "we believe the call for closure or consolidation really is a call for the Board to take whatever action is necessary, however drastic it may be, to keep the cost of higher education within the financial means of the state."[42]

Like most previous consultants, Foster implored the board to take an active rather than a reactive role in the governance of higher education. He suggested appointing a commissioner of higher education and requiring university presidents to report to the board through the commissioner. The autonomy of each institution, he insisted, would have to be surrendered in the interest of an overall statewide system of higher education. Finally, Foster criticized the funding formula and recommended that the board reexamine the process of allocating funds to the eight universities.[43]

The Foster study's criticism of the funding process was corroborated by another independent study of the formula conducted by Joseph E. Johnson, whose report was filed with the board on January 16, 1985. Johnson found that the existing formula, which the board had adopted in 1974, funded the "comprehensive universities less adequately than [the] regional universities," and he recommended "major revisions."[44]

The board of trustees as constituted in 1985 was by far the most enlightened and most intelligent board in the state's history; it was also the least influenced by institutional loyalty. Sensitive to the mounting criticism that it had failed to avert the financial crisis facing higher education in Mississippi, the board in the spring of 1985 reviewed a wide range of options that might avert or at least lessen the funding crisis. At the March 1985 meeting the trustees seriously considered consolidating Mississippi University for Women and Mississippi State, as well as closing Mississippi Valley and several off-campus centers. After lengthy deliberations and discussions with alumni groups from Mississippi University for Women and Mississippi Valley, however, they decided to maintain Mississippi University for Women "as a separate institution with its own mission." The board also voted to continue Mississippi Valley and adopted several measures to enhance the quality of education there. And, in order to stop the drain of funds from the parent campuses to branch campuses, the board directed that all off-campus centers, with three exceptions, become self supporting.[45]

Actually, the trustees did not have the constitutional or statutory authority to close a university. They were blamed, nevertheless, for the deepening financial crisis, and public support for closing or consolidating some of Mississippi's universities mounted. Governor Bill Allain became one of the most vocal critics of the board of trustees, reiterating his claim that Mississippi could not support eight universities. Representative H. L. Meridith, chairman of the house ways and means committee, warned university presidents: "This business of having eight [universities] is gone. The only question is when."[46]

The criticism increased. Some dissension within the ranks of higher education surfaced after November 2, 1985, when a revenue shortfall forced a $14 million reduction in the general support funds for higher education. That reduction was followed two months later by an additional one of $767,829. While the board of trustees and university officials were scurrying to find items in the budget to cut, the legislative budget office was forecasting an even gloomier prospect for the following fiscal year. On November 21, 1985, the joint legislative budget committee projected a general support appropriation of $149,043,447 for higher education for 1986–87, a reduction of $17,595,714 from the previous year's appropriation. When that projection was announced, the board directed the staff to prepare several contingency plans for consideration at the December meeting. Those options became moot, however, because the legislative budget committee soon announced that revenue projections had again been adjusted downward.[47]

As board members prepared for their January 15, 1986, meeting, they realized that they were facing major budget reductions, a governor who had denigrated the board for not closing some of the universities, a sometimes hostile legislature, and an unsympathetic public. On the eve of the January meeting, several board members met with the legislative leadership. There was straight talk, and the trustees left the discussion convinced that things were even worse than they had imagined.[48] When the board convened the next morning, Thomas Bourdeaux moved that the trustees recommend to the legislature the closing of Mississippi University for Women, Mississippi Valley, the veterinary school, the dental school, and all off-campus centers. He further recommended that the amount of state funds used for intercollegiate sports be limited to $300,000 at each of the three comprehensive universities and $500,000 at each of the other five. Bourdeaux's motion also directed university officials to eliminate or consolidate as many existing degree programs as feasible. That blockbuster motion was passed by a vote of nine to three. The three black members of the board cast the dissenting votes.[49]

While the news of that proposal was ricocheting throughout Mississippi, the legislative budget committee again reduced its recommendation for higher education for fiscal year 1986–87 to $50 million below what the board was asking. That figure translated into reductions for individual universities ranging from 50 percent at MUW to 33.96 percent at Alcorn and 10 percent at Mississippi State.[50] Many educational and business leaders, the governor, and the general public presumed that the financial crisis would force the legislature to implement at least some of the board's recommendations. However, the senate committee on colleges and universities and its counterpart in the house were chaired by black legislators who were also faculty members at Jackson State and Alcorn University. Senator Douglas Anderson and Representative Charles Shepphard announced that their committees would take no action on the board's recommendations until thorough consideration had been given to the impact of the closings. The decision to close the two universities and the two professional schools was of such enormous political sensitivity, and the opposition so furious and well organized, that the legislature did not give any serious consideration to the proposal during the 1986 session.[51]

The funding crisis remained unresolved, however, and lobbying by university groups intensified. Some higher education forces even suggested new taxes. In the face of the monetary crisis, which showed no signs of abating in the immediate future, powerful legislators—preferring coordination to closing or consolidating universities—stepped up their demands that university presidents pare programs and establish new priorities. "Until those presidents openly say, 'Here are our priorities,' I am going to sit there on the money," warned Chairman Meridith of the ways and means committee. He predicted that the presidents would try to "spook this legislature into raising taxes." But, he proclaimed, "I'm spook proof."[52]

Chancellor R. Gerald Turner of the University of Mississippi acknowledged that "there must be some difficult decisions made" and expressed his willingness to accept those decisions. President Donald Zacharias of Mississippi State was even more emphatic. "If something dramatic is not done," he said, "something dramatic will happen by default." The recent budget cuts and the increasing likelihood that the formula would be revised in favor of the comprehensive universities had intensified the rivalry between the five regional universities and the big three. The presidents of the latter realized that many of the decisions dictated by the current circumstances would be unpopular with the smaller schools and that institutional loyalties and rivalries could weaken the resolve of the board of trustees to make those hard decisions.[53]

Consequently, the university presidents, at the urging of Turner and Zacharias, called for a special, impartial, broadly based, statewide committee, which would include legislators, to study the funding formula and the general condition of higher education in Mississippi. On the basis of its study the committee would "recommend long-range solutions—even program closures or consolidation—to avoid a repeat of the present financial crisis." The presidents of the comprehensive universities agreed to "follow the recommendations of an impartial committee made up of concerned Mississippi citizens, educators and lawmakers." But the presidents of the regional schools, who stood to lose the advantage they had under the current formula, were skeptical that a truly objective study could be made. President James Strobel of Mississippi University for Women said he would be hesitant to endorse any study before it was conducted and saw little advantage in yet another study. "I've only been here nine years," he said, "and I have a roomful of studies."[54]

Governor Allain and several influential legislators shared President Strobel's skepticism about the utility of another study and accused higher education officials of trying to avoid the hard decisions which they themselves should make. Douglas Anderson, chairman of the senate committee on colleges and universities, claimed that another study would be "an exercise in futility" and would have the same goal as earlier studies, which was to close "some of the state's regional universities and funnel the money" to the three comprehensive universities.[55] Because of the opposition of Governor Allain and several powerful legislators, the "impartial" study of higher education was not made. And the difficult decisions, which almost everyone agreed had to be made, were left for another time.

The fact that some presidents believed an impartial study was necessary and were willing to resort to a committee of concerned citizens revealed a structural flaw in the state's system of higher education. Every study of higher learning in Mississippi since 1925 had cited that flaw and had recommended a variety of ways to correct it. But all agreed on two fundamentals. First, if the eight individual institutions were to function as a coordinated state system of higher education, institutional autonomy would have to be surrendered. Second, if the board of trustees was to function as a governing rather than administrative board, it had to remove itself from operational decisions by establishing an operational officer or commissioner of higher education who would carry out the board's policies and decisions.

The financial crisis of the 1980s forced the board of trustees to reexamine the tradition of institutional autonomy. Perhaps even more important, Executive Secretary E. E. Thrash's retirement in August 1986 prompted the board to consider creating a commissioner of higher education. Thrash, whose distinguished if sometime stormy tenure as executive secretary dated back to 1968, had long been a champion of institutional autonomy. He had shared that belief with strong-willed board members of varying philosophical persuasions, including Verner Holmes, M. M. Roberts, Bobby Chain, Miriam Simmons, and Robert Harrison. But those trustees were no longer on the board, and after Thrash's retirement there were no determined advocates of autonomy on the board staff.

Shortly after Thrash announced his resignation, the board of trustees appointed a special committee to redefine the role of executive secretary. The committee eventually recommended that this office be superseded by a commissioner of higher education with broader authority and responsibility. The board accepted that recommendation and established the new office.[56] Following an extensive nationwide search, the board of trustees appointed William Ray Cleere as Mississippi's first commissioner of higher education. At the time of his appointment in November 1987, Cleere was the vice-chancellor for academic affairs of the University System of Georgia. Although the board of trustees drafted a job description outlining the powers and responsibilities of the new position, Commissioner Cleere is in large measure defining the office as he exercises his duties. By design the eight university presidents report to the board of trustees through the commissioner and are subordinate to him. The actual working relationship between the university presidents and the commissioner of higher education, however, is predicated on the commissioner's official duty to delimit the office of president and Ray Cleere's personal desire not to diminish it.[57]

While the commissioner of higher education is shaping the contours of his office, the board of trustees is altering the traditional relationship among the eight universities. Under the old system the eight institutions were a confederacy of colleges, each autonomous and bound to the others only through a common funding source and through the general policies of the consolidated board of trustees. Under the new system now taking shape, the eight institutions resemble a federation of universities in which each maintains a certain measure of independence but each is an integral part of the state system of higher education. By the board's definition, the eight institutions of higher learning now constitute not a university system but a "system of universities" that can make possible the extensive coordination of course offerings and degree programs. Though all the intricacies of a system of universities have yet to be discerned, the governing structure of higher education in Mississippi today is stronger and more sound than it has ever been. When the current financial crisis is resolved, Mississippi's eight public universities have the potential at last to become the state system of higher education—offering excellence in a few areas—which the people of Mississippi have long awaited.

Afterword

The history of higher education in Mississippi has been shaped by two persistent themes: the search for a structure of governance that would make the institutions responsive to the genuine educational needs of the state and at the same time protect them from factional politics, and the failure of the various governing boards to coordinate the institutions into a state system of higher education with a minimum of unnecessary duplication.

The search for a structure of governance that would protect the institutions from the incursion of politics, which began as early as 1856, was complicated until very recently by the fact that the governor was chairman of the boards of trustees and was also considered head of the state's higher educational institutions. Moreover, the governor had power to appoint the members of the governing boards, and he always appointed his political allies. Drawn into the political canvas every four years, the colleges and universities felt the aftershock of election turmoil. With the creation of the constitutional board of trustees and the designation of twelve-year terms for members, the opportunity for the governor to intervene in higher education was dramatically and almost immediately reduced. Except for the Meredith crisis at Ole Miss, the members of the constitutional board of trustees have been basically free of political influence.

But the solution to one problem created another. The independence derived from constitutional autonomy and twelve-year terms did more than insulate the board members; it isolated them from the body politic and often kept them from being responsive to the state's genuine educational needs. On one occasion the board president said that Mississippi's institutions of higher learning should not be expected to train people for the jobs available in the state. The state, he said, should provide jobs for the people trained by the institutions. Worse still, for many years the board conducted its affairs behind closed doors and with a mentality more befitting a corporate than a public enterprise. The board's relationship with the legislature, the building commission, the attorney general, and state agencies was characterized by an independence that some called arrogance. On one occasion the state sued the board, and on another the board chose not to use the attorney general but instead paid a private attorney over $400,000 dollars to defend it in a sex discrimination suit that could have been settled for less than $10,000.

While it may have eventually been shielded from factional politics, the board of trustees and the colleges and universities it governed were not free from institutional politics. Until Mississippi's closed society was opened, a racial orthodoxy based on white supremacy controlled board decisions; as a result the protected interests of the white colleges inevitably produced separate and unequal facilities for blacks. But beyond race, institutional favoritism and the promotion of an educational hierarchy with the state university as the capstone generated a bitter rivalry among the institutions, spawned the academic equivalent of insurrection, and made coordination virtually impossible. Most members of the governing boards, especially after 1910, were alumni of the institutions they governed. Until very recently, few could resist the temptation to place the short-term interest of their alma mater above the long-term interest of the state. College presidents, in seeking a new degree program or some other favorable decision, sometimes exploited the ties that bound board members to their institutions. When two or three presidents worked together, that strategy could neutralize the best efforts of the executive secretary and the board to coordinate institutional programs and policies.

The ill effects of institutional loyalty, competition, and duplication were so pronounced by the beginning of the 1980s that William Winter pledged during his successful campaign for governor in 1979 to appoint to the college board only individuals committed to the larger interests of higher education rather than the immediate interests of the institutions from which they graduated. Governor Winter's appointments, the appointments by his successors, WIlliam Allain and Ray Mabus, as well as the policies the current board has pursued presage a departure from the tradition of institutional autonomy. With the recent appointment of a commissioner of higher education, Mississippi now has in place a structure of governance that can make wisest use of the state's educational resources. It remains to be seen whether function will follow form.

Notes

The following journal abbreviations are used throughout the Notes:

HEQ   *History of Education Quarterly*
JNE   *Journal of Negro Education*
JNH   *Journal of Negro History*
JMH   *Journal of Mississippi History*
JSH   *Journal of Southern History*
PMHS *Publications of Mississippi Historical Society*

Preface

1. Bernard Bailyn, *Education in the Forming of American Society* (Chapel Hill, 1960), 14; Harvey Neufeldt and Clinton Allison, "Education and the Rise of the New South: An Historiographical Essay," in *Education and the Rise of the New South,* ed. Ronald K. Goodenow and Arthur O. White (Boston, 1981), 250. See also Thomas G. Dyer, "Higher Education in the South Since the Civil War: Historiographical Issues and Trends," in *The Web of Southern Social Relations: Women, Family, and Education,* ed. Walter J. Fraser, Jr., R. Frank Saunders, Jr., and Jon L. Wakelyn (Athens, 1985), 127–45.

2. Frederick Rudolph, *The American College and University: A History* (New York, 1962).

Chapter 1. Jefferson College and the Origins of Higher Education, *1802–1830*

1. On the Harvard code see Richard Hofstadter and Wilson Smith, eds., *American Higher Education: A Documentary History* (Chicago, 1961), 1:8; for President Clap's quote see John S. Brubacher, *A History of the Problems of Education* (New York, 1966), 448; and for the last quote see David W. Robson, *Educating Republicans: The College in the Era of the American Revolution, 1750–1800* (Westport, Conn., 1985), 7. See also Bernard J. Kohlbrenner, "Religion and Higher Education: An Historical Perspective," *HEQ* 1 (June 1961): 45–57; John D. Guice, "Log Colleges and Legacies of the Great Awakening," *Southern Quarterly* (January 1972): 117–37; George P. Schmidt, *The Liberal Arts College: A Chapter in American Cultural History* (New Brunswick, N.J., 1957), 23; Donald Tewksbury, *The Founding of American Colleges and Universities Before the Civil War* (New York, 1932), 55; Frederick Rudolph, *The American College and University: A History* (New York, 1962), 61.

2. Alma Pauline Foerster, "The State University in the Old South" (Ph.D.

diss., Duke University, 1939), 14; Rudolph, *American College,* 36, 40–41; Albea Godbold, *The Church College in the Old South* (Durham, N.C., 1944), 147.

3. During the early 1800s the area from Georgia to the Mississippi River was known as the Southwest. For a brief discussion of Claiborne's educational philosophy see Joseph Hatfield, *William Claiborne, Jeffersonian Centurion in the American Southwest* (Lafayette, La., 1976), 77–80; Dunbar Rowland, ed., *Official Letter Books of W. C. C. Claiborne, 1801–1816,* 6 vols. (Jackson, 1917), 6:100–101.

4. Douglas C. McMertrie, ed., *The Mississippi Territorial Session Laws of May, 1802* (Chicago, 1938), not paginated. In antebellum America institutions of higher learning were designated by a variety of names including college, seminary, institute, academy, and university.

5. Foerster, "State University," 2, 4, 6, 212 [Jefferson quote]; Clement Eaton, *The Freedom of Thought Struggle in the Old South* (Durham, N.C., 1940), chap. 3.

6. Foerster, "State University," 216, 219 [general assembly quote], 234–37; David W. Robson, "College Founding in the New Republic, 1776–1800," *HEQ* 23 (Fall 1983): 326. For a recent study of the University of Georgia see Thomas G. Dyer, *The University of Georgia: A Bicentennial History* (Athens, 1985). For a survey of college life in the antebellum South see Jon L. Wakelyn, "Antebellum College Life and the Relations between Fathers and Sons," in Walter J. Fraser, Jr., R. Frank Saunders, Jr., and Jon L. Wakelyn, eds., *The Web of Southern Social Relations, Women, Family, and Education* (Athens, Ga., 1985), 107–26.

7. McMertrie, *Session Laws,* not paginated.

8. William T. Blain, *Education in the Old Southwest: A History of Jefferson College* (Washington, Miss., 1976), 2–6; William B. Hamilton, "Jefferson College and Education in Mississippi, 1798–1817," *Journal of Mississippi History* 3 (1941): 266–67. See also Sharron Lynn Dobbs, "Jefferson College: A Study of the Origins of Higher Education in Mississippi, 1802–1848" (Ph.D. diss., University of Mississippi, 1987).

9. Blain, *Education in Old Southwest,* 206; Hamilton, "Jefferson College," 266–67.

10. Blain, *Education in Old Southwest,* 206; Hamilton, "Jefferson College," 266–67.

11. Blain, *Education in Old Southwest,* 206; Hamilton, "Jefferson College," 266–67.

12. J. K. Morrison, "Early History of Jefferson College," *PMHS* 2 (1898): 181–83.

13. Ibid., 181–82.

14. Ibid. [quote]; Blain, *Education in Old Southwest,* 10–11.

15. Blain, *Education in Old Southwest,* 11–14; Board of Trustees, *The Charter and Statutes of Jefferson College* (Natchez, 1840), 57, 74–76; Hamilton, "Jefferson College," 268–69, 271.

16. Charles Sydnor, *A Gentleman of the Old Natchez Region: Benjamin L. C. Wailes* (Durham, N.C., 1938), 49; Blain, *Education in Old Southwest*, 23–26.

17. Blain, *Education in Old Southwest*, 23–26; Trustees, *Charter and Statutes*, 76; Sydnor, *Gentleman of Old Natchez*, 49 [quote], 205.

18. Trustees, *Charter and Statutes*, 16, 77; Sydnor, *Gentleman of Old Natchez*, 204.

19. Morrison, "History of Jefferson College," 185–86; Trustees, *Charter and Statutes*, 77.

20. Morrison, "History of Jefferson College," 185–86; Trustees, *Charter and Statutes*, 77.

21. Charles Betts Galloway, "Elizabeth Female Academy: Mother of Female Colleges," *PMHS* 2 (1898): 169–78; Anne Firor Scott, "The Ever Widening Circle: The Diffusion of Feminist Values from the Troy Female Seminary, 1822–1872," *HEQ* 19 (Spring 1979): 3–27; William H. Weathersby, *History of Educational Legislation in Mississippi from 1798–1860* (Chicago, 1921), 66; Edward Mayes, *History of Education in Mississippi* (Washington, 1899), 38; John B. Cain, *Methodism in the Mississippi Conference, 1846–1870* (Jackson, 1939), 20, 23. In *A Burning Torch and a Flaming Fire: The Story of Centenary College of Louisiana* (Nashville, 1931), 109, William Hamilton Nelson cites Elizabeth Female Academy as the first college in the world chartered to grant degrees to women. Neither Thomas Woody in *A History of Women's Education in the United States* (New York, 1929), 481ff., nor Mabel Newcomer, in *A Century of Higher Education for American Women* (New York, 1959), 12, 33 n. 17, acknowledges Elizabeth Female Academy as a degree-granting college; however, Claribel Drake in "Mississippi's Elizabeth Female Academy: Its Claim to be the Mother of Women's Colleges in America," *Daughters of the American Revolution Magazine* (May 1962): 96, 487ff., makes a strong case for the academy as a collegiate institution. Trey Berry, in "A History of Higher Education for Women in Mississippi" (M.A. thesis, University of Mississippi, 1987), accepts Newcomer's conclusion. Shirley Ann Hickson does not mention Elizabeth Female Academy in "The Development of Higher Education for Women in the Antebellum South" (Ph.D. diss., University of South Carolina, 1985). For a more recent study of women's higher education see Barbara Soloman, *In Company of Educated Women: A History of Women and Higher Education in America* (New Haven, 1985).

22. Mayes, *History of Education*, 42–43, 55; Cain, *Methodism 1846–1870*, 20–23. Nelson, *A Burning Torch*, 109, states that the academy awarded a degree in 1826 but does not name the graduate. He also says that the suspension of Elizabeth Female Academy prompted another group of Methodists to establish a new female college, named Whitworth, at Brookhaven. Kathleen George Rice, in "A History of Whitworth College for Women" (Ph.D. diss., University of Mississippi, 1985), also links the establishment of Whitworth College to the suspension of Elizabeth Female Academy.

23. Trustees, *Charter and Statutes*, 78; Blain, *Education in Old Southwest*, 84;

Morrison, "History of Jefferson College," 186; *Mississippi Republican,* December 1, 1818.

24. Trustees, *Charter and Statutes,* 78; Blain, *Education in Old Southwest,* 84; Sydnor, *Gentleman of Old Natchez,* 205.

25. Trustees, *Charter and Statutes,* 79; Sydnor, *Gentleman of Old Natchez,* 205; *Senate Journal 1825,* 12–16 [Grayson quotes], 23, 92, 132, 159, 163. See Richard A. and Nannie Pitts McLemore, *A History of Mississippi College* (Clinton, Miss., 1979), for the early history of Hampstead Academy.

26. *House Journal 1825,* 23, 92.

27. Trustees, *Charter and Statutes,* 18, 79.

28. Trustees, *Charter and Statutes,* 83–84; Brandon quoted in *House Journal 1829,* 10; Morrison, "History of Jefferson College," 187.

29. Trustees, *Charter and Statutes,* 83–84; Morrison, "History of Jefferson College," 187; *House Journal 1829,* 10–11 [Brandon quote].

30. *House Journal 1829,* 14–15; *Mississippi Laws 1826,* 23–24 [cited hereafter as *Laws* and date]; McLemore and McLemore, *Mississippi College,* 7–8; Weathersby, *Educational Legislation,* 86.

31. Caldwell's letter to Quitman is quoted in Mayes, *History of Education,* 81–82.

32. *Laws 1829,* 54–55; *Laws 1830,* 101–2; McLemore and McLemore, *Mississippi College,* 10; Weathersby, *Educational Legislation,* 86.

33. Blain, *Education in Old Southwest,* 76, 80; Trustees, *Charter and Statutes,* 85; Sydnor, *Gentleman of Old Natchez,* 205–8 [quote, 205].

34. Sydnor, *Gentleman of Old Natchez,* 207; Blain, *Education in Old Southwest,* 77 [quote]. On white Mississippians' fondness for military splendor see Reuben Davis, *Recollections of Mississippi and Mississippians* (New York, 1889), 137–41.

35. Trustees, *Charter and Statutes,* 62–68, 85–86; Sydnor, *Gentleman of Old Natchez,* 206–7.

36. Sydnor, *Gentleman of Old Natchez,* 208–9; Rudolph, *American College,* 131–35. For a brief examination of the various interpretations of the Yale Report and an analysis of what the report was intended to do see Jack C. Lane, "The Yale Report of 1828 and Liberal Education: A Neorepublican Manifesto," *HEQ* 27 (Fall 1987): 325–38.

37. Sydnor, *Gentleman of Old Natchez,* 208–9.

38. Ibid., 145.

39. Ibid., 209. See also Suanna Smith, "Washington, Mississippi: Antebellum Elysium," *JMH* 15 (1978): 143–65; Laura D. Harrell, "The Development of the Lyceum Movement in Mississippi," *JMH* 31 (1969): 187–201; Arthur H. DeRosier, Jr., "William Dunbar: A Product of the Eighteenth Century Scottish Renaissance," *JMH* 28 (1966): 185–227; James R. Dungan, "'Sir' William Dunbar of Natchez: Planter, Explorer, and Scientist, 1792–1810," *JMH* 24 (1961): 211–28; Eron Rowland, *Life, Letters, and Papers of William Dunbar of Elgin, Morayshire, Scotland, and Natchez, Mississippi: Pioneer*

Scientist of the Southern United States (Jackson, 1930); William B. Gates, "The Theater in Natchez," *JMH* 3 (1941), 71–129; D. Clayton James, *Antebellum Natchez* (Baton Rouge, 1968). A set of the *Southwest Journal* is in the Louisiana State University Library.

40. Trustees, *Charter and Statutes*, 85; Blain, *Education in Old Southwest*, 69; Joseph Holt Ingraham, *The South-West, by a Yankee* (New York, 1835), 2:212.

41. Blain, *Education in Old Southwest*, 71–72.

42. Trustees, *Charter and Statutes*, 89–90; Sydnor, *Gentleman of Old Natchez*, 211. On President Lindsley see LeRoy J. Halsey, ed., *The Works of Philip Lindsley, D.D.* (Philadelphia, 1866). For a very brief analysis of Lindsley's educational reforms see Merle Borrowman, "The False Dawn of the State University," *HEQ* 1 (June 1961): 18–21.

43. Trustees, *Charter and Statutes*, 10–11, 38–39, 54–55; Foerster, "State University," 318–19.

44. Foerster, "State University," 318–19; James Allen Cabaniss, *The University of Mississippi: Its First One Hundred Years* (Oxford, 1949), 5–6.

45. Blain, *Education in Old Southwest*, 84 n. 86; McLemore and McLemore, *Mississippi College*, 27–30, 36, 45; Dawn Maddox, "The Buildings and Grounds of Jefferson College in the Nineteenth Century," *JMH* 35 (February 1973): 40 n. 3; James J. Piller, *The Catholic Church in Mississippi, 1837–1865* (New Orleans, 1964), 28 [quote].

46. James, *Antebellum Natchez*, 105; Hamilton, "Jefferson College," 276.

Chapter 2. Old-Time Colleges in Mississippi, 1830–1840

1. Frederick Rudolph, *The American College and University, A History* (New York, 1962), 48; Donald G. Tewksbury, *The Founding of American Colleges and Universities Before the Civil War* (New York, 1932), 3; David Robson, *Educating Republicans: The College in the Era of the American Revolution, 1750–1800* (Westport, Conn., 1985), 228–36; Daniel Boorstin, *The Americans: The National Experience* (New York, 1965), 152–61. On the continuing effort to establish a national university see David Madsen, *The National University: Enduring Dream of the United States of America* (Detroit, 1966). While Americans rejected the idea of a national university, many southern sectionalists advocated a regional university to promote southern views on states' rights and slavery and to train the best of the southern elite. The establishment of the University of the South at Sewanee was partly in response to that sentiment. See J. M. Richardson, "Central Southern University: Political and Educational Necessity for Its Establishment," *De Bow's Review* 23 (1857): 490–503; "University of the South," ibid. 26 (1859): 330–35; John S. Ezell, "A Southern Education for Southrons," *JSH* 17 (August 1951): 303–28.

2. John K. Bettersworth, *Mississippi, Yesterday and Today* (Austin, 1964), 132. The number of antebellum colleges in Mississippi is based on a compilation of those institutions which, in my judgment, were of collegiate rank and

includes all schools that were chartered even if they did not open. Elizabeth Female Academy is included in this compilation. I relied to a large extent on William H. Weathersby, *History of Educational Legislation in Mississippi from 1798–1860* (Chicago, 1921), although he did not list the female academy as a collegiate institution.

3. Charles Sydnor, *The Development of Southern Sectionalism, 1819–1848* (Baton Rouge, 1948), 303–4; Weathersby, *Educational Legislation*, 92–93; Thomas O. Summers, ed., *Autobiography of the Rev. Joseph Travis, A.M.* (Nashville, 1856), 68 [Travis quote]; William B. Hamilton, "Holly Springs, Mississippi to 1878" (M.A. thesis, University of Mississippi, 1931), 120, 122; Rudolph, *American College*, 47; Tewksbury, *Founding of American Colleges*, 28. The number of antebellum colleges that were established and subsequently failed has been revised downward by Natalie A. Naylor, "The Ante-bellum College Movement: A Reappraisal of Tewksbury's *The Founding of American Colleges and Universities*," *HEQ* 13 (Fall 1973): 261–75, and more recently by Colin B. Burke, *American Collegiate Populations: A Test of the Traditional View* (New York, 1987). Burke notes that Tewksbury's figures include all the institutions that were chartered, including those that never opened. Some chartered institutions in Mississippi did not open, but there were several more antebellum colleges in Mississippi than the seven Burke lists on page 308.

4. On the regional differences in public schools see Carl F. Kaestle, *Pillars of the Republic: Common Schools and American Society* (New York, 1983), 182–218; George P. Schmidt, *The Liberal Arts College, A Chapter in American Cultural History* (New Brunswick, N.J., 1957), 103; Clement Eaton, *The Freedom of Thought Struggle in the Old South* (Durham, N.C., 1940), 216; Rudolph, *American College*, 48. The traditional view of antebellum liberal arts colleges, which depicted them as sectarian, inefficient, and inflexible institutions that reflected the pre-modern attitude and values of their sponsors (in particular Richard Hofstadter's assertion that they were "The Great Retrogression" in American higher education), has been challenged by a host of revisionist historians. For the traditional view see Richard Hofstadter and Walter P. Metzger, *The Development of Academic Freedom in the United States* (New York, 1955), pt. 1. For the best brief statement of the traditional view, and a convincing challenge to that interpretation, see Burke's introduction to *American Collegiate Populations*. In addition to Burke and Naylor, "Ante-bellum College Movement," among the other historians who have challenged the traditional view are George Peterson, *The New England College in the Age of the University* (Amherst, 1964); Codman Hislop, *Eliphalet Nott* (Middletown, Conn., 1971); James L. Axtell, "The Death of the Liberal Arts College," *HEQ* 11 (Winter 1971): 330–53; David F. Allmendinger, Jr., "The Strangeness of the American Education Society; Indigent Students and the New Charity, 1815–1840," *HEQ* 11 (Spring 1971): 3–23, "New England Students and the Revolution in Higher Education 1800–1900," *HEQ* 11 (Winter 1971): 381–89, and *Paupers and Scholars: The Transformation of Student Life in Nineteenth Century New England* (New York, 1975);

David B. Potts, "American Colleges in the Nineteenth Century: From Localism to Denominationalism," *HEQ* 11 (Winter 1971): 363–80; Thomas S. Harding, *Collegiate Literary Societies: Their Contributions to Higher Education in the United States, 1815–1876* (New York, 1971); Jurgen Herbst, "American College History: Re-examination Underway," *HEQ* 14 (Summer 1974): 259–66; Wilson Smith, "Apologia pro Alma Matre: The College as Community in Antebellum America," in *The Hofstadter Aegis: A Memorial,* ed. Stanley Elkins and Eric McKitrick (New York, 1974), 125–54; and James McLachlan, "The American Colleges in the Nineteenth Century: Towards a Reappraisal," *Teachers College Record* 86 (December 1978): 287–306.

5. For Sharon College see Edward Mayes, *History of Education in Mississippi* (Washington, 1899), 51–57, 64; John B. Cain, *Methodism in Mississippi Conferences, 1846–1870,* (Jackson, 1939), 19, 231; Tommy Wayne Rogers, "The Schools of Higher Learning at Sharon, Mississippi," *JMH* 28 (February 1966): 40–56; *Biographical and Historical Memoirs of Mississippi* (Chicago, 1891), 2:315 [cited hereafter as *Goodspeed*]; Dunbar Rowland, *Mississippi, Compromising Sketches . . . Arranged in Cyclopedia Form* (Atlanta, 1907), 2:658. On Centenary's pledge not to teach sectarian dogma see Mayes, *History of Education,* 112, and on Mississippi Female College see the college's 1856 catalog, 14. Centenary College was relocated from Brandon Springs, Mississippi, to Jackson, Louisiana, and then later to Shreveport. For Chamberlain's statement see Mississippi Legislature, *House Journal 1840,* 308–10 [cited hereafter as *House* or *Senate Journal* and year]. President Chamberlain did indicate in a report to the governor that Oakland intended to enlarge the chair of theology into a theological seminary. On the development of American theological seminaries see Natalie A. Naylor, "The Theological Seminary in the Configuration of Higher Education: The Ante-bellum Years," *HEQ* 17 (Spring 1977): 17–31. Whether the college mania of the 1830s to 1850s was a great retrogression may be arguable, but it is a fact that most of the colleges founded during that period were denominationally connected. The link should not be understated because, as William Hamilton Nelson, *A Burning Torch and a Flaming Fire: The Story of Centenary College of Louisiana* (Nashville, 1931), 105, has correctly noted, "the college follows the church." Many of the South's church schools such as Emory, Davidson, Richmond, Wake Forest, Spring Hill, and Randolph-Macon date from this period. In Mississippi the Presbyterians established Oakland College, the Methodists founded Centenary, and the Baptists acquired ownership of Mississippi College. Although the Mississippi Baptist Convention did not officially establish or financially support any colleges before 1850, it did encourage and endorse the work of any college that was compatible with Baptist doctrines and principles. Philip Lindsley was scornful of colleges that pretended to be nonsectarian but proselytized their students; see Merle Borrowman, "The False Dawn of the State University," *HEQ* 1 (June 1961): 18–21. Chancellor F. A. P. Barnard of the University of Mississippi, who was often criticized by Mississippi's evangelical leadership, claimed that

the denominational colleges were "instrumentalities through which the peculiarities of their founders are to be maintained, propagated, and defended" (Tewksbury, *Founding of American Colleges,* 5). See Samuel C. Mitchell, ed., *The South in the Building of the Nation* (Richmond, 1909), 10:249–50; Z. T. Leavell, *A Complete History of Mississippi Baptists from the Earliest Times* (Jackson, 1904), 2:1243. For denominational competition in the Southwest see Brownlow Posey, *Religious Strife on the Southern Frontier* (Baton Rouge, 1965).

    6. Tommy Wayne Rogers, "T. C. Thornton: A Methodist Educator in Antebellum Mississippi," *JMH* 44 (May 1982): 138, Rudolph, *American College,* 48.

    7. Tewksbury, *Founding of American Colleges,* 5.

    8. Rudolph, *American College,* 139; Wayne J. Urban, "History of Education: A Southern Exposure," *HEQ* 21 (Summer 1981): 137; Anne Firor Scott, "The Ever Widening Circle: The Diffusion of Feminist Values from the Troy Female Seminary, 1822–1872," *HEQ* 19 (Spring 1979): 3.

    9. John N. Waddel, *The Evils of Unsanctified Ambition* (Meridian, Miss., 1870); Charles L. Dubuisson, *Inaugural Address Delivered by Charles L. Dubuisson, President of Jefferson College* (Natchez, 1835), 9.

    10. *Goodspeed,* 2:310; Michael Wayne, *The Reshaping of Plantation Society: The Natchez District, 1860–1880* (Baton Rouge, 1983), 12. Rudolph, in *American College,* found that state aid to private colleges was not uncommon in the antebellum period and that lotteries and land grants were the "favorite forms of state assistance," 185–86.

    11. Schmidt, *Liberal Arts College,* 211; Laurence R. Veysey, *The Emergence of the American University* (Chicago, 1965), 22–23; Richard Hofstadter and C. DeWitt Hardy, *The Development and Scope of Higher Education in the United States* (New York, 1952), 15; Thomas C. Thornton, *Inaugural Address Delivered at the First Commencement of Centenary College* (Jackson, 1842), 21; *Rules for the Government of the Methodist Female Academy Near Washington Enacted By the Trustees in October 1818* (Natchez, 1818). 1.

    12. Schmidt, *Liberal Arts College,* 153.

    13. For a brief discussion of the influence of Benjamin Franklin's imaginary "College of Mirania," with its nontraditional curriculum, see Schmidt, 58–59, and Rudolph, *American College,* 36. On the rise and spread of entrepreneurialism and the American college's response to it see Jack C. Lane, "The Yale Report of 1828 and Liberal Education: A Neorepublican Manifesto," *HEQ* 27 (Fall 1987): 326. On the development of the collegiate curriculum see Douglas Sloan, "Harmony, Chaos, and Consensus: The American College Curriculum," *Teachers College Record* 73 (December 1971): 221–51, and Frederick Rudolph, *Curriculum: A History of the American Undergraduate Course of Study Since 1636* (San Francisco, 1977).

    14. Schmidt, *Liberal Arts College,* 55–56; Rudolph, *American College,* 134–35 [quoting Yale Report]; quote by Rowland Bertoff, "Peasants and Artisans, Puritans and Republicans: Personal Liberty and Communal Equality in American History," *JAH* 69 (December 1982): 579–98. For a history of the develop-

ment of liberal education see Bruce A. Kimball, *Orators and Philosophers: A History of the Idea of Liberal Education* (New York, 1986).

15. Weathersby, *Educational Legislation,* 98, 92, 159; Alma Pauline Foerster, "The State University in the Old South" (Ph.D. diss., Duke University, 1939), 357; Katie M. Headley, *Claiborne County, Mississippi: The Promised Land* (Port Gibson, Miss., 1976), 166. See Francis Wayland, *Thoughts on the Present Collegiate System in the United States* (Boston, 1842), and LeRoy J. Halsey, ed., *The Works of Philip Lindsley, D.D.* (Philadelphia, 1866).

16. William B. Hamilton, "Jefferson College and Education in Mississippi, 1798–1817," *JMH* 3 (1941): 260–61; Horace Mann Bond, *The Education of the Negro in the American Social Order* (New York, 1934), 178; William R. Hogan and Edwin Davis, eds., *William Johnson's Natchez: The Antebellum Diary of a Free Negro* (Baton Rouge, 1951); see also their biography of Johnson, *The Barber of Natchez* (Baton Rouge, 1973). For a brief discussion of the education of slaves see Charles Sydnor, *Slavery in Mississippi* (New York, 1933), 53–56. For general studies of the education of blacks before the Civil War see Carter G. Woodson, *The Education of the Negro Prior to 1861* (New York, 1919); Thomas L. Webber, *Deep like the River: Education in the Slave Quarter Community, 1831–1865* (New York, 1978); and Henry A. Bullock, *A History of Negro Education in the South From 1619 to the Present* (Cambridge, 1967). For a bibliographical essay on education of American blacks see Ronald E. Butchart, "'Outthinking and Outflanking the Owners of the World': A Historiography of the African American Struggle for Education," *HEQ* 28 (Fall 1988): 333–67.

17. *Rules for the Methodist Female Academy,* 1; Cain, *Methodism 1846–1870,* 275. See also Kathleen George Rice, "A History of Whitworth College for Women," (Ph.D. diss., University of Mississippi, 1985).

18. Weathersby, *Educational Legislation;* see 154–61 for abstracts of college charters.

19. Trustees, *Charter and Statutes of Jefferson College* (Natchez, 1840), 31; Weathersby, *Educational Legislation,* 156; Ray Holder, "Centenary: Roots of a Pioneer College (1838–1844)," *JMH* 42 (1980): 77–99. For a study of academic government that is generally favorable to an authoritarian board of trustees see W. H. Cowley, *Presidents, Professors, and Trustees: The Evolution of American Academic Government* (San Francisco, 1980). For Winans's educational endeavors see Ray Holder, *William Winans: Methodist Leader in Antebellum Mississippi* (Jackson, 1977), 138–39, 140, 146, 177, 181.

20. Nelson, *A Burning Torch,* 128–32; John D. Wade, *Augustus Baldwin Longstreet: A Study in the Development of Culture in the South* (New York, 1924), 294.

21. Rudolph, *American College,* 170; *House Journal 1840,* 294 (quote about Stephens); Rogers, "Higher Learning at Sharon," 51–54; Mayes, *History of Education,* 55; Summerville Institute, *Catalog* (n.p., 1866), 9 [quote at end of paragraph]; Charles Betts Galloway, "Elizabeth Female Academy: Mother of Female Colleges," *PMHS* 2 (1898): 172. See also George P. Schmidt, *The Old-Time College President* (New York, 1930).

22. Mayes, *History of Education*, 64–65; Reverend J. R. Hutchinson, D.D., *Reminiscences, Sketches, and Speeches* (Houston, 1874), 22–25; *House Journal 1840*, 308–10; Tommy Wayne Rogers, "Oakland College, 1830–1871," *JMH* 26 (May 1974): 143–61 [Parker quote, 150]; For a fuller discussion of Chamberlain and Oakland College see Melvin K. Bruss, "History of Oakland College (Mississippi), 1830–1871" (M.A. thesis, Louisiana State University, 1965).

23. *Goodspeed* 2:310; Rogers, "Oakland College," 150. For a brief discussion of the bowie knife stabbing of President Chamberlain see Bruss, "Oakland College," 63–65.

24. Mayes, *History of Education*, 67.

25. Rogers, "Oakland College," 159; Edward D. Eddy, Jr., *Colleges for Our Land and Time* (New York, 1957), 257. See also Merlerson Guy Dunham, *The Centennial History of Alcorn Agricultural and Mechanical College* (Hattiesburg, Miss., 1971), xii. On early black colleges see Rufus B. Atwood, "The Origin and Development of the Negro Public College, with Special Reference to the Land-Grant College," *JNE* 31 (Summer 1962): 240–50.

26. David L. Smiley, "William Carey Crane, Professor of Old Mississippi," *JMH* 12 (April 1950): 98–104; Weathersby, *Educational Legislation*, 158, 160. Mississippi Female College had a nominal relationship with the Baptists, but it received no funds from the Mississippi Baptist Convention. Semple Broaddus was a college for boys at Center Hill in De Soto County which received some but not much support from several nearby Baptist associations. The college's charter authorized its founders to use the name "The University of De Soto County" but they did not exercise that option.

27. Smiley, "Crane," 102–3 [quotes]; Jessie L. Boyd, *A Popular History of Baptists in Mississippi* (Jackson, 1930), 315; Schmidt, *Liberal Arts College*, 71. See also Mayes, *History of Education*, for a discussion of several old-time colleges in Mississippi.

28. For a generally positive assessment of teaching in the old-time college see Smith, "Apologia pro Alma Matre."

29. E. Merton Coulter, *College Life in the Old South* (New York, 1928), 86.

30. Foerster, "State University," 201; Rudolph, *American College*, 88 [first quote], 86; Mayes, *History of Education*, 58; *Forty-fourth Announcement of the Union Female College, 1897–1898* (n.p., n.d.); Grover C. Cleveland, "The Origin and Development of the University of Mississippi with Special Reference to Its Legislative Control" (Ph.D. diss., Stanford University, 1932), 81–82.

31. Professor Gale's letter of January 6, 1840, to Governor Alexander McNutt is published in *House Journal 1840*, 296–97. David Allmendinger has found that the essential features of the corporate collegiate community had disappeared in New England by 1840, at the time Professor Gale made his comparison of northern and southern students. The loss of that corporate character was caused by a shift in the social origins of New England college students. A combination of demographics and new scholarship funds brought

"poor students" and older students to northern colleges in large numbers. The advent of older students, from the lower class, changed the housing and dining arrangements, admission standards, and codes of conduct and "shattered the order and uniformity" of New England colleges. See Allmendinger, "New England Students" and *Paupers and Scholars.* The residential colleges in antebellum Mississippi did not experience a similar transformation, in part because there were few scholarships available to poor students and few takers for those that were available. J. E. B. De Bow complained that "it is a common difficulty at the South to get persons to accept free instruction in our colleges" (*De Bow's Review* 27 [1860]: 239). For scholarships that were untaken see Ezell, "Education for Southrons," 325. Free schooling was considered "a bounty to the indigent," and few southern men wanted to reveal that they could not pay for their sons' educations; see Foerster, "State University," 210–11, 315, 391.

32. Holder, "Centenary," 77–99; John N. Waddel, *Memorials of Academic Life* (Richmond, 1891), 267; Foerster, "State University," 344.

33. The 1853 examination at the Presbyterian Female Collegiate Institute at Pontotoc attracted such a large crowd from the surrounding counties that the exam had to be moved from the college building to the local Presbyterian church. See Edna Haley Lowe, *Sketch of Chickasaw College, Pontotoc, Mississippi* (Oxford, 1951), 10; Charles Sydnor, *A Gentleman of the Old Natchez Region: Benjamin L. C. Wailes* (Durham, N.C., 1933), 207; Boyd, *Baptists in Mississippi,* 316; Coulter, *College Life,* 36; *Rules and Regulations of the University of Mississippi* (Holly Springs, Miss., 1850), 6; Mayes, *History of Education,* 58.

34. For Thwing's quote see Cowley, *Presidents, Professors and Trustees,* 99. During the Christmas season of 1855 southwest Mississippi experienced a rare snowfall, and the student poet makes reference to it in "A Parody," which appeared in the *Oakland Magazine* (July 1856), 21. Verner Smith Holmes, a student at Mississippi College in the late 1920s, tells stories of late-night raids on nearby chicken coops that were very similar to the episode celebrated in this verse.

35. See Rudolph, *American College,* 137–46, and Harding, *Literary Societies.* For a discussion of the importance of literary societies in the antebellum college see Bruss, "Oakland College," 33–50.

36. Chamberlain's letter to Governor McNutt is published in *House Journal 1840,* 310.

37. See *House Journal 1842,* 1075–82, for Governor Tucker's veto message.

38. Grenada *Weekly Register* quoted in Mayes, *History of Education,* 112.

Chapter 3. Founding the State University, 1840–1865

1. *Southern Reformer* quoted in Alma Pauline Foerster, "The State University in the Old South," (Ph.D. diss., Duke University, 1939), 391; John D. Wade, *Augustus Baldwin Longstreet: A Study in the Development of Culture in the South,* (New York, 1924), 228; Albea Godbold, *The Church College in the Old South* (Durham, N.C., 1944), 149. On sectionalism see Samuel T. Lyles,

"Conditions Relating to Sectionalism in Mississippi from 1838 to 1852," (M.A. thesis, University of Mississippi, 1932), 1–9; Charles Sydnor, *The Development of Southern Sectionalism, 1819–1848* (Baton Rouge, 1948), 60–63; Charles W. Dabney, *Universal Education in the South* (Chapel Hill, 1936), 350.

2. Nathaniel C. Hathorn, "A Financial History of the University of Mississippi from Its Endowment in 1819 to 1900," (M.A. thesis, University of Mississippi, 1938), 2–5, 7, 9, 22–23.

3. Wilbur J. Cash, in *Mind of the South* (New York, 1941), 93–94, says that by the 1830s "the South was enroute to the savage ideal: to that ideal whereunder dissent and variety are completely suppressed and men became, in all their attitudes, professions, and actions, virtual replicas of one another." For the collegiate official's quote see Board of Trustees, *The Charter and Statutes of Jefferson College* (Natchez, 1840), 10–11. For the quotes concerning Henry II and the German principalities see W. H. Cowley, *Presidents, Professors, and Trustees* (San Francisco, 1980), 18, 23; Foerster, "State University," 2, discusses the colonial fathers' complaint. For Brown's quote see Mississippi *House of Representatives Journal 1840,* 17–18 [cited hereafter as *House* or *Senate Journal* and date], and for a study of Governor Brown see James B. Ranck, *Albert Gallatin Brown: Radical Southern Nationalist* (New York, 1937). For the last quote see Bernard Bailyn, *Education in the Forming of American Society* (Chapel Hill, 1960), 14. James L. Axtell, "The Death of the Liberal Arts College," *HEQ* 11 (Winter 1971): 330–53, suggests that historians of education should take "a cue from cultural anthropologists" and "make continuity and conservatism our working assumptions about societies and the educational institutions they create to preserve and transmit their ideals and social character." But see also Laurence Veysey, "Toward a New Direction in Educational History: Prospect and Retrospect," *HEQ* 9 (Fall 1969): 343–59.

4. Reverend J. R. Hutchinson, D.D., *Reminiscences, Sketches, and Speeches* (Houston, 1874), 22–23, stating that it was customary in antebellum America to locate colleges in a "sylvan exile prepared deliberately to curb the normal wildness of youth"; Neal C. Gillespie, "Ole Miss: A New Look at Her First President," *JMH* 30 (1968): 282–83; James Allen Cabaniss, *The University of Mississippi: Its First Hundred Years,* 2d ed. (Hattiesburg, 1970), 6–7; Frederick Rudolph, *The American College and University: A History* (New York, 1962), 92–93; Lyles, "Sectionalism," 1–9.

5. *Woodville Republican,* March 14, 1846, quoting the *Natchez Courier.*

6. Edward Mayes, *History of Education in Mississippi* (Washington, 1899), 133–34; *Woodville Republican,* January 31, 1846; *House Journal 1846,* 232–34 [Simrall quotes].

7. Cabaniss, *University of Mississippi,* 7–8; *Laws of Mississippi 1844,* 227–28; *Laws 1846,* 248–49. James Alexander Ventress was such an influential supporter of a state university that he is considered the "father of the University of Mississippi." For his efforts in behalf of the university and for his long ten-

ure on the board of trustees see Lynda Lasswell Crist, "'Useful in His Day': James Alexander Ventress (1805–1867)" (Ph.D. diss., University of Tennessee, 1980), esp. 191–236.

8. *Senate Journal 1846,* 14.

9. John N. Waddel, *Memorials of Academic Life* (Richmond, 1891), 248; *Historical Catalogue of the University of Mississippi, 1849–1909* (Nashville, 1910), 74; Foerster, "State University," 197; Florence E. Campbell, "Journal of the Board of Trustees of the University of Mississippi" (M.A. thesis, University of Mississippi, 1939), July 12, 1848 [a typed copy of the manuscript minutes of the board, to be cited hereafter as Campbell, Minutes, and date]; Cabaniss, *University of Mississippi,* 10.

10. Waddel, *Memorials,* 249–50, 252–53, 288; Campbell, Minutes, July 12, 1848, and see p. 459; Cabaniss, *University of Mississippi,* 165–66, n. 49.

11. Waddel, *Memorials,* 252; Wade, *Longstreet,* 289–90, 292.

12. Gillespie, "Ole Miss: First President," 282; Foerster, "State University," 342–43; Waddel, *Memorials,* 254; Cabaniss, *University of Mississippi,* 14–17. For a study of Bledsoe's career see Willard M. Hayes, "Polemics and Philosophy: A Biography of Albert Taylor Bledsoe (Ph.D. diss., University of Tennessee, 1971).

13. Gillespie, "Ole Miss: First President," 284–85 [quotes]; Foerster, "State University," 344; Waddel, *Memorials,* 267.

14. Wade, *Longstreet,* 296; Gillespie, "Ole Miss," 289–90; Foerster, "State University," 275–76.

15. Wade, *Longstreet,* 297; Campbell, Minutes, July 12, 1849.

16. Wade, *Longstreet,* 297–98; Cabaniss, *University of Mississippi,* 21–23; Foerster, "State University," 345.

17. Foerster, "State University," 181, 183, 277, 287; *De Bow's Review* quoted in Sydnor, *Southern Sectionalism,* 303; William H. Weathersby, *History of Educational Legislation in Mississippi from 1798 to 1860* (Chicago, 1921), 126–27, 189–90; Mayes, *History of Education,* 20; Frederick A. P. Barnard, *Letter to the Honorable The Board of Trustees of the University of Mississippi* (Oxford, 1858), 53.

18. Weathersby, *Educational Legislation,* 127; *Historical Catalogue,* 40–41; *Laws 1852,* 189–90; John Fulton, *Memoirs of Frederick A. P. Barnard* (New York, 1896), 231.

19. Foerster, "State University," 354–55, 454. See also Gillespie, "Ole Miss: First President"; Gladys Bryson, "The Emergence of the Social Sciences From Moral Philosophy," *International Journal of Ethics* 42 (April 1932): 304–23.

20. Mayes, *History of Education,* 142 [Thompson quote]; Cabaniss, *University of Mississippi,* 31; Waddel, *Memorials,* 483.

21. Cabaniss, *University of Mississippi,* 24.

22. Wade, *Longstreet,* 302, 304.

23. Wade, *Longstreet,* 307–8; Cabaniss, *University of Mississippi,* 32–33.

24. Foerster, "State University," 392, 407.

25. Wade, *Longstreet,* 305–6; Foerster, "State University," 413.

26. *House Journal 1856,* 22.

27. Wade, *Longstreet,* 310.

28. Foerster, "State University," 414. See also J. W. Johnson, "Sketches of Judge A. B. Longstreet and Dr. F. A. P. Barnard," *PMHS* 12 (1912): 122–48.

29. Johnson, "Longstreet and Barnard," 143.

30. Rudolph, *American College,* 99, 108; Fulton, *Memoirs,* 237; Barnard quoted in William J. Chute, *Damn Yankee! The First Career of Frederick A. P. Barnard* (New York, 1978), 161.

31. Cabaniss, *University of Mississippi* (see following p. 50 for a picture of the gymnasium); Campbell, Minutes, November 9, 1857; Foerster, "State University," 433.

32. Chute, *Damn Yankee,* see chap. 18.

33. Wade, *Longstreet,* 299; Frederick A. P. Barnard, "Autobiographical Sketch of Dr. F. A. P. Barnard," *PMHS* 12 (1912): 112–13; Chute, *Damn Yankee,* 143, quoting Mrs. Barnard.

34. Chute, *Damn Yankee,* 167; Hathorn, "Financial History," 36ff.; Cabaniss, *University of Mississippi,* 43; Grover C. Hooker, "The Origin and Development of the University of Mississippi with Special Reference to Its Legislative Control," (Ph.D. diss., Stanford University, 1932), 21ff.

35. Hathorn, "Financial History," 38–39; *Laws 1856,* 76.

36. Weathersby, *Educational Legislation,* 90–91; *House Journal 1856,* 22 [McRae quote]; *Laws 1856,* 383–84; Mayes, *History of Education,* 245–46.

37. Fulton, *Memoirs,* 204 [first Barnard quote]; Campbell, Minutes, July 8–14, 1857; Chute, *Damn Yankee,* 160.

38. Campbell, Minutes, November 9, 1857; *Laws 1857,* 109–10, 439–40, 447; Mayes, *History of Education,* 151; Barnard, "Autobiographical Sketch," 121.

39. Barnard, *Letter,* 7. See also Frederick A. P. Barnard, *Report on the Organization of Military Schools* (Jackson, 1861), 31.

40. Chute, *Damn Yankee,* 163. See Rudolph, *American College,* 110–36.

41. Barnard, *Letter,* 104.

42. Ibid., 100.

43. Ibid., 82–86.

44. Ibid., 85.

45. Ibid., 110.

46. Frank Keyes, *An Address Delivered Before the Alumni Association of the University of Mississippi, on the Fifth Day of July, 1859* (Oxford, 1859), 16, 19.

47. Campbell, Minutes, November, 24, 1859; Chute, *Damn Yankee,* 167.

48. Cabaniss, *University of Mississippi,* 46–49; Foerster, "State University," 379; Chute, *Damn Yankee,* 162, 168.

49. For Davis's quote see Barnard, "Autobiographical Sketch," 115.

50. Fulton, *Memoirs,* 279; Keyes, *Address,* 23.

Chapter 4. Expansion of Higher Education, 1865–1900

1. Frederick Rudolph, *The American College and University: A History* (New York, 1962), 243–45; Joseph Stetar, "In Search of Direction: Southern Higher Education After the Civil War," *HEQ* 25 (Fall 1985): 341.

2. Joseph W. Taylor, *An Address Delivered Before the Phi Sigma and Hermean Societies at the Commencement . . . on June 25, 1869* (Memphis, 1869), 8–10.

3. John N. Waddel, *Memorials of Academic Life* (Richmond, 1891), 446–49; James Allen Cabaniss, *The University of Mississippi: Its First Hundred Years* (Hattiesburg, 1970), 6off.; Edward Mayes, *History of Education in Mississippi* (Washington, 1899), 159; Edward Mayes, *The State University: A Reply by Professor Edward Mayes to Senator James Z. George* (n.p., 1887), 24.

4. Waddel, *Memorials,* 449; Rudolph, *American College,* 267. Cornell and other universities throughout the country faced similar though less extreme admission problems. Some Cornell students who were given a basic geography test in 1869 listed Portugal as the capital of Spain, Borneo as the capital of Russia, India as a part of Africa, and Egypt as a province of Russia. Cornell rejected the fifty students who could not meet its admission standards.

5. Waddel, *Memorials,* 453–55; Dunbar Rowland, *Mississippi, Comprising Sketches . . . Arranged in Cyclopedic Form* (Atlanta, 1907), 2:617.

6. For studies of Reconstruction in Mississippi see James W. Garner, *Reconstruction in Mississippi* (New York, 1901); William C. Harris, *Presidential Reconstruction in Mississippi* (Baton Rouge, 1967) and *Day of the Carpetbagger* (Baton Rouge, 1978); Vernon L. Wharton, *The Negro in Mississippi, 1865–1890* (Chapel Hill, 1947). For the views of a black participant in Reconstruction see John Roy Lynch [with an introduction by John Hope Franklin], *Reminiscences of an Active Life: The Autobiography of John Roy Lynch* (Chicago, 1970), and on Mississippi scalawags see David G. Sansing, "The Role of the Scalawag in Mississippi Reconstruction" (Ph.D. diss., University of Southern Mississippi, 1969).

7. Harris, *Day of the Carpetbagger,* 345. For a biography of Governor Alcorn see Lillian Pereyra, *James L. Alcorn, Persistent Whig* (Baton Rouge, 1966).

8. Harris, *Day of the Carpetbagger,* 345–47 [*Clarion* quote, 345]; Edward Mayes, *L. Q. C. Lamar: His Life, Times, and Speeches* (Nashville, 1896), 131–34. For a more recent biography of Lamar see James L. Murphy, *L. Q. C. Lamar: Pragmatic Patriot* (Baton Rouge, 1973).

9. Harris, *Day of the Carpetbagger,* 345–47.

10. Ibid., 345; Mayes, *History of Education,* 162; Cabaniss, *University of Mississippi,* 81. For a biography of Ames see Blanche Ames, *Adelbert Ames, 1835–1933* (New York, 1964). Governor Ames was a former Union general who had won the Congressional Medal of Honor at the first Battle of Bull Run. He was despised by Mississippi's "unreconstructed rebels," and the passing years did little to diminish their cordial dislike of the Yankee officer. In 1958 a "76-year-old unreconstructed Rebel" was "shocked beyond words" that General Ames's portrait in his union blue uniform, which was adorned with medals

"earned by blood of Confederate soldier boys," was hanging in the Hall of Governors in the state capitol and he demanded its immediate removal. For a brief discussion of this episode see David G. Sansing and Carroll Waller, *A History of the Mississippi Governor's Mansion* (Jackson, 1977), 157 n. 9, 210.

11. Laurence R. Veysey, *The Emergence of the American University* (Chicago, 1965), 1.

12. Grover C. Hooker, "The Origin and Development of the University of Mississippi with Special Reference to Its Legislative Control" (Ph.D. diss., Stanford University, 1932), 103; Board of Trustees, Minutes, June 21, 1867 [Waddel quote], June 19, September 22–23, 1869, August 17, October 26, 1870 [cited hereafter as Minutes and date]. For a brief report on his trip see Waddel, *Memorials,* 478.

13. Waddel, *Memorials,* 478–79; University of Mississippi, *Historical Catalogue, 1849–1909,* 12; Cabaniss, *University of Mississippi,* 75–76, 109, 112; Mayes, *History of Education,* 174–75.

14. For Hilgard's report on the organization of the Department of Agriculture and Mechanic Arts see Mayes, *History of Education,* 170–73, and John K. Bettersworth, *People's College* (Birmingham, 1953), 18ff. On the politics of agricultural education see Francis B. Simkins, *Pitchfork Ben Tillman* (Baton Rouge, 1944). For Burkitt and Vardaman see Albert Kirwan, *The Revolt of the Rednecks: Mississippi Politics, 1876–1925* (Lexington, Ky., 1951), esp. 40–50, and William F. Holmes, *The White Chief: James Kimble Vardaman* (Baton Rouge, 1970).

15. Wharton, *Negro in Mississippi,* 250–51, 254–55; Harris, *Day of the Carpetbagger,* 343; Mayes, *History of Education,* 260–63, 267–70. See also Webster B. Baker, *History of Rust College* (Greensboro, 1924); Clarice T. Campbell and Oscar Allen Rogers, Jr., *Mississippi: The View From Tougaloo* (Jackson, 1979), 3–9; Charles H. Wilson, Sr., *Education for Negroes in Mississippi Since 1910* (Boston, 1947), 516–24; Mississippi *Senate Journal 1896,* 39. For a survey of higher education for blacks in this period see Robert L. Jenkins, "The Development of Black Higher Education," *JMH* 45 (November 1983): 272–83. The designation of institutions that provided teacher training as normal schools or colleges was derived from the French word *normal* (model) and popularized by Victor Cousin, a professor at the Sorbonne.

16. Mayes, *History of Education,* 164. The University of South Carolina was the only southern state university to integrate during Reconstruction. See David W. Hollis, *The University of South Carolina* (Columbia, 1956), 2:61–79. On the education of blacks after the Civil War see Robert C. Morris, *Reading, 'Riting and Reconstruction: The Education of the Freedmen in the South, 1861–1870* (Chicago, 1981); William Vaughn, *Schools for All: Blacks and Public Education in the South, 1865–1877* (Lexington, 1974); and James D. Anderson, *The Education of Blacks in the South, 1860–1935* (Chapel Hill, 1988).

17. Waddel, *Memorials,* 465ff. [Waddel quote]; *Historical Catalogue, 1849–1909,* 74 [Sharkey quote]; Garner, *Reconstruction in Mississippi,* 369.

18. Garner, *Reconstruction in Mississippi,* 369; Mayes, *History of Education,* 164.

19. Mississippi *Laws 1871*, 716–21. For a biographical sketch of Revels see George A. Sewell and Margaret L. Dwight, *Mississippi Black History Makers* (Jackson, 1984), 7–16; Harris, *Day of the Carpetbagger*, 347–48; Mayes, *History of Education*, 271; Rufus B. Atwood, "The Origin and Development of the Negro Public College, with Special Reference to the Land-Grant College," *JNE* 31 (Summer 1962): 240–50.

20. Mayes, *History of Education*, 174; Wharton, *Negro in Mississippi*, 253; Merlerson Guy Dunham, *The Centennial History of Alcorn Agricultural and Mechanical* (Hattiesburg, 1971), 45. For the development of coeducation at Alcorn see W. Milam Davis, *Pushing Forward: A History of Alcorn A & M College and Portraits of Its Successful Graduates* (Okolona, Miss., 1938), 27–29; *Official and Statistical Register of Mississippi, 1917*, 653.

21. *Catalogue of Alcorn University, 1871*, 12–17; Dunham, *Alcorn*, 17–22; Mayes, *History of Education*, 173; Wharton, *Negro in Mississippi*, 160; Harris, *Day of the Carpetbagger*, 350.

22. Dunham, *Alcorn*, 22; Harris, *Day of the Carpetbagger*, 351.

23. Bettersworth, *People's College*, 26, 33. After the Mississippi Agricultural and Mechanical College had been named Mississippi State University, and during its centennial, Bettersworth published an enlarged and revised *People's University: The Centennial History of Mississippi State* (Jackson, 1980). See also Earle D. Ross, *Democracy's College: The Land-Grant Movement in the Formative Stages* (Ames, Iowa, 1942), and J. B. Edmond, *The Magnificent Charter: The Origin and Role of the Morrill Land-Grant Colleges and Universities* (Hicksville, N.Y., 1978).

24. For biographical information on Lee see Herman Hattaway, *General Stephen D. Lee* (Jackson, 1976); on the selection of President Lee see Bettersworth, *People's College*, 42; for Lee's failure to make "Devereaux," his Noxubee County plantation, a successful operation see 49–50; and for the appointment of Governor Stone see 180.

25. For Morrill's quote see Rudolph, *American College*, 249; for Lee's quote see Bettersworth, *People's College*, 77.

26. Bettersworth, *People's College*, 77–80 [Lee quote, 77]; Hattaway, *Lee*, 189.

27. See *Report of Joint Select Committee Appointed to Inquire Into . . . the A & M College of Mississippi* (Jackson, 1882), 7. Auburn University in neighboring Alabama experienced a similar development.

28. Bettersworth, *People's College*, 80 [Lee quote], 147–48; Mayes, *History of Education*, 231, 242.

29. Bettersworth, *People's College*, 80–84.

30. Ibid., 118ff.; Mayes, *History of Education*, 240–41. On the farmer's stubborn resistance to agricultural education see Roy V. Scott and James G. Shoalmire, *The Public Career of Cully Cobb* (Jackson, 1973).

31. Bettersworth, *People's College*, 84.

32. Cabaniss, *University of Mississippi*, 51; Mayes, *History of Education*, 245–

46. See also Bridget Smith Pieschel and Stephen Robert Pieschel, *Loyal Daughters: One Hundred Years at Mississippi University for Women, 1884–1984* (Jackson, 1984).

33. *Laws 1884*, 50–55; Mayes, *History of Education*, 246–47, 249–50, 252–53 [Jones quote, 250]; *Official and Statistical Register, 1904*, 279–84; Richard A. McLemore, ed., *A History of Mississippi* (Jackson, 1973), 2:317.

34. Mayes, *History of Education*, 252–53; *Official and Statistical Register, 1917*, 633; *House Journal 1896*, 84; Cabaniss, *University of Mississippi*, 122–23.

35. McLemore, *History of Mississippi*, 2:418; Rowland, *Mississippi*, 2:619, 633; see Senate bills 202 and 226 in *Senate Journal 1884*, 242, 344, 477, 490. In 1903 the state superintendent of education again cited the lack of competent teachers as the state's major educational problem and recommended the establishment of a normal college. On the development of professional education for teachers see John S. Brubacher, *A History of the Problems of Education* (New York, 1966), 465–506.

36. See Patrick H. Thompson, *The History of Negro Baptists in Mississippi* (Jackson, 1898), 12–13, 15–27. On black junior colleges and four-year church schools see Wilson, *Education for Negroes in Mississippi*, 455–531; Lelia Gaston Rhodes, *Jackson State University: The First Hundred Years, 1877–1977* (Jackson, 1979), 15–34; and Z. T. Leavell, *A Complete History of Mississippi Baptists from the Earliest Times* (Jackson, 1904), 2:1266–68, 1275–76. For a summary of higher education in Mississippi during the late nineteenth century see McLemore, ed., *History of Mississippi*, 2:625–28.

37. Cabaniss, *University of Mississippi*, 109–10; Rudolph, *American College*, 283; Michael V. O'Shea, *Public Education in Mississippi* (Jackson, 1927), 204–5.

38. Cabaniss, *University of Mississippi*, 101ff.; Mayes, *History of Education*, 178; Veysey, *Emergence of the University*, 182, 193.

39. Cabaniss, *University of Mississippi*, 103–4.

40. Rudolph, *American College*, 297–98; Veysey, *Emergence of the University*, 234.

41. Rudolph, *American College*, 303; H. E. Shepard, "Higher Education in the South," *Sewanee Review* (May 1893), 289; University of Mississippi, *Historical and Current Catalogue, 1893–1894*, 145, 162–63.

42. Cabaniss, *University of Mississippi*, 104, 107.

43. For a study of Mississippi's racial policy of this era and its effect on the state see Neil R. McMillen, *Dark Journey: Black Mississippians in the Age of Jim Crow* (Urbana, 1989). See also Lester Milton Salamon, "Protest, Politics, and Modernization in the American South: Mississippi as a 'Developing Society,'" (Ph.D. diss., Harvard University, 1971).

44. Mayes, *The State University*, 21; Bettersworth, *People's University*, 99–100; *Chickasaw Messenger*, September 6, 1887; Cabaniss, *University of Mississippi*, 99 [quote], 102–3.

45. Mayes, *The State University*, 4, 27.

46. Dunbar Rowland, *Courts, Judges, and Lawyers of Mississippi* (Jackson, 1935), 99–103; *Biographical Directory of the United States Congress, 1774–1949* (Washington, D.C., 1950), 1203. For a biographical sketch of George see James Lloyd, ed., *Lives of Mississippi Writers* (Jackson, 1980), 195–96; for a sketch of Mayes see David G. Sansing, "Edward C. Mayes," in *Mississippi Writers*, ed. Lloyd, 327–30.

47. *Senate Journal 1886*, 504.

48. Bettersworth, *People's College*, 155; Kirwan, *Revolt of the Rednecks*, 165 [Burkitt quote]; Bettersworth, *People's University*, 98; Mayes, *History of Education*, 231.

49. *Senate Journal 1886*, 501–3; Mayes, *History of Education*, 248 [Jones quote]; Bettersworth, *People's University*, 98 ["imported scholars" quote]; Hooker, "University of Mississippi," 132; Cabaniss, *University of Mississippi*, 104; Dunham, *Alcorn*, 41.

Chapter 5. A State System of Higher Education, 1900–1928

1. David G. Sansing and Carroll Waller, *A History of the Mississippi Governor's Mansion* (Jackson, 1977), 91–94; Robert E. McArthur, ed., *Inaugural Addresses of the Governors of Mississippi, 1890–1980* (University, Miss., 1980), 13–14, 16.

2. McArthur, *Inaugural Addresses*, 13–14, 16.

3. John K. Bettersworth, *People's University: The Centennial History of Mississippi State* (Jackson, 1980), 90.

4. Ibid., 87–90.

5. Ibid., 117–21.

6. Ibid., 109, 146.

7. Albert Kirwan, *The Revolt of the Rednecks: Mississippi Politics, 1876–1925* (Lexington, 1951), 165–66, 145–46; Bettersworth, *People's University*, 133; Vardaman quoted in McArthur, *Inaugural Addresses*, 29–30.

8. William F. Holmes, *The White Chief: James K. Vardaman* (Baton Rouge, 1970), 121–22; Richard Wright, *Black Boy, A Record of Childhood and Youth* (New York, 1945), 186–87. For a recent study of Richard Wright see Margaret Walker (Alexander), *Richard Wright, Daemonic Genius: A Portrait of the Man, A Critical Look at His Work* (New York, 1988). For a brief study of black education in Mississippi during this period see Neil R. McMillen, *Dark Journey: Black Mississippians in the Age of Jim Crow* (Urbana, 1989), 72–111.

9. Holmes, *White Chief*, 182.

10. Ibid., 167–76; James Allen Cabaniss, *The University of Mississippi: Its First One Hundred Years* 2d ed. (Hattiesburg, 1970), 119–20; Holmes, *White Chief*, 171–72; University of Mississippi, *Historical Catalogue, 1849–1909*, 78.

11. Holmes, *White Chief*, 172.

12. Ibid., 174–76 [Fulton quote, 174]; Grover C. Hooker, "The Origin and Development of the University of Mississippi with Special Reference to

its Legislative Control," (Ph.D. diss., Stanford University, 1932), 165–67. For a friendly explanation of Governor Vardaman's role in the removal of Chancellor Fulton see the Greenville *Times*, June 23, 1906.

13. *House Journal 1910*, 348, 885, 1157, 1275, 1311; *Senate Journal 1910*, 772; *Clarion-Ledger*, April 8, 1910; *Laws 1910*, 105–9. One trustee was designated the LaBauve Trustee to superintend a small scholarship fund at the University of Mississippi established by Felix LaBauve for orphan boys from De Soto County. That special trustee eventually became identified as the "Ole Miss Trustee," a position that remained very controversial until it was abolished by a constitutional amendment in 1987.

14. Board of Trustees, State Institutions of Higher Learning, *First Biennial Report*, 5, 16, 44–45. For a discussion of the vocational makeup of college boards see W. H. Cowley, *Presidents, Professors, and Trustees: The Evolution of American Academic Government* (San Francisco, 1980), 202–3. For the changing character of the American college and university during the early twentieth century see David O. Levine, *The American College and the Culture of Aspiration, 1915–1940* (Ithaca, 1986), esp. 45–68.

15. Sexton's speech is printed in *Mississippi School Journal* (October 1910): 1–12.

16. Laurence R. Veysey, *The Emergence of the American University* (Chicago, 1965), 252.

17. *Senate Journal 1912*, 223, 232, 240, 480; *Laws 1912*, 179–80, 180–81; Hardy Poindexter Graham, "Bilbo and the University of Mississippi, 1928–1932" (M.A. thesis, University of Mississippi, 1965), 118.

18. *Senate Journal 1912*, 379, 664, 706.

19. Bettersworth, *People's University*, 159. Bettersworth writes, "Presidents and governors went in together and out together." When President Robert C. Cook arrived at Mississippi Southern College in Hattiesburg in 1945, faculty members were still introducing themselves as a "Governor Bilbo appointee" or "Governor Conner appointee" or "Governor Johnson appointee." See Robert C. Cook Interview, Oral History Collection, University of Southern Mississippi, Hattiesburg, Miss.

20. *Senate Journal 1912*, 746–47; Cabaniss, *University of Mississippi*, 128, 143; Hooker, "University of Mississippi," 214–15 [Kincannon quote]. Some of Chancellor Kincannon's most serious problems stemmed from athletics. Ole Miss was suspended from the Southern Intercollegiate Athletic Association in 1914 for illegal aid to athletes.

21. Bettersworth, *People's University*, 178; *Jackson Daily News*, July 2, 1916.

22. *Itta Bena Times*, undated clipping in Institutions of Higher Learning, Subject File, Mississippi Department of Archives and History, Jackson, Miss.; *Commercial Appeal*, undated clipping in same file.

23. Bill Baker, *Catch the Vision: The Life of Henry L. Whitfield* (Jackson, 1974), 73–74; Willard F. Bond, *I Had A Friend: An Autobiography* (Kansas City, 1958), 139.

24. *House Journal 1920*, 367, 384, 1216, 1228, 1371; *Senate Journal 1920*, 466–67; *Jackson Daily News*, January 21, 22, 23, 25, 1920.

25. *Jackson Daily News*, January 23, 1920.

26. *House Journal 1920*, 1374, 1029, 1217, 1235, 1505, 1542, 1592–93.

27. Ibid., 231, 324, 488; Baker, *Catch the Vision*, 71–73; *Jackson Daily News*, January 21, 1920.

28. *Senate Journal 1922*, 591–92.

29. Board of Trustees, *Minutes*, July 23, 1923 [quotation]; Baker, *Catch the Vision*, 81–82, 89, 92; Graham, "Bilbo and the University," 32.

30. Hooker, "University of Mississippi," 251, 255–56. For biographical information on Alfred Hume see Francis Egger Watson, "Dr. Alfred Hume: His Leadership as Vice Chancellor, Acting Chancellor, and Chancellor of the University of Mississippi (1905–1945)," (Ph.D. diss., University of Mississippi, 1987), 13–23.

31. Baker, *Catch the Vision*, 78–116 [quote, 109–10].

32. On the link between the state and the state university see Frederick Rudolph, *The American College and University: A History* (New York, 1962), 362–65 and Governor Henry L. Whitfield, *Know Mississippi: A Syllabus on Present Conditions in Mississippi* (n.p. n.d), esp. 21–36, 42–53. For a study of the Wisconsin Idea see Merle Curti and Vernon Cartensen, *The University of Wisconsin*, 2 vols. (Madison, 1959), and Mary Content, "The National Implications of the Wisconsin Idea: A Bibliographic Study" (M.A., George Washington University, 1964).

33. Baker, *Catch the Vision*, 111; Michael V. O'Shea, *Public Education in Mississippi* (Jackson, 1927).

34. O'Shea, *Public Education in Mississippi*, 200–201, 325–35, 348, 351.

35. Ibid., 32–34, 214.

36. Ibid., 221–23.

Chapter 6. The Bilbo Purge, 1928–1932

1. *Jackson Daily News*, May 27, 1927; *Clarion-Ledger*, August 19, 1927.

2. Interview with Robert Farley at Oxford, May 15, 1979; Hardy Poindexter Graham, "Bilbo and the University of Mississippi, 1928–1932" (M.A. thesis, University of Mississippi, 1965), 14.

3. Thomas Turner Interview, Oral History Collection, University of Southern Mississippi, Hattiesburg, Miss.

4. T. Harry Williams, *Huey Long* (New York, 1969), 491–526; Bilbo quoted in Robert E. McArthur, ed., *Inaugural Addresses of the Governors of Mississippi, 1890–1980* (University, 1980), 146. For a study criticizing American state universities for being precisely what Governor Bilbo wanted the University of Mississippi to become see Norman Foerster, *The American State University: Its Relation to Democracy* (Chapel Hill, 1937).

5. Graham, "Bilbo and the University," 5, 12.

6. Larry T. Balsamo, "Theodore G. Bilbo and Mississippi Politics,

1877–1932" (Ph.D. diss., University of Missouri, 1967), 163; *Mississippian,* October 8, 1927.

7. James Allen Cabaniss, *The University of Mississippi: Its First One Hundred Years* (Oxford, 1949), 142. See Charles R. Wilson, *Baptized in Blood: The Religion of the Lost Cause, 1865–1920* (Athens, Ga., 1980).

8. *Mississippian,* January 7, 1928.

9. Ibid., January 13, 1928.

10. Balsamo, "Bilbo," 163, 166; Sullens quoted in *Jackson Daily News,* January 18, 1928. For a discussion of Bilbo's second administration and the politics of this era see William D. McCain, "The Triumph of Democracy, 1916–1932" in *A History of Mississippi,* ed. Richard A. McLemore (Jackson, 1973), 2:59–97. See also Albert Kirwan, *The Revolt of the Rednecks: Mississippi Politics, 1876–1925* (Lexington, Ky., 1951), 241–59.

11. McArthur, ed., *Inaugural Addresses,* 146–47, 152–53.

12. Ibid.

13. Ibid.

14. *Jackson Daily News,* January 19, 1928; *Clarion-Ledger,* January 19, 20, 1928.

15. Cabaniss, *University of Mississippi,* 141–42. For a text of this and other speeches by Chancellor Hume see Myra Hume Jones, "Tenets and Attitudes of an Old-Time Teacher (Alfred Hume)" (M.A. thesis, University of Mississippi, 1949). For additional arguments against moving the university see Friends of the University, *Some Facts Against Removal of the University of Mississippi* (Oxford, n.d.).

16. *Oxford Eagle,* February 23, March 8, 1928; *Jackson Daily News,* February 15, March 7, September 18, 1928; *Mississippian,* January 13, 1928.

17. Graham, "Bilbo and the University," 3.

18. McLemore, ed., *History of Mississippi,* 2: 430; Graham, "Bilbo and the University," 37–38.

19. *Mississippian,* April 6, 1928.

20. Cabaniss, *University of Mississippi,* 135, 141–43; Graham, "Bilbo and the University," 32 [Hume quote], 36.

21. Graham, "Bilbo and the University," 32–33, 36–37; William D. McCain Interview at Hattiesburg, Mississippi, on January 30, 1979; Graham, "Bilbo and the University," 32–33; Francis Egger Watson, "Dr. Alfred Hume: His Leadership as Vice Chancellor, Acting Chancellor, and Chancellor of the University of Mississippi (1905–1945)" (Ph.D. diss., University of Mississippi, 1987), 71–73.

22. Balsamo, "Bilbo," 210; *Hattiesburg American,* June 20, July 1, 1928; New Orleans *Times Picayune,* May 31, 1928; *Jackson Daily News,* June 12, 1930; Memphis *Commercial Appeal,* June 2, 1930; *Jackson Daily News,* March 6, 1940; Willard F. Bond, *I Had a Friend: An Autobiography* (Kansas City, 1958), 80–81; Alma Hickman, *Southern As I Saw It: Personal Remembrances of an Era, 1912 to*

1954 (Hattiesburg, 1966), 73, 84; Chester Morgan, *Dearly Bought, Deeply Treasured: The University of Southern Mississippi, 1912–1987* (Jackson, 1987), 45–52.
    23. *Mississippian,* April 27, September 28, 1929; Board of Trustees, *Biennial
Report, 1927–1929,* 14–21.
    24. Graham, "Bilbo and the University," 13–15. *Mississippian,* September
28, 1929 [quoting Hume].
    25. University of Mississippi, *Biennial Report, 1927–1929,* 14, 17.
    26. *Jackson Daily News,* June 20, 1929. For a study of Ole Miss alumni see
Franklin E. Moak, *A History of the Alumni Association of the University of Mississippi, 1852–1986* (University, 1986).
    27. *Senate Journal 1930,* 8–9.
    28. *Clarion-Ledger,* June 14, 1930; *Jackson Daily News,* January 7, 1930.
    29. John K. Bettersworth, *People's College* (Birmingham, 1953), 280; Bal-
samo, "Bilbo," 208; *Clarion-Ledger,* June 11, 14 [Sutherland quote], July 6,
1930; *Jackson Daily News,* June 12, 15, 1930; Memphis *Commercial Appeal,* August 5, 1930.
    30. Graham, "Bilbo and the University," 15. In 1930 the chancellor's sal-
ary was considerably lower than that of presidents of other southern universities. The University of Alabama was paying its president $12,000 annually;
the University of Arkansas, $10,000; the University of Tennessee, $12,000;
Louisiana State University, $10,000; and Mississippi A & M, $6,000. The University of Mississippi chancellor's salary was $4,800. The salary had been
$5,000, but in 1922 the legislature reduced it to $4,800. The average full professor's salary at the University of Mississippi in 1930 was $3,600. That same
year the board of trustees appointed Christian Keener ("Red") Cagle, "West
Point football star," as an assistant football coach at A & M at a salary
of $3,500.
    31. Bond, *I Had a Friend,* 141; *Clarion-Ledger,* June 12, 1930; Jack W. Gunn
and Gladys C. Castle, *A Pictorial History of Delta State University* (Jackson,
1980), 27.
    32. *Jackson Daily News,* June 11, 15, 1930; *Clarion-Ledger,* June 12, 15, 1930;
Bridget Smith Pieschel and Stephen Robert Pieschel, *Loyal Daughters: One
Hundred Years at Mississippi University for Women, 1884–1984* (Jackson, 1984),
88–90 [quote concerning Keirn]; Board of Trustees, Minutes, June 13, 1930
[cited hereafter as Minutes and date].
    33. *Clarion-Ledger,* June 5, 11, 1930; Minutes, June 13, 1930.
    34. *Clarion-Ledger,* June 5, 11, 1930; *Jackson Daily News,* June 12, 1930.
    35. Minutes, June 13, 1930; *Clarion-Ledger,* June 14, 1930.
    36. Minutes, June 13, July 5, 1930; *Clarion-Ledger,* June 12, 28, July 3, 6,
1930; *Jackson Daily News,* June 16, 1930; Pieschel and Pieschel, *Loyal Daughters,* 90–91. Bettersworth, *People's College,* was not very helpful in determining
the exact number of faculty members fired or reassigned.
    37. Minutes, June 13, 1930; Graham, "Bilbo and the University," 40; *Offi-*

cial and Statistical Register of the State of Mississippi, 1920–1924, 135–40; *Jackson Daily News*, June 13, 1930.

38. For a comparison of the credentials of the dismissed faculty and their replacements see Graham, "Bilbo and the University," 44–64. The names of the faculty who were dismissed are also listed in a letter from Alfred Hume to Chancellor A. B. Butts, dated January 22, 1942, a copy of which was provided the author by Vice-chancellor Emeritus Alton Bryant.

39. Theodore G. Bilbo Papers, William D. McCain Library, University of Southern Mississippi, Hattiesburg, Miss. When the Bilbo Papers were first used by the author they had not been cataloged, and these letters were in a folder marked "Higher Education." Other Bilbo partisans at the university who were dismissed or demoted included John Dorroh, Robert Torry, and Murry C. Faulkner (Graham, "Bilbo and the University," 76).

40. *Jackson Daily News*, June 15, 1930.

41. John Hudson, "The Spoils System Enters College," *New Republic* 64 (September 17, 1930): 123–24.

42. Clarence Cason, "The Mississippi Imbroglio," *Virginia Quarterly Review* 7 (April 1931): 229–140; *Advance* (October 1930): 9 and (November 1930): 41. John K. Bettersworth, *People's College*, 208, relies on Hudson's figures and concludes: "Before the 'terror' ended 112 members of the faculty at A & M had been dismissed and the positions of 233 others were in jeopardy." James Allen Cabaniss, *University of Mississippi*, is more careful in describing the purge but does not challenge Hudson's figures.

43. Graham, "Bilbo and the University," 78–79, 80–85.

44. Ibid., 98–100.

45. Ibid., 91–94, 95–98; *Proceedings of the Thirty-fifth Annual Meeting of the Association of Colleges and Secondary Schools of the Southern States, Atlanta, Georgia, December 4–5, 1930* (Birmingham, n.d.), 35–36 for the report of the executive committee and 54–55 for the action taken by the association. On the admission of Delta State Teachers College see 34. For a brief discussion of the Mississippi case and similar cases involving Governor Huey P. Long of Louisiana and Governor Eugene Talmadge of Georgia see Guy E. Snavely, *A Short History of the Southern Association of Colleges and Secondary Schools* (Durham, N.C., 1945), 57–62.

46. *Proceedings 1930*, 37; *Jackson Daily News*, December 7, June 15, 1930.

47. A. Wigfall Green, *The Man Bilbo* (Baton Rouge, 1963), 72; William Alexander Percy, *Lanterns on the Levee: Recollections of a Planter's Son* (New York, 1941), 148. See Chester Morgan, *Redneck Liberal: Theodore G. Bilbo and the New Deal* (Baton Rouge, 1985), for a revisionist interpretation of Bilbo's senate career.

Chapter 7. A Constitutional Board of Trustees, 1932–1944

1. Mississippi Senate, *Journal 1932*, 40, 91, 100 [cited hereafter as *Senate Journal* and year]; *Laws of Mississippi 1932*, 383–88. See Brookings Institution,

Report on a Survey of the Organization and Administration of State and County Government in Mississippi (Jackson, [1932]), 514–45.

2. *Mississippi Laws 1932*, 383–88.

3. Ibid.

4. Ibid.

5. Ibid., 387.

6. Hardy Poindexter Graham, "Bilbo and the University of Mississippi, 1928–1932," (M.A. thesis, University of Mississippi, 1965), 107–18; Board of Trustees, Minutes, March 1, 1932 [cited hereafter as Minutes and date]; John K. Bettersworth, *People's College* (Birmingham, 1953), 293–94.

7. *Proceedings of the Thirty-seventh Meeting of the Southern Association of Colleges and Secondary Schools at New Orleans, Louisiana. December 1–2, 1932* (Birmingham, n.d.), 36; Bettersworth, *People's College*, 296–97.

8. James Allen Cabaniss, *The University of Mississippi: Its First Hundred Years* (Oxford, 1949), 148; Richard A. McLemore, ed., *A History of Mississippi* (Jackson, 1973), 2: 432; Bettersworth, *People's College*, 313. Mississippi A & M was renamed Mississippi State College in 1932.

9. Board of Trustees, *Biennial Report 1934–1935*, 4 [cited hereafter as *Biennial Report* and date].

10. See Frank P. Bachman, *Report of Functions of State Institutions of Higher Learning in Mississippi* (Nashville, 1933) [cited hereafter as Bachman, *Peabody Study*].

11. Ibid., 1, 12–14; Michael V. O'Shea, *Public Education in Mississippi* (Jackson, 1927), 200–205, 351. On socialization and higher education see Oscar and Mary Handlin, *The American College and American Culture: Socialization as a Function of Higher Education* (New York, 1970).

12. *Biennial Report 1934–1935*, 6–7.

13. Ibid.

14. David O. Levine, *The American College and the Culture of Aspiration, 1915–1940* (Ithaca, 1986), 170–72; Myra Hume Jones, "Tenets and Attitudes of an Old-Time Teacher (Alfred Hume)" (M.A. thesis, University of Mississippi, 1949), 84–89.

15. *Mississippian*, February 17, 1932; *House Journal 1934*, 193–94, 270, 311.

16. *Jackson Daily News*, February 18, 21, 1936.

17. Ibid., February 18, 1936; *Clarion-Ledger*, February 21, 1936.

18. *Jackson Daily News*, February 18, 19, 1936.

19. Ibid., February 20, 1936.

20. Ibid., February 18, 1936, quoting the Columbus *Commercial Dispatch*.

21. *Jackson Daily News*, February 18, 20, 1936; *Mississippian*, March 7, 1936; University of Mississippi, Subject File, Mississippi Department of Archives and History, Jackson, Miss. [cited hereafter as MDAH].

22. *Jackson Daily News*, February 18, 1936.

23. *Jackson Daily News*, February 21, 1936; *Senate Journal 1936*, 241 [Harper quote].

24. *Laws of Mississippi 1936,* 322–26; *Clarion-Ledger,* February 21, 1936. See copies of bills in University of Mississippi, Subject File, in MDAH.

25. McLemore, ed., *History of Mississippi,* 2:435; *Hattiesburg American,* May 29, December 13, 1940; *Jackson Daily News,* March 7, 8, 1940; *Clarion-Ledger,* March 7, 1940.

26. *Jackson Daily News,* March 7, 8, 1940.

27. *Biennial Report 1939–1941,* 53. A house resolution to change the name to Jackson State College failed. See also Lelia Gaston Rhodes, *Jackson State University: The First Hundred Years, 1877–1977* (Jackson, 1979), 25–27, 155.

28. McLemore, ed., *History of Mississippi,* 2:435; *Jackson Daily News,* January 26, 1945.

29. McLemore, ed., *History of Mississippi,* 2:435.

30. Interview with Senator John C. Stennis at Starkville, Miss. on May 30, 1979. See the John C. Stennis Collection at Mitchell Memorial Library, Mississippi State University, for letters, documents, and clippings concerning the establishment of the constitutional board of trustees.

31. *Jackson Daily News,* February 27, 1942; *Mississippi Laws 1942,* 438–39; *Mississippi Laws 1944,* 454–69.

32. *Jackson Daily News,* May 19, 1944. The *Clarion-Ledger* cut line read: "New College Board to Resume Football Schedules."

33. For the impact of World War II on American colleges see Frederick Rudolph, *The American College and University: A History* (New York, 1962), 483–87.

Chapter 8. The College Boom, 1944–1954

1. J. Oliver Emmerich Interview, Oral History Collection, University of Southern Mississippi, Hattiesburg, Miss. For his reminiscences see J. Oliver Emmerich, *Two Faces of Janus: The Saga of Deep South Change* (Jackson, 1973).

2. James C. Read, "The Williams Chancellorship at the University of Mississippi, 1946–1968" (Ph.D. diss., University of Mississippi, 1978), 158.

3. Board of Trustees, *Biennial Report 1945–1947,* 27, 29 [cited hereafter as *Biennial Report* and date].

4. Benjamin Fine, *Democratic Education* (New York, 1945), 71–79; Oliver Cromwell Carmichael, *The Changing Role of Higher Education* (New York, 1949), 11; Frederick Rudolph, *The American College and University: A History* (New York, 1962), 479. For Hutchins's views see Robert Maynard Hutchins, *The Higher Learning in America* (New Haven, 1936, 1961 [with new preface]).

5. Fine, *Democratic Education,* 71, 75, 70.

6. Fine, *Democratic Education,* 9–10. For contrasting views on what a university is, or should be, see Clark Kerr, *The Uses of a University* (Cambridge, 1963), and Robert P. Wolff, *The Ideal of the University* (Boston, 1969).

7. President's Commission on Higher Education, *Higher Education for American Democracy,* 6 vols. (Washington, 1947), 1:v, 101, 102.

8. Carmichael, *Changing Role of Higher Education,* 95, 98, 101.

9. Rudolph, *American College*, 486, 494; Carmichael, *Changing Role of Higher Education*, 96.

10. Richard A. McLemore, ed., *History of Mississippi* (Jackson, 1973), 2:438.

11. *Biennial Report 1943–1945*, 47; *Biennial Report 1945–1947*, 8–9, 21, 26, 33, 36, 40, 44; *Biennial Report 1947–1949*, 2; John K. Bettersworth, *People's University: The Centennial History of Mississippi State* (Jackson, 1980), 307; James Allen Cabaniss, *The University of Mississippi: Its First Hundred Years* (Oxford, 1949), 159–160. State Teachers College was renamed Mississippi Southern College in 1940, and Mississippi Negro Training School was renamed Jackson College for Negro Teachers in 1944.

12. Board of Trustees, Minutes, August 23, 1944 [cited hereafter as Minutes and date].

13. Memphis *Commercial Appeal*, December 22, 1945; *Jackson Daily News*, December 22, 1946, January 5, 1947; Minutes, June 15, 1944; Merlerson Guy Dunham, *Centennial History of Alcorn A & M College* (Hattiesburg, 1971), 67–68, 72; Charles H. Wilson, Sr., *Education for Negroes in Mississippi Since 1910* (Boston, 1947), 497–99.

14. *Jackson Daily News*, January 26, 1945; *Clarion-Ledger*, June 15, 1945; Alma Hickman, *Southern As I Saw It: Personal Remembrances of an Era, 1912 to 1954* (Hattiesburg, 1966), 115–16 [George quote]; interview with Reece D. McLendon, September 21, 1981, Senatobia, Miss. McLendon, a member of the board of trustees in 1945 and a former student of President George, personally delivered the board's request that George resign. When George refused, McLendon moved that he be dismissed.

15. Minutes, June 14–15, 1945, January 25, July 15, 1946.

16. Bridget Smith Pieschel and Stephen Robert Pieschel, *Loyal Daughters: One Hundred Years at Mississippi University for Women, 1884–1984* (Jackson, 1984), 106; Minutes, January 24–31, 1952; *Jackson Daily News*, January 24, 1952.

17. Joseph E. Gibson, *Mississippi Study of Higher Education* (Jackson, 1945), 31–33, 38, 46–48.

18. Ibid., 332–33, 337.

19. Ibid. See chapter 11 of the Gibson report for the study and recommendation concerning medical education, specifically 151–66; see also Lucie Robertson Bridgforth, *Medical Education in Mississippi: A History of the School of Medicine* (Jackson, 1984), 104–5.

20. John E. Brewton, *Higher Education in Mississippi* (Jackson, 1954), 278–79; McLemore, ed., *A History of Mississippi*, 2:439.

21. Memphis *Commercial Appeal*, July 22, 1948.

22. Hickman, *Southern As I Saw It*, 119, 122; *Biennial Report 1951–1953*, 34.

23. Robert Cecil Cook Interview, Oral History Collection, University of Southern Mississippi.

24. Ibid.; Minutes, March 16, 1948; Hickman, *Southern As I Saw It*, 121.

25. *Biennial Report 1949–1951,* 38.

26. *Biennial Report 1947–1949,* 20–21; Bettersworth, *People's University,* 304–6.

27. *Biennial Report 1945–1947,* 26–27; Bettersworth, *People's University,* 314–18.

28. Pieschel and Pieschel, *Loyal Daughters,* 107.

29. Ibid., 111–17, 119–21.

30. See Minutes, January 18, 1951, for the role-and-scope assignment of the black colleges; Sammy Jay Tinsley, "A History of Mississippi Valley State College" (Ph.D. diss., University of Mississippi, 1972), 10, 12, 20.

31. *Biennial Report 1947–1949,* 7. For the tribulations of black college presidents in Mississippi see W. A. Butts, ed., *Up from a Cottonpatch: J. H. White and the Development of Mississippi Valley State College* (Itta Bena, Miss., 1979); Jacob L. Reddix, *A Voice Crying in the Wilderness: The Memoirs of Jacob L. Reddix* (Jackson, 1974); and B. Baldwin Dansby, *A Brief History of Jackson College* (Jackson, 1953). Dansby was president of Jackson College, now Jackson State University, from 1927 to 1940 and was succeeded by Reddix who served until 1967. On the increasing militancy of black students see Anne Moody, *Coming of Age in Mississippi* (New York, 1968).

32. *Biennial Report 1947–1949,* 42.

33. Minutes, January 18, 1951; *Biennial Report 1949–1951,* 7; Tinsley, "Mississippi Valley," 63–64; Lelia Gaston Rhodes, *Jackson State University: The First Hundred Years, 1877–1977* (Jackson, 1979), 116–20.

34. Hickman, *Southern As I Saw It,* 122.

35. *Biennial Report 1947–1949,* 10; *Biennial Report 1949–1951, 18.*

36. Biennial Report 1949–1951, 18.

Chapter 9. Race, Rights, Riots, Role and Scope, 1954–1962

1. Neil R. McMillen, *The Citizens' Council: Organized Resistance to the Second Reconstruction* (Urbana, Ill., 1971), 336–37; Russell Barrett, *Integration at Ole Miss* (Chicago, 1965), 48–49 [quote, 49].

2. Merlerson Guy Dunham, *Centennial History of Alcorn A & M College* (Hattiesburg, 1971), 70–71.

3. Chancellor Alfred Butts to Calvin Wells, July 11, 1939, and Wells to Butts, July 12, 1939, in Chancellor's Correspondence, University of Mississippi. A copy of these letters was provided by Vice-chancellor Gerald Walton.

4. Lucie Robertson Bridgforth, *Medical Education in Mississippi: A History of the School of Medicine* (Jackson, 1984), 130; Board of Trustees, Minutes, August 15, 1950 [cited hereafter as Minutes and date].

5. Interview with Dean Robert J. Farley, Oxford, Miss. May 15, 1979; Barrett, *Integration at Ole Miss,* 25.

6. Farley Interview.

7. Mrs. Medgar Evers, *For Us, The Living* (Garden City, 1967), 114–19; Minutes, September 16, December 16, 1954.

8. *Jackson Daily News,* December 2, 1954.

9. Ibid., February 17, 1955. For Faulkner's quote see Barrett, *Integration at Ole Miss,* 31.

10. Joint Interviews with Verner Smith Holmes and Euclid R. Jobe, Jackson, Miss., July 24–November 20, 1978, 56–61, transcriptions in Holmes Collection, John Davis Williams Library, University of Mississippi [cited hereafter as Holmes-Jobe Interviews]; Minutes, February 21, March 9, 1957.

11. Holmes-Jobe Interviews, 26.

12. Minutes, July 18, 1957; Holmes-Jobe Interviews, 66–67.

13. Hugh Clegg, "Someone Jumped the Gun" (unpublished manuscript), 19–22; *Mississippian,* May 16, 1958. Clegg, a former aide to J. Edgar Hoover, was the assistant to Chancellor John D. Williams during the late 1950s and early 1960s. A copy of his manuscript, which chronicles those troubled years, was provided by his daughter through the assistance of George Street, former director of development at the University of Mississippi.

14. Interview with Judge James P. Coleman, Oxford, Miss., June 16–17, 1979. A few months before his attempt to register, King had been involved in a church squabble that required the intervention of law enforcement authorities. University authorities put him in a room by himself and closed the door. This isolation apparently triggered the screaming. King was rolling on the floor when authorities took him from the room.

15. James C. Read, "The Williams Chancellorship at the University of Mississippi, 1946–1968," (Ph.D. diss., University of Mississippi, 1978), 181; Minutes, September 18, 1958; Wilburn Hooker to E. R. Jobe, November 28, 1958, copy in James Wesley Silver Papers, John D. Williams Library, University of Mississippi; statement of Edwin White, dated May 20, 1958, in Silver Papers; Interview with James W. Silver, Dunedin, Fla., March 15–17, 1982.

16. A complete list of the allegations, together with the written replies provided by the various individuals or groups, may be found in Clegg, "Someone Jumped," 35–94 [quote, 61]. See clippings, letters, and documents in Silver Papers; Silver Interview. Mrs. Peel Cannon, president of the United Daughters of the Confederacy in Holly Springs, wrote to Professor Silver on September 5 that she was pleased he had agreed to speak to the group on October 21, 1959. She stated that she would not require a copy of his speech before the meeting, although she and the organization had been offended by a recent speaker on Jefferson Davis who used the occasion to solicit contributions for the Citizens' Council. In closing she said she would "grieve" over the "unfair charges" against him except for the fact that he was probably enjoying the whole affair. See also *Jackson Daily News,* July 9, 1959; *Clarion-Ledger,* July 10, 1959; and *Delta Democrat Times,* undated clipping in Silver papers. A copy of the allegations against Professor Silver may be found in the Silver Papers.

17. For the charges against Professor Lyon see Clegg, "Someone Jumped," 65–71 [quote, 70]; undated clipping of *Oxford Eagle* in Silver papers.

18. *Jackson Daily News,* July 9, 1959; *Clarion-Ledger,* July 10, 1959; *Daily Mississippian,* September 13, 1959; *Madison County Herald,* August 13, 1959; "Statement of the Board of Trustees concerning Allegations Relative to the University of Mississippi," August 27, 1959, copy in Holmes Collection.

19. Zack J. Van Landingham, "Report on Clyde Kennard to the State Sovereignty Commission" (December 1, 1958–January 29, 1960). This dossier was compiled by the chief investigator of the Sovereignty Commission during Clyde Kennard's second attempt to enroll at Mississippi Southern College. It was found in Governor Ross Barnett's papers in the Mississippi Department of Archives and History in Jackson. The dossier is arranged chronologically but is not paginated. It will be cited hereafter as Kennard Dossier. A copy is in the Holmes Collection.

20. Ibid.; Ronald Hollander, "One Mississippi Negro Who Didn't Go To College," *The Reporter* 27 (November 8, 1962): 30–34. For Kennard's letter see *Hattiesburg American,* December 6, 1958.

21. Barrett, *Integration at Ole Miss,* 28–29; McMillen, *Citizens' Council,* 336–37; Kennard Dossier.

22. Kennard Dossier.

23. Ibid.

24. Ibid.

25. Ibid.; Coleman Interview.

26. Coleman Interview; interview with President Emeritus William D. McCain, Hattiesburg, Miss., on January 30, 1979.

27. McCain Interview; Kennard Dossier.

28. Kennard Dossier; McCain Interview.

29. Kennard Dossier.

30. Ibid.

31. Hollander, "Mississippi Negro," 31; Coleman Interview; James W. Silver, *Mississippi: The Closed Society* (New York, 1966), 94; Kennard Dossier.

32. Kennard Dossier; Hollander, "Mississippi Negro," 32–34; Monte Piliawsky, *Exit 13: Oppression and Racism in Academia* (Boston, 1982), 23–25, quoting the Jackson *State Times.*

33. Hollander, "Mississippi Negro," 34; Piliawsky, *Exit 13,* 25–27; Silver, *Closed Society,* 93–95.

34. *Mississippian,* October 6, 1959. State planning and coordination of higher education was a growing national concern in 1959. For contrasting views see Malcolm Moos and Francis Rouke, *The Campus and the State* (Baltimore, 1959), who opposed any state or political controls on higher education, and Lyman A. Glenny, *Autonomy of Public Colleges: The Challenge of Coordination* (New York, 1959), who saw no inherent danger in statewide coordination of public institutions of higher learning. For a brief but instructive analysis of statewide coordination of higher education see Hugh Davis Graham "Structure and Governance in American Higher Education: Historical and Compara-

tive Analysis in State Policy," *Journal of Public Policy History* 1 (1989): 80–107, and Aubrey K. Lucas, "The Mississippi Legislature and Mississippi Public Higher Education, 1890–1960" (Ph.D. diss., Florida State University, 1966).
  35. Minutes, May 19, 1960.
  36. *Mississippian,* March 16, 1961; Read, "Williams Chancellorship," 174.

Chapter 10. The Meredith Crisis: NEVER
  1. *Daily Mississippian,* July 5, 1962. For a chronology of the legal steps leading to Meredith's admission see Russell Barrett, *Integration at Ole Miss* (Chicago, 1965), Appendix A, 247–51.
  2. James H. Meredith, *Three Years in Mississippi* (Bloomington, Ind., 1966), 20–22.
  3. For copies of these letters see ibid., 54–55, 57–58.
  4. Ibid., 58. For dates on the integration of southern public universities see Roger D. Russell, "Negro Publicly-Supported Colleges in Mississippi and South Carolina," *JNE* 31 (Summer 1962): 310–21. On desegregation of some other southern universities see James Montgomery, Stanley Folmsbee, and Lee Greene, *To Foster Knowledge: A History of the University of Tennessee, 1794–1970* (Knoxville, 1984); Paul Conklin, *Gone with the Ivy: A Biography of Vanderbilt University* (Knoxville, 1985); and Thomas Dyer, *The University of Georgia: A Bicentennial History, 1785–1985* (Athens, 1985).
  5. Hugh Clegg, "Someone Jumped the Gun" (an unpublished manuscript written by Clegg after his retirement from the university), 122. Clegg explains: "This practice was continued for weeks as written documents were received from the applicant. . . . I had been designated by the Chancellor and the Division Heads to coordinate the handling of this matter."
  6. Meredith, *Three Years in Mississippi,* 58.
  7. Ibid., 59.
  8. Ibid., 61.
  9. Board of Trustees, Minutes, February 7, 1961 [cited hereafter as Minutes and date].
  10. Barrett, *Integration at Ole Miss,* 52–53; Meredith, *Three Years in Mississippi,* 66–67, 64 [quoting letter].
  11. Meredith, *Three Years in Mississippi,* 65–77 [quote from March 26 letter, 69].
  12. Ibid., 71, 74.
  13. Barrett, *Integration at Ole Miss,* 43, 50, 53; University of Mississippi, *Bulletin 1962,* 81–82.
  14. Meredith, *Three Years in Mississippi,* 77.
  15. Ibid., 105ff.
  16. *Meredith* v. *Fair, Transcript of Record,* 2:217, 220. A copy of this transcript is in the chancellor's office at the University of Mississippi.
  17. Ibid., 228, 238–39, 241–43.
  18. Ibid., 232.

19. *Meredith* v. *Fair,* 3:361, 370, 381, 385–87, 389–410, 411–22, 423–30, 515, 4:482, 501–2 (Riddell quote).

20. Ibid., 509, 501, 558–59. See *Jackson Daily News* and *Clarion-Ledger,* January 25–27, 1962.

21. *Meredith* v. *Fair,* 3:563.

22. Ibid., 5:661–70.

23. Ibid., 690–91.

24. Ibid., 725–26.

25. *Meredith* v. *Fair,* 5:734, 737–39; Jack Bass, *Unlikely Heroes* (New York, 1981), 172–201.

26. Meredith, *Three Years in Mississippi,* 143.

27. Jack Bass, *Unlikely Heroes,* 180–81; Barrett, *Integration at Ole Miss,* 82.

28. Minutes, September 4, 1962.

29. Barrett, *Integration at Ole Miss,* 249.

30. *Clarion-Ledger,* September 14, 1962, [complete text of Governor Barnett's speech] and Clegg, "Someone Jumped," 32; interview with Charles Fair at Louisville, Miss., on September 18, 1978; *Jackson Daily News–Clarion-Ledger,* September 16, 1962. In the 1978 interview, Fair stated that he did not believe the university would be closed.

31. Minutes, September 14, 1962.

32. Ibid. This assessment of the division of the board is based on interviews with S. R. Evans (October 13, 1978), Thomas Tubb (September 20, 1978), M. M. Roberts (September 23, 1978), Charles Fair (September 18, 1978), William O. Stone (September 20, 1978), Tally Riddell (June 10, 1980), Mrs. Harry Carpenter (October 12, 1978), Verner Smith Holmes and Euclid R. Jobe (July 24–November 20, 1978); many conversations with Edward Morgan (son of Ira Morgan); an analysis of newspaper coverage of the board through the few weeks before Meredith's admission; and information in Walter Lord, *The Past That Would Not Die* (New York, 1966), Barrett, *Integration at Ole Miss,* and James W. Silver, *Mississippi: The Closed Society* (New York, 1966). The transcripts of the interviews cited in this chapter are in the Verner Smith Holmes Collection, John Davis Williams Library, University of Mississippi.

33. Transcripts of interviews in Holmes Collection; *Jackson Daily News,* September 16, 1962.

34. A copy of the transcripts of the Barnett-Kennedy tapes were provided by Marcia Synott of the University of South Carolina. Professor Synott reproduced the transcripts from the Burke Marshall Papers at the Kennedy Library in Boston. The transcripts were prepared for Leon Jaworski in January 1963 for his use in the Justice Department's contempt of court proceedings against Governor Barnett. Those charges were later dropped, and the transcripts remained unpublished and unused by historians for several years. They will be cited hereafter as "Transcripts" and date. A complete copy of the transcripts, arranged by date and hour, is in the Holmes Collection. For an account of the Meredith crisis from the vantage of the Kennedy administra-

tion see Carl M. Brayer, *John F. Kennedy and the Second Reconstruction* (New York, 1977), 180–205, Victor S. Navasky, *Kennedy Justice* (New York, 1971), 154–243, and Leon Jaworski, *Confessions and Avoidance: A Memoir* (New York, 1979), 145–73.

35. Minutes, September 17, 1962.

36. See interviews with Tubb, Fair, Stone, Roberts, Evans. Also see Holmes-Jobe Interviews for a long, often rambling discussion of the Meredith crisis.

37. Ibid.

38. *Jackson Daily News,* September 18, 1962; Verner Holmes–James P. Coleman Interview, June 16–17, 1979, Oxford, Miss. See Clegg, "Someone Jumped," 32, for the names of an alumni steering committee which Clegg said "saved" the University of Mississippi.

39. *Jackson Daily News,* September 19, 1962; *Washington Post,* September 20, 1962.

40. *Jackson Daily News,* September 18, 19, 1962; Clegg, "Someone Jumped," 32; interview with William H. Mounger at Jackson, Miss., on September 21 and 28, 1978.

41. "Transcripts," September 17, 1962 [Kennedy memorandum]; *Jackson Daily News,* September 18, 1962.

42. Barrett, *Integration at Ole Miss,* 102. See telegram in Holmes Collection from Attorney General Kennedy to board members.

43. Barrett, *Integration at Ole Miss,* 103; *Jackson Daily News,* September 19, 1962.

44. William H. Mounger, former president of Lamar Life Insurance Company, which owned WLBT-TV and WJDX, provided copies of this and other editorials, telegrams, and letters from his personal files. These copies are in the Holmes Collection.

45. *Jackson Daily News,* September 19, 1962; *The Chronicle,* September 19, 1962. See also Ira Harkey, . . . *dedicated to the proposition . . . Editorials from the Chronicle* (Pascagoula, Miss., 1963) and *The Smell of Burning Crosses* (Jacksonville, Ill., 1967), as well as Carl Wiesenburg, *The Oxford Disaster . . . The Price of Defiance* (Pascagoula, Miss., 1962). Wiesenburg, from Jackson County and Joe Wroton of Greenville were the only two state legislators who publicly opposed Barnett's policy of defiance.

46. Minutes, September 19, 1962. See interviews with Tubb, Fair, Evans, Riddell, Stone, and Holmes-Jobe.

47. Interviews with Tubb, Fair, Evans, Riddell, Stone, and Holmes-Jobe.

48. Ibid.

49. Ibid.

50. Minutes, September 20, 1962; Tubb Interview, Riddell Interview; Holmes-Jobe Interviews. A copy of Riddell's statement is in the Holmes Collection.

51. Minutes, September 20, 1962; Tubb Interview; Holmes-Jobe Interviews.

52. Minutes, September 20, 1962; Tubb Interview; Holmes-Jobe Interviews; *Jackson Daily News,* September 21, 1962.

Chapter 11. The Meredith Crisis: НƆ∀ƎИ

1. *Jackson Daily News,* September 21, 1962. For Thomas Tubb's quote see David Halberstram, "Starting Out to Be a Famous Reporter," *Esquire* (November 1981): 70–80. For Meredith's account of these events see James H. Meredith, *Three Years in Mississippi* (Bloomington, Ind., 1966).

2. Thomas Turner Interview, Oral History Collection, University of Southern Mississippi.

3. New Orleans *Times Picayune,* September 22, 1962; Russell Barrett, *Integration at Ole Miss* (Chicago, 1965), 109; Walter Lord, *The Past That Would Not Die* (New York, 1966), 157.

4. *Jackson Daily News,* September 21, 1962.

5. Interview with S. R. Evans on October 13, 1978, at Vaiden, Miss.

6. *Jackson Daily News,* September 22, 1962.

7. Interview with William H. Mounger on September 21 and 28, 1978, at Jackson, Miss.

8. Interview with Verner S. Holmes and James P. Coleman on June 16–17, 1979, at the University of Mississippi. Coleman represented several members of the board of trustees.

9. Almost every board member has his own version of this story. It is best told, however, by Ed Morgan, the son of "Shine" Morgan.

10. Interview with Thomas J. Tubb on September 18, 1978, at West Point, Miss.

11. Mounger Interview.

12. "Transcripts of the Barnett-Kennedy Tapes," September 24, 1962 [cited hereafter as "Transcripts" and date].

13. Verner S. Holmes and Euclid R. Jobe Interviews, July 24–November 20, 1978, at Jackson, Miss.

14. "Transcripts," September 24, 1962.

15. Holmes-Coleman Interview.

16. Jack Bass, *Unlikely Heroes* (New York, 1981), 193.

17. *Daily Mississippian,* September 26, 1962.

18. Tubb Interview.

19. Ibid.; Holmes-Jobe Interviews.

20. Tubb Interview.

21. "Transcripts," September 25, 1962.

22. Ibid.

23. *Jackson Daily News,* September 26, 1962; *Times Picayune,* September 26, 1962.

24. Interview with Emma Holmes on March 24, 1979, at McComb, Miss; Meredith, *Three Years in Mississippi,* 196.

25. "Transcripts," September 26, 1962.

26. *Daily Mississippian,* September 27, 1962; Meredith, *Three Years in Mississippi,* 202–3; "Transcripts," September 27, 1962.

27. "Transcripts," September 26, 1962.

28. Ibid., September 26 and 27, 1962.

29. A transcript of this conversation between President Kennedy and Governor Barnett is not included in the transcripts prepared for Leon Jaworski. Excerpts of the conversation, from which the above quotation is reproduced, may be found in Hugh Clegg, "Someone Jumped the Gun" (an unpublished manuscript written after Clegg's retirement from the university), 179–81.

30. Ibid.

31. Ibid.

32. Ibid.; George B. Leonard, T. George Harris, and Christopher S. Wren, "How a Secret Deal Prevented a Massacre at Ole Miss," *Look* (December 31, 1982): 22.

33. Mounger Interview. Copies of those telegrams are in the Holmes Collection.

34. *Jackson Daily News–Clarion-Ledger,* September 30, 1962.

35. Interview with Gerald Blessey on July 22, 1975, by Hank Holmes, in Mississippi Department of Archives and History, Jackson, Miss.

36. Holmes-Coleman Interview.

37. Leonard, Harris, and Wren, "Secret Deal," 22ff.

38. Holmes-Coleman Interview.

39. "Transcripts," September 30, 1962.

40. Ibid.; Barrett, *Integration at Ole Miss,* 136.

41. Clegg, "Someone Jumped," 189ff. [Marshall quotes, 190–91].

42. Barrett, *Integration at Ole Miss,* 146.

43. Willie Morris, "At Ole Miss: Echoes of a Civil War's Last Battle," *Time* (October 4, 1982): 8–11. For the best and most objective account of the riot see Barrett, *Integration at Ole Miss,* 123–63. Hugh Clegg, "Someone Jumped," 220–39, blamed the riot on the marshals whom he described as "trigger happy exhibitionists on a safari." He claims that the marshals "jumped the gun" and fired the tear gas before it was necessary.

44. Clegg, "Someone Jumped," 242–43.

45. Fair Interview; Tubb Interview.

46. Evans Interview; Holmes-Coleman Interview; Clegg, "Someone Jumped," 243.

47. Clegg, "Someone Jumped," 243; Evans Interview; Barrett, *Integration at Ole Miss,* 123–63.

48. Clegg, "Someone Jumped," 246.

49. Holmes-Jobe Interviews; Meredith, *Three Years in Mississippi*, 212–13.
50. Clegg, "Someone Jumped," 246–49. On October 2, 1962, the *Clarion-Ledger* reported that Senator Eastland had ordered a probe that might lead to the arrest of some federal marshals. On the legislative investigation see Barrett, *Integration at Ole Miss*, 169, 173–78.
51. Barrett, *Integration at Ole Miss*, 221.

Chapter 12. In Defense of Yesterday, 1962–1972
1. Richard A. McLemore, ed., *A History of Mississippi* (Jackson, 1973), 2:162–63; David G. Sansing, *Mississippi, Its People and Culture* (Minneapolis, 1981), 320.
2. Board of Trustees, Minutes, August 15, 1963 [cited hereafter as Minutes and date]; *Clarion-Ledger*, August 16, 1963; *Commercial Appeal*, August 16, 1963.
3. *Jackson Daily News*, August 16, 1963; *Clarion-Ledger*, August 16, 1963; interview with Verner S. Holmes and James P. Coleman at Oxford, Miss., June 16–17, 1979.
4. *Newsweek* (October 14, 1963): 35–36.
5. Governor Paul B. Johnson Inaugural Address, January 21, 1964, in *Inaugural Addresses of the Governors of Mississippi, 1890–1980*, ed. Robert E. McArthur, (University, Miss., 1980), 327–34.
6. Ibid. For a general study of this period see Neil McMillen, *The Citizens' Council: Organized Resistance to the Second Reconstruction* (Urbana, Ill., 1971).
7. *Clarion-Ledger*, March 10, 1963; Minutes, April 18, 1963; interview with M. M. Roberts at Hattiesburg, Miss., on September 23, 1978. See Robert Dubay, "Pigmentation and Pigskin: A Jones County Junior College Dilemma," *JMH* 46 (February 1984): 43–50.
8. *Daily Mississippian*, February 21, March 7, 1963; Minutes, February 21, 1963. For a discussion of this episode see Dean Wallace Colvard, *Mixed Emotions* (Danville, Ill., 1985), 41–95, 156.
9. The minutes of the March 9 meeting were not included in the published minutes of the board; See *Jackson Daily News–Clarion-Ledger*, March 10, 1963; Roberts Interview; Verner Smith Holmes and Euclid R. Jobe Interviews, July 24–November 20, 1978, at Jackson, Miss.; *Commercial Appeal*, March 10, 1963. See also the *Clarion-Ledger*, March 15, 1983, for a twenty-year retrospective report on this event.
10. Colvard, *Mixed Emotions*, 41–95; Roberts quoted in *Clarion-Ledger*, March 10, 1963.
11. Holmes-Jobe Interviews.
12. Minutes, August 8, 1964. For accounts of that summer see Len Holt, *The Summer That Didn't End* (New York, 1965), Tracy Sugarman, *Stranger at the Gates: A Summer in Mississippi* (New York, 1966), and Sally Belfrage, *Freedom Summer* (Greenwich, Conn., 1966).

13. AAUP *Bulletin* (Autumn 1965): 347; James W. Silver, *Mississippi: The Closed Society* (New York, 1966), 319–20.

14. Silver, *Mississippi: The Closed Society*, 319–20; Minutes, September 17, 1964.

15. Minutes, November 21, 1963; interview with Professor James W. Silver at Dunedin, Fla., March 16–17, 1982.

16. *Clarion-Ledger*, April 1, 1964; *Commercial Appeal*, March 28, 1964.

17. Undated memorandum from E. R. Jobe to members of the board of trustees in the Verner S. Holmes Collection, John Davis Williams Library, University of Mississippi.

18. E. R. Jobe to James W. Silver, April 27, 1964; James W. Silver to E. R. Jobe, May 6, 1964; Landman Teller to E. R. Jobe, May 30, 1964, in Holmes Collection. Copies of this correspondence were provided by Professor Silver. The originals are in the James W. Silver Papers, John Davis Williams Library, University of Mississippi. Most are published in James W. Silver, *Running Scared: Silver in Mississippi* (Jackson, 1984), 183–206.

19. John Emmerich to Verner S. Holmes, April 29, 1964, Holmes Collection.

20. Silver, *Running Scared*, chaps. 4, 5, 6, and appendix F; Silver Interview. For an assessment of the Silver case see also AAUP *Bulletin* (Autumn 1965): 351–55.

21. AAUP *Bulletin* (Autumn 1962): 248–52; *Times Picayune*, October 10, 1962; *Jackson Daily News*, September 7, 1970; Minutes, January 18, 1972; *Daily Mississippian*, January 9, February 11, 12, 1970; AAUP *Bulletin* (Spring 1970): 76–80. See also Ken Vinson, "Mississippi: Signs of Life, The Lawyers of Ole Miss," *The Nation* (June 23,1969): 791–93; Minutes, January 15, 1970; *Clarion-Ledger*, December 29, 1970; Monte Piliawsky, *Exit 13: Oppression and Racism in Academia* (Boston, 1982), 76–92.

22. Minutes, March 21, 1957, August 19, 1971, April 20, 1972. Bowen defeated Butler by a vote of nearly two to one.

23. Minutes, February 17, 1955. For a study of the speaker ban controvesy see Lucie Robertson Bridgforth, "'Bomb the Ban': A Study of the Legal Controversy Surrounding Off-Campus Speakers at Mississippi Institutions of Higher Learning" (M.A. thesis, University of Mississippi, 1979).

24. Minutes, March 20, November 17, 1966; Bridgforth, "Bomb the Ban," 51–52; interview with President William Giles at Starkville, Miss., on May 30, 1979.

25. Bridgforth, "Bomb the Ban," 55ff. See also John Carter, "A Boll Weevil Six Feet Long," *Library Journal* (October 15, 1969): 3615–19. Carter, the assistant director of libraries at Mississippi State University in 1968, spoke at a rally at the university on October 23, 1968, calling on the college board to open up Mississippi's campuses to a diversity of speakers and ideas.

26. Minutes, November 21, February 20, 1968; Bridgforth, "Bomb the Ban," 93–94, 98–104.

27. Bridgforth, "Bomb the Ban," 116–18.

28. Ibid., 122ff; Giles Interview.

29. Giles Interview; M. M. Roberts to All Members of the Board, March 10, 1970, a copy in Holmes collection.

30. Minutes, March 19, 1970. For Giles's expression of appreciation to Holmes for his support see Giles to Holmes, March 20, 1970, in Holmes Collection.

31. Giles Interview.

32. Minutes, May 8, 1965; Silver, *Mississippi: The Closed Society*, 322–23.

33. Minutes, April 12, 21, 1966.

34. Minutes, March 24, April 12, 21, 1966; Holmes Interview; Minutes, June 29, 1967, March 20, 1969.

35. University of Southern Mississippi, *The Student Printz*, December 11, 1969.

36. *Daily Mississippian*, January 12, February 13, 25, 26, March 2, 3, 8, 1970; *Newsweek* (March 30, 1970): 83.

37. *Daily Mississippian*, January 12, February 13, 25, 26, March 2, 3, 8, 1970; *Newsweek* (March 30, 1970): 83. W. A. Butts, ed., *Up from a Cottonpatch: J. H. White and the Development of Mississippi Valley State College*, (Itta Bena, Miss., 1979) does not address student unrest in any detail; see 107, 110, 112, 114.

38. *Daily Mississippian*, March 18, 1970; Minutes, April 24, 1970.

39. For an analysis of the Jackson State riot see William W. Scranton, Chairman, *The Report of the President's Commission on Campus Unrest, Including Special Reports: The Killings at Jackson State, the Kent State Tragedy* (New York, 1970), 411–65. See also Lelia Gaston Rhodes, *Jackson State University: The First Hundred Years, 1877–1977* (Jackson, 1979), 176–80. For a more recent study of the riot see Tim Spofford, *LYNCH STREET, The May 1970 Slayings at Jackson State College* (Kent, Ohio, 1988).

40. Scranton, *Report of President's Commission*, 411–65; *New York Times*, May 16, 1970.

41. Rhodes, *Jackson State University*, 177; *Jackson Daily News*, May 15, 19, 1970; *New York Times*, May 16 [quotes], 23, 1970; Minutes, May 21, June 18, 1970. See also John R. Salter, *Jackson, Mississippi: An American Chronicle of Struggle and Schism* (Hicksville, N.Y., 1979).

42. *New York Times*, May 16, 23, 1970.

43. Scranton, *President's Commission on Campus Unrest*, 444; Stephen Lesher, "Jackson State a Year After," *New York Times Magazine* (March 21, 1971): 56. On the increasing militancy among Mississippi black college students see Anne Moody, *Coming of Age in Mississippi* (New York, 1968).

44. *Clarion-Ledger*, October 20, August 27, 1970.

45. *McComb Enterprise Journal*, October 7, 1970. See also J. Oliver Emmerich, *Two Faces of Janus: The Saga of Deep South Change* (Jackson, 1973).

46. Sansing, *Mississippi*, 354.

47. Roberts Interview.
48. Ibid.
49. Holmes Interview.
50. Ibid.; interview with President Robert Marston, University of Florida, Gainesville, on March 18, 1982.
51. See *Memorandum Opinion, Ayers, Jake, Sr., et al. United States of America v. Allain, William, Governor, et al.,* 16–17. On December 10, 1987, Federal District Judge Neal B. Biggers, Jr., ruled in favor of the state and dismissed the Ayers complaint, which is now on appeal. A copy of the *Memorandum Opinion* was provided by Judge Biggers and is in the Verner Smith Holmes Collection, John D. Williams Library, University of Mississippi.
52. Minutes, January 19, September 2, 1967, May 28, 1953, June 17, 1960, February 17, 1966, February 19, 1976, May 15, 1969; Rhodes, *Jackson State University,* 142; Minutes, April 15, May 20, 1971, December 14, 1967, January 18, 1968, April 19, 1962.
53. Minutes, May 18, 1972.

Chapter 13. A System of Universities, 1972–1990
1. Robert Berdahl, *Statewide Coordination of Higher Education* (Washington, D.C., 1971). See also Hugh Davis Graham, "Structure and Governance in Higher Education: Historical and Comparative Analysis in State Policy," *Journal of Policy History* 1 (1989): 80–107. John D. Millett, *Conflict in Higher Education: State Government Versus Institutional Independence* (San Francisco, 1984), is very skeptical about coordination if it is imposed upon higher education by political circumstances and cites the governance of higher education in Mississippi as a highly commendable system.
2. *Clarion-Ledger,* April 16, 1974; *Jackson Daily News,* April 19, 1974; *Commercial Appeal,* April 19, 1974.
3. Eugene W. Hickock, Jr., "Higher Education, the State, and the Politics of Administration in Mississippi," (Ph.D. diss., University of Virginia, 1983), 10.
4. *Jackson Daily News,* February 15, 1974; interview with Governor William L. Waller in Jackson, Miss., on February 29, 1979.
5. *Clarion-Ledger,* October 2, 1974.
6. Unauthored, untitled, unpublished, twenty-four-page typed manuscript narrative of the evolution of Mississippi's compliance plan, Verner S. Holmes Collection, John Davis Williams Library, University of Mississippi, [cited hereafter as "Compliance"]; Board of Trustees, Minutes, March 20, April 17, September 18, 1969, January 15, 1970 [cited hereafter as Minutes and date]; New Orleans *Times Picayune,* April 22, 1973. The compliance plan manuscript was probably prepared by the board staff.
7. Interviews with Verner S. Holmes and Euclid R. Jobe, July 24–November 20, 1978, at Jackson, Miss.
8. "Compliance," 3–4.

9. *Jackson Daily News,* November 30 [Waller quotes], December 21, 1973; *Clarion-Ledger,* November 29, 1973. For a good summary of compliance plans see Norma Fields's article in Tupelo *Daily Journal,* December 12, 1973.

10. Minutes, January 28, 31, 1974; for Turner's quote see *Jackson Daily News,* February 12, 1974.

11. *Clarion-Ledger,* February 22, March 7, 1974; Jackson *Daily News,* January 30, 1974; interview with Commissioner of Higher Education Ray Cleere on February 13, 1989, at Jackson, Miss. See also *Memorandum Opinion, Ayers, Jake, Sr., et al. United States of America* v. *Allain, William, Governor, et al.,* copy in Holmes Collection.

12. Minutes, February 2, 1976. For a discussion of the desegregation of one of Mississippi's most famous churches see W. J. Cunningham, *Agony at Galloway: One Church's Struggle With Social Change* (Jackson, 1980).

13. Undated clipping from the *Reflector* (September 1976) in the Holmes Collection.

14. *Student Printz,* March 15, 1977.

15. *Times Picayune,* November 11, 1973; Minutes, April 17, 1975, July 15, 1976, June 15, December 20, 1978; *Clarion-Ledger,* July 16, 1976; Monte Piliawsky, *Exit 13: Oppression and Racism in Academia* (Boston, 1982), 42–43.

16. Minutes, November 11, 1977.

17. This information was obtained in conversations with Professor Barrett and Professor Evans Harrington at the University of Mississippi.

18. Minutes, May 18, 1978; interview with Verner Holmes on May 18, 1978, in Biloxi, Miss.

19. Minutes, January 17, 1980.

20. *Clarion-Ledger,* May 17, 1974.

21. *Jackson Daily News,* May 17, 1974.

22. Minutes, April 19, December 20, 1973.

23. *Clarion-Ledger,* February 20, 1975; *Daily Corinthian,* June 19, 1974.

24. Minutes, August 21, 1975; *Clarion-Ledger,* September 16, 1975.

25. Minutes, January 15, 1976; *Jackson Daily News,* January 15, 1976; *Oxford Eagle,* January 16, 1976; Tupelo *Daily Journal,* January 27, 1976.

26. *Jackson Daily News,* January 15, 1976.

27. *Biloxi Sun-Herald,* January 24, 1976.

28. Minutes, July 15, 1976.

29. Ibid., February 17, 1977.

30. *Natchez Democrat,* February 24, 1977.

31. Ibid.

32. Minutes, March 15, 1979.

33. Academy for Educational Development, Inc., *Program Review: A Structure for Mississippi's Public Universities* (Washington, D.C., 1979), vol. 11, p. 1, 1–3.

34. Minutes, November 18, 1981. A copy of the mission statement and the "Official Explanation," dated March 21, 1982, is in the Holmes Collection.

35. Ibid.

36. Board of Trustees, "Centers of Excellence." A copy of this document, along with a letter explaining the rationale for centers of excellence, is in the Holmes Collection. The letter, dated February 2, 1983, is from Executive Secretary Thrash to Senator John T. Fraiser, Jr., chairman of the senate appropriations committee.

37. Tupelo *Daily Journal*, July 20, August 16, 1984; *The Daily Mississippian*, July 26, 1984.

38. See detailed article by Andy Kanengiser in *Jackson Daily News-Clarion-Ledger*, January 5, 1986.

39. Denton Rogers to Editor Robert Gordon, January 19, 1986. A copy of this letter is in the Holmes Collection.

40. Interview with Representative Glenn Endris and Representative Ed Perry on February 26, 1986, in Jackson, Miss.

41. Board of Trustees, "Appropriations and Reductions, 1981–82 through 1985–86," Holmes Collection; Jack D. Foster, *Restructuring Higher Education: Choices and Analysis for Mississippi* (Jackson, 1985).

42. Foster, *Restructuring Higher Education*, 60–63.

43. Ibid., 54–57, 70–72.

44. Joseph E. Johnson, *Review of Funding and Allocation Formula* (Jackson, 1985), 2.

45. Minutes, March 14, 1985.

46. *Clarion-Ledger*, March 6, 1986.

47. See Board of Trustees, "Alternative I, Allocation of January 1986 Reductions," "Joint Legislative Budget Committee Recommendations for FY 1986–87," and "Analysis of Joint Legislative Budget Committee's Recommendations, 1986–87." Copies of these documents are in the Holmes Collection.

48. Interviews with Representative Endris and Representative Perry.

49. A copy of the Bourdeaux motion is in the Holmes Collection.

50. Board of Trustees, "FY 1987 Senate Recommendations." A copy of this document is in the Holmes Collection.

51. *Clarion-Ledger*, February 2, 1986.

52. Ibid., March 9, 1986.

53. Ibid., March 5, 24, 1986.

54. Ibid., March 5, 1986; interview with Chancellor R. Gerald Turner on February 20, 1989, at the University of Mississippi.

55. *Clarion-Ledger*, March 5, 1986.

56. Interview with Will Hickman, member of the board of trustees, on February 29, 1989, at Oxford, Miss. *Clarion-Ledger*, August 21, 1986.

57. Interview with Commissioner Cleere.

Bibliography

A Note on Sources

Though higher education in Mississippi has been the subject of at least a dozen studies, and even more investigations, and though it has often received extensive press coverage, it has not attracted the attention of historians. That is true of the nation generally. Except for a series of state studies sponsored by the United States Bureau of Education between 1887 and 1903, there are only four state histories of higher education: Willis F. Dunbar, *The Michigan Record in Higher Education* (Detroit, 1963); Saul Sack, *History of Higher Education in Pennsylvania*, 2 vols. (Harrisburg, 1963); Michael McGiffert, *The Higher Learning in Colorado: An Historical Study, 1860–1940* (Denver, 1964); and Samuel R. Granade, "Higher Education in Antebellum Alabama" (Ph.D. diss., Florida State University, 1972). Nevertheless, the sources for state histories are rich, varied, and readily available. Perhaps historians will begin to give this neglected field the attention it warrants.

The study of higher education in Mississippi begins and ends with legislative documents. This author found that the laws and charters establishing colleges and universities included significant information on the sponsors as well as the nature and function of institutions. For church schools, denominational histories, which are listed in the Bibliography, offered sparse but helpful information on many of the short-lived liberal arts colleges in antebellum Mississippi. For state institutions the reports of both standing and special legislative committees provided very important data through which the progression of higher education could be traced. The biennial reports that the legislature required of the various governing boards after 1910, the minutes of the boards, the reports required of college presidents by those boards, and official college publications were among the most useful sources of information. The annual addresses and special messages of Mississippi's governors also frequently included information about the state's educational institutions. Of particular importance were the various studies of higher education listed in the Bibliography.

For the more recent period the author conducted a series of interviews with current and former board members, four former governors, and several university officials. Those interviews, together with the ones in the Oral History Collection at the University of Southern Mississippi and the Department of Archives and History in Jackson, provided information that was not available from any other source. The interviews conducted by the author, which are cited in the Notes, have been transcribed and housed in the Verner Smith

Holmes Collection at the University of Mississippi. The James Wesley Silver Papers and the Russell Barrett Papers at the University of Mississippi, the Theodore G. Bilbo Papers at the University of Southern Mississippi, and the John C. Stennis Papers at Mississippi State University also included sources useful for this study.

Since the Mississippi press regularly and routinely covered higher education, various state newspapers were consulted for the entire period covered by this study. These journals are cited in the Notes. Most important were the Jackson papers, primarily because they covered the meetings of the board of trustees, which after 1910 were normally held in Jackson.

The following Bibliography includes the published primary and secondary sources, articles, theses and dissertations that were consulted for this study.

Academy for Educational Development, Inc. *Program Review: A Structure for Mississippi's Public Universities.* 11 vols. Washington, D.C., 1979.

Advisory Study Groups. *Public Education in Mississippi, Institutions of Higher Learning.* N.p.: n.p., 1961.

Allmendinger, David F., Jr. "The Strangeness of the American Education Society: Indigent Students and the New Charity, 1815–1840." *History of Education Quarterly* 11 (Spring 1971): 3–23.

———. "New England Students and the Revolution in Higher Education 1800–1900." *History of Education Quarterly* 11 (Winter 1971): 381–89.

———. *Paupers and Scholars: The Transformation of Student Life in Nineteenth Century New England.* New York: St. Martins, 1975.

American Association of University Professors. *Bulletin.* Autumn 1962, Autumn 1965, Spring 1970.

Ames, Blanche. *Adelbert Ames, 1835–1933.* New York: Argosy-Antiquarian, 1964.

Anderson, James D. *The Education of Blacks in the South, 1860–1935.* Chapel Hill: University of North Carolina Press, 1988.

Atwood, Rufus B. "The Origin and Development of the Negro Public College, with Special Reference to the Land-Grant College." *Journal of Negro Education* 31 (Summer 1962): 240–50.

Axtell, James L. "The Death of the Liberal Arts College." *History of Education Quarterly* 11 (Winter 1971): 330–53.

Bachman, Frank P. *Report of Functions of State Institutions of Higher Learning in Mississippi.* Nashville: George Peabody College, 1933.

Bailyn, Bernard. *Education in the Forming of American Society.* Chapel Hill: University of North Carolina Press, 1960.

Baker, Bill. *Catch the Vision: The Life of Henry L. Whitfield.* Jackson: University Press of Mississippi, 1974.

Baker, Webster B. *History of Rust College.* Greensboro: n.p., 1924.

Balsamo, Larry T. "Theodore G. Bilbo and Mississippi Politics, 1877–1932." Ph.D. diss., University of Missouri, 1967.

Barnard, Frederick A. P. *Letter to the Honorable The Board of Trustees of the University of Mississippi.* Oxford, 1858.

———. "Autobiographical Sketch of Dr. F. A. P. Barnard." *Publications of the Mississippi Historical Society* 12 (1912): 112–13.

———. *Report on the Organization of Military Schools.* Jackson, n.p., 1861.

Barnett, Ross. Speech on September 13, 1963. *Clarion-Ledger,* September 14, 1963.

Barrett, Russell. *Integration at Ole Miss.* Chicago: Quadrangle Books, 1965.

Bass, Jack. *Unlikely Heroes.* New York: Simon and Schuster, 1981.

Belfrage, Sally. *Freedom Summer.* Greenwich, Conn.: Fawcett Publications, 1966.

Berdahl, Robert. *Statewide Coordination of Higher Education.* Washington, D.C.: American Council on Education, 1971.

Berry, Trey. "A History of Higher Education for Women in Mississippi." M.A. thesis, University of Mississippi, 1987.

Bertoff, Rowland. "Peasants and Artisans, Puritans and Republicans: Personal Liberty and Communal Equality in American History." *Journal of American History* 69 (December 1982): 579–98.

Bettersworth, John K. *People's College.* Birmingham: University of Alabama Press, 1953.

———. *Mississippi, Yesterday and Today.* Austin: Steck-Vaughn, 1964.

———. *People's University: The Centennial History of Mississippi State.* Jackson: University Press of Mississippi, 1980.

Biographical and Historical Memoirs of Mississippi. 2 vols. Chicago: Goodspeed Publishing Company, 1891.

Blain, William T. *Education in the Old Southwest: A History of Jefferson College.* Washington, Miss.: Friends of Jefferson College, Inc., and Mississippi Department of Archives and History, 1976.

Board of Trustees. *Laws of Jefferson College.* Natchez: Board of Trustees, 1820.

Board of Trustees. *The Charter and Statutes of Jefferson College.* Natchez: Board of Trustees, 1840.

Board of Trustees, Mississippi Institutions of Higher Learning. *Biennial Reports.*

Bond, Horace Mann. *The Education of the Negro in the American Social Order.* New York: Prentice-Hall, 1934.

Bond, Willard F. *I Had A Friend: An Autobiography.* Kansas City: E. L. Mendenhall, 1958.

Boorstin, Daniel. *The Americans: The National Experience.* New York: Random House, 1965.

Booze-Allen and Hamilton, Inc. *State-wide Education Study, State of Mississippi.* N.p.: n.p., 1979.

Borrowman, Merle. "The False Dawn of the State University." *History of Education Quarterly* 1 (June 1961): 18–21.

Boyd, Jessie L. *A Popular History of Baptists in Mississippi.* Jackson: Baptist Press. 1930.

Brayer, Carl M. *John F. Kennedy and the Second Reconstruction*. New York: Columbia University Press, 1977.

Brewton, John E. *Higher Education in Mississippi*. Jackson: Board of Trustees, 1954.

Bridgforth, Lucie Robertson. "'Bomb the Ban': A Study of the Legal Controversy Surrounding Off-Campus Speakers at Mississippi Institutions of Higher Learning." M.A. thesis, University of Mississippi, 1979.

————. *Medical Education in Mississippi: A History of the School of Medicine*. Jackson: University Press of Mississippi, 1984.

Brookings Institution. *Report on a Survey of the Organization and Administration of State and County Government in Mississippi*. Jackson: n.p., 1932. Chapter 33, "Higher Education," 514–45.

Brubacher, John S. *A History of the Problems of Education*. New York: McGraw, 1966.

Bruss, Melvin K. "History of Oakland College (Mississippi), 1830–1871." M.A. thesis, Louisiana State University, 1965.

Bryson, Gladys. "The Emergence of the Social Sciences From Moral Philosophy." *International Journal of Ethics* 42 (April 1932): 304–23.

Bullock, Henry A. *A History of Negro Education in the South From 1619 to the Present*. Cambridge: Harvard University Press, 1967.

Burke, Colin B. *American Collegiate Populations: A Test of the Traditional View*. New York: New York University Press, 1987.

Butchart, Ronald E. "'Outthinking and Outflanking the Owners of the World': A Historiography of the African American Struggle for Education." *History of Education Quarterly* 28 (Fall 1988): 333–67.

Butts, W. A., ed. *Up from a Cottonpatch: J. H. White and the Development of Mississippi Valley State College*. Itta Bena: Mississippi Valley State College, 1979.

Cabaniss, James Allen. *The University of Mississippi: Its First Hundred Years*. University: University of Mississippi, 1949. Reissued 1971.

Cain, John B. *Methodism in the Mississippi Conference, 1846–1870*. Jackson: Hawkins Foundation, 1939.

Campbell, Clarice T., and Oscar Allen Rogers, Jr., *Mississippi: The View From Tougaloo*. Jackson: University Press of Mississippi, 1979.

Campbell, Florence E. "Journal of the Board of Trustees of the University of Mississippi." M.A. thesis, University of Mississippi, 1939.

Carmichael, Oliver Cromwell. *The Changing Role of Higher Education*. New York: Macmillan, 1949.

Carter, John. "A Boll Weevil Six Feet Long," *Library Journal* (October 15, 1969): 3615–3619.

Cash, Wilbur J. *Mind of the South*. New York: Knopf, 1941.

Cason, Clarence. "The Mississippi Imbroglio." *Virginia Quarterly Review* 7 (April 1931): 229–40.

Chute, William J. *Damn Yankee! The First Career of Frederick A. P. Barnard*. New York: Kennikat Press, 1978.

Clegg, Hugh. "Someone Jumped the Gun." Unpublished manuscript.

Cleveland, Grover C. "The Origin and Development of the University of Mississippi with Special Reference to Its Legislative Control." Ph.D. diss., Stanford University, 1932.

Colvard, Dean Wallace. *Mixed Emotions.* Danville, Ill.: Interstate Printers, 1985.

Conklin, Paul. *Gone with the Ivy: A Biography of Vanderbilt University.* Knoxville: University of Tennessee Press, 1985.

Content, Mary. "The National Implications of the Wisconsin Idea: A Bibliographic Study." M.A. thesis, George Washington University, 1964.

Coulter, E. Merton. *College Life in the Old South.* New York: Macmillan Company, 1928.

Cowley, W. H. *Presidents, Professors, and Trustees: The Evolution of American Academic Government.* San Francisco: Jossey-Bass, 1980.

Crist, Lynda Lasswell. "'Useful in His Day': James Alexander Ventress (1805–1867)." Ph.D. diss., University of Tennessee, 1980.

Cunningham, W. J. *Agony at Galloway: One Church's Struggle With Social Change.* Jackson: University Press of Mississippi, 1980.

Curti, Merle, and Vernon Cartensen, *The University of Wisconsin.* 2 vols. Madison: University of Wisconsin Press, 1959.

Dabney, Charles W. *Universal Education in the South.* Chapel Hill: University of North Carolina Press, 1936.

Dansby, B. Baldwin. *A Brief History of Jackson College.* Jackson: Jackson College, 1953.

Davis, Rueben. *Recollections of Mississippi and Mississippians.* New York: Houghton-Mifflin, 1889.

Davis, W. Milam. *Pushing Forward: A History of Alcorn A & M College and Portraits of Its Successful Graduates.* Okolona, Miss.: Okolona Industrial School, 1938.

De Bow, J. E. B. *De Bow's Review.* "University of the South." 26 (1859): 330–35.

DeRosier, Arthur H., Jr. "William Dunbar: A Product of the Eighteenth Century Scottish Renaissance." *Journal of Mississippi History* 28 (1966): 185–27.

Dobbs, Sharron Lynn. "Jefferson College: A Study of the Origins of Higher Education in Mississippi, 1802–1848." Ph.D. diss., University of Mississippi, 1987.

Drake, Claribel. "Mississippi's Elizabeth Female Academy: Its Claim to be the Mother of Women's Colleges in America." *Daughters of the American Revolution Magazine* (May 1962): 96, 487–88, 514.

Dubay, Robert. "Pigmentation and Pigskin: A Jones County Junior College Dilemma." *Journal of Mississippi History* 46 (February 1984): 43–50.

Dubuisson, Charles L. *Inaugural Address Delivered by Charles L. Dubuisson, President of Jefferson College.* Natchez: Courier and Journal, 1835.

Dungan, James R. "'Sir' William Dunbar of Natchez: Planter, Explorer, and Scientist, 1792–1810." *Journal of Mississippi History* 24 (1961): 211–28.

Dunham, Merlerson Guy. *The Centennial History of Alcorn A & M College.* Hattiesburg: University and College Press of Mississippi, 1971.

Dyer, Thomas G. "Higher Education in the South Since the Civil War: Historiographical Issues and Trends." In *The Web of Southern Social Relations: Women, Family and Education,* edited by Walter J. Fraser, Jr., R. Frank Saunders, Jr., and Jon L. Wakelyn, 127–45. Athens: University of Georgia Press, 1985.

————. *The University of Georgia: A Bicentennial History.* Athens: University of Georgia Press, 1985.

Eaton, Clement. *The Freedom of Thought Struggle in the Old South.* Durham: Duke University, 1940.

Eddy, Edward D., Jr. *Colleges for Our Land and Time.* New York: Harper, 1957.

Edmond, J. B. *The Magnificent Charter: The Origin and Role of the Morrill Land-Grant Colleges and Universities.* Hicksville, N.Y.: Exposition Press, 1978.

Emmerich, J. Oliver. *Two Faces of Janus: The Sage of Deep South Change.* Jackson: University and College Press of Mississippi, 1973.

Evers, Mrs. Medgar. *For Us, The Living.* Garden City: Doubleday, 1967.

Ezell, John S. "A Southern Education for Southrons," *Journal of Southern History* 17 (August 1951): 303–28.

Fine, Benjamin. *Democratic Education.* New York: Crowell, 1945.

Foerster, Alma Pauline. "The State University in the Old South." Ph.D. diss., Duke University, 1939.

Foerster, Norman. *The American State University: Its Relation to Democracy.* Chapel Hill: University of North Carolina Press, 1937.

Foster, Jack D. *Restructuring Higher Education: Choices and Analysis for Mississippi.* Jackson: n.p., 1985.

Fraser, Walter J., Jr., R. Frank Saunders, Jr., Jon L. Wakelyn, eds. *The Web of Southern Social Relations: Women, Family and Education.* Athens: University of Georgia Press, 1985.

Friends of the University. *Some Facts Against Removal of the University of Mississippi.* Oxford: n.p., n.d.

Fulton, John. *Memoirs of Frederick A. P. Barnard.* New York: Macmillan and Company, 1896.

Galloway, Charles Betts. "Elizabeth Female College: Mother of Female Colleges." *Publications of the Mississippi Historical Society* 2 (1898): 169–78.

Garner, James W. *Reconstruction in Mississippi.* New York: Macmillan, 1901.

Gates, William B. "The Theater in Natchez." *Journal of Mississippi History* 3 (1941): 71–129.

Gibson, Joseph E. *Mississippi Study of Higher Education.* Jackson: Board of Trustees, 1945.

Gillespie, Neal C. "Ole Miss: A New Look at Her First President." *Journal of Mississippi History* 30 (1968): 275–90.

Glenny, Lyman A. *Autonomy of Public Colleges: The Challenge of Coordination.* New York: McGraw, 1959.

Godbold, Albea. *The Church College in the Old South.* Durham: Duke University Press, 1944.

Goodenow, Ronald K. and Arthur O. White, eds. *Education and the Rise of the New South.* Boston: G. K. Hall and Co., 1981.

Graham, Hardy Poindexter. "Bilbo and the University of Mississippi, 1928–1932." M.A. thesis, University of Mississippi, 1965.

Graham, Hugh Davis. "Structure and Governance in American Higher Education: Historical and Comparative Analysis in State Policy." *Journal of Public Policy History* 1 (1989): 80–107.

Green, A. Wigfall. *The Man Bilbo.* Baton Rouge: Louisiana State University Press, 1963.

Guice, John D. "Log Colleges and Legacies of the Great Awakening." *Southern Quarterly* (January 1972): 117–37.

Gunn, Jack W., and Gladys C. Castle. *A Pictorial History of Delta State University.* Jackson: University Press of Mississippi, 1980.

Halberstram, David. 'Starting Out to Be a Famous Reporter." *Esquire* (November 1981): 70–80.

Halsey, LeRoy J., ed. *The Works of Philip Lindsley, D.D.* 2 vols. Philadelphia: J. B. Lippincott, 1866.

Hamilton, William B. "Holly Springs, Mississippi to 1878." M.A. thesis, University of Mississippi, 1931.

———. "Jefferson College and Education in Mississippi, 1798–1817." *Journal of Mississippi History* 3 (1941): 259–77.

Handlin, Oscar, and Mary Handlin. *The American College and American Culture: Socialization as a Function of Higher Education.* New York: McGraw-Hill, 1970.

Harding, Thomas S. *Collegiate Literary Societies: Their Contributions to Higher Education in the United States, 1815–1876.* New York: Pagent Press, International, 1971.

Harkey, Ira. . . . *dedicated to the proposition . . . Editorials from the Chronicle.* Pascagoula, Miss.: n.p., 1963.

———. *The Smell of Burning Crosses.* Jacksonville, Ill.: Harris-Wolfe, 1967.

Harrell, Laura D. "The Development of the Lyceum Movement in Mississippi." *Journal of Mississippi History* 31 (1969): 187–201.

Harris, William C. *Presidential Reconstruction in Mississippi.* Baton Rouge: Louisiana State University Press, 1967.

———. *Day of the Carpetbagger.* Baton Rouge: Louisiana State University Press, 1978.

Hatfield, Joseph. *William Claiborne, Jeffersonian Centurion in the American Southwest.* Lafayette, La.: Southwestern Louisiana University, 1976.

Hathorn, Nathaniel C. "A Financial History of the University of Mississippi from Its Endowment in 1819 to 1900." M.A. thesis, University of Mississippi, 1938.

Hattaway, Herman. *General Stephen D. Lee.* Jackson: University Press of Mississippi, 1976.

Hayes, Willard M. "Polemics and Philosophy: A Biography of Albert Taylor Bledsoe. Ph.D. diss., University of Tennessee, 1971.

Headley, Katie M. *Claiborne County, Mississippi: The Promised Land.* Port Gibson, Miss.: Port Gibson-Claiborne County Historical Society, 1976.

Herbst, Jurgen. "American College History: Re-examination Underway." *History of Education Quarterly* 14 (Summer 1974): 259–66.

Hickman, Alma. *Southern As I Saw It: Personal Remembrances of an Era, 1912 to 1954.* Hattiesburg: University of Southern Mississippi, 1966.

Hickock, Eugene W., Jr. "Higher Education, the State, and the Politics of Administration in Mississippi." Ph.D. diss., University of Virginia, 1983.

Hickson, Shirley Ann. "The Development of Higher Education for Women in the Antebellum South." Ph.D. diss., University of South Carolina, 1985.

Hislop, Codman. *Eliphalet Nott.* Middletown, Conn.: Wesleyan University Press, 1971.

Historical Catalogue of the University of Mississippi, 1849–1909. Nashville: n.p., 1910.

Hofstadter, Richard, and C. DeWitt Hardy, *The Development and Scope of Higher Education in the United States.* New York: Columbia University Press, 1952.

——, and Walter P. Metzger. *The Development of Academic Freedom in the United States.* New York: Columbia University Press, 1955.

——, and Wilson Smith, eds. *American Higher Education: A Documentary History.* Chicago: University of Chicago Press, 1961.

Hogan, William R., and Edwin Davis, eds. *William Johnson's Natchez: The Antebellum Diary of a Free Negro.* Baton Rouge: Louisiana State University Press, 1951.

——. *The Barber of Natchez.* Baton Rouge: Louisiana State University Press, 1973.

Holder, Ray. *William Winans: Methodist Leader in Antebellum Mississippi.* Jackson: University Press of Mississippi, 1977.

——. "Centenary: Roots of a Pioneer College (1838–1844)." *Journal of Mississippi History* 42 (1980): 77–99.

Hollander, Ronald. "One Mississippi Negro Who Didn't Go To College." *The Reporter* 27 (November 8, 1962): 30–34.

Hollis, David W. *The University of South Carolina.* 2 vols. Columbia: University of South Carolina Press, 1956.

Holmes, William F. *The White Chief: James K. Vardaman.* Baton Rouge: Louisiana State University Press, 1970.

Holt, Len. *The Summer That Didn't End.* New York: Morrow, 1965.

Hooker, Grover C. "The Origin and Development of the University of Mississippi with Special Reference to Its Legislative Control." Ph.D. diss., Stanford University, 1932.

Hudson, John. "The Spoils System Enters College," *New Republic* 64 (September 17, 1930): 123–24.

Hutchins, Robert Maynard. *The Higher Learning in America.* New Haven: Yale University Press, 1936, 1961.

Hutchinson, Reverend J. R., D.D. *Reminiscences, Sketches, and Speeches.* Houston, Tex.: E. H. Cushing, 1874.

Ingraham, Joseph Holt. *The South-West, by a Yankee.* 2 vols. New York, Harper and Brothers, 1835.

Institutions of Higher Learning. Subject File. Mississippi Department of Archives and History, Jackson, Mississippi.

James, D. Clayton. *Antebellum Natchez.* Baton Rouge: Louisiana State University Press, 1968.

Jaworski, Leon. *Confessions and Avoidance: A Memoir.* New York: Anchor Press, 1979.

Jenkins, Robert L. "The Development of Black Higher Education," *Journal of Mississippi History* 45 (November 1983): 272–83.

Jobe, E. R. *The Status of Planning for Postsecondary Education in Mississippi, 1979.* Jackson: n.p., 1979.

Johnson, J. W. "Sketches of Judge A. B. Longstreet and Dr. F. A. P. Barnard." *Publications of the Mississippi Historical Society* 12 (1912): 122–48.

Johnson, Joseph E. *Review of Funding and Allocation Formula.* Jackson: n.p., 1985.

Jones, Myra Hume. "Tenets and Attitudes of an Old-Time Teacher (Alfred Hume)." M.A. thesis, University of Mississippi, 1949.

Kaestle, Carl F. *Pillars of the Republic: Common Schools and American Society.* New York: Hill and Wang, 1983.

Kerr, Clark. *The Uses of a University.* Cambridge: Harvard University Press, 1963.

Keyes, Frank. *An Address Delivered Before the Alumni Association of the University of Mississippi, on the Fifth Day of July, 1859.* Oxford: n.p., 1859.

Kimball, Bruce A. *Orators and Philosophers: A History of the Idea of Liberal Education.* New York: Columbia University Press, 1986.

Kirwan, Albert. *The Revolt of the Rednecks: Mississippi Politics, 1876–1925.* Lexington: University of Kentucky Press, 1951.

Kohlbrenner, Bernard J. "Religion and Higher Education: An Historical Perspective." *History of Education Quarterly* 1 (June 1961): 45–57.

Lane, Jack C. "The Yale Report of 1828 and Liberal Education: A Neorepublican Manifesto." *History of Education Quarterly* 27 (Fall 1987): 325–38.

Leavell, Z. T. *A Complete History of Mississippi Baptists from the Earliest Times.* 2 vols. Jackson: Mississippi Baptist Publication Corp., 1904.

Leonard, George B., T. George Harris, and Christopher S. Wren. "How a Secret Deal Prevented a Massacre at Ole Miss." *Look* (December 31, 1982): 22.

Lesher, Stephen. "Jackson State a Year After." *New York Times Magazine* (March 21, 1971): 56.

Levine, David O. *The American College and the Culture of Aspiration, 1915–1940.* Ithaca: Cornell University Press, 1986.

Lloyd, James, ed. *Lives of Mississippi Writers.* Jackson: University Press of Mississippi, 1980.

Lord, Walter. *The Past That Would Not Die.* New York: Harper, 1966.

Lowe, Edna Haley. *Sketch of Chickasaw College, Pontotoc, Mississippi.* Oxford: University of Mississippi, 1951.

Lucas, Aubrey K. "The Mississippi Legislature and Mississippi Public Higher Education, 1890–1960." Ph.D. diss., Florida State University, 1966.

———. "Education in Mississippi from Statehood to the Civil War." In *A History of Mississippi,* edited by Richard A. McLemore, 1:352–78. Jackson: University and College Press of Mississippi, 1973.

Lyles, Samuel T. "Conditions Relating to Sectionalism in Mississippi from 1838 to 1852." M.A. thesis, University of Mississippi, 1932.

Lynch, John Roy. *Reminiscences of an Active Life: The Autobiography of John Roy Lynch.* Introduction by John Hope Franklin. Chicago: University of Chicago Press, 1970.

McArthur, Robert E., ed. *Inaugural Addresses of the Governors of Mississippi, 1890–1980.* University, Miss.: Bureau of Governmental Research, 1980.

McCain, William D. "The Triumph of Democracy, 1916–1932." In *A History of Mississippi,* edited by Richard A. McLemore, 2: 59–97. Jackson: University and College Press of Mississippi, 1973.

McLachlan, James. "The American Colleges in the Nineteenth Century: Towards a Reappraisal." *Teachers College Record* 86 (December 1978): 287–306.

McLemore, Richard A. and Nannie Pitts. *A History of Mississippi College.* Clinton: Mississippi College, 1979.

———, ed. *A History of Mississippi.* 2 vols. Jackson: University and College Press of Mississippi, 1973.

McMertrie, Douglas C., ed. *The Mississippi Territorial Session Laws of May, 1802.* Chicago: University of Chicago Press, 1938.

McMillen, Neil R. *The Citizens' Council: Organized Resistance to the Second Reconstruction.* Urbana: University of Illinois Press, 1971.

———. *Dark Journey: Black Mississippians in the Age of Jim Crow.* Urbana: University of Illinois Press, 1989.

Maddox, Dawn. "The Buildings and Grounds of Jefferson College in the Nineteenth Century," *Journal of Mississippi History* 35 (February 1973): 37–55.

Madsen, David. *The National University: Enduring Dream of the United States of America.* Detroit: Wayne State University Press, 1966.

Martorana, S. V. *Strengthening Mississippi's Higher Education Through Diversification, Cooperation, and Coordination.* Jackson: Board of Trustees, 1960.

Mayes, Edward. *The State University: A Reply by Professor Edward Mayes to Senator James Z. George.* N.p.: n.p., 1887.

―――. *L. Q. C. Lamar: His Life, Times, and Speeches.* Nashville: Publishing House of the Methodist Episcopal Church, 1896.

―――. *History of Education in Mississippi.* Washington: Government Printing Office, 1899.

Meredith, James H. *Three Years in Mississippi.* Bloomington: University of Indiana Press, 1966.

Meredith v. *Fair, Transcript of Record.* 5 vols. Chancellor's Office, University of Mississippi, 1961–62.

Millett, John D. *Conflict in Higher Education: State Government Versus Institutional Independence.* San Francisco: Jossey-Bass, 1984.

Mississippi Law Research Center. *An Analysis of the Law of Separation of Powers Applicable to the Governance of Higher Education.* University: University of Mississippi Law Research Center, 1978.

"Mississippi's Compliance Plans." Verner Smith Holmes Collection, John Davis Williams Library, University of Mississippi.

Mitchell, Samuel C., ed. *The South in the Building of the Nation.* Richmond: Southern Historical Publication Society, 1909.

Moak, Franklin E. *A History of the Alumni Association of the University of Mississippi, 1852–1986.* University: Alumni Association of The University of Mississippi, 1986.

Montgomery, James, Stanley Folmsbee, and Lee Greene. *To Foster Knowledge: A History of the University of Tennessee, 1794–1970.* Knoxville: University of Tennessee Press, 1985.

Moody, Anne. *Coming of Age in Mississippi.* New York: Dial Press, 1968.

Moos, Malcolm, and Francis Rouke. *The Campus and the State.* Baltimore: Johns Hopkins Press, 1959.

Morgan, Chester. *Redneck Liberal: Theodore G. Bilbo and the New Deal.* Baton Rouge: Louisiana State University Press, 1985.

―――. *Dearly Bought, Deeply Treasured: The University of Southern Mississippi, 1912–1987.* Jackson: University Press of Mississippi, 1987.

Morris, Robert C. *Reading, 'Riting and Reconstruction: The Education of the Freedmen in the South, 1861–1870.* Chicago: University of Chicago Press, 1981.

Morris, Willie. "At Ole Miss: Echoes of a Civil War's Last Battle." *Time* (October 4, 1982): 8–11.

Morrison, J. K. "Early History of Jefferson College." *Publications of the Mississippi Historical Society* 2 (1898): 179–89.

Murphy, James L. *L. Q. C. Lamar: Pragmatic Patriot.* Baton Rouge: Louisiana State University Press, 1973.

Navasky, Victor S. *Kennedy Justice.* New York: Atheneum, 1971.

Naylor, Natalie A. "The Ante-bellum College Movement: A Reappraisal of Tewksbury's *The Founding of American Colleges and Universities.*" *History of Education Quarterly* 13 (Fall 1973): 261–75.

―――. "The Theological Seminary in the Configuration of Higher Education: The Ante-bellum Years." *History of Education Quarterly* 17 (Spring 1977): 17–31.

Nelson, William Hamilton. *A Burning Torch and a Flaming Fire: The Story of Centenary College of Louisiana.* Nashville: Methodist Publishing House, 1931.

Neufeldt, Harvey, and Clinton Allison. "Education and the Rise of the New South: An Historiographical Essay." In *Education and the Rise of the New South,* edited by Ronald K. Goodenow and Arthur O. White, 250–93. Boston: G. K. Hall, 1981.

Newcomer, Mabel. *A Century of Higher Education for American Women.* New York: Harper, 1959.

O'Shea, Michael V. *Public Education in Mississippi.* Jackson, Miss.: Jackson Printing Company, 1927.

Percy, William Alexander. *Lanterns on the Levee: Recollections of a Planter's Son.* New York: Knopf, 1941.

Pereyra, Lillian. *James L. Alcorn, Persistent Whig.* Baton Rouge: Louisiana State University Press, 1966.

Peterson, George. *The New England College in the Age of the University.* Amherst: Amherst College Press, 1964.

Pieschel, Bridget Smith, and Stephen Robert Pieschel. *Loyal Daughters: One Hundred Years at Mississippi University for Women, 1884–1984.* Jackson: University Press of Mississippi, 1984.

Piliawsky, Monte. *Exit 13: Oppression and Racism in Academia.* Boston: South End Press, 1982.

Piller, James J. *The Catholic Church in Mississippi, 1837–1865.* New Orleans: Hauser Press, 1964.

Posey, Brownlow. *Religious Strife on the Southern Frontier.* Baton Rouge: Louisiana State University Press, 1965.

Potts, David B. "American Colleges in the Nineteenth Century: From Localism to Denominationalism." *History of Education Quarterly* 11 (Winter 1971): 363–80.

President's Commission on Higher Education. *Higher Education for American Democracy.* 6 vols. Washington: Government Printing Office, 1947.

Proceedings of the Thirty-fifth Annual Meeting of the Association of Colleges and Secondary Schools of the Southern States, Atlanta Georgia, December 4–5, 1930. Birmingham: Premier Printing Company, n.d.

Proceedings of the Thirty-seventh Meeting of the Southern Association of Colleges and Secondary Schools at New Orleans, Louisiana, December 1–2, 1932. Birmingham: Premier Printing Company, n.d.

Ranck, James B. *Albert Gallatin Brown: Radical Southern Nationalist.* New York: Appleton-Century, 1937.

Read, James C. "The Williams Chancellorship at the University of Mississippi, 1946–1968." Ph.D. diss., University of Mississippi, 1978.

Reddix, Jacob L. *A Voice Crying in the Wilderness: The Memoirs of Jacob L. Reddix.* Jackson: University and College Press of Mississippi, 1974.

Report of the Joint Select Committee Appointed to Inquire Into . . . the A & M College of Mississippi. Jackson: J. L. Power State Printer, 1882.

Rhodes, Lelia Gaston. *Jackson State University: The First Hundred Years, 1877–1977.* Jackson: University Press of Mississippi, 1979.

Rice, Kathleen George. "A History of Whitworth College for Women." Ph.D. diss., University of Mississippi, 1985.

Richardson, J. M. "Central Southern University: Political and Educational Necessity for Its Establishment." *De Bow's Review* 23 (1857): 490–503.

———. "University of the South." *De Bow's Review* 26 (1859): 330–35.

Roberts, M. M. Letter to All Members of the Board, March 10, 1970. Verner Smith Holmes Collection, John Davis Williams Library, University of Mississippi.

Robson, David W. "College Founding in the New Republic, 1776–1800." *History of Education Quarterly* 23 (Fall 1983): 323–41.

———. *Educating Republicans: The College in the Era of the American Revolution, 1750–1800.* Westport, Conn.: Greenwood Press, 1985.

Rogers, Tommy Wayne. "The Schools of Higher Learning at Sharon, Mississippi." *Journal of Mississippi History* 28 (February 1966): 40–56.

———. "Oakland College, 1830–1871," *Journal of Mississippi History* 26 (May 1974): 143–61.

———. "T. C. Thornton: A Methodist Educator in Antebellum Mississippi." *Journal of Mississippi History* 44 (May 1982): 136–46.

Ross, Earle D. *Democracy's College: The Land-Grant Movement in the Formative Stages.* Ames: Iowa State College Press, 1942.

Rowland, Dunbar. *Mississippi, Comprising Sketches . . . Arranged in Cyclopedia Form.* 3 vols. Atlanta: Southern Historical Publishing Association, 1907.

———. *Courts, Judges, and Lawyers of Mississippi.* Jackson: Mississippi Historical Society, 1935.

———, ed. *Official Letter Books of W. C. C. Claiborne, 1801–1816.* 6 vols. Jackson: Department of Archives and History, 1917.

Rowland, Eron. *Life, Letters, and Papers of William Dunbar of Elgin, Morayshire, Scotland, and Natchez, Mississippi: Pioneer Scientist of the Southern United States.* Jackson: Mississippi Historical Society, 1930.

Rudolph, Frederick. *The American College and University: A History.* New York: Knopf, 1962.

———. *Curriculum: A History of the American Undergraduate Course of Study Since 1636.* San Francisco: Jossey-Bass, 1977.

Rules and Regulations of the University of Mississippi. Holly Springs: University of Mississippi, 1850.

Rules for the Government of the Methodist Female Academy Near Washington Enacted By the Trustees in October 1818. Natchez: n.p., 1818.

Russell, Roger D. "Negro Publicly-Supported Colleges in Mississippi and South Carolina." *Journal of Negro Education* 31 (Summer 1962): 310–21.

Salamon, Lester Milton. "Protest, Politics, and Modernization in the American South: Mississippi as a 'Developing Society.'" Ph.D. diss., Harvard University, 1971.

Salter, John R. *Jackson, Mississippi: An American Chronicle of Struggle and Schism.* Hicksville, N.Y.: Exposition Press, 1979.

Sansing, David G. "The Role of the Scalawag in Mississippi Reconstruction." Ph.D. diss., University of Southern Mississippi, 1969.

————. *Mississippi, Its People and Culture.* Minneapolis: T. S. Denison and Co., 1981.

————, and Carroll Waller, *A History of the Mississippi Governor's Mansion.* Jackson: Mississippi Executive Mansion Commission, 1977.

Schmidt, George P. *The Old-Time College President.* New York: Columbia University Press, 1930.

————. *The Liberal Arts College: A Chapter in American Cultural History.* New Brunswick, N.J.: Rutgers University Press, 1957.

Scott, Anne Firor. "The Ever Widening Circle: The Diffusion of Feminist Values from the Troy Female Seminary, 1822–1872." *History of Education Quarterly* 19 (Spring 1979): 3–27.

Scott, Roy V., and James G. Shoalmire, *The Public Career of Cully Cobb.* Jackson: University and College Press of Mississippi, 1973.

Scranton, William W., *The Report of the President's Commission on Campus Unrest, Including Special Reports: The Killings at Jackson State, the Kent State Tragedy.* New York: Arno Press, 1970.

Secretary of State, *Official and Statistical Register of Mississippi.* Published quadrennially.

Sewell, George A., and Margaret L. Dwight. *Mississippi Black History Makers.* Jackson: University Press of Mississippi, 1984.

Shepard, H. E. "Higher Education in the South." *Sewanee Review* 1 (May 1893): 283–89.

Silver, James W. *Mississippi: The Closed Society.* New York: Harcourt, 1966.

————. *Running Scared: Silver in Mississippi.* Jackson: University Press of Mississippi, 1984.

Simkins, Francis B. *Pitchfork Ben Tillman.* Baton Rouge: Louisiana State University Press, 1944.

Sloan, Douglas. "Harmony, Chaos, and Consensus: The American College Curriculum." *Teachers College Record* 73 (December 1971): 221–51.

Smiley, David L. "William Carey Crane, Professor of Old Mississippi." *Journal of Mississippi History* 12 (April 1950): 98–104.

Smith, Suanna. "Washington, Mississippi: Antebellum Elysium." *Journal of Mississippi History* 15 (1978): 143–65.

Smith, Wilson. "Apologia pro Alma Matre: The College as Community in

Antebellum America." In *The Hofstadter Aegis: A Memorial*, edited by Stanley Elkins and Eric McKitrick, 125–54. New York: Knopf, 1974.

Snavely, Guy E. *A Short History of the Southern Association of Colleges and Secondary Schools.* Durham: Duke University Press, 1945.

Soloman, Barbara. *In Company of Educated Women: A History of Women and Higher Education in America.* New Haven: Yale University Press, 1985.

Spofford, Tim. *LYNCH STREET, The May 1970 Slayings at Jackson State College.* Kent, Ohio: Kent State University Press, 1988.

Stetar, Joseph. "In Search of Direction: Southern Higher Education After the Civil War." *History of Education Quarterly* 25 (Fall 1985): 341–67.

Sugarman, Tracy. *Stranger at the Gates: A Summer in Mississippi.* New York: Hill and Wang, 1966.

Summers, Thomas O., ed. *Autobiography of the Rev. Joseph Travis, A.M.* Nashville (n.p.), 1856.

Sydnor, Charles. *Slavery in Mississippi.* New York: Appleton-Century, 1933.

———. *A Gentleman of the Old Natchez Region: Benjamin L. C. Wailes.* Durham: Duke University Press, 1938.

———. *The Development of Southern Sectionalism, 1819–1848.* Baton Rouge: Louisiana State University Press, 1948.

Taylor, Joseph W. *An Address Delivered Before the Phi Sigma and Hermean Societies at the Commencement . . . on June 25, 1869.* Memphis: Hite and Corwine, 1869.

Tewksbury, Donald. *The Founding of American Colleges and Universities Before the Civil War.* New York: Teachers College, Columbia University, 1932. Reprint. New York: Arno Press, 1969.

Thompson, Patrick H. *The History of Negro Baptists in Mississippi.* Jackson: R. W. Bailey Print Company, 1898.

Thornton, Thomas C. *Inaugural Address Delivered at the First Commencement of Centenary College.* Jackson: n.p., 1842.

Tinsley, Sammy Jay. "A History of Mississippi Valley State College." Ph.D. diss., University of Mississippi, 1972.

Urban, Wayne J. "History of Education: A Southern Exposure." *History of Education Quarterley* 21 (Summer 1981): 131–45.

Van Landingham, Zack J. "Report on Clyde Kennard to the State Sovereignty Commission." December 1, 1958–January 29, 1960.

Vaughn, William. *Schools for All: Blacks and Public Education in the South, 1865–1877.* Lexington: University Press of Kentucky, 1974.

Veysey, Laurence R. *The Emergence of the American University.* Chicago: University of Chicago Press, 1965.

———. "Toward a New Direction in Educational History: Prospect and Retrospect." *History of Education Quarterly* 9 (Fall 1969): 343–59.

Vinson, Ken. "Mississippi: Signs of Life, The Lawyers of Ole Miss." *The Nation* (June 23, 1969): 791–93.

Waddel, John N. *The Evils of Unsanctified Ambition.* Meridian, Miss.: Sherman and Company, 1870.

———. *Memorials of Academic Life.* Richmond: Presbyterian Committee of Publications, 1891.

Wade, John D. *Augustus Baldwin Longstreet: A Study in the Development of Culture in the South.* New York: Macmillan, 1924.

Wakelyn, Jon L. "Antebellum College Life and the Relations between Fathers and Sons." In *The Web of Southern Social Relations, Women, Family, and Education,* edited by Walter J. Fraser, Jr., R. Frank Saunders, Jr., and Jon L. Wakelyn, 107–26. Athens: University of Georgia Press, 1985.

Walker (Alexander). Margaret. *Richard Wright, Daemonic Genius: A Portrait of the Man, A Critical Look at His Work.* New York: Warner Books, 1988.

Watson, Francis Egger. "Dr. Alfred Hume: His Leadership as Vice Chancellor, Acting Chancellor, and Chancellor of the University of Mississippi (1905–1945)." (Ph.D. diss., University of Mississippi, 1987).

Wayland, Francis. *Thoughts on the Present Collegiate System in the United States.* Boston, 1842. Reprint. New York: Arno Press, 1969.

Wayne, Michael. *The Reshaping of Plantation Society: The Natchez District, 1860–1880.* Baton Rouge: Louisiana State University Press, 1983.

Weathersby, William H. *History of Educational Legislation in Mississippi from 1798–1860.* Chicago: University of Chicago Press, 1921.

Webber, Thomas L. *Deep like the River: Education in the Slave Quarter Community, 1831–1865.* New York: Norton, 1978.

Wharton, Vernon L. *The Negro in Mississippi, 1865–1890.* Chapel Hill: University of North Carolina Press, 1947.

Whitfield, Henry L. *Know Mississippi: A Syllabus on Present Conditions in Mississippi.* N.p.: n.p., c. 1924.

Wiesenburg, Karl. *The Oxford Disaster . . . The Price of Defiance.* Pascagoula, Miss.: *The Chronicle,* 1962.

Williams, T. Harry. *Huey Long.* New York: Knopf, 1969.

Wilson, Charles H., Sr. *Education for Negroes in Mississippi Since 1910.* Boston, Meador Publishing Co., 1947.

Wilson, Charles R. *Baptized in Blood: The Religion of the Lost Cause, 1865–1920.* Athens: University of Georgia Press, 1980.

Wolff, Robert. *The Ideal of the University.* Boston: Beacon Press, 1969.

Woodson, Carter G. *The Education of the Negro Prior to 1861.* Washington: Associated Publishers Inc., 1919.

Woody, Thomas. *A History of Women's Education in the United States.* New York: The Science Press, 1929.

Wright, Richard, *Black Boy, A Record of Childhood and Youth.* New York: Harper and Brothers Publishers, 1945.

Index

Academic freedom, 200–06, 215
Academic standards, 20–21, 56–57
Academy for Educational Development, *Program Review*, 226–27
Admissions policies, 56–57, 70–71,
  161–62
African-Americans, education of,
  23–24, 27, 56, 61–64, 69, 75,
  79–80, 90, 115, 122, 129, 130,
  132, 136–37, 140–51, 157,
  210–11, 218, 237. *See also* Meredith, James Howard; Alcorn University, Jackson College
  (Mississippi), Mississippi Vocational College, and their respec-
  tive later manifestations; State
  Normal School
Alabama, University of, 45, 158, 167
Alcorn, James L., 58, 59, 62
Alcorn Agricultural and Mechanical
  College, 64, 68, 69, 76, 80, 81, 90,
  102, 109, 114, 115, 117, 129, 130,
  132, 133, 136, 140–41, 142, 144–
  45, 146, 202, 205, 207, 214; 1951
  mission statement, 137; student
  unrest, 207; and integration, 213.
  See also Alcorn University; Alcorn
  State University
Alcorn State University, 232, 233,
  235; and Ayers case, 218; nursing
  program, 225–26; 1982 mission
  statement, 227–28; and funding,
  232
Alcorn University, 27, 63–64; and
  funding, 63; reorganizations, 64;
  reestablished as Alcorn Agricultural and Mechanical College, 64

Allain, William, 213, 233, 237
American Pharmaceutical Associa-
  tion, 108
American Association of State Uni-
  versities, 108
American Association of University
  Professors, 108
American Association of University
  Women, 108
American Missionary Society, 61
Ames, Adelbert, 59
Amherst College, 21, 60
Anderson, Douglas, 232, 233
Angell, James B., 55
Antioch College, 127
Association for American Univer-
  sities, 108
Atlanta Constitution, 155
Audubon, John James, 15
Ayers v. *Allain*, 218

Backstrom, John W., 134
Bailey, J. A., 65
Bailey, Thomas L., 120, 123, 125
Bard College, 127
Barnard, Frederick Augustus Porter,
  26, 36, 41, 43, 45–47, 48–54, 60,
  72, 138; *Art Culture*, 46; and *Universitas Scientiarium*, 50, 51, 52; *Letter to the Honorable The Board of
  Trustees of the University of Mississippi*, 49–52
Barnard, Mrs. Frederick A. P., 47
Barnett, Ross, 151, 153, 154–55,
  156, 157, 168, 169, 170, 171, 172,
  173–76, 177–79, 180, 181, 182,
  183–84, 185–87, 188–89, 190–

Barnett, Ross (*continued*)
  91, 192, 193, 195, 196, 197, 202,
  214
Barrett, Russell, 202, 220; *Integration
  at Ole Miss,* 167, 220
Barton, Bill, 155
Bascom, John, 71
Bass, Jack, 166
Baylor University, 28
Belhaven College, 70, 129
Bell, William H., 130
Bennett, Claude, 100, 103, 114
Bennington College, 127
Berdahl, Robert, *Statewide Coordina-
  tion of Higher Education,* 215–16
Bettersworth, John K., 134
Bilbo, Theodore G., 37, 84, 85, 87,
  88, 90, 91–93, 94–97, 98, 99, 100,
  101–02, 103, 104, 105, 106–07,
  109–10, 111, 112, 114, 115, 119,
  125, 157
Billingsly, Charles, 194
Birdsong, T. B., 191, 193
Black, Hugo, 168
Black Mississippi Council on Higher
  Education, 218
Bledsoe, Albert Taylor, 39
Blue Mountain College, 70, 129
Board of Trustees, Mississippi Institutions of Higher Learning,
  81–84, 87, 92, 102, 103, 104, 106,
  109, 114, 115–17, 118, 119–22,
  123–24, 125–26, 130, 131, 132–
  34, 136, 137, 138, 140, 141–42,
  143, 144–45, 146, 147–48, 152,
  154–55, 157, 159–60, 162, 163–
  64, 166, 167–72, 173–76, 177,
  178, 179–83, 189, 193, 196, 197,
  198, 199–201, 202–08, 210, 211,
  212, 213, 214, 216, 217, 218, 219–
  23, 227, 230, 236–37; 1932 statute
  reorganizing, 111–13; executive
  secretary of, 112, 118, 121, 125,
  143, 159, 163, 164, 168–69, 171,
  175, 178, 182, 183, 201, 205, 214,

  221, 224, 234, 237; and 1942 constitutional amendment, 123, 236;
  LeBauve Trustee ("Ole Miss
  Trustee"), 123, 155, 225; Committee on Negro Education, 144;
  Special Committee on Charges of
  Apostasy at the University of
  Mississippi, 147–48; "Mississippi
  Southern board member," 212;
  comprehensive reviews of state
  institutions, 223–26, 227, 228–29,
  230, 231–32, 237; Medical Affairs
  Committee, 226; role and scope
  study, 225–26; 1982 mission
  statements for institutions, 226–
  27; and funding crisis of 1980s,
  229–34; and institutional auton-
  omy, 234; and commissioner of
  higher education, 234–35, 237
Bond, Nathaniel, 106
Bond, Willard F., 88, 104
Boston University, 142
Bourdeaux, Thomas, 231–32
Bowen, David, 203
Bowdre, Paul, 104
Boyd, John D., 145, 207, 214
Boyer, Roscoe, 146
Boykins, Ernest, 214
Brandon, Gerard C., 11–12, 13
Branham, Henry, 53
Branham Affair, 53
Brewer, Earl Leroy, 84
Brister, Milton, 219, 221–22
Brookings Institution, *Report on a
  Survey of the Organization and Ad-
  ministration of State and County
  Government in Mississippi,* 110, 111,
  112, 115
Brown, Albert Gallatin, 34, 35, 37
Brown, Benjamin, 209
Brown University, 60
Brown v. *Board of Education,* 140, 142,
  144, 149, 164
Brunini, Ed, 180, 188
Bryan, Harry, 87

Bryan, William Jennings, 73
Bryn Mawr College, 72
Burgin, Bill, 121
Burkitt, Frank, 55, 61, 66, 75, 79, 83
Butler, Carl, 203
Butts, Alfred, 103, 104, 131, 141

Cabaniss, James Allen, *The Univer-
  sity of Mississippi: Its First Hundred
  Years,* 72
Caldwell, Isaac, 12, 13
Calhoun, John C., 38
California Board of Regents, 116
California, University of, 60
Campbell, Will, 146
Campbell College, 70, 129
Carmichael, Oliver, *The Changing
  Role of Higher Education,* 128
Carnegie, Andrew, 55
Carpenter, Corrine T., 202
Carpenter, H. G., 144–45, 155, 169
Carrollton Female College, 70
Carter, Hodding, Sr., 140–41
Cates, Edward L., 164, 165
Centenary College, 20, 22, 25–26,
  30, 31, 40
Central High School (Little Rock,
  Arkansas), 194
Centre College (Kentucky), 26
Central Female Institute, 28
Chadwick, W. D., 104
Chain, Bobby, 226, 228, 234
Chamberlain, Duncan H., 80
Chamberlain, Jeremiah, 20, 26–27,
  28, 32
Chanche, John Joseph, 17
Chattanooga, University of, 105
Chicago, University of, 83, 102, 105,
  148; Chicago Plan, 126–27
Chickasaw College, 70
Chulahoma College and Commer-
  cial Institute, 23
Citizens' Council, 149, 179
Civil Rights Act of 1964, Mississippi
  compliance with, 217–19

Civil Rights movement, 199,
  212–13. *See also* Meredith, James
  Howard; Evers, Charles; Evers,
  Medgar
Claflin College (SC), 142
Claiborne, W. C. C., 4, 7
Clark, Charles, 165, 169, 170, 183
Clark, Walter, 85
Clap, Thomas, 3
Cleaver, Eldridge, 208
Cleere, William Ray, 234, 235
Clegg, Hugh, 192, 193, 194, 195
Clinton Presbytery, 17
Coahoma Junior College, 136
Coleman, James P., 145–46,
  150–51, 152, 154, 181, 189–90,
  196, 197, 204
College preparatory divisions in in-
  stitutions of higher education, 70
Columbia College, 22
Columbia University, 36, 60
Columbus Commercial Dispatch,
  119–20
Colvard, Dean W., 198, 214
Conner, Martin Sennett, 85, 111,
  113, 114, 121
Cook, Joseph Anderson, 87,
  99–100, 111, 113, 120
Cook, Robert Cecil, 131, 133–34,
  137, 226
Cornell University, 60
Crane, Henry Hitt, 203
Crane, William Carey, 28
Crawley, David E., 111, 121
Critz, Hugh, 104, 107, 114
Crystal Springs *Monitor,* 59
Curriculum, 4, 10, 14–15, 16, 21,
  22–23, 24, 28–29, 38, 40–41, 45,
  46, 50, 56, 60–61, 63–64, 65–67,
  68–69; elective principle in,
  71–72, 126
Currie, J. H., 118

Davis, Jefferson, 53
Davis, Russell, 209, 210, 211

Day, Jeremiah, 127
De Bow, James E. B., 40
Delta State College, 154, 157, 214;
    Vietnam War demonstration, 207;
    and integration, 213, 214. *See also*
    Delta State University
Delta State Teachers College, 82,
    90, 102, 109, 114, 117, 125, 129,
    131, 133, 141; role and scope de-
    fined in 1934–35, 116; renamed
    Delta State College, 154
Delta State University, 226, 233,
    235; 1982 mission statement,
    227–28; funding of intercollegiate
    sports, 231
Denison College, 21
Dent, Jessie, 208
Doar, John, 182, 183–84, 185, 186
Donald, Cleveland, 213
Dorman, Clarence, 126
Douglass, Frederick, 63
Drane, James, 48
Dubra, Charles, 142, 159
Dubuisson, Charles L., 21
Duke, Washington, 55
Duke University, 106
Dunbar, William, 15

Eastland, James, 194, 195
Eliot, Charles W., 60
Elizabeth Female Academy, 10–11,
    22, 24
Ellard, J. A., 125
Ellis, Robert B., 158, 159, 160, 161,
    163, 164–65, 166, 177, 178, 182,
    183
Ellis, William A., 83
Emmerich, J. Oliver, 123, 125, 202,
    211
Emmerich, John, 202
Emory College, 38, 40
Endris, Glenn, 229
Englehardt, N. L., 137
Enlightenment influences, 3, 4

Entrepreneuralism, 22–23
Equal Rights, 62
Ervin, Sam, 195
Eskridge, J. C., 106
Evans, S. R., 155, 169, 178, 193–94
Evers, Charles, 205, 206, 207, 209
Evers, Medgar, 142–43, 159, 207
Ewing, James, 207, 214

Fair, Charles, 155, 169, 170, 193,
    194
Fant, John C., 91, 103
Farley, Robert J., 92, 142, 146
Faulkner, William, 144
Fayetteville State College (NC), 148
Female Collegiate Institute (Holly
    Springs, MS), 21
Financing higher education, 21–22.
    See also funding under individual
    institutions
Fine, Benjamin, 127; *Democratic Edu-*
    cation, 127
Finley, Robert H., 5
Flexner, Abraham, 126
Flournoy, Robert W., 62–63
Foerster, Alma Pauline, 34, 46
Foote, Henry S., 27
Forrest County Cooperative, 152,
    153
Forshey, C. G., 15
Fortune, Porter L., Jr., 209, 214
Foster, Jack D., 229; *Restructuring*
    Higher Education (Foster study),
    229–30
Foster, James, 6
Foster, John, 6
Frank, Glenn, 102
Franks, Ross, 225
Freedmen's Bureau, 61
French liberalism, influence, 4–5
Fulton, Robert, 76, 80–81

Gainey, John Lee, 118
Gale, Leonard D., 29–30

Gartin, Carroll, 151
George, James Z., 73–74
George, Jennings Burton, 114, 118, 121, 130–31
Georgia State Bureau of Investigation, 155
Georgia, University of, 5, 29, 31, 36, 38, 40, 60, 234
Gibbs, Phillip L., 210
Gibson, Joseph E., 130, 131; *Mississippi Study of Higher Education*, 131–32, 223
Gibson, Randall, 6
Giles, William, 203–04, 205, 206, 214
Graham, Hardy Poindexter, 99, 105, 107, 108
Grant University (TN), 105
Grayson, B. B., 11
Green, James Earl, 210
Green, Wigfall, 109
Gregory, Dick, 153
Greenville *Delta-Democrat Times*, 140
Grenada College, 25
Grenada *Weekly Register*, 33
Griffin, John Howard, 153
Guest, W. D., 200
Gulf Coast Research Laboratory, 221
Guthman, Edwin, 191

Haile, William, 11
Hamilton, William B., 17
Hampstead Academy, 11, 12. See *also* Mississippi Academy
Hardy, John C., 79, 134
Harkey, Ira, 173
Harper, Frank, 121
Harrison, Robert, 214, 224–25, 234
Harvard University, 3, 60, 66, 67, 71, 127, 147, 224
Hattiesburg American, 148–49
Hazard, B. H., 118
Hederman, Tom, 179

Hemingway, William, 92
Henry, Aaron, 203–04
Henry, J. M., 43
Henry II, of England, 35
Herrin, Bob, 180
Hickman, Will, 215
Hickock, Eugene W., Jr., 216
Highgate, W. B., 75
Hightower, George R., 84
Hilbun, Ben, 214
Hilgard, Eugene, 48, 50, 61
Hinds Junior College, 103
Hogarth, Charles Pinckney, 131, 136
Holbrook, John, 13
Holly Springs, University of, 19
Holmes, David, 8
Holmes, George Frederick, 39–40, 41
Holmes, Emma, 184
Holmes, Verner Smith, 144–45, 155, 164, 169, 170, 171, 173, 176, 180–81, 182–83, 184, 189–90, 193, 194, 198, 199, 202, 205, 206, 213, 218, 220–21, 222, 225, 226, 234
Hooker, Wilburn, 146
Hopkins, Mark, 36
Hudson, John, "The Spoils System Enters College," 107, 108
Hudson, Robert S., 62
Hume, Alfred, 87, 88, 92, 93–94, 97, 98–99, 100–01, 102, 104, 106, 107, 114, 116
Humphrey, George Duke, 114, 116, 131
Hunnicutt, W. L. C., 26
Hunt, David, 21
Hutchins, Robert Maynard, 102, 126–27, 128, 138

Industrial Institute and College, 68–69, 75–76, 76, 81, 85; renamed Mississippi State College for Women, 86

Illinois Wesleyan University, 105
Ingraham, Joseph Holt, 15
Itta Bena Times, 84–85
Ivy, H. M., 133, 142
Izard, Ray, 155, 169, 170, 174, 175,
    198

Jackson *Clarion,* 58, 62
Jackson *Clarion-Ledger,* 103, 121,
    179, 221, 224
Jackson College (Louisiana), 26
Jackson College (Mississippi), 29,
    30, 70, 122. *See also* Mississippi
    Negro Training School; Jackson
    College for Negro Teachers; Jack-
    son State College; Jackson State
    University
Jackson College for Negro Teachers,
    129, 130, 131, 132, 136, 137; 1951
    mission statement, 137; renamed
    Jackson State College, 154
Jackson Daily News, 84, 88, 94, 96,
    101–02, 105, 118–19, 124, 143,179
Jackson Daily News—Clarion-Ledger,
    228
Jackson *Mississippian,* 3
Jackson State College, 154, 158, 161,
    202, 214; student unrest, 207,
    209–10; 1970 killings, 210, 211;
    Blue and White Flash, 210; and in-
    tegration, 213–14. *See also* Jack-
    son State University
Jackson State University, 70, 122,
    224, 232, 233, 235; and Ayers
    case, 218; memorial garden for
    past presidents, 220–21; 1982
    mission statement, 227; and fund-
    ing of intercollegiate sports, 231
Jefferson, Thomas, 4–5
Jefferson College, 4, 5–12, 13–17,
    21, 22, 25, 26, 29, 31, 37; estab-
    lishment, 4, 5–9; and Tombigbee
    River land grant, 7–8, 9, 13–14,
    47; and Natchez land grant, 8, 47;
    reorganization of, 11, 12; and for-

mer Choctaw and Chickasaw land
    grant exchange, 13–14; cur-
    riculum, 14–15, 16; and second
    federal land grant of 1819, 16
Jobe, Euclid R., 143, 144–45, 150,
    163, 164, 168–69, 171, 175, 178,
    182, 183, 201, 214
Johns Hopkins University, 60
Johnson, Joseph E., *Review of Funding
    and Allocation Formula,* 230
Johnson, Paul B., Sr., 117–18, 121,
    122, 123
Johnson, Paul B., 185, 186, 196–97
Johnson, William, 24
Johnston, Means, 123
Jones, R. H., 68, 75–76
Jones, Thomas, 24
Jones County Junior College, 198

Kansas, University of, 127
Keady, William, 205
Keirn, Nellie, 103
Kelly, A. B., 104
Kennard, Clyde, 148–54
Kennedy, John F., 156–57, 158, 186,
    188, 190, 191, 192, 195, 196
Kennedy, Robert F., 170, 172, 180,
    181, 183, 185–87, 189, 190–91,
    192, 195, 197, 203
Kent State University, riots, 210
Ker, David, 6, 15
Kershaw, Alvin, 203
Kethley, William M., 102, 131
Keyes, Frank, *An Address Delivered
    Before the Alumni Association of the
    University of Mississippi,* 54
Kincannon, Andrew, 69, 84
King, B. B., 208
King, Clennon, 144, 145–46
King, Martin Luther, Jr., 153, 209

Lamar, Lucius Quintus Cincinnatus,
    43, 53, 58, 59, 74
Lamar Life Insurance Company,
    179, 180

Latham, Joe, 180
Lawrence, Mrs. O. F., 91
Lee, J. P., 24
Lee, Robert E., 101
Lee, Stephen D., 64–66, 67–68, 78
Lesher, Steven, 210–11
Levine, David O., *The American College and the Culture of Aspiration, 1915–1940,* 116
Lewis, A. B., 163, 178
Lindsley, Philip, 16, 18, 23, 50
Lipscomb, J. N., 155, 169
Lomax, W. A., 93, 94, 98
Long, Huey P., 92
Longino, Andrew H., 77–78
Longstreet, Augustus Baldwin, 26, 38, 39, 40, 41–45, 46, 49, 53, 58; and political controversy, 43–44
Love, John Clark, 164–65
Love, L. L., 192
Lowell, James Russell, 71
Lowry, Leon, 155, 169
Loyola University of Chicago, 198
Lucas, Aubrey, 214, 225
Lucy, Autherine, 158, 167
Lumpkin, Sam, 120
Lyon, Quinton, 147; *The Great Religions,* 147

McAllister, James, 9, 10
Mabus, Ray, 237
McCain, William D., 125, 134, 150, 151, 152, 207
McCarthy, James, 198
McCaughan, John J., 38, 39
McComb Enterprise Journal, 211
McCosh, James, 72
McDowell, Cleve, 213
McElroy, Taylor, 97
McNutt, Alexander G., 16, 17, 32
McRae, John J., 43, 44, 48, 49
McShane, James, 183–84, 185, 186
Madison College, 24; Madison County interdenominational college, 19

Malott, Deane W., 127
Manly, Basil, 45
Marquette, Clare, 194
Marshall, Burke, 183, 184, 185, 191, 192
Marshall, Thurgood, 159, 160
Marston, Robert, 213
Massachusetts Institute of Technology, 60
May, Joseph, 121
Mayes, Edward, 59, 62, 71, 72, 73, 74, 76, 138
Memphis State University, 200
Meredith, James Howard, 63, 155, 156–95, 196, 197, 198, 213, 236; *Three Years in Mississippi,* 156
Meredith, Larry, 165
"Meredith law" (Mississippi Senate Bill 1501), 172–73
Meredith v. *Fair,* 163–66
Meridith, H. L., 231, 232
Michigan, University of, 55, 60, 71, 130
Michigan State University, 134
Midderhoff, J. A., 16
Millington, John, 30, 39
Millington, Mrs. John, 30
Millsaps College, 70, 129
Mississippi Academy, 12–13. *See also* Hampstead Academy; Mississippi College
Mississippi Agricultural and Mechanical College, 64–68, 70, 73, 74, 75, 76, 78–79, 81, 83, 84, 85, 86, 91, 96, 102, 103, 104; and Hatch Act, 67; Department of Mechanic Arts and Electricity, 78; textile school, 78, 79; 1930 reorganization, 104–05, 106, 107–08, 109; and accreditation, 109, 113; renamed Mississippi State College, 114
Mississippi Baptist Convention, 17
Mississippi College, 13, 17, 22, 37, 70, 129; and Clinton Presbytery,

Mississippi College (*continued*)
17; and Mississippi Female College, 20
Mississippi Board of Education,
95–96, 101
Mississippi commissioner of higher
education, 96, 101, 112
Mississippi Conference of the Methodist Episcopal Church, 61
Mississippi Education Association,
Advance, 107–08
Mississippi Female College, 20, 28
Mississippi Farm Bureau Federation,
219
Mississippi Methodist Conference,
33
Mississippi National Guard, 189,
190, 191
Mississippi Negro Training School,
122. *See also* Jackson College
(Mississippi); Jackson College for
Negro Teachers
Mississippi Normal School, 81–82,
90. *See also* Mississippi State
Teachers College
Mississippi Power and Light Company, 104, 107, 179
Mississippi Presbytery, 26
Mississippi Southern College, 129,
130–31, 133–34, 138–39, 141,
154, 203, 226; department of commerce, 134; and integration, 148,
149–53; Vietnam War demonstration, 207; becomes University of
Southern Mississippi, 212. *See also*
Mississippi State Teachers
College
Mississippi state building commission, 217, 220, 236
Mississippi State College, 114, 117,
126, 129, 131, 133, 134–35, 138–
39, 141; engineering program,
114; role and scope defined in
1934–35, 115–16; school of business, 116, 135; graduate school,

117, 135; library, 135; sociology
department, 135; becomes Mississippi State University, 135. *See
also* Mississippi Agricultural and
Mechanical College
Mississippi State College for
Women, 86, 87, 91, 102, 103, 114,
117, 118–19, 129, 131, 133, 134,
135–36, 141; 1930 reorganization,
104, 106, 109; and accreditation,
109, 113; role and scope defined
in 1934–35, 116. *See also* Industrial Institute and College; Mississippi University for Women
Mississippi State Female College, 48
Mississippi State Sovereignty Commission, 149, 150, 152–53, 155
Mississippi State Teachers College,
87, 91, 99–100, 102, 103, 109,
111, 113, 114, 117, 118, 121,
122–23; role and scope defined in
1934–35, 116. *See also* Mississippi
Normal School
Mississippi State University, 135,
154, 157, 197, 203–04, 206, 212,
219, 221, 224, 225, 230, 232, 233,
235; and NCAA basketball tournaments, 197–98; Young Democrats, 205, 206; Speakers Review
Committee, 205; and integration,
213, 214; *Reflector,* 219; 1982 mission statement, 227; areas of academic excellence defined, 228; and
funding, 231, 232. *See also* Mississippi Agricultural and Mechanical
College; Mississippi State College
Mississippi Superintendent of Education, 104, 112
Mississippi Supreme Court, 153
Mississippi University for Women,
233, 235; and integration, 213,
214; 1982 mission statement,
227–28; closing of, 229, 230, 231,
232; and funding, 231, 232. *See
also* Industrial Institute and Col-

lege; Mississippi State College for Women

Mississippi, University of, 21, 22, 26, 30, 31, 56, 62–63, 68, 69, 70, 73, 74–75, 76, 80, 81, 82, 83, 84–86, 87, 88–89, 91–92, 98, 101, 102–04, 114, 117, 118, 120, 123, 126, 129, 131, 133, 138–39, 146, 199, 202, 203, 214, 221, 224, 225, 232, 233, 235; and integration, 63, 142–43, 145–48, 155, 156–95, 198, 200, 207, 208, 213, 214, 236; establishment of, 32–33, 34–38; and the natural sciences, 40–41; funding of, 41, 46–48, 56, 63, 73, 74, 97, 98, 114, 212; and social sciences, 41; School of Law and Governmental Science, 42, 60–61, 93, 97, 108, 142–43, 204, 208, 213; and board of visitors, 44; and federal land grants, 47; governance, 48–49; and the Civil War, 53–54; reforms of 1889, 56; admission policy, 56–57, 70–71, 161–62; statute reorganizing the university, 58; 1870 reorganization, 60; department of science, literature and arts, 60, 71; professional department, 60–61; School of Medicine and Surgery, 61, 93, 97–98, 108, 132, 141; Department of Agriculture and Mechanic Arts, 61; 1889 reorganization, 71–72; library, 71, 98; "Ole Miss Trustee" (LaBauve Trustee), 123, 155, 225; and athletics, 198, 231; and O'Shea study, 90; and relocation, 93–94, 95, 96–97; yearbook, 100; *Daily Mississippian*, 93, 94, 98, 208; and academic freedom, 100–01, 200–05; salaries, 102; 1930 reorganization, 104, 105–06, 107–09; expulsions and loss of accreditations, 108–09; school of pharmacy, 108; restoration of accreditation, 113–

14; engineering program, 114, 116; role and scope defined in 1934–35, 115; school of education, 146; charges of communism and apostasy at, 147–48; Mortar Board and Omicron Delta Kappa resolution, 201–02; Young Democrats, 204; AAUP chapter, 204, 220; violence at Southern Literary Festival, 207; student unrest, 207–09; Black Student Union, 208; board of trustees arbitrary treatment of faculty and staff, 220; 1982 mission statement, 227; areas of academic excellence defined, 228

Mississippi Valley State College, 214; student unrest, 207, 208; and integration, 213, 214. *See also* Mississippi Vocational College; Mississippi Valley State University

Mississippi Valley State University, 233, 235; 1982 mission statement, 227–28; closing of, 229, 230, 231, 232; and funding of intercollegiate sports, 231

Mississippi Vocational College, 136, 150; 1951 mission statement, 137. *See also* Mississippi Valley State College

Mitchell, Fred Tom, 131, 134–35

Mize, Sidney, 162–63, 164, 166, 167, 168, 178

Montgomery, G. V., 211

Morgan, Ira, 155, 169, 179–80

Morrill, Justin, 65

Morris, Willie, 193

Morrow, R. D., 142

Motley, Constance Baker, 160, 161, 162, 163, 164, 165

Mounger, William H., 179, 180, 188

Murphree, Dennis, 91

NAACP, 142, 143, 144, 147, 148, 150, 203, 207; Legal Defense Fund, 158, 159, 160

Nashville, University of, 16
Natchez College, 70
Natchez College of Commerce, 23
Natchez Courier, 36
Natchez-Democrat, 226
National university, idea of, 18
New Republic, 107, 108
New York State board of regents, 124
New York Times, 127
New York, University of the City of, 60
Nixon, Richard M., 210
Noblin, Jim, 224
Noel, Edmund F., 84
Normal schools or colleges, 62, 69, 81–82
North, Linton Glover, 96
North Carolina, University of, 36
Norwood, W. D., 202
Notre Dame University, 202

Oakland College, 20, 21, 23, 26–27, 31–32, 63
Oakland Magazine, 32
Ohio State University, 108
"Old-time colleges," 19; governing boards of, 24–26
O'Shea, Michael V., 89–90, 92, 95, 96, 99, 112; *Public Education in Mississippi,* 89–90, 91, 92, 109, 111, 114–15, 131, 134
Otis, Jesse R., 130, 144–45, 207

Panama, University of, 147
Parker, Joel, 27
Parkinson, Burney L., 114, 117, 118–19, 121, 131
Pascagoula *Chronicle,* 173
Patterson, Joe, 145, 169, 170
Peabody study (Frank P. Bachman, *Report of Functions of State Institutions of Higher Learning in Mississippi*), 114, 115, 116–17
Pennsylvania, University of, 22

Peoples, John A., 209, 214, 220
Percy, William Alexander, 109
Perry, Ed, 229
Peters, Absalom, 18
Pettus, John J., 53
Peyton, Annie Coleman, 68
Phares, D. L., 67
Phillips, M. W., 28
Phillips, Rubel, 197
Piliawsky, Monte, 202
Pipes, William H., 130
Planters College, 24
Politics and higher education, 83–88, 91–97, 102–04, 106–07, 111–13, 117–23, 125–26, 151, 154–55, 157, 176, 201, 203, 216, 223, 229, 231, 232, 233, 236–37
Polk, Leonidas K., 50
Pontotoc College, 129
Porter, Noah, 60
Powell, Robert, 81
Powers, Joseph Neely, 87–88, 92, 104, 105, 107–08, 114
President's Commission on Campus Unrest, 209, 210–11
President's Commission on Higher Education, 128; *Higher Education for American Democracy,* 128
Presidents Council, 115
Princeton University, 14, 60, 72
Public school system of Mississippi, 56, 57, 58, 75, 79, 82, 96, 229; integration of, 211–12
Puget Sound, University of, 105

Quintus Fabius Maximus, 167
Quitman, John A., 12, 13, 27

Rainey, Kenneth, 202
Ralston, Mrs. Robert, 91
Raymond *Hinds County Gazette,* 64
Reconstruction, 57–59, 60–63
Reddix, Jacob, 129, 131, 214
Regional (Southern) university, idea of, 243 n.1

Religion and higher education, 3, 5, 10, 17, 19–20, 25, 26, 32, 33, 34, 38–39, 41–42, 70, 99
Reneau, Sallie Eola, 48, 68; and Reneau Female University of Mississippi, 68
Rensselaer Polytechnic Institute, 23
Rent, Clyda, 103
Revels, Hiram, 63, 64
Reynolds, Earl, 204–05
Rice, James C., 121–22
Richardson, John, 53
Ricks, J. R., 104
Riddell, Tally, 155, 164, 169, 170, 175
Rives, Richard T., 163
Roberts, Johnny, 153
Roberts, Malcomb Metts, 154, 169, 170–71, 174, 175, 176, 196, 198, 199, 200, 202, 203, 204, 205–06, 207–08, 212–13, 214, 217, 218, 234
Robertson, Stokes V., 146
Rockefeller, John D., 54
Rogers, Denton, 228–29
Rosenwald Fund, 122
Roudebush, G. S., 65
Rowen, Levi, 102
Rudolph, Frederick, *The American College and University: A History,* 18, 19, 20, 23, 54, 72, 128
Russell, Lee, 85, 87
Rust College, 70. *See also* Shaw University
Rust University. *See* Shaw University

St. John's College (Maryland), 127
Sanger, W. T., 130, 132
Sarah Lawrence College, 127
Schauber, Ambrose, 87, 104
Schlei, Norbert A., 187–88
Sectionalism, 35, 43, 44, 45; states' rights, 52–53, 59
Semple Broaddus College, 24–25, 28, 30

Sewanee Review, 72
Sexton, James, 82–83, 222
Shands, Garvin, 80, 81
Sharkey, William L., 56, 62
Sharon College, 10, 19–20
Shaw University, 61–62. *See also* Rust College
Shattuck, David O., 25
Sheldon, George L., 85
Shepard, H. E., 72
Shepphard, Charles, 232
Sillers, Walter, 120, 141
Silver, James Wesley, 146–47, 200, 201, 202; "Mississippi: The Closed Society," 200
Simmons, Miriam, 214, 227, 234
Simmons, William, 179
Simrall, Horatio Fleming, 36–37
Smith, Fred, 178
Smith, R. B., Jr., 134, 155, 169, 170, 178
Smith, R. F. N., 10
Smith, Theodore, 120, 224
Smith, William H., 118, 121
Smylie, James, 8
Smylie, James M., 27
Society of Civil Engineers, 108
South Carolina, University of, 45
South Florida, University of, 202
Southern Association of Colleges and Secondary Schools, 98, 109, 113–14, 120, 122, 157, 161
Southern Farm Bureau Insurance Company, 152
Southern Historical Association, 200
Southern Mississippi, University of, 125, 202, 207, 212, 221, 224, 225, 233, 235; funding of, 212, 231; and integration, 213, 214; *Student Printz,* 219; board of trustees dismissal of faculty and staff, 220; ACLU chapter, 220; Natchez branch, 225–26; 1982 mission statement, 227; areas of academic excellence defined, 228. *See also*

Southern Mississippi (*continued*)
Mississippi State Teachers College; Mississippi Southern College
Southern Reformer, 34
Southern Scientific Institute, 23
Stanford University, 127
State Normal School, 62, 68, 75, 76, 79
State supervisor of public schools, 96
Stennis, John C., 123, 194
Stephens, Abednego, 16, 26
Stetar, Joseph, "In Search of Direction," 55, 56
Stevens, Boswell, 219
Stevens, Mrs. Daisy McLaurin, 91
Stone, John M., 62, 64, 65
Stone, William O., 155, 169
Stratton, Joseph B., 27
Strickler, George, 202
Strobel, James, 233
Students, discipline of, 29–31, 39, 40, 45–46
Sullens, Fred, 84, 94, 101, 104, 107, 109, 118–19, 122
Sullivan, W. J. T., 65
Summer, A. F., 211
Summerville Institute, 21
Sutherland, Robert E. Lee, 100, 102, 103, 114
Sydnor, Charles, 106

Tarbell, Jonathan, 59
Taylor, O. B., 123
Teacher training, 69–70. *See also* Normal schools or colleges
Teller, Landman, 201
Thomas, Carey, 72
Thompson, Jacob, 41, 42, 46–47
Thompson, W. O., 108
Thornton, Thomas C., 20, 22, 26
Throckmorton, Mordecai, 6
Thrash, E. E., 205, 214, 221, 224, 234
Thwing, Charles F., 31

Tillman, Ben, 61
Tougaloo, College, 61–62, 207
Travis, Joseph, 19
Triplett, Edward H., 76
Trister, Michael, 202
Troy (New York) Institute, 10
Truman, Harry, 128. *See also* President's Commission on Higher Education
Tubb, Thomas, 155, 169, 170, 171, 174, 175, 176, 180, 182, 183, 193–94
Tucker, Tilghman, 32–33
Turner, R. Gerald, 232, 233
Turner, Thomas, 92, 177, 216, 218, 219
Tuskegee Institute, 130
Tuttle, Elbert, 163, 166, 167, 183

Union Female College, 29
United States Military Academy, 14–15, 22, 39, 65
U.S. Court of Appeals for the Fifth Circuit, 156, 162, 163, 166, 167, 168–69
U.S. Department of Health, Education, and Welfare, Office of Civil Rights, 217–18, 219
U.S. Department of Justice, 159, 170, 174, 181
U.S. Supreme Court, 153, 172
University Medical Center, 132, 193, 213
Utica Institute, 145

Van Landingham, Jack J., 149, 150, 151–53
Vance, Cyrus, 189
Vardaman, James K., 61, 76, 79–81
Veysey, Laurence, *The Emergence of the American University,* 59, 83
Virginia, University of, 4, 14, 22, 40

WLBT-WJDX (Jackson radio-television station), 173, 180

Waddel, John Newton, 21, 30, 38, 39, 40, 45, 56, 57, 59, 60, 62, 63
Waddel, Moses, 29, 38
Wade, John D., *Augustus Baldwin Longstreet*, 39, 43
Wailes, Benjamin L. C., 13–14, 15
Waites, Hilton, 120
Walker, Buz M., Jr., 86
Walker, Buz M., Sr., 86, 102, 103, 104, 107
Walker, Edwin, 194
Waller, William, 214, 216–17, 218, 219; his committee to study higher education in Mississippi, 216
Walton, Thomas L., 59, 146
Washington, Walter, 214
Washington Academy, 8
Washington and Jefferson College Lyceum, 15; *Southwest Journal*, 15
Watkins, H. B., 123
Watkins, Tom, 184, 185, 186, 190, 191
Wayland, Francis, 23, 50
Wells, Calvin, 141, 179, 180
West, Cato, 8
White, Edwin, 146
White, Hugh, 117–18, 119–21, 189
White, James H., 150, 208, 214
Whitfield, Henry L., 85, 86, 87–88, 89, 91, 92, 95
Whitfield State Hospital, 146
Whitworth College, 24, 70, 129
Wiechardt, A. J., 78
Wilkerson, E. C., 38–39
William and Mary College, 4, 39
William Carey College, 129
Williams, John Bell, 209, 210, 211
Williams, John Davis, 126, 131, 138, 142, 146, 147–48, 154, 155, 163, 167, 172, 175, 178, 192, 193–94, 196, 200, 204, 214

Williams, John Sharp, 81
Williams, Lucius Quintus Cincinnatus, 86
Williston, E. B., 13, 14; *Eloquence in the U.S.*, 13; *Williston's Tacitus*, 13
Wilson, Baxter, 179, 180
Wilson, Charles R., *Baptized in Blood*, 93
Wilson, R. S., 104
Winans, William, 25, 30
Winter, William, 237
Wisconsin, University of, 88, 89, 102
Wisdom, John Minor, 163, 167
Women, higher education of, 9–10, 24, 48, 56, 63, 68–69, 70, 75–76, 84, 86, 103
Wood, Sanford, 202
Woodville Republican, 36
World War II, the effect of on higher education (postwar college boom), 124, 127–30, 132, 137–39, 141, 215, 217; GI Bill, 124, 126
Wright, Fielding L., 126, 141, 143, 144
Wright, Richard, 79–80
Wyche, J. J., 15

YWCA, 135–36
Yale University, 3, 23, 45, 53, 60, 72; "A Report on the Course of Liberal Education" (Yale Report of 1828), 14, 23, 127; Sheffield School, 61
Yarbrough, George, 200

Zacharias, Donald, 232–33
Zeller, Julius Christian, 85–86, 96, 105